EDUCATING THE ACADEMICALLY ABLE

A Book of Readings

EDUCATING THE ACADEMICALLY ABLE

A Book of Readings

Edited by

LESTER D. CROW, Ph.D. *, 1897-* ^(onald)

Professor of Education
Brooklyn College

and

ALICE CROW, Ph.D. *, 1894-* ^(Von Bauer)

Formerly Associate Professor of Education
Brooklyn College

DAVID McKAY COMPANY, INC.

New York

EDUCATING THE ACADEMICALLY ABLE: A BOOK OF READINGS

LIBRARY OF CONGRESS CATALOG CARD NUMBER: 63–20857

MANUFACTURED IN THE UNITED STATES OF AMERICA

Preface

THE DEVELOPMENT of the learning potential of the gifted or talented learner is receiving considerable attention in many school systems and in institutions of higher learning. We have come to realize that not enough has been done to develop the mental capacity of many of our academically able learners. Fortunately, many educators are giving considerable thought to ways and means of dealing with this problem.

Educating the Academically Able: A Book of Readings brings together basic principles and practices dealing with the education of gifted learners. The editors have attempted to select material that presents the thinking of many writers concerned with the education of gifted and talented young people. Special consideration has been given to the identification and needs of the gifted, as well as to their personal and educational problems.

Included in the *Readings* are some excellent programs for gifted learners. These represent various types of programs in operation in every section of the country: east, south, midwest and far west. Thus, the reader is introduced to a wide range of practical, ongoing programs and a wealth of expert opinion on the subject.

Educating the Academically Able offers valuable resource material to students in college and university classes, and to teachers and administrators on the job who are wrestling with the problem of educating the gifted. The coverage also is sufficiently extensive to make it a valuable text in a college course dealing with gifted or talented learners.

The editors wish to thank all who have given permission to reprint material included in *Educating the Academically Able: A Book of Readings.* The superintendent of schools is listed as author of many of the excerpts included from ongoing-programs in school systems, although, in most instances, multiple authorship can be assumed.

LESTER D. CROW
ALICE CROW

Contents

EDUCATING THE ACADEMICALLY ABLE

A Book of Readings

1. Education of Our Talented Children * 1

HYMAN G. RICKOVER, *Rear Admiral, USN*

Is Special Education for the Talented "Undemocratic"?

I am aware that any change in the American public school system will meet opposition. Special schooling for the mentally superior will be branded as "undemocratic" and as "class" education. It will be considered "unfair" to give the talented child education superior to that offered the average. It will be said that the separation of children according to mental capacity will deny them valuable experience in living together with other children of varied background and ability, and that this constitutes an important ingredient in the smooth functioning of American democracy—so it will be said. None of these objections, however, bear critical examination.

It would, indeed, be "undemocratic" to propose a cleavage along class lines, but not one along the lines of natural ability, which hardly anyone will claim is limited to the children coming from better homes. It is, however, often forgotten that we already have just such a separation along class lines in large American cities where schools draw their pupils from a particular neighborhood rather than from the whole population, as is the case in smaller towns. Neighborhoods in America are usually homogeneous,

---

* From *The Education of Our Talented Children,* Thomas Alva Edison Foundation, Inc., New York, N.Y., February 1957. Reprinted with permission.

1 This is a portion of an address by Rear Admiral H. G. Rickover given at the Seventh Institute of the Thomas Alva Edison Foundation. Additional views of his may be found in *Education and Freedom,* E. P. Dutton & Co., Inc., 1959; *Swiss Schools and Ours—Why Theirs Are Better,* Atlantic-Little, Brown & Co., 1962; and *Education for All Children—What We Can Learn from England,* Hearings before the Committee on Appropriations of the U.S. House of Representatives.

at least as far as the finances of the families are concerned. Parents in better-class neighborhoods generally succeed in obtaining better schools for their children. Finally, we must not forget that well-to-do parents always have it in their power to assure their children a good education by sending them to private preparatory schools. But the talented *poor* child must depend solely on the public school. Education in a democracy must not only be democratic, it must also be education.

Education is not a commodity such as a house, a television set, or an automobile. Everyone can use and enjoy a house, a TV set, or a car; it would indeed be "unfair" if the state distributed these commodities free of charge but limited them to only part of the population. The ability to use and enjoy academic training, on the other hand, is *not* universal; therefore, to limit it to those who can benefit from it is not unfair; but, to deny it to the minority who *can* use and derive benefit from academic training is both unfair and undemocratic, as well as a waste of our most valuable national asset.

Finally, as to the objection that experiences valuable for democratic living will be lost if the talented are separated, this again would be true only if all the talented came from the same type of home. As long as pupils in *all* public schools, including those giving college preparatory courses, are drawn from the whole population and all are given the same opportunity to advance in accordance with their ability, the social values of learning to live together with children of varying backgrounds will still be preserved.

A Searching Comparison

In considering ways to improve our schools, we must recognize that no institution is so hallowed by age or tradition that it ought to be exempt from periodic examination and appraisal in terms of whether it accomplishes the goals for which it was established; in particular, whether it is adjusting itself to the realities of a rapidly changing world. Measured by these tests, the American school system must be judged to need a thorough overhaul. Now that ours is no longer the only school system with an open educational ladder, the time has come when we should subject it to a searching comparison with school systems in England and on the continent of Europe. It should be easy to obtain from foreign school authorities such information as:

1. The subjects taught in the several types of secondary schools, with data on the number of class periods and length of class periods devoted to each subject.

2. The extent to which mastery in each subject is achieved, as measured by examinations at the end of each period of schooling.

3. School fees, if any, and scholarships granted to poor children.

4. Requirements for entrance into different types of secondary schools and universities, with samples of examinations needed to obtain the school-leaving certificates that are required for study at a European university.

5. Extent to which such certificates are given credit in foreign universities.

6. Extent to which courses taken in the university of one European country are given credit by other European universities.

7. Scholastic requirements demanded of American students wishing to enroll at European universities.

In addition, school textbooks could easily be obtained for comparison with those used in American public schools.

We need not slavishly copy the schools of other countries; neither should we succumb to the happiness of ignorance. In studying their ways of educating the young, we may discover valuable ideas. To these we could add the experiences of those American secondary schools that have already instituted special accelerated courses for the talented. On the basis of this information, it would then be possible to work out a course of schooling—open to all children but on a basis of entrance examination—that would proceed alongside our present junior and senior high school courses. Such schooling would begin after the fourth or fifth grade and be dovetailed into the four-year liberal arts course in such a manner that the student could attain a Bachelor of Arts degree by 20 years of age.

The necessary steps to bring about this educational reform will be taken as soon as the American public has been made aware of the great need to cultivate our now most neglected national resource—the talented child. But it will require the devoted efforts of many men and women who are willing to make this problem their own personal responsibility, perhaps as many as it took a hundred years ago when it was first proposed to remove all financial bars to higher education so that no child might be denied equal educational opportunity. That was a hard fight too, but it was won because those who fought had the inspiration and the inner force. Later developments have, however, diminished the splendor of what, up to that time, was one of the noblest achievements of American democracy.

Let's Make a Start

I am not an educator, but I have interviewed more than 1,000 young college graduates. These interviews have made it plain to me that our

educational system needs considerable improvement. It has, therefore, been
a great disappointment to me that, despite the vast amount that has been
said about it in recent years, so little is being done. We must, somehow,
make a start. We cannot keep on just talking while our ruthless opponent
acts. How can any American remain complacent about our educational
dilemma?

Is money the problem? Then what are we going to do with all our
wealth? If an additional four billion dollars a year—*1* per cent of our
gross national product—makes the difference between good teachers and
mediocre ones, good schools and poor ones, can we afford not to spend that
sum? Is our end aim merely to become more wealthy, to acquire more
things?

Can we afford to make our talented children remain in school any
longer than they have to, when our schools are already so overcrowded and
the teachers so few?

Last year I suggested that industry's growing need for trained personnel
made it good business for them to take active steps to help. I proposed
that industry make available its scientists and engineers for one-year periods
to teach in our high schools—in this way helping to relieve the teacher
shortage. I pointed out that in present day America the business corporation is not a business device alone; that is has become a social institution
and has acquired the obligations inherent in this concept; that there is
justification for industry to assume a responsibility for financing education because the college graduates they obtain have been trained at public
expense; that such expenditures are vital for the future, and should be
considered as part of the routine expense of running the business.

Today I should like to plead earnestly for even greater help from industry.

A Proposal for Twenty-five Model Schools

I suggest that industry, together with our educational foundations,
undertake the setting up of model academic secondary schools in perhaps
twenty-five different centers in the United States. These schools would be
on a par with our best academic secondary schools. They would be free;
the ability to pass an entrance examination of a kind that would weed out
those not mentally capable of absorbing an academic secondary education
would be the only requirement for admission. The schools would be staffed
by teachers truly capable of teaching talented children; teachers whose
qualifications place less emphasis on training in teaching *methods* and
more on graduate study in their fields. The competence of European

secondary school teachers, based as it is on years of postgraduate study in their fields, is one of the main reasons why they can teach as much in twelve years as ours do in fourteen or fifteen.

Teachers' salaries in these schools would be in accord with the high scholastic qualifications required and, therefore, equal to those paid for comparable positions in industry. Such salaries would attract competent teachers.

These model schools should aim at a ratio of at least one teacher for every twenty pupils. One of the reasons why the private English boarding schools, such as Eton, Harrow, etc., contribute so large a percentage of England's leaders is their ratio of teachers to pupils—one for every twelve students.

The schools would start with the fifth grade so as to have the pupils ready for college at sixteen. To do this, it may be necessary to provide a choice: students could complete the course the regular way in seven years, or they could finish in six years by taking extra courses during three summers. We must find a way for our children to attend school for more than the present 180 days. Lengthening the time in school might most easily be done through the medium of voluntary summer courses.

Teachers in these schools would be given no extracurricular work of any kind, because a teacher, as does any professional person, requires time for thought and study. The schools would be scholastic institutions, so social activities would be kept at a minimum.

The management of these schools, qualifications and salaries of teachers, entrance requirements, curricula, and standards would be left to an independent body not connected directly with the donor. But I see no reason why the schools could not be given names to indicate the corporation, or industry, or labor organization—for labor ought to participate in this endeavor no less than industry—that contributes financial support. This seems to me fair and legitimate, and even desirable; it would win friends for industry as a whole, and for the donor in particular.

I estimate that the cost of operating each model school for a period of five years will be about ten million dollars. At the end of that period the community ought to have an option to take over the school, provided it agrees to continue the high scholastic standards set under private management.

These model schools would demonstrate what could be accomplished by competent teachers, a proper curriculum, and an adequate school year. They would be goals and living examples of what can be done by the community for the education of its children.

These are my suggestions. Others can and will be made. But let us

make a start. As a beginning, let us get the data on European curricula
and teaching methods and then let us devise a way to make our schools as
good, and even better, than those of any other country. We have the ability
to do this. We are rich enough to do this. All we need is the will to do it and
to recognize that "the inevitable comes to pass through effort."

2. New Perspectives in the Education of the Gifted *

VIRGIL S. WARD, *Professor of Education, University of Virginia*

Introduction

The fact that America has failed to utilize its human resources wisely,
especially with respect to the care devoted to the discovery and development of the intellectual powers and special talents latent in its youth, has
become startlingly clear in the mid-twentieth century struggle for advantage
among nations. The national shock that followed upon finding our own
scientific and technological progress paralleled or exceeded by nations
striving for increased domain in the modern world has had at least one
fortunate consequence for education—that is a public will and demand in
support of the educator's quest to provide exceptional education for those
of exceptional capabilities. The inadequacy of the typical school regimen
in preparing able youth for the demanding and creative social roles that
they typically face as adults, and for their own more generous self-realization as human beings, was recognized by educational theorists for many,
many years before the present crisis. Only with sustained public understanding and support, however, could the schools begin and can they now
expand upon efforts to find significant means for upgrading the educational
process to meet these needs.

However, the nature of the problem is of such magnitude that mere re-

* From *The Educational Forum,* March 1960, pp. 329–35. Reprinted with permission.

arrangements among the present educational practices will scarcely suffice. The breakthrough in education that has been variously called for by Lippmann, Conant, and other insightful observers of American public education demands extraordinary imagination. Only thinking of the sort that Harold Rugg has termed "radical—of the root" is likely to provide the fresh orientation necessary to lift the American school forward into the space age in the differential education of that topmost percentage of its youth that need not, and should not, be bound by the limited potentiality in the school curriculum that serves the middle mass of future citizenry. The untapped intellectual potential of the most perceptive of American youth can and should be developed so as to advance the welfare, not only of their own nation, but of mankind generally.

What, then, would be the nature of such unaccustomed ways of thinking about the educative process for exceptional youth? It is our contention that the breakthrough must come both at the level of educational aim, and at that of the corresponding processes through which the enlarged vision is implemented. We have attemped in this presentation to examine three elements of the conception upon which practices in the contemporary American school are based, with a view toward suggesting through these the type of emergent thought that must be applied to all elements of the educational endeavor if it is to be geared to the current mandate. We shall call these points of view "Perspectives," in the sense that they attempt to represent both ideas in themselves essential to the task, and a plane of thought concerning knowledge and its uses not presently active in the development of the most common school curricula.[1]

Perspective One: Treatment of Knowledge in the Enriched Curriculum

The division into unit courses of knowledge selected from the cumulative cultural heritage, with the attendant practice of electing from these courses at secondary levels of schooling, allows for missing strands in the whole cloth of knowledge. The purposes of a more fitting education for the gifted, then, can better be served by a conception of the curriculum throughout the period of general education as divided into broad segments, allowing for economy in educational planning, assignment, and appraisal of prog-

---

[1] These principles are developed to pertain chiefly to the general education of intellectually superior students, rather than to the training of specific aptitudes. It is recognized that children with superior talent in given fields tend to possess a superior general level of intelligence, as well, rather than an inferior. They would, therefore, also be subject to these principles to the extent of their intellectual capacity.

ress. Traditionally, higher education has been considered to divide into major fields such as the humanities, the natural sciences, inclusive sometimes of mathematics, and the social sciences.

Since intensive and extensive adaptations of the curriculum, as well as the integration of more than one field of knowledge, involves cutting across course boundaries as presently conceived, such a broad division is more manageable. Accordingly it is recommended that teachers at the elementary school level and the secondary, and the general college level as well, plan enrichment units as integral to four areas: (1) the humanities, including language arts, literature, foreign languages, aesthetics, logic, etc.; (2) mathematics; (3) the natural sciences; and (4) the social sciences, including history, government, economics, geography, etc.

It is further appropriate, rather than that the gifted youth investigate only certain discrete bodies of knowledge from these broad areas, that he should be led toward a perspective upon *all* epistemological branches. The intellectually superior individual is likely to be, and should be treated as a life-long learner, tending to engage throughout his life in the continuing expansion of his knowledge. Thus a choice can be made by the teacher against leading the child explicitly through all phases of selected subject matter desirable for learning, in favor of adequate introductions embracing all areas of knowledge, typical problems and techniques peculiar to these broad fields, and interrelationships that exist among them. Specific fact and principle within the various phases of a given subject such as physics, or grammar, or political science can be learned by the bright student quite largely through his own efforts. The school's chief responsibility should lie in the artful and adequate introduction of all fields of knowledge in proper perspective with respect to techniques, problems, applications, and interrelationships, leaving the acquisition of a presently appropriate body of fact largely to individual or peer group pursuit, and trusting that through the perspectives established upon all knowledge, successive acquisition of fact and principle within any area of concern to the individual can and will be accomplished.

Accordingly, electives from the broad fields would largely be eliminated in the interest of pursuing in the manner indicated all bodies of knowledge within these areas. The gifted youth in practical effect would, instead of electing either biology or chemistry or physics or geology, be required to know the facts from *all* of these that pertain to his present developed capacity or functional need. These extensive levels of understanding pertain both to the superior learner's unique manner of learning and to his needs in the advancement of frontiers of knowledge, or in creative and complicated applications thereof.

Still a third treatment of knowledge appears to pertain. The highly selective content from the entire realm of knowledge in a subject area that finds its way into the standard school text is concerned chiefly with the present state of knowledge, contemporaneous fact, and principle. This singular type of emphasis fails to yield an appreciation of knowledge as continuously unfolding, and particularly as dependent upon the efforts and the imagination of men and women in past and present times. To the contrary, knowledge appears generally to be presented as a state of affairs that exists presently in a form not especially expected to change with time, or at least with no understandings presented as to how the individual can cope with changes.

The history [2] of the various academic disciplines is fruitful in presenting developing knowledge as an evolutionary process, idea built upon idea in the minds of men, a progressive movement in which it is not unrealistic to expect that the talented youth of today will take rightful place.

The full application of this principle, again, bespeaks a somewhat radical departure from pedagogical methods in common use for the generality, the uniqueness of the capacity level of the superior learner and his anticipated social role dictating the changed procedure. Summarily, the differences involve utilizing the teacher's skills and mature insights for *providing introduction to and perspectives upon all adventures in knowledge that lie ahead,* forms of understanding that cannot be acquired so economically by individual pursuit, and the greater utilization of the child's own capacity for one-to-one acquisition of fact and principle. By this rearrangement in curricular economy, the broader scope that is indicated can be accomplished, and the concomitant learnings for the developing individual will yield increasing freedom from the necessity for direct instruction. This form of "preparation for life" is both as possible and as pertinent for the education of the gifted, as it is impracticable and unrealistic in the education of the generality.

Perspective Two: Education in the Abstract for the Intellectually Able

The role of direct experience in the learning process is well recognized in modern school practices. The sand table, the field trip, the school laboratory all testify to an imbedded respect for the inductive mode in education, the development of the abstract concept by way of concrete ex-

---

[2] Leta Hollingworth was possibly the first to discover, in the practical school setting, how special groups of bright children were immediately receptive to the search for origins of things generally.

perience. "Learning by doing" is, virtually, a cornerstone in the school process today.

Furthermore, whereas in general as the experience of the individual broadens with age and education, he tends to summon past concrete experience to the present situation and thus to minimize the need for some levels of concreteness, the need for the direct experience in doing with ideas and problems to be learned remains essential at even the top level of complexity. The medical student "interns"; the young lawyer practices in partnership; the doctoral student in research principles practices the design and conduct of experiments; in short, concrete, direct performance in the realm of real things and situations is essential to learning of the new at whatever age or stage of advancement the learning might occur.

However, the necessary ratio of amount of concrete experience to the intellective ramification of that experience in the development of generalizations is a variable factor in the learning situation. A rough negative correlation is suggested between the intelligence of the individual and the amount of concrete experience essential to the understanding of a concept. Therefore, it is suggested that at all points in the educative process where the concrete can be abbreviated for gifted youth, in recognition of its diminished necessity, that this be accomplished, in the interest of utilizing the saved time in pursuits more nearly essential to the fullest rounding of the intellectually superior youth's understanding.

The presentation of curricular material in text and in lecture should be couched at a level of generalization that recognizes the amount of direct experience that the gifted individual will have undergone in formal school and informal environment, and tend to bring to the learning situation. Textbooks written at advanced levels, encyclopedic articles on specific problems (these being noted for compactness and comprehensiveness), and original writings by critics, historians, and scientists on the level of the academic and professional world, as distinct from the standard textual presentation—all these are indicated as more likely to approximate a convenient ratio between the concrete and the abstract than does the text and lesson presentation, at normal grade levels, through which the generality are schooled.

Yet a further use of the abstraction possesses fascinating educational potential. In his *Education As the Cultivation of Higher Mental Processes,* published in 1936, Charles Hubbard Judd spoke of ". . . the end and goal of all education (as) the development of systems of ideas which can be carried over from the situations in which they were acquired, to other situations." "Systems of general ideas illuminate and clarify human experiences," Judd says, "by raising them to the level of abstract, generalized, conceptual understanding." This concept, we hold, relates more realistically to the education for creative and productive behavior of intellectually superior individuals, than to the possible attainment of all children.

Instruction in ideas as such, and in their relative magnitudes, and curricular traffic in literature conceived at a high level of ideational structure should contribute to the ability to reconstruct, to apply, and to produce or originate novel conceptions and practices. In the education of the gifted, the "idea" can and should receive central emphasis. Gifted children reach out for ideas; and thought in terms of ideas, as opposed to the material accouterment and instruments following from them, appeals to their intellectual interest. Thus the *idea* of psychological measurement is likely to be attractive, in addition to the study and application of instruments of measurement; the *idea* of electricity as a controlled natural energy, in addition to the mechanics of control; the *idea* of social security, and so on, *ad infinitum*. Such ideas exist in every subject area. They are found in the history of the subject, from which history "creative moments" may be selected for particular examination. The isolation of "great experiments" in psychology or in physics contains the same potentiality. Reflection upon major and minor discoveries in the development of man's complex technology, upon "accidents that have influenced history," are further indications of the educational potential in the selection of ideas per se for study. Instruction in ideas such as these would contribute, it is held, to the facility of the superior individual in reckoning with generic ideas as such, among which ideas and at which levels of thought, origination is likely to eventuate.

In conclusion of these particulars, it follows that the representation of knowledge acquired by the gifted youth should take the more general and the more abstract form, and should reveal understandings in terms of such systems of ideas. Expectations by the teacher that classroom contributions and individual reports reflect the higher intellectual process are appropriate; merely average quality in thought and performance are not appropriate, and should not be acceptable. In like fashion, teacher-made tests should contain exercises that tap the superiority of the gifted through discussions that demand greater precision in significant fact, more elaborate cognizance of the related variables in a problem, more penetrating inference beyond fact, and more responsible judgment. Without such advanced expectations at all levels in the educative process, the education of the gifted falls short of evoking his finest potential; and school experiences, rather, conduce toward his mediocrity.

Perspective Three: Universal Orientation for World Leadership

The final suggestive "perspective" to be treated here relates to man's capacity for enlarging upon that particular body of culture into which the individual is born, toward an understanding and appreciation for all human culture. Theories of social parallelism suggest the inherent relationship between schools and their supporting societies. It is a defensible primary consideration that publicly supported institutions loyally sustain the basic beliefs and practices of the parent society. There is philosophical sanction, however, for progressive reconstruction within the democratic society, in a movement that anticipates at each stage a more perfect implementation of the democratic idea. An extension of the same position brings to the fore the idea of evolving relationships in the international arena. In a world contracted by media of transportation and communication, and possessed of power devices that threaten the surival of nations, a world view seems urged upon men generally, and especially upon their leaders. By virtue of his capacity for learning, of his ability to acquire that subtlety of understanding and that flexibility of response necessary to an adequate reckoning with ideologies international in scope, and by virtue of the probabilities that men of his caliber are destined to reckon therewith, it is reasonable that the school conduce toward the development of responsible attitudes and information cognizant of the realities of present and emerging relationships among nations. Justifiably, world needs will first be considered as the present welfare of the parent society is concerned; beyond this, real possibilities of more adequate international relationships should be in explicit focus.

In practical effects upon the school program, this would mean that those studies grounded in Western culture alone would now be accompanied by others exploring the determinants of Oriental and Slavic civilizations. Relationships as significant as those that brought into the American school curriculum a reflection of European cultures, now exist between this country and newer national forces. "Modern languages" as a curricular concept should be expanded to include languages other than the conventional French, German, and Spanish, for instance, on justifiable theoretical grounds. International politics, law, and economy; anthropology, generic studies of the nature of human nature, and sociology—concepts from such disciplines, adapted functionally to the age level of the child and youth, are inexcusably omitted from educational substance offered the abler child, particularly in favor of experiences far less significant that presently crowd his school day. A statement from the Educational Policies Commission is specifically directed to this point [3]:

> Far too many Americans in positions of influence both in government service and in private life are handicapped by insufficient acquaintance with foreign cultures and inadequate command of any foreign language. That our leaders in the future may not be so handicapped, the schools and colleges must give them today the kind of education that is clearly indicated by the need.

Education for frontier roles in all phases of human culture suggests a continuous development of the capacity for evaluating observations and information, testing these against various sanctions and in view of various purposes, and reordering through discussion the contemporaneous state of affairs in improved harmony with chosen purposes. This conscious ideational management of the objects and institutions in man's affairs, if the management is to be progressive and constructive, demands implicit or explicit awareness of criteria by which human institutions, given existences, are evaluated; and an understanding of means through which the revision of these elements in the real world of affairs can be accomplished.

In sum, this principle indicates that the superior abilities characteristic of the gifted child should be related through the educative process to the probable role of reconstruction in world affairs that, in more than a proportionate share, will be thrust upon the gifted individual. Preparation for leadership in the international scene urges insight into the historical foundations of societies, and the dynamics upon which they are maintained. Ideals generic to his own society must be reckoned with those of others, and the education of the gifted child can serve him best if it includes experiences designed to produce the skills and the understandings basic to such reckoning.

* * *

We have attempted to demonstrate through these three illustrations how various educational aims and practices must be reexamined in order to meet the challenge of education for the intellectually superior youth scattered throughout our schools today. These emerging social philosophers and natural scientists have a tremendous capacity for ingesting and for transmuting culture, and turning it to human advantage. Let those charged with the responsibility for arranging formal school experiences that will

[3] Educational Policies Commission, *Education of the Gifted* (Washington, D.C.: National Education Association, 1950), p. 9.

capitalize adequately upon this biological potential not fail through limited imagination. Theirs is a great task; they have the public will behind them now as never before. What will history have to say of the manner in which they carry this responsibility?

3. What Is the Extent of the Problem? *

CHARLES E. BISH, *Director, NEA Project on the Academically Talented Student*

D EPENDING upon our definition of "gifted children" and upon the criteria we use to identify them, varying but always impressively large numbers of school-age youngsters fall within the group with which we must be concerned.

Based upon the revised Stanford-Binet scale and assuming a total school population of thirty million, the upper 1 per cent of that population (which percentage is clearly a conservative delimitation of the "gifted" group) would total 300,000 gifted children.

Setting the lower limit at 130 IQ, 4 per cent of the school population, or 1,200,000 children, may be classified as gifted. And if, as in Cleveland, the cutting-off point is set at 125 IQ, 6½ per cent would be included. This would mean that there are 1,950,000 gifted children in the United States.[1]

Some of these, of course, are being adequately and appropriately handled. Nevertheless, the National Manpower Council and the National Education Association estimate that 400,000 bright children each year are being denied a chance to develop their potential.

All these estimates are, if anything, conservative. Can we, as a nation, really afford a loss of this magnitude? And can they, as individuals, afford it? The answer is clearly no.

* From *Administration Procedures and School Practices for the Academically Talented Student in the Secondary School* (Washington, D.C.: National Education Association), pp. 15–18. Reprinted with permission.

[1] Arch O. Heck, *The Education of Exceptional Children* (2d ed.; New York: McGraw-Hill Book Co., Inc., 1953), p. 390.

What Must Be Our Aims?

It is a frequently repeated truism that gifted children are children first and gifted second. In other words, whatever is appropriate for children in general will to a great degree be appropriate for the gifted. It is not necessary, therefore, to belabor the point that gifted children need to acquire those skills and understandings that form a basic part of the overall educational program in America.

The aims of education for children with high mental ability are not appreciably different from those for all children. They are dependent upon the abilities, interests, and aspirations of the children themselves and on the needs of society that the children eventually will serve. Any program for bright children must stimulate positive attitudes, promote good work habits, and encourage worthwhile purposes that are necessary to their success in school and imperative if these boys and girls are to become effective adults.[2]

But neither can it be forgotten that there is a second element in their definition. What must be done because of their giftedness? This question demands an answer before a concrete program can be undertaken.

As is true for every child, then, the educational program must strive to meet the needs created by his own individual capacities and limitations. Because of the general abilities of most gifted children, which will be examined in greater detail somewhat later, certain basic aims must be kept constantly in sight. While by no means an exhaustive list, the following items represent goals toward which the efforts of educators could well be directed in approaching the complex problem of educating gifted children:

1. Foster the integration of knowledge, regardless of the special interests of either the student or the teacher.
2. Develop the student's own broad cultural background.
3. Recognize the earmarks of intelligence and understand their implications for learning and for teaching.
4. Realize that the intellectual qualities of giftedness render superfluous much of the traditional pattern of classroom instruction, and thus imply special methods such as problem-centered teaching and pupil-teacher planning.
5. Recognize the basic uniquenesses of the talented, understanding those who have been identified as talented.

[2] James M. Dunlap, "The Education of Children with High Mental Ability," *Education of Exceptional Children and Youth,* ed. by William M. Cruickshank and G. Orville Johnson (Englewood Cliffs, N.J.: Prentice-Hall, Inc., 1958), p. 172.

6. Realize particularly the guidance needs of the talented.
7. Gain skill in providing a wide variety of learning activities, especially those that will bring about higher, broader, and deeper levels of experience.
8. Teach with the enthusiasm that transmits a love for learning.
9. Learn when to guide, when to direct, when to "get out of the way."
10. Help students reach a self-satisfying degree of achievement commensurate with their ability.
11. Provide for young minds a new freedom of ideas and explorations.
12. Develop intrinsic rather than extrinsic motivation.

These goals for the educator must be kept in mind in order to guarantee the education needed by the gifted members of our society. They should be supplemented, however, by student-related goals. Gifted students must, through the enlightened programming and teaching that are the essence of special provisions for the gifted, be helped to achieve the following broad objectives:

1. Become intellectually curious, searching for meanings and seeking to find new relationships rather than old facts.
2. Improve the ability to do independent study and carry on research with attention to basic work habits, study skills, and methodology.
3. Learn to apply a wide range of knowledge and principles to the solution of many life problems.
4. Gain skill in self-evaluation.
5. Develop skills in critical thinking, gain a passion for truth, become open-minded with a sense of suspended judgment.
6. Realize the responsibilities as well as the power of knowledge.
7. Develop leadership ability including personal poise, respect for the worth of others, and skill in group dynamics and person-to-person relationships.
8. Extend any tendency toward creativeness of various types.
9. Sense the implications of change.
10. Perfect skills in communication.
11. Develop the breadth of vision to see the possibilities of the future, the realities of the present, and the heritage of the past; to see in all this the continuing stream of man's ideas and questions and concerns.

When these aims, both educator- and student-oriented, are kept in mind, the development of a practical and meaningful program to do justice to the challenge of the gifted children in our schools will be facilitated because of the clarity with which we see exactly what we want to do. That something must be done is now generally recognized. Enough activity is already afoot throughout the land to enable us to examine some general patterns that can serve as guideposts for schools or systems approaching this fascinating and challenging problem for the first time.

4. General Policies Concerning Education of Intellectually Gifted Pupils *

EVERETT CHAFFEE, *Associate Superintendent, Division of Instructional Services, Los Angeles City Schools*

Basic Philosophy

The basic point of view of the Los Angeles City Schools is that every pupil be expected to make the most of his potentialities; that every pupil be helped to attain as high a level of intellectual development as is possible; that there be deliberate plans made to identify individual differences; and that provisions be made for learning situations for pupils of varied abilities, interests, and talents.

Pupils with Special Abilities and Talents

Gifted pupils may have special talents in nonacademic areas, such as in the fine and practical arts, or they may possess unusual leadership ability or athletic skills. They may excel in some areas and be average or below average in others. Many intellectually gifted pupils have special talents. Identification of and adequate provision for pupils with special abilities and talents are parts of the educational program of the Los Angeles City Schools. This report, however, is concerned primarily with the provisions for pupils who have unusual ability to deal with abstract concepts, symbols, and ideas—the intellectually gifted.

* From *Education of Intellectually Gifted Pupils in Los Angeles City Schools*, rev., May 1962, pp. 1–2. Reprinted with permission.

Intellectually Gifted Pupils

Intellectually gifted pupils differ from the majority of their classmates in their ability to master abstract concepts and in their speed and depth of comprehension. These differences emphasize the importance of individualized instruction to challenge the interests and abilities of pupils who are intellectually gifted.

There is probably no single best way to educate pupils of this type. The general approach of the Los Angeles City Schools is characterized by flexibility and a willingness to plan and to utilize the methods that seem best fitted to given situations. Measures to assist with the program for the gifted include development of courses of study and instructional guides; establishing of criteria for the selection of textbooks and library materials; provision of institute and in-service activities for teachers; conduct of faculty and departmental meetings to foster, guide, and evaluate the program in the schools; and enlisting the aid of parents, both in planning and conducting the special programs.

Identification of the Intellectually Gifted

Intellectually gifted pupils are defined as those who are in approximately the top 2 per cent of the total school population as measured by intelligence tests. Within this classification, two groups are considered: "gifted" pupils whose intelligence quotients are about 130; and "highly gifted" pupils whose intelligence quotients are above 160. A child with an IQ of 160 occurs only once among 10,000 pupils; thus, he needs a highly individualized instructional program.

Characteristics of the Intellectually Gifted

Although there is a broad range of individual differences among all pupils for any given trait or achievement, it is generally recognized that intellectually gifted pupils can learn with remarkable speed and depth; meet normal standards of achievement with relatively little effort; and, with adequate motivation, are capable of setting their own goals and working independently.

Intellectually gifted pupils may possess some or all of the following additional characteristics. Such pupils:

1. Are alert, intellectually curious, and keenly observant.
2. Have a wide variety of interests and versatility.

3. Are perceptive.
4. Are creative and inventive.
5. Understand concepts, recognize relationships, make generalizations, and reason clearly.
6. Learn easily and rapidly with a minimum of drill.
7. Are highly verbal.
8. Are persistent and have power of concentration and retention.
9. Have the ability to work independently and responsibly.

5. A Study of the Family Background of the Gifted *

WALTER B. BARBE, *Kent State University*

O F WHAT influence has heredity and environment been in the development of the gifted child? Specifically, how does the family background of the gifted child differ from that of the child who is average in intelligence? Unfortunately, it is not possible to determine from such a study as this whether heredity or environment played a larger part in the development of the superior intellect of the subject.

. . . .

The 456 subjects in such a study received an IQ of 120 or above on the 1917 Form of the Stanford-Binet. These data were taken from the records of the Psychological Clinic of the Cleveland Board of Education. The range of IQ is from 120 to 164, with a mean IQ of 130.2. The largest number of subjects were in the 125–29 range (37.3 per cent), while almost 62 per cent were between 125 and 135. This placed all of the subjects in about the upper 10 per cent (2) of the population of the United States at the time they were tested. A large percentage of the group (44 per cent) were in the upper 1 per cent of the population in intellectual ability as measured by this particular test.

All of the subjects were graduates of the Major Work Program of special classes for public school children in Cleveland, Ohio. The data for

* From *The Journal of Educational Psychology,* May, 1956, pp. 302–9. Reprinted with permission.

this study were obtained from information reported on a five-page printed questionnaire that was distributed to the graduates of the program over the last fifteen years. Of those who received the questionnaire, a return of 77 per cent was received.

. . . .

Economic Background

An important phase of a study of the gifted that has not received adequate attention is their socioeconomic background. This is difficult to determine and, when done in retrospect, is subject to many errors. The procedure followed in this study was to locate the economic tenth of the census tract in which the subject had lived while he was in public school (7). This gave an indication of the rent and property value of the neighborhood in which the gifted subject had been reared. The results of this phase of the study are presented in Table 1.

TABLE 1
THE ECONOMIC STATUS OF 456 GIFTED SUBJECTS

Economic Tenths	Per Cent
Highest	1.1
Ninth	7.9
Eighth	10.3
Seventh	37.1
Sixth	21.3
Fifth	11.0
Fourth	5.0
Third	3.5
Second	2.2
Lowest	0.7

The economic tenth from which the greatest number of subjects came was the seventh, while the sixth and seventh economic tenths included more than 58 per cent of the subjects. This indicates that the background of the majority of the subjects in the study may accurately be described as "upper middle-class."

Order of Birth and Size of Family

It has long been a popular belief that the gifted child is an only child, or, perhaps, has one sibling. In a study of 253 subjects (8), Goddard reported half as being first-born and three-fourths as being either first- or second-born. Of the first-born, forty-five (about 18 per cent) were only children.

Hollingworth reported that the gifted child had few siblings. In a study by Cobb and Hollingworth, fifty-seven gifted children averaged less than one sibling each (3). With respect to the order of birth, they found that more than one-half of their subjects were first-born.

In 1940, Terman reported that "the parents of the gifted subjects had produced . . . an average of 3.09 (children) per family. He states that this rate would more than maintain the stock, but "it appears likely that the subjects themselves will not equal the fertility rate of their parents (5, p. 18)."

In the present study two questions were asked to determine the size of the family and the order of birth of the gifted child. About 21.8 per cent of the subjects had no siblings, while 42.6 per cent had only one. Almost 20 per cent had two siblings, and 7 per cent three.

About 22 per cent of the subjects in this study are only children. This is not as large a number as that found by Cobb and Hollingworth, although their finding that "more than half were first-born (3, p. 180)" is substantiated by the fact that 52.5 per cent of the subjects in this study were first-born. About 29 per cent are second-born, and only 9.3 third-born. The data indicate that in this group the gifted child was the first-born in a family of two children.

Parent or Guardian of Gifted Subjects

Eighty-seven and a half per cent of the gifted subjects were reared by their own parents. The next largest group, 7.2 per cent, were reared by only their mothers. Two per cent were reared by their own mother and a stepfather, and 1.5 per cent by their own father and a stepmother. The father or foster parents each reared 0.9 per cent of the total number of subjects.

TABLE 2
PERCENTAGE OF PARENTS OF GIFTED SUBJECTS WHO
WERE BORN OUTSIDE THE UNITED STATES

Both parents U.S. born	51.3
One parent foreign born	21.1
Both parents foreign born	27.5

Witty (9), in studying one hundred gifted children in Kansas, found that most of their parents were American-born. This was not true of the subjects in this study. Slightly less than 50 per cent of the subjects had one or both parents who were foreign born. This is partially due to the large foreign element in the population of Cleveland.[1] It emphasizes the contribution of the immigrant to the mentally superior groups of the country. Table 2 presents these data.

Even though more rigid government controls have been placed on immigration, no trend is noted that would indicate that fewer of the subjects have parents who are foreign born.

Education of Parents

Hollingworth states (*3*) that the educational level of the parents of gifted subjects is far above the average for their generation. "In the majority of the cases where the gifted child has been born since 1915, both parents are graduates of high school, and in far more cases than in the population at large both parents are college graduates (*3*, p. 180)." Since all of the subjects in the present study were born after 1915, it is interesting to compare Hollingworth's statements with the data obtained for this group.

Of the fathers of the subjects, 38.4 per cent had a grammar school education or less; 33.6 per cent had a high school education; 8.8 per cent trade or business school; and 19.2 per cent had some college. Of the mothers of the subjects, 32.5 per cent had a grammar school education or less; 42.2 per cent had a high school education; 12.3 per cent trade or business school; and 13.0 per cent had some college. The mothers of the gifted subjects on the average appeared to be slightly better educated than the fathers through the high school and business school levels. However, there were more fathers than mothers who attended college.

Marital Status of Parents

Terman reported (*5*) that until 1922, 5.2 per cent of the parents of his gifted group had been divorced and 1.9 per cent were separated. By 1940, the percentage of divorced and separated parents had risen to 13.9.

The data in the present study are not exactly comparable to the results of Terman's study. The information obtained in this study deals with the marital status of the parents while the subject was in public school. It is perhaps comparable to Terman's 1922 data but is definitely not comparable to his 1940 data.

Eighty-eight per cent of the parents of the subjects were living together while the subject was in public school. About 6.3 per cent were either divorced or separated. This is only slightly higher than the report for

[1] About 20 per cent of the population of Cleveland were foreign born.

Terman's 1922 group and is certainly lower than that of the general population. The remaining 5 per cent consists of cases where one or both of the parents were deceased.

Occupational Level of Parents of Gifted Subjects

The occupations of the parents were listed according to the U.S. census classification. The *Dictionary of Occupational Titles* (*10*) was used to classify the occupations into seven distinct groups: professional and managerial; clerical and sales; service; agriculture, fishery, forestry, etc.; skilled; semiskilled; and unskilled. The subjects were asked the title and description of the father's occupation. It was possible to classify all but a few of the occupations listed. Where descriptions were not given and two classifications were possible, the data were omitted. Classifications of the parent's occupation were made for four hundred and thirty-seven subjects. Three of the remaining nineteen were on government pensions, while the rest gave no response to the questions at all. The data are presented in Table 3.

TABLE 3
OCCUPATIONAL LEVEL OF PARENTS OF GIFTED SUBJECTS

	Per Cent
Professional and managerial	40.3
Clerical and sales	22.4
Service	3.7
Agriculture, fishery, forestry, etc.	0.2
Skilled	21.5
Semiskilled	8.2
Unskilled	3.7

Hollingworth reports (*3*) that more than 50 per cent of the children testing above 140 IQ have fathers who are professional men or proprietors. The IQ's of the subjects in the present study are not this high, which may partly explain why only about 40 per cent of the parents fall into the professional and managerial group. Hollingworth also states (*3*) that half of the remaining fathers are in semiprofessional and clerical occupations. This corresponds to the clerical and sales group of the U.S. Census Bureau, and the data for this group agree with the data in Hollingworth's study.

The fact that over 30 per cent of the parents are in the laboring class, and about 40 per cent of these are semiskilled or unskilled, is noteworthy. It indicates that while the majority of gifted children do come from parents of higher occupational status, the laboring class also contributes a sizable number.

Summary

In this study, data were presented concerning the composition of the group being studied and their family backgrounds.

1. The range in IQ of the four hundred and fifty-six subjects was from 120 to 164 with a mean IQ of 130.2. Almost 62 per cent of the group were within the 125–35 range.

2. Slightly less than 52 per cent of the subjects are females; slightly more than 48 per cent are males.

3. Of the total samples, only 2.6 per cent are Negroes.

4. About 39 per cent of the subjects are Jewish. The Jewish group is represented in far greater numbers than the size of this group in the total population would lead one to expect.

5. The economic tenth of the census tract in which the subjects lived while in public schools was most frequently the sixth and seventh. This would characterize the gifted child as being upper middle class.

6. The gifted child appears to be either an only child or firstborn in a family of two.

7. Eighty-seven and one-half per cent of the gifted subjects were reared by their own parents.

8. Almost 50 per cent of the subjects had one or both parents who were foreign-born. These data indicate that the group studied is quite unlike other studies of gifted groups. Previously, the gifted child was found to have American parentage. The high percentage of foreign-born in Cleveland (approximately 20 per cent) partially explains these data.

9. The education of the mothers of gifted subjects is slightly higher than that of the fathers, even though more of the fathers went to college.

10. Forty per cent of the parents were in the professional and managerial group, 22.5 per cent in the clerical and sales, and 30 per cent in the laboring class.

The subjects in this study come from about average backgrounds with respect to occupational level, educational level, and marital adjustment of their parents. Economically the majority of them come from an upper middle-class group.

References

1. Jenkins, Martin David. "A Socio-Psychological Study of Negro Children of Superior Intelligence." Unpublished Ph.D. dissertation, Graduate School, Northwestern University, Evanston, Ill., June, 1935. P. 53.

2. SUMPTION, MERLE R. *Three Hundred Gifted Children.* Yonkers, N.Y.: World Book Co., 1941.

3. HOLLINGWORTH, LETA A. *Gifted Children.* New York: Macmillan Co., 1926.

4. WITTY, PAUL A. "A Study of One Hundred Gifted Children," *Bulletin of Education, University of Kansas,* 2:8, February, 1930.

5. TERMAN, LEWIS M., and ODEN, MELITA H. *The Gifted Child Grows Up.* Stanford, Calif.: Stanford University Press, 1947.

6. U. S. DEPARTMENT OF COMMERCE, BUREAU OF THE CENSUS, SIXTEENTH CENSUS OF THE UNITED STATES 1940. *Population,* 11:712, Part 5, Washington, D.C.: U. S. Government Printing Office, 1943.

7. GREEN, HOWARD WHIPPLE. *Census Tract Street Index for Cuyahoga County,* fifth ed. Cleveland Health Council, 1951.

8. GODDARD, HENRY H. *School Training of Gifted Children.* Yonkers, N.Y.: World Book Co., 1928. P. 129.

9. WITTY, PAUL A. "A Genetic Study of Fifty Gifted Children," In *Intelligence: Its Nature and Nurture,* Thirty-Ninth Yearbook, Part II, National Society for the Study of Education. Chicago: University of Chicago Press, 1940.

10. JOB ANALYSIS AND INFORMATION SECTION, DIVISION OF STANDARDS AND RESEARCH, UNITED STATES DEPARTMENT OF LABOR. *Dictionary of Occupational Titles, Part I,* second ed. Washington, D.C.: Government Printing Office, 1949.

6. The Academically Talented *

CHARLES E. BISH, *Director, NEA Project on the Academically Talented Student*

What Are They Like? How Can We Identify Them?

Your class probably has its share of academically talented children. They, along with an estimated seven million other elementary and secondary school children, constitute the upper 15 to 20 per cent of the public school students in the United States.

But whether you have one or one hundred of these children, your attitude toward them and your understanding of them will have an effect not only on their progress in school but on their role in the world.

WHAT ARE THEY LIKE?

There are certain observable characteristics, in a variety of combinations, in talented children. Most of these students learn quickly without much drill, organize data efficiently, reason clearly, and show an interest in a wide range of abstract concepts. As a rule, they are above-average in their use of vocabulary and in reading skills.

Creativity and originality are often distinguishing characteristics. These children are generally persevering; they are capable of a considerable amount of independent study, possess more than the normal amount of stamina, and are usually above-average physically.

All things being equal, they are fully capable of profiting by unusual academic challenge. But, unfortunately, all things are never equal.

* From *The NEA Journal*, February, 1961, pp. 33–37. Reprinted with permission. (Pictures omitted.)

The intelligence test, our most widely used instrument for identifying academic talent and predicting academic success, measures primarily those factors that have been most heavily emphasized in the classroom—verbal comprehension, general reasoning, and memory.

The fact that academic talent is not a single identifiable quality is another complicating factor. Two children, each with an IQ of 130, may be entirely different in aptitude, interest, motivation, and even in academic standing.

Then, too, individual IQ's change. In some cases, a child's IQ may rise (or fall) as much as fifty points as he grows older.

Obviously, then, many indicators of talent and ability must be used in the school situation, and tests must be made at regular intervals throughout a child's school career. Grades, personal records, teacher evaluations, and tests of achievement, aptitude, and interest should supplement the information obtained from the intelligence test.

It is generally conceded, says James J. Gallagher, who has done much research on giftedness, that the outstanding strengths of gifted children are centered in the following abilities:

1. The association and interrelation of concepts.
2. The critical evaluation of facts and arguments.
3. The creation of new ideas and origination of new lines of thought.
4. The ability to reason complex problems through.
5. The ability to understand other situations, other times, and other people; to be less bound by one's own peculiar environmental settings.

If we are to challenge bright youngsters, we must teach with such strengths in mind.

MASQUERADE

Even when the most judicious testing program is in operation and when excellent provisions for differences in ability are made, many talented children will either escape detection altogether or persistently resist efforts in their behalf. Some will masquerade behind certain behavior patterns; the talent of others will be so submerged in social, economic, and ethnic environmental conditions that our most sensitive testing devices and careful observations may not be able to identify them.

Bright children, especially the very young, are notorious conformists. Their precocious grasp of cause-and-effect, however, brings them to some strange conclusions. An affable youngster, for example, may resort to pretending not to know things so that his teacher will be pleased at his "efforts to learn." Most quick children—and this is particularly apparent at the elementary level—are eager to please even at the cost of considerable discomfort to themselves.

Then there are those of high intelligence who simply do not respond to the formal academic program although they may in private enjoy the Federalist papers or the poetry of Conrad Aiken, rebuild a jet motor, or exhibit an astonishing grasp of the social or natural world.

And finally, there are those from intellectually impoverished backgrounds who are identifiable and who respond up to a point, only to slip quietly back into the rank and file. Intuitively, or consciously, they have weighed their chances of achievement at a higher socioeconomic level and have chosen to live within a stratum of society that is less demanding and more familiar. These youngsters often grow up in an atmosphere that actively discourages the development of high potential. Many of these youths may never have the slightest suspicion that they possess unusual creative or intellectual ability.

MOTIVATING FACTORS

Many studies of motivation among ethnic groups have been reported. Most of these conclude that the significant factor is the "value pattern" that prevails in the individual's social world.

Other and related studies point to the importance of background, family interest, and dominance of one or both parents. In one study, the top 15 per cent of a group of academically talented high school students was surveyed following high school graduation. Twenty per cent of the boys and 40 per cent of the girls had not gone on to college! Why? The reasons were many, but in almost all of the cases the parents of these youngsters had shown little interest in higher education for them even though they had been informed that the boys and girls were exceptionally capable.

The young men were for the most part engaged in unskilled, semiskilled, or service jobs; the young women were in office positions. Almost all the boys expressed a desire to further their education; the girls seemed more content and appeared to be waiting to get married.

Another interesting piece of information was gleaned from a study concerned with motivational differences between the sexes in terms of achievement. It was found that girls at the tenth grade level who were able to surpass the boys did so, but that the girls at the twelfth grade level who had the capacity to make higher grades than the boys chose to make lower grades in order to avoid being considered unfeminine. Social approval was to them more important than academic success.

THE BANDWAGON FOR TALENT

These research studies disclose the overwhelming influence of early home training as well as the attitudes and values in our society that operate against the fulfillment of certain potentials. But there is much that is encouraging. It has been estimated that about seven out of ten secondary schools are now "doing something" for the academically talented student.

A survey of high school principals made by the NEA in 1959 found that nearly all believed that "school provisions for the superior students should differ in important respects from those for students of average ability," and that "whether in separate or in regular classes, superior students should be given specially enriched programs of class work."

Other desirable factors at work include the enrichment of the out-of-school environment by all types of mass media, an increasing interest throughout the community in academic achievement, the impetus toward strengthening the guidance and testing programs at all levels of instruction because of the National Defense Education Act, and the increased cooperative activities of the college and secondary schools such as the Advanced Placement Program.

Is It Undemocratic to Give Them Special Attention?

A guidance director in a small, Midwestern school expressed concern about community feeling over a program for academically talented youth. The school proposed an honors seminar for outstanding senior high school science students, and the project had apparently been launched with faculty and administrative enthusiasm.

However, a whole series of questions was raised at a midterm PTA meeting: "Are we providing opportunities for some at the expense of others?" "Will this project produce an 'elite group' in our student body?" "Will the more difficult work mean lower grades and therefore less chance for college admission or scholarship assistance?"

There are many people who feel that giving special attention to the needs of the academically talented is inconsistent with ideals of equality. It is time to consider this question. I believe that every youth is equally worthy of concern and that each youth must be given equal opportunity in terms of his needs and his capacity. This concept recognizes individual differences and variance in motivation, and accepts disparities in achievement.

Of course, I do not believe in developing an elite group; I believe, instead, that those youths whose mental growth is more rapid than some can be educated in the same school—indeed, if need be, in the same classroom with others—without lessening opportunity for their classmates and without loss of democratic values.

The problem of marks arises in many schools that have ability grouping. Even the best teachers sometimes lose their perspective and mark a selected group as though they were an unselected group, causing the most intense and unwarranted competition. As one troubled supervisor said: "The whole class of topnotch students now must compete for the few A's to be given out."

This is unnecessarily poor classroom management. If each mark has the same meaning among both slow and fast learners, then certainly most in the selected group who work up to their ability level ought to be given high grades. If for some reason the student fails to work up to the level of the class, the program should be flexible enough so that he can be reassigned, without prejudice, to a more suitable class.

If grades are tagged as honors grades and this is made sufficiently clear on the record of each pupil in the selected group, then this is the needed safeguard for college admission.

The marking problem involved in grouping is serious only if school administrators and faculty fail to set up all the administrative safeguards needed for an effective program.

If we are both to cultivate the ideal of excellence and to protect the moral values of equality, we must be extremely sensitive to principles rooted deep in the American conscience.

John Gardner, president of the Carnegie Corporation of New York, writing in one of the reference publications prepared for the 1960 White House Conference, has skillfully described these principles, all dear to the heart of the American people and all to be taken into account in any attempt to deal with the differences in children.

He says that, first, we must avoid any arrangement that diminishes the dignity of the less able. Second, we must preserve the principle of multiple chance. Every individual has the right to try and try again if he so desires. There must be no permanently closed doors. Third, we must recognize that there are many kinds and levels of excellence, all of which we need and all of which must be nourished in a healthy society.

As Dr. Gardner so aptly puts it: "We must have respect for both our plumbers and our philosophers, or neither our pipes nor our theories will hold water."

In applying these principles to the school situation, our major goal must be to deal wisely and constructively with individual differences. And while we will respect all our children and all their degrees of talent, we will make sure to provide for the academically superior on their own level; for contrary to traditional theory, only a few of them will achieve maximum potential without assistance.

Identification and counseling programs presuppose an appropriate curriculum. Here is the hardest part of the task. The academically talented student at the secondary level needs a general education in the areas usually offered in an academic program. He also needs a well-planned array of electives that will broaden and enrich his school life. This calls for a more flexible program of studies and a school day in which there is an adequate number of periods.

Most above-average pupils can profit best from a seven-period day without study halls. In many instances such pupils will need to attend class no more than three periods per week to meet acceptably high standards, thus having time for depth study in areas of specific interest.

A six-subject program, with classes meeting three times a week, can be quite satisfactorily carried by the able student in a seven-period day.

Fully as important as the content of a course is the "method of the discipline." For example, one purpose of studying history is to learn the method of the historian, to think like an historian. And certainly an important purpose in studying chemistry, physics, or biology is to learn how to follow the systematic procedures of the scientist, to think as a scientist has to think.

A special anthropology class for highly capable ninth graders was set up several years ago in Connecticut in which the *method* of anthropology was followed, allowing for a view of the whole culture under study.

A combination music and art conference that met at NEA headquarters last year showed interest in "depth" for the talented. The conferees asked: "What can we do about teaching music and art to academically talented students who are not talented performers?" "How can we avoid teaching *about* art or *about* music?" "How can we bring intellectual challenge to appreciation courses?"

A similar conference at the NEA, concerned with business education, noted that only a few of the academically talented people in the United States will be teachers, research scientists, writers, or philosophers and that many of our finest minds will be in industry, government, and business.

This group declared that special programs for the academically talented in business education would be highly beneficial. Special courses would include not only an understanding of business procedures but also the method underlying the management of our economy.

The schools and the curriculums of the next decade are already on the drawing table. Pacesetting schools are experimenting with all sorts of arrangements in grouping, team teaching, electronic aids, and flexible scheduling. Elementary schools are trying out the ungraded program. Combinations of large-group instruction, small-group discussion, and individual study are being explored in a number of high schools.

Most exciting of all, appropriately differentiated education for the talented, as well as research related to it, is contributing positively to the improvement of education for all of our children.

We have discovered that it is impossible to identify the talented through a comprehensive testing program without also identifying abilities of the entire student body. We have also found out that it is equally impossible to devise appropriate content or methodology of instruction for one segment of the school population without considering what might be excellent for all youth.

The demands that the next decade will impose upon these youths are unclear. We must prepare them to assess and deal with whatever problems emerge in their time.

How Can We Provide a Better Program for Them?

During the past two and a half years, I have made visits to some 110 schools (perhaps one of them was yours) that revealed a "change in climate." This change is reflected in youngsters' remarks such as: "It's smart around here to be intelligent."

High schools, particularly (for here the greatest changes are taking place), are bringing their total programs into better balance. There is less emphasis on marching bands, twirler groups, and interscholastic athletics. These activities are good, but in the past they often have been too big and expensive in relation to available funds for classroom teaching materials.

Entertainment of the community per se has confused both pupils and parents *concerning the purpose for which the school building was built*. But this is changing, and the change has brought decision making to a new high in many, many school systems.

No longer is the principal submerged in housekeeping and management. Rather, he is becoming more and more an educational leader; responsible for a strengthened guidance program; a more comprehensive testing program; a master schedule better articulated with feeder schools, as well as more flexible and more in keeping with pupil needs.

Where, traditionally, schools have held inviolate the allocation of content for each grade level, they now are relocating content in accordance with pupil readiness and capacity. The good student need not be held back nor graduated earlier. There is both enrichment and the movement of content down—a very substantial step toward better education for the bright student.

The task of helping youth to *capture excellence* and thereby make their best contribution to the decades ahead is indeed difficult, since the demands of the future are so unclear. More and better-trained teachers and more money, while clearly necessary, will not suffice to do the job. Experimentation with administrative procedures and with teaching methods is also needed: team teaching; functional grouping; flexible programming; more effective use of electronic devices, including the teaching machine; pupil assignments consistent with what is now being revealed concerning the development of pupil creativity.

And yet, in our enthusiasm for early development of talent, we must avoid being merely spectacular. It has been demonstrated that very bright third graders are able to learn Sanskrit and that very bright pupils in the intermediate grades are able to learn advanced college astronomy. But just because something *can* be done does not mean it should be done. Decisions concerning curriculum organization and content allocation, particularly for the academically talented student, should be justified on philosophical grounds as well as on objective test data and what is known about human growth and the learning process.

Classroom centered research is badly needed. It seems likely that many questions about the academically talented can be answered, at least in part, through classroom research by the teachers in cooperation with the counselor and others on the staff.

During the next few years there will surely be abundant opportunity to move forward on educational frontiers. Teachers and administrators who can use the past as a springboard for future development, who can safeguard the present and at the same time move ahead—these will be the leaders who will contribute most to the soundness of tomorrow's schools and indeed to the security of tomorrow's democracy.

7. Human Resources and the Aptitude Inventory *

HAROLD G. SEASHORE, *Director of the Test Division, The Psychological Corporation*

Some Questions the Aptitude Inventory Can Help Answer

Here are two questions that every school should be able to answer about its pupils:

1. How many—or what proportion—of our students are *superior?* That is, how many rank high on most or all of the abilities commonly considered necessary for advanced training at the college or technical school level?
2. How many—or what proportion—of our students are *inferior?* That is, how many rank so low on so many commonly demanded abilities that they will have difficulty in profiting from the usual academic and technical school programs?

These are not new questions. Educators and social philosophers have been concerned with them for many years. Many volumes have appeared on the "gifted" and the "mentally retarded." Others have been written about the requirements and standards for college education. Currently many are concerned with the problem of allocating the less academic student to appropriate trade school courses and are unhappy about the dumping of the less able into the "general course," whatever that means.

Consider the data available on about 1,400 boys and about 1,700 girls who took the *Differential Aptitude Tests* in their ninth grade. These pupils are from several school systems but are gathered here into one analysis to provide large enough samples to yield stable, illustrative data. There are several possible analyses of their talents but only a few are shown here to illustrate how an *objective analysis of measured abilities* can yield stimulating information to administrators, counselors, and teachers.

* From *Test Service Bulletin*, Nos. 41–43 (1951–52), pp. 4–5. Reprinted with permission.

For our first analyses we decided that ranking at or below the 40th percentile score on a given test would identify a "less able" person on the ability measured by that test, and that ranking at the 60th percentile score or above would be considered indicative of superior ability. With these standards, Table 1 was prepared.

TABLE 1
PROPORTION OF PUPILS DEFINED AS SUPERIOR BY TESTS

PERCENTAGE OF PUPILS AT 60TH PERCENTILE OR ABOVE		
	Boys	Girls
1. On the Verbal Reasoning Test	47	40
2. On both the Verbal Reasoning *and* the Numerical Ability Tests	32	28
3. On the Verbal Reasoning, Numerical Ability, *and* Sentences Tests	24	21
4. On the Verbal Reasoning, Numerical Ability, Sentences, *and* Spelling Tests	18	15
5. On the above tests *and* the Abstract Reasoning Test	14	12
6. On the above tests *and* the Mechanical Reasoning Test	9	9
7. On the above tests *and* the Space Relations Test	8	7
8. On the above tests *and* the Clerical Speed and Accuracy Test	5	5

The Superior Group

While it is impossible to state exactly what ability levels in particular talents are necessary for successful work in a college with reasonable standards, we are willing to assume the "upper 40 per cent rule" as being an approximately correct and tenable standard. We also know that the first four of these tests in the aforementioned analysis—Verbal Reasoning, Numerical Ability, and Language Usage (Sentences and Spelling)—are consistently good predictors of academic success.

Thus it appears that about one-sixth of the pupils (18 per cent of the boys and 15 per cent of the girls) should *certainly* have an *opportunity* to prepare for post-high-school education of some sort. If we assume high *V* and *N* abilities to be evidence of college-level aptitude for learning, the proportion is about 30 per cent. These boys and girls probably can complete almost any college curriculum. There will be reasons why not all of them will want to plan for college; some will not see their way clear to plan for college. But if a community really believes in conserving and developing its human resources, it will see to it that *not one of its boys and girls who meet the aforementioned standards of aptitude excellence will fail to prepare for college just because the talents were unrecognized* by the pupil, the family, or the school. Furthermore, a responsible school will try to recognize these talents early, at least as early as the ninth grade.

The modern community will ask its schools to provide counseling services for those with high talents whose aspirations stop short of their potentialities or who, for some reason, do not seem able to function at a high level. Such a school will insist on appropriate remedial programs to help these generally bright students overcome any special handicaps that are holding them back, such as inadequate reading skills or language skills.

This modern school will not force nor coerce its superior students to plan for a formal college education, but it will encourage those who have other plans to set their sights high in preparing for whatever vocation they choose to enter. For example, our best secretaries tend to come from among girls with high abilities who do not go to college.

Look now at a smaller group—the 5 to 8 per cent of boys and girls who are defined as superior on seven, or all eight, of the tests. These youngsters are "naturals" for the professions and scholarly careers. A talent-conscious school will at least be aware of these boys and girls—*name by name*—and leave no administrative stone unturned to help each of them know and appreciate the academic and technical levels to which he or she can reasonably aspire. Naturally, most of these bright pupils will be high-level achievers, but this is not necessarily so; our casebooks are full of under-achievers—each of whom is a counselor's challenge.

8. Who Are the Gifted Children?
North Dakota *

JANET M. SMALTZ, *Director, Division of Special Education* AND
JAMES D. MATHISEN, *Director, Division of Guidance Services*

THERE ARE a score of different used words to convey the concept of superior ability. Some of these are: exceptional, talented, genius, bright, accelerated, rapid learner, superior, gifted, advanced. Likewise, there is

* From *Guides to Special Education in North Dakota: IX. The Gifted Child*, pp. 1–4, 10–13, Department of Public Instruction, Bismarck, N.D. Reprinted with permission.

some confusion as to the statistical definition of superior ability. Some writers identify the gifted as the upper 1 per cent of the school population, while others include the upper 15 to 20 per cent.

Definitions of Terms

For the purpose of clarity the basic frame of reference in this booklet will be as follows:

The Gifted Pupils—an all-inclusive term referring to the upper 15 per cent of the school population. The intellectually superior, talented, skillful, and able leader.

The Intellectually Superior—those endowed with highly superior mental ability who score an IQ of 135 or above on an individual intelligence test administered by a qualified psychologist.

The Talented—those children who have special scientific, musical, artistic, dramatic, dancing, or writing ability.

The Skillful—those with special ability in physical or mechanical skill.

Leadership Ability—those who show particular ability in social skills and ability to work with and to lead others.

Indications of Giftedness

As already indicated, a gifted child may possess a high level of general intelligence as measured by tests or he may have special abilities that are not necessarily associated with a high intelligence quotient. Giftedness may be found in any group and manifest itself in many forms during the life of an individual.

Some of the identifying characteristics of giftedness are listed in the following. For convenience, they are grouped by type of giftedness as defined earlier.

THE INTELLECTUALLY SUPERIOR

1. Learns rapidly and without much effort.
2. Uses much common sense and practical knowledge.
3. Reasons things out well.
4. Thinks clearly, comprehends meanings, recognizes relationships.
5. Retains what he has heard or read without much rote drill.
6. Uses a large number of words easily and accurately.

7. Can read books that are one or two years in advance of the rest of the class.
8. Performs difficult mental tasks.
9. Asks many questions—is interested in many subjects.
10. Does some academic work one or two years in advance of his class.
11. Is original in methods or ideas.
12. Is alert, keenly observant, responds quickly.

THE TALENTED

1. Wants to know causes and reasons.
2. Can do arithmetic or mathematics one or two years ahead of his class.
3. Has good gross and minute motor coordination.
4. Reads a considerable amount of scientific literature and enjoys scientific discussions.
5. Is not easily discouraged by failure of experiments and projects and spends a great deal of time on projects of his own.
6. Enjoys music more than others in the group.
7. Uses music to express his feelings and experiences.
8. Makes up original tunes.
9. Plays one or more musical instruments well and/or sings well.
10. Shows ability to draw a variety of things and originality in artwork.
11. Uses prospective ink drawing.
12. Uses art to express his feelings and experiences.
13. Can assume characterizations easily.
14. Writes original plays or makes up plays from stories; shows interest in dramatic activities.
15. Enjoys evoking emotional responses from listeners and shows unusual ability to dramatize feelings and experiences.
16. Enjoys writing prose or poetry.
17. Can develop a story well.
18. Makes the characters seem lifelike in his writing and chooses descriptive words that show perception.

THE SKILLFUL

1. Is interested in mechanical gadgets and machines and can repair gadgets and put together mechanical devices.
2. Has hobbies involving mechanical devices.
3. Comprehends mechanical problems, puzzles, and trick questions, and reads widely on mechanical subjects.

4. Is consistently outstanding in and enjoys many kinds of competitive games.
5. Is well coordinated in physical skills.
6. Is energetic and seems to need considerable exercise to stay happy.
7. Is willing to spend much time practicing physical activities.

LEADERSHIP ABILITY

1. Is looked up to by others and sought out for opinions and ideas.
2. Can take charge of a group.
3. Judges abilities of other children accurately and places them well in group activities.
4. Guides others effectively toward goals.
5. Is enthusiastic.
6. Is liked and respected by others in the group.
7. Is a leader in several kinds of activities.
8. Is elected to offices.

Methods for Identification of the Gifted

As can be seen by the previously mentioned characteristics, the factors involved in the identification of the gifted are physical, intellectual, emotional, and social. None of these should be considered in isolation. The superior child has all the fundamental needs of childhood: comfort, affection, exercise, play, security, self-respect, and the right to mature unhampered by fears, pressures, or exploitation.

Teachers and other interested persons may use both subjective and objective means for identifying the gifted.

Subjective Methods
1. Observation
2. School marks
3. Age-grade status
4. Interest inventories
5. Interviews
6. Rating scales
7. Autobiography
8. Sociometry

Objective Methods
1. Work samples
2. Group readiness tests
3. Group mental ability tests
4. Achievement tests
5. Aptitude tests

9. What Are Gifted Children Like? *

JAMES J. GALLAGHER, *Professor of Education, University of Illinois*

WHAT ARE the behavioral characteristics by which the teacher could identify and plan for gifted children? The general characteristics of these children have been a focus of research for many years. Comparisons of groups of gifted children with groups of children of average and dull intelligence on various characteristics have indicated the characteristics we may expect in the *usual* gifted child.

As a group, gifted children compare favorably with other groups of children. However, gifted children may be small for their age, socially ill at ease, emotionally disturbed, and intellectually unmotivated. All these unfavorable traits may be crammed together in one unpleasant package seated in your classroom. Thus, individual case studies that describe the interrelationship of factors within particular gifted children often help us to understand their problems more thoroughly than general facts about groups of gifted children.

Family Background

The nearly unanimous finding of all research studies has been that the family background of these children, as a group, has been better than average no matter what the characteristic under question. These families tend to have a favorable socioeconomic background, better than average education, less divorce, and above average income.

In all these studies, however, there has also been a fascinating minority of families that deviate from this general picture. A few gifted children come from home backgrounds that would not be considered the usual breeding places for intellectual superiority. *The teacher should not dismiss*

* From *What Research Says to the Teacher: The Gifted Child in the Elementary School,* Department of Classroom Teachers, American Educational Research Association of the National Education Association, Washington, D.C., 1959, pp. 10–17. Reprinted with permission.

the possibility that a child could possess intellectual gifts even if he wears poor or inadequate clothing, or comes from a slum, or has parents who never attend PTA meetings.

Puny or Strong?

Gifted children, as a group, are not the puny and physically underdeveloped youngsters that composed the public stereotype of a few years ago. A large body of research collected in different places and at different times suggests that gifted children are equal to, or slightly better than, their average-ability classmates on such physical characteristics as height, weight, strength of grip, and resistance to physical illness.

At the same time, no physical attribute can be used as an identifying feature of giftedness. Neither good looks nor a healthy body are exclusively the property of gifted children. They come in all shapes and defy easy identification.

Are the Gifted Unstable?

Of all the myths surrounding the gifted child, the idea that intellectual superiority is related to emotional instability has been one of the most persistent. Current research does not support this idea. If anything, gifted children, *as a group,* are more emotionally stable, less tense, and more able to handle personal problems than average-ability children.

This does not mean that you will not encounter emotionally disturbed gifted children. There are all too many of them in our schools. What it does mean is that if one appears in your classroom, the chances are he is not emotionally disturbed *because* of his intellectual gifts. Instead, his emotional problems probably have sources similar to those of average children.

Since the idea that high intelligence is accompanied by emotional disturbance has persisted, we pause to ask ourselves, "Why?" First, because there is a general tendency to call anything that is different "unhealthy." The child who is interested in atomic physics rather than baseball is thought to be queer. The idea that emotional health is represented by the average of most people has been attacked deservedly in recent years.

We must also recognize that valuable work in the creative arts has been produced by persons whose expressive activities represented a release of their emotional tensions. Beethoven, Poe, and Van Gogh are obvious examples. Value was received by the culture, if not the artists, through their attempts to relieve their personal tensions.

Finally, the general public tends to resist discarding the idea of "oddness" in the gifted, one of the fondest rationalizations of parents of intellectually average children. How often have you heard the following statement from parents? "Well, my Johnny is not a genius, but at least he is all right in the head."

Who Likes the Gifted Child?

Is intellectual ability an asset or liability among one's peers? A large and rapidly growing body of knowledge has given a clear and unambiguous answer to this question. Recent reviews of the literature indicate that social acceptance is positively related to intellectual ability. The more intelligent the child, the more likely it is that he will be socially popular and accepted. It is not true that gifted children, as a group, tend to face social ostracism or rejection from their peers in elementary school.

Early investigators were concerned that the extremely gifted child (IQ of 160 or over) might face special adjustment problems because of difficulties in communicating and because of having interest patterns markedly different from those of his age peers. More recent studies have shown that this need not be the case. Many of these youngsters make excellent social adjustments to their age group. No simple rule of thumb or cliché, such as "Mary is disliked because she is so smart," is defensible with the knowledge now available. Each individual case of poor social adjustment needs to be studied on its own merits to discover the cause of the problems.

We are not saying that gifted children may not have serious social problems. If you find such a child, in all likelihood his problems are more directly caused by factors other than his high intellectual status. Probably the reason for his inability to get along will be similar to the reasons why children of average ability do not get along with their fellows. Predominant among these reasons would be marked emotional immaturity, hostile and aggressive attitudes, or values markedly different from those of the peer group.

Teachers often fear the formation of an intellectual clique in their classrooms that might be created through the interlocking friendships of the brightest youngsters. Further, they fear that this clique could develop and propagate an attitude of intellectual snobbery that would be difficult to handle. One of the most consistent reasons given for resisting the establishment of special classes is that such arrangements would encourage the development of an attitude of intellectual superiority in the gifted children.

It is foolish to suggest that this sort of thing never happens. The evidence, however, suggests that these fears are more anticipated than realized. For one thing, friendship choices of both gifted and average children depend upon many factors in addition to intellectual ability; for example, distance between residences. In the elementary school, the gifted child will choose many children of average or even below average ability for his (or her) friends and will receive friendship choices from children of all ability levels. If cliques form, they may be more attributable to peculiar residential grouping or reflections of already existing parental cliques rather than the intense attraction of children of high-level ability to each other.

How Good Is Good School Achievement?

The research of pioneer investigators has shown that gifted children, *as a group,* perform more successfully on achievement tests than groups of students with average intellectual ability. In the absence of other information the classroom teacher traditionally has been satisfied with a child's academic performance if he was able to perform at his grade level. There is serious question as to whether this particular standard should be accepted for intellectually superior children. Should we accept only a fifth-grade performance from a ten-year-old with an IQ of 150?

Many persons have tried to adopt an alternate way of determining a reasonable expectation of achievement for bright children. One popular device has been the use of the "Achievement Quotient," which is obtained by the following formula:

$$\frac{\text{Age Score on Achievement Test}}{\text{Mental Age on Intelligence Test}} \times 100 = \text{Achievement Quotient.}$$

Thus, if a seven-year-old child obtained a mental age score of ten years, he would have to obtain an achievement age of ten years on the reading tests in order to obtain an achievement quotient of 100. Experts on tests and measurements have written scathing articles, pointing out the obvious statistical flaws in such a procedure, but the practice still continues. The desire for a practical formula, any practical formula, is great.

At extremely high levels of intellectual ability the absurdity of the achievement quotient (AQ) becomes quite apparent. Let us suppose that a child of seven years obtains a *Binet* IQ of 170. The child's mental age would be around twelve years. Using mental age as a criterion, we would then expect sixth-grade performance of this child if he were merely to hold his own with an average AQ of 100. To show superior educational efficiency this seven-year-old child would have to perform at the seventh-

or eighth-grade level. The manifest absurdity of such an expectation speaks for itself.

This misleading formula has been responsible for several studies that have attempted to show that mentally retarded children are more efficient learners (have higher AQ's) for their ability than are gifted children. Whether they are or not is an unanswered question because the achievement quotient (AQ) is too faulty to be used as a basis for such conclusions.

But if we can use neither the life age nor the mental age, how can we obtain a "rule of thumb" to determine the level of expected achievement of the gifted child? One method uses a formula for obtaining an expected achievement score in both reading and arithmetic tests for intellectually superior children. By assuming a correlation of .67 between reading tests and intelligence scores, we can obtain the following formula:

$$\text{Expected Achievement} = \frac{2 \times \text{Mental Age} + 1 \times \text{Life Age}}{3}.$$

Thus, if a child is eight years old with a mental age of 11, his expected reading age would be:

$$\text{Expected Achievement} = \frac{2 \times 11 + 1 \times 8}{3} = 10.0 \text{ years.}$$

The expected achievement of ten years (approximately fifth grade) is a more reasonable and valid approximation of expected achievement. More important, it indicates that such a child would be well below expectation in achieving at the third-grade level. Thus, he would be underachieving even though his reading skills might be equal to, or even better than, his third-grade classmates.

Using the same procedure with an estimated correlation of .50 between arithmetic tests and intelligence scores, the formula for expected achievement in arithmetic test is:

$$\text{Expected Achievement} = \frac{\text{Mental Age} + \text{Life Age}}{2}.$$

In this instance the same child would have an expectation in arithmetic as follows:

$$\text{Expected Achievement} = \frac{11 + 8}{2} = 9.5 \text{ years.}$$

The calculation suggests that his expected achievement in arithmetic would be somewhat lower than his expected achievement in reading, and this difference in expectation is in accord with both test theory and observable facts.

The Case of the Dragging Arithmetic

Many teachers have noted that gifted children score lower on arithmetic tests than they do on tests of reading. A recent study showed that of 35 highly gifted children, 34 obtained a higher age equivalent score in reading than on arithmetic in subtests of a comprehensive test. There is every reason to believe that these lower arithmetic scores can be attributed, in large measure, to the structure of the achievement test.

The arithmetic tests in most standard achievement batteries have been developed on a vertical basis so that there are a few problems in addition, another few in subtraction, and so on to cover briefly each of the major operations. While it does seem quite possible for intellectually gifted children to learn to read more or less independently, and thus to develop these skills through practice, it is less likely that the child will learn the proper arithmetic processes without systematic instruction.

The attempt of gifted children to derive the concepts of borrowing and carrying in advance of instruction can be quite creative but, for the most part, inefficient. Also, trial-and-error methods of self-teaching often have the effect of making more difficult the instruction of more effective methods and may discourage the child from future creative attempts in this area.

The really pertinent question is, "What depth of understanding does the child have of the number system, or of basic concepts in social studies, or of science?" This, unfortunately, is a question that cannot be answered by many of our present achievement measures. Even the better-constructed tests rely heavily upon factual material. A gifted child could obtain a significant insight between the relationship of famine to aggressiveness in nations, or how a number system could operate from a base of 2 rather than a base of 10, or how light waves are related to sound waves without raising his scores on achievement tests one point.

Therefore, one of our first needs is for tests that measure the significant associations and insights that a child has obtained through his studies.

Those That Can But Don't

Of all frustrating experiences that can befall a teacher, one of the most irritating is to be confronted by a child with obviously great potential who does not learn efficiently. At any rate, he does not learn what you want him to. These youngsters with superior ability but limited achievement have been labeled "underachievers."

Obviously there have to be many reasons children do less well in school than their intellectual potential would predict. Research studies comparing gifted underachievers with gifted achievers have found certain patterns of adjustment that are unique to the underachievers. Some children use their poor achievement as a passive-aggressive attempt to strike back at parents and a culture whose values they wish to reject. Underachievement is a particularly powerful weapon for a child to use against parents who value school achievement highly. In other cases underachievement appears to be the by-product of an emotional problem. The child's inner tensions have so drained his energies that he has little left for his school work. In still other instances, these underachieving children are reflecting the anti-intellectual and anti-educational attitudes of their parents.

A recent study, using the techniques of role playing, supports the general conclusion that underachievement is related more closely to the emotional life of the child than to the type of instruction he receives. It was found that the low achievers see themselves as less free to pursue their own interests, to express their own feelings, and to respond adequately to their environments than do adequately achieving children.

In short, the teacher, in order to plan most effectively for the child, should understand that underachievement seems to be strongly related to personal problems of adjustment or attitude formation. It probably means that in many instances the underachieving child might profitably receive guidance from a psychologist or school social worker. Most classroom teachers, when confronted by the underachiever, try to present different and more stimulating lessons or materials to arouse the bored and unmotivated child to greater effort. While teachers *should* try to motivate and interest every child, they should also realize, when they are not succeeding, that other professional people (e.g., school psychologist) might be more qualified to handle the *sources* of the problems.

10. The More Able Student: Described and Rated *

ERNEST O. BUHLER, *Counselor, Winona, Minnesota,* AND
EUGENE N. GUIRL, *Counselor, Palo Verde High School, Tucson Public Schools*

THE MORE able students are a controversial minority these days. They are frequently stereotyped, often misunderstood, revered by some of their peers and feared by others. The public's picture of them is changing from one of the puny, bespectacled little pedant to a child who is happier, healthier, friendlier, smarter, more reasonable, and better adjusted than other children.[1]

At no time in our national history has the discovery and development of the more able children been as important as it is today. Today everyone —especially the academically superior, the talented and creative, and those with superior leadership qualities—must be trained to lead and guide the nation in the way of life that utilizes the democratic values and individual initiative. In developing this leadership, George Counts and others have emphasized the need for equilibrium between scientific knowledge and effective leadership in the humanities.

In one of Pearl Buck's stories of Chinese life, Wong the Tiger says, "The thing to do when one kills a centipede is to crush its head and then its hundred legs are in confusion and they run hither and thither against each other and are harmless." If we neglect the superior children of this nation, America may find itself to be a nation with a hundred well-trained legs but without a head that would make effective work of those legs.

James B. Conant makes frequent reference to the more able youth in his writings, and the National Defense Act of 1958 specifically refers to and is intended to find and train them.

* From *Vocational Guidance Quarterly,* Summer, 1960, pp. 217–21. Reprinted with permission.
[1] Dorothy Barclay, "The Challenge of the Gifted Child," *New York Times Magazine,* February 22, 1959, p. 46.

Identification Imperative

It is the responsibility of the school and the nation to give the more able youth every opportunity to develop to his fullest in order that he may take his leadership role in society. But, before this can be effectively accomplished, we must understand who he is and how he is different from other children.

This article, based on a review of existing literature, attempts to determine and define the characteristics that best identify the more able student and to incorporate these characteristics into a comprehensive, yet concise and workable evaluative checklist for school personnel. This is in accordance with Henry Winthrop's idea that "It would be well worth investing funds in a project devoted to the rigorous construction of such a standardized checklist by psychologists and educators, and it could be of immediate use on a national scale." [2]

In developing such a checklist it has been necessary to answer two questions. First, what do professional educators, congressmen, and the lay public mean when they say the "more able" student? Second, what evidence has been presented to substantiate the identifying characteristics of the more able?

The authors have reviewed existing professional literature and have selected those characteristics and their definitions that are most often used in the identification of the more able students. These characteristics and definitions are listed in the following:

Characteristics of the More Able Student

High Academic Achievement [1, 3–5, 7–10, 12, 13]. The more able student shows as much unevenness in subject matter abilities as do other children, but his overall grade point average is usually high and is the best single predictor of college success. He requires less detailed and fewer repeated instructions, often anticipating them. He works readily with symbols, such as words and numbers, in place of direct experience and the actual objects.

Advanced Vocabulary and Reading Level [1, 3–5, 7–10, 12, 13]. The more able student has a large vocabulary that he uses easily and accurately. He retains what he has heard or read without much rote or drill. He can

---

[2] Henry Winthrop, *Discovery of the Gifted Child,* Bulletin of the Menninger Clinic, May, 1959, p. 93.

read books that are one to two years in advance of the rest of the class. He usually reads at an early age.

Expressive Fine Arts Talent [1, 4, 5, 7–10, 12, 13]. The more able student's wide range of interests stems from his vivid imagination. He is able to solve problems in aesthetic fields and can visualize actions and things from descriptions. He frequently creates original stories, plays, poetry, tunes, and sketches. He can use materials, words, or ideas in new ways.

Wholesome Personal-Social Adjustment [1, 4, 5, 7–10, 12, 13]. The more able student adjusts easily to new associates and situations. He is alert, keenly observant, and responds quickly. He possesses a keen sense of humor and incorporates suggestions from others into his own thinking and actions. His companions are often one or two years older, but they recognize his superior ability in planning, organizing, and promoting. He also displays evidence of emotional stability in ordinary behavior.

Early Physical Competence [1, 3, 5, 8–10, 12, 13]. The more able student is characterized by his early physical development. He has a tendency to be taller, heavier, and has fewer physical defects. Not only does he enjoy outdoor games preferred by average children, but tends to excel in these games. He usually enjoys superior health and, as a result, has fewer absences from school due to illness. He also possesses especially good eye-hand coordination.

Superior Intellectual Ability [1, 4, 7–10, 12]. The more able student exhibits superior ability in reasoning, generalizing, thinking logically, and comprehension. He is able to perform highly difficult mental tasks and to learn more rapidly and more easily than most children. This child also has a longer concentration span and is keenly aware of the processes of his environment.

Effective Independent Work [1, 7–10, 12, 13]. The more able student displays his competence for effective independent work by criticizing himself and modifying his behavior accordingly. He possesses superior insight into problems, is not easily influenced, and is less prone to change his mind once an opinion is formed. His effectiveness is also displayed by applying learning from one situation to more difficult situations.

Persistent Curiosity [1, 3, 7, 9, 10, 12]. The more able student displays a deep-seated interest in some subject or field. In an attempt to gratify this insatiable curiosity he may display a dislike for rote memory and busy work. He also enjoys using encyclopedias, dictionaries, maps, globes, and other references.

Strong Creative and Inventive Power [1, 4, 5, 8, 10, 12]. The more able student possesses high-powered intellectual curiosity, imagination, and creativity. He has unusual power to see new structures and processes and to express his visions in speaking, writing, art, music, or some other form. His work has freshness, vitality, and uniqueness. An individual may create new ideas and substances or he may invent and build new mechanical devices. He sometimes runs counter to tradition and is continually questioning the status quo. He may do the unexpected.

Special Scientific Ability [1, 4, 5, 8, 10, 12]. The more able student with scientific talent will use the scientific method of thinking. He will employ scientific research methods and will grasp scientific concepts in short periods of time. He will display a curiosity of the natural world. He is not easily discouraged by failure or experiments or projects and will seek causes and reasons for things. He will spend much time on special projects of his own such as making collections, constructing radios, and making electronic computors.

High Energy Level [1, 7, 9, 10, 12]. The more able student displays a high level of energy. He keeps active by undertaking and completing task after task. He participates in various extracurricular activities, holding leadership roles in many, and frequently concentrates on long-range, unattainable, and poorly defined goals.

Demonstrated Leadership Ability [4, 5, 10, 12]. The more able student displays an ability to help a group reach its goals. He often will improve human relationships within a group and will achieve prominence by individual effort. He enters into activities with enthusiasm and is able to influence others to work toward desirable or undesirable goals. He can take charge of the group.

Well-Developed Mechanical Skills [4, 5, 10]. The more able student who possesses mechanical ability may be identified by unusual manipulative skills and spatial ability. He perceives a visual pattern complete with details, similarities, and differences. He excels on craft projects and is interested in mechanical gadgets, devices, and machines. He comprehends mechanical problems and puzzles and likes to draw plans and sketches of mechanical objects.

The aforementioned characteristics have been incorporated into a checklist that the authors believe can be used by a school staff to identify the more able students. The checklist presented as follows is intended not as an end product but rather as a guide to be modified and improved as experience warrants.

Checklist for Identifying the More Able Student

Name _____ School _____

Age: Years _____ Months _____ IQ _____

Place a check mark ( ) on the scale at a point where you think the pupil under consideration rates in the characteristics named. Please make your estimate in relation to all other pupils in this age group.

	LOW	2	3	4	HIGH
High academic achievement					
Advanced vocabulary and reading level					
Expressive fine arts talent					
Wholesome personal-social adjustment					
Early physical competence					
Superior intellectual ability					
Effective work independently					
Persistent curiosity					
Strong creative and inventive power					
Special scientific ability					
High energy level					
Demonstrated leadership abilities					
Well-developed mechanical skills					

In conclusion it can be said that existing intelligence tests inadequately identify the gifted. They give high scores to students with sponge-type minds but fail to measure generative and explosive powers of the brain. As Dean Lindley Stiles of the School of Education, University of Wisconsin has said, "We do not know how to predict with accuracy such important factors as drive, persistence, inclination to work, patience, self-direction, and discipline. The school should take the lead in identifying accurately the more able and in planning appropriate educational programs for them. The entire community should educate the more able child and parents should be given full information about abilities, interests, strengths, and weaknesses that tests and counseling reveal. More able students should be taught by more able challenging creative teachers."

The foregoing description of characteristics of the more able student and the accompanying checklist may help in this challenge. The most encouraging part of this report is that you can begin using it in your own classroom, today.

References

1. ABRAHAM, WILLARD. *Common Sense About Gifted Children.* New York: Harper, 1958.

2. BARCLAY, DOROTHY. "The Challenge of the Gifted Child," *New York Times Magazine,* February 22, 1959. P. 46.

3. CRUICKSHANK, WILLIAM M. *Psychology of Exceptional Children and Youth.* Englewood Cliffs, N.J.: Prentice-Hall, 1955.

4. DeHAAN, ROBERT F., and HAVIGHURST, ROBERT J. *Educating Gifted Children.* Chicago: The University of Chicago Press, 1957.

5. ————, and JACK KOUGH. *Identifying Students with Special Needs,* Science Research Associates, 1956.

6. HILDRETH, GERTRUDE H. *Educating Gifted Children.* New York: Harper, 1952.

7. *Identification and Education of the Academically Talented Student in the American Secondary School.* The Conference Report, National Education Association, February, 1958.

8. OTTO, HENRY J. *Curriculum Enrichment for Gifted Elementary School Children in Regular Classes,* Bureau of Laboratory Schools, University of Texas, 1957.

9. SCHWIFELE, MARIAN. *The Gifted Child in the Regular Classroom.* Teachers College, Columbia University, New York, 1953.

10. TERMAN, LEWIS M., and ODEN, MELITA H. *The Gifted Group at Mid-Life.* Stanford: Stanford University Press, 1959.

11. WINTHROP, HENRY. *Discovery of the Gifted Child,* Bulletin of The Menninger Clinic, May, 1959.

12. WITTY, PAUL (ed.). *The Gifted Child.* Boston: D. C. Heath & Co., 1951.

13. WOMER, FRANK B. "Programs in Schools Which Will Aid in Identifying the More Able Students." Unpublished mimeographed pamphlet.

11. Learning Characteristics and Problems of Gifted Children *

HELEN HAY HEYL, *Chief, Bureau of Elementary Curriculum Development, New York State Education Department*

INTELLECTUALLY gifted children learn in ways that sometimes create learning problems. They have what might be described as "special" learning characteristics and "special" learning problems, resulting in learning needs that are distinctive and that call for challenge and enrichment within the framework of the regular curriculum.

In many respects, however, the learning characteristics of the gifted child are similar to those of the child with average intelligence. Both learn by direct, concrete experience and by associating desirable and undesirable consequences to their acts. Both profit from the exercise of their abilities. The gifted child must be ready to learn before he actually learns as well as anyone else. Again, the differences between the two types of learners are mainly differences of degree.

But these differences are still important. The gifted child, for example, learns more from less experience. His powers of perception are keener. The quality of his reflective thinking is such that the association of stimuli with desirable response takes place rapidly. He is able to reach a higher level of proficiency than most other children with less repetitive exercise of his abilities. His readiness to learn abstractions is invariably in advance of the other children in his age group.

There are other ways in which the learning of the intellectually able pupil differs markedly from other children. Chief among these different ways of learning is the high degree of self-activity in which this child engages. Not content with merely formulating purposes, he considers possible procedures, selects what seems to be an appropriate course of action, puts his plan to work, and then evaluates the results. He does this quickly, and, what is more, he does it continuously rather than in a

* From *Curriculum Adaptations for the Gifted,* Bureau of Elementary Curriculum Development, New York State Education Department, Albany, 1958, pp. 17–20. Reprinted with permission.

53

disjointed fashion. He is more easily motivated than other children, finding in situations that may seem inconsequential to his classmates many opportunities for intellectual stimulation. He brings much more to a new situation than one might ordinarily expect. Based on the richness of his past experiences, his apperceptions are characterized by depth of understanding as well as breadth of knowledge.

An understanding of the learning characteristics of the gifted and superior child leads to a consideration of educational implications. This child will need time to employ what he has learned. He will need guidance to pace the experiences to which he is exposed with his state of readiness. He will need an abundance of the kinds of literature that will help him to crystallize his thinking. Such literature should introduce to the child the reasoned conclusions that others have drawn from observations similar to those made by the child.

Special Learning Problems of the Gifted

The fact that a child has a high capacity for learning does not necessarily mean that he will automatically "become all he is capable of becoming." Ability needs to be developed and harnessed if it is ever going to help the child of superior mental endowment achieve self-realization. He needs to subject himself to the disciplines of scholarship. This he finds hard to do. It is so easy to see the answer without doing any work. It is so easy to write poorly and spell inaccurately while doing things "like a flash." It is not easy to subject oneself to the repetitive practice that even a bright child must have as a basic ingredient of scholarship.

The exceptionally bright child must learn to be precise in areas such as science where precision is important. As a balance he must be tolerant and learn to suspend judgment until he has sufficient data in certain areas of study, such as the social sciences, where opinion may play a major role. He will need help in learning to distinguish facts from opinions, in learning to see things objectively apart from what he had hoped to see, and in developing valid criteria to serve as a reliable basis for critical analysis. His use of constructive imagination in visualizing a desirable state of affairs will need to be tempered by practical considerations. He will have to learn to respect the judgments of others, even those less able than he, giving credit where credit is due.

He must be helped over the quagmire of indeciveness when confronted by multiple alternatives so that he may finish a task once he has begun. A characteristic of the gifted child not too uncommon is his tendency frequently to discontinue a project once the outcome becomes evident.

Some people have used the expression "a grasshopper mind" to identify this tendency. They refer, of course, to the frequent and sudden changes in activity of the gifted child before work aspects of a project begin. A puzzle, an experiment, or a story may be set aside once the end becomes apparent. Because the gifted child can often solve problems at the abstract level, he may lose some of the values that work could develop. Consequently, the gifted child needs to learn that the knowing and the doing are two different things. He needs some experiences that will teach him that not all of his solutions arrived at in the abstract are correct or as accurate as his practical efforts would reveal. He needs to make himself go through the process so that when he encounters a problem too hard even for him he will know the steps to take to arrive at a solution. The danger, of course, is that in attempting to respond superficially to a diversity of stimuli his energy is dissipated. That is why a good teacher can exert a steadying influence on the gifted child and help him to draw from a learning situation all its inherent values. This child has a rich fantasy life. He is often distracted from the work at hand by the richness of his own imaginative interplay. His teacher needs to reach into this inner creativity to capitalize upon it.

Another problem of the gifted is to overcome learning aversions so that he may become a well-rounded learner. This is particularly important in the elementary school years. Oftentimes, he will pursue an interest so intently that his work in certain other areas will be neglected. There is some evidence that the gifted child is not so proficient in handwriting and spelling as he is in other areas. If this is true with respect to an individual child, the sooner this problem is faced the better. Most gifted children will readily understand the necessity for a well-rounded education. They will often acknowlege their difficulties more readily than they will work to surmount them. Here, again, is a situation in which the gifted child needs his teacher's support. He will need help to keep himself at the task of improving his skills through properly paced practice. He will need to discipline himself in learning to spell, for example, by a process that he tends to dislike—rote memorization, although he will be better able to profit from spelling rules and from a study of roots, prefixes, and suffixes than most children. He must learn that there are some skills in life that require painstaking effort and for which there are no shortcuts, although the amount of time he will need to spend on repetitive practice will usually be less than for other pupils.

An additional problem of the superior learner should be mentioned here, although it does not usually affect his education very much at the elementary school level. It is that his high potential is such that he could succeed almost equally well in a wide range of occupations and professions. This makes the matter of vocational choices difficult for the gifted child when the time comes that he must choose. Teachers, pupil personnel workers, school administrators, and parents all need to cooperate to help the gifted child find his own best place in life.

Special Needs Other Than Intellectual

If the school is to meet the intellectual needs of exceptionally bright children, certain other factors that have a bearing on learning must be given consideration. The emotional well-being of such people, as well as of all other individuals, depends in large part upon self-acceptance and accept- ance by others. In the case of this child, he must be provided with an environment that will encourage him to accept and to appreciate and understand others whom he may find objectionably slow and with whom he tends to become impatient. He must also learn to accept himself and to find for himself acceptance from others.

The child is usually aware to some degree of the learning differences between himself and the other children with whom he lives. Younger children may not be able to articulate this awareness, and many of the older children have learned from their age-mates not to flout the ways of the average or slow learner. An important learning for the gifted child is that of accepting and appreciating these differences in other people. In similar manner, average children must come to understand and accept the gifted even though the gifted outstrip them at many points. It is here that a teacher's guidance is important. This kind of appreciation on each side is much more than tolerance, for it is based on the under- standing that people are valued for many reasons other than their ability in sheer intellectual learning. Furthermore, the gifted child, if properly guided, will come to know that some of his age-mates of lesser intellectual ability may be superior in certain academic areas, and in other areas of living not strictly thought of as academic. Moreover, they may have de- veloped their skills to levels of proficiency that exceed that of the gifted through an industrious self-application. They may have unusual gifts of leadership.

The gifted child must learn to appreciate the learning differences in others in another sense, that of taking into account the slower and less powerful intellectual functioning of those with whom he lives when sharing ideas. He must be encouraged to think as well and as fast as he can, but at the same time he must learn to express this high-powered thinking simply and in terms that others can understand. This will not be easy for him to do. It will frequently result in a sense of frustration for him. Nevertheless, unless he learns to be patient with others early in life and to develop a true understanding of the worth of all people, this sense of frustration may trouble him as long as he lives. Fortunately, the gifted child is also usually well adjusted. Research has shown that he is usually successful in his human relations. Since his brilliance helps him to have unusual insight, he can be led to understand how others are thinking and feeling; and with skillful guidance on the part of the classroom teacher, others will learn to appreciate and to accept him.

12. Identification and General Placement Procedures for Pupils of Superior Learning Abilities *

Division of Curriculum and Instruction and the Department of Psychological Services, Milwaukee Public Schools

General Principles

1. Academic abilities exist on a continuum in the Milwaukee school population. No clear-cut marked division exists between those children defined as above average in academic ability at any grade level and those children defined as superior. By utilizing well-defined screening and selection criteria, the identification of a group to be known as Children and Youth of Superior Ability can be accomplished with reasonable accuracy based upon arbitrary but generally accepted criteria.

2. Identification and placement procedures will need to be citywide in scope. These procedures must provide for the earliest possible identification of such pupils as well as for flexibility and reappraisal at all grade levels where special educational plans may be available for such pupils (kindergarten through grade 12). These procedures are based, first, upon group test scores of ability, group test scores of

* From *Program for Children and Youth of Superior Ability,* pp. 15–20, Milwaukee, Wis. Reprinted with permission.

achievement, teacher ratings, past classroom accomplishments of the students, and secondly, upon individual psychological studies of the pupils who were screened by group techniques.

3. Placement procedures for students beyond the intermediate grades will need to take account of the level of overall academic ability established by the student and at the same time provide for the student's areas of strongest motivation and achievement. That is, certain students of superior ability by the time they reach the junior high school may evidence high language achievements but lower patterns of achievement in numerical areas. Other students may reverse this pattern or show other definite patterns of strengths and weaknesses in academic achievement. Differentiated interests and abilities will likely be even more evident at the senior high school level.

4. Extraneous factors such as irregularities of physiological development, of social adjustments, and of emotional stability may have a deleterious effect upon learning and the functioning of pupils, including those pupils identified as having superior ability. These factors will be considered in the individual psychological study of each pupil referred for possible placement in the program.

5. Placement recommendations will be made by personnel of the Department of Psychological Services to the Division of Curriculum and Instruction. Written substantiation of such recommendations in the form of a report will be made to the principal of the school the pupil attends and to the appropriate personnel in the Division of Curriculum and Instruction. Division of Curriculum and Instruction personnel will decide as to individual pupil placement.

6. Once a pupil has been identified as a pupil of superior ability, and he has been placed in any special program developed for such pupils, he may be reevaluated upon written referral to the Department of Psychological Services. This referral may be initiated by either the school principal or by authorized persons in the Division of Curriculum and Instruction. Any decision for reassignment of a pupil will be based upon individual psychological study, teacher appraisal, parental request, group test results, and present achievement records. This is essentially the same procedure used for placement in the program. Each year all pupils of superior ability in special arrangements will be systematically reviewed through the use of an evaluation form filed by the teacher.

7. Specific identification procedures for pupils of superior ability are based on the need for as careful a study of these students as is required for the identification of other exceptional pupils. The educational programs for such pupils will need to be founded upon a careful identification of the population involved.

Specific Identification Procedures at Instructional Levels

THE PRIMARY SCHOOL

1. All P3 children each school year are to be given a group intelligence test during the last month of the semester. The test will be selected by Psychological Services in collaboration with the Division of Curriculum and Instruction.

2. The results of this group test are to be carefully examined by the classroom teacher and building principal to screen all pupils who are at or above the 90th percentile level of this test—(cutoff points in terms of IQ, MA, or raw scores to be furnished by Psychological Services).

3. Teachers will fill out a rating scale and recommendation sheet for all students who meet the aforementioned criterion. (These forms will be furnished by Psychological Services.) These forms will be attached to a regular referral for Psychological Services and mailed to the Department of Psychological Services. Each pupil will be seen by the regularly assigned psychologist at the school where the child is enrolled. The psychologist will confer with the teacher of the student, will study the cumulative record, and will then prepare a written recommendation. Recommendations will be sent to the school and to the Division of Curriculum and Instruction. Depending upon findings, parental conferences at the school may then be held involving the concerned parties.

4. Children who either do not meet the group test criterion or who have not taken the group test but about whom teachers and principals have strong evidence that they might be students of superior ability should be referred at any time for individual psychological study. This would mean that some students will be studied on an individual basis as early as during kindergarten. It would also mean a check of group test results for students where those results seemed inconsistent with teacher observations.

THE INTERMEDIATE GRADES

1. All 4B students and all 6B students will be given, as a part of the citywide testing program, a group intelligence test and a group achievement test.

2. Upon receiving the rosters of the test results, the elementary schools that have been designated as having a part in any special arrangement for students of superior ability will examine these rosters to screen such students.

3. All students who establish an intelligence quotient at the 95th percentile level on the group intelligence test and also establish a 90th percentile level on the battery mean of the group achievement test will be designated as meeting screening criteria for the program of superior ability students. (Cutoff scores in terms of IQ, MA, GP, etc., will be furnished by Psychological Services.)

4. Teachers of students so designated will fill out rating sheets and recommendation forms (to be supplied by Psychological Services) on each student and attach them to a regular referral for Psychological Services. As many of these students as possible will be individually studied by the regularly assigned school psychologist during the regular school year in the child's own school. Some of these students will be seen during the summer prior to the school year of contemplated placement. Appropriate recommendations will be made to the school, to the Division of Curriculum and Instruction, and to the parents.

5. All students who meet one or the other of the screening criteria, as stated in the aforementioned paragraph, but who do not meet both criteria and who are strongly recommended by their teachers will also be referred for individual psychological study. Rating sheets and recommendation forms will be made for these students in a manner similar to that made in the preceding paragraph.

6. Any pupil who is once identified as a student of superior ability and placed in any special arrangement and who does not adjust well to the program should be reappraised by the teacher and reevaluated by the psychologist. Recommendations will be made with appropriate action decided by personnel in the Division of Curriculum and Instruction in collaboration with unit school personnel.

7. Identification procedures for students new to the system, for students who miss the citywide test experience, and other exceptional cases

may be instituted by the unit school through individual referral to the Department of Psychological Services at any time during grades 4, 5, and 6. Subsequent recommendations will be made.

8. All students who are engaged in any phase of the special program provided for students of superior ability will be evaluated each year during grades 5 and 6 by a teacher rating instrument. All students who have established doubtful ratings should be restudied during the second semester of grade 6 and careful recommendations made as to continuance at the junior high level.

JUNIOR HIGH SCHOOL (GRADES 7–8–9)

1. Students previously identified at the primary and elementary levels and performing satisfactorily according to teacher ratings will enter their district junior high school without intensive individual study. However, all students where prognosis for success in a junior high program is questionable will be subject to careful review using all previous substantiating data before being dropped from the program or allowed to proceed in the program or in parts of the program. No student will be dropped from the program without a parental conference.

2. All students will be reassessed routinely at the 6B level through the use of group intelligence tests and group achievement tests. Any student after being placed in the program who falls below the 95th percentile on the ability test and/or below the 90th percentile on the battery mean of the group achievement test will be routinely referred to Psychological Services for reassessment. Appropriate recommendations will be made for this student following such a study.

3. Personnel in the elementary schools will further examine the group test results of all 6B students and make recommendations and referrals in the same manner previously done with the 4B students for students who were not identified at the 4B level. This will include new students as well as those students who were unable to meet the criteria at the fourth grade level but who now meet the criteria.

4. At the junior high level all student records will be reappraised to ascertain proper placement for the total program offered or for specific parts of that program. For example, identified students who have met the initial criteria of establishing a 95th percentile level on a group intelligence test and a 90th percentile level on the battery mean of the group achievement test may have established through

testing and classroom achievement well-defined peak areas of performance. Students dropping below the 80th percentile level in a subject area and/or establishing less than a grade of B in the immediate past semester should be carefully considered prior to being permitted to participate in a program designed for students of superior learning ability in the low subject matter area. Denial of participation in one part of the special program should not mean denial of participation in other areas of the specially designed program.

5. All 6B students who fail to meet the 95th percentile level on the group intelligence test and fail to meet the 90th percentile level on the group achievement battery but who do establish achievement at the 95th percentile level in some one achievement area in which there is a special program should be identified and considered for placement in that particular area at the beginning of grade 7. This provision holds if the group intelligence IQ does not fall below the 75th percentile level. All such students should be referred for individual psychological service as soon as possible either before or after entrance into the program.

6. Guidance personnel in the junior high schools should examine the results of the citywide testing program at the 8B level of all students previously identified for the program for students of superior ability. Students falling below the criteria used for initial selection should be reviewed and a restudy made of their response to the program. In some instances, such students not recently studied individually by the psychologist should be restudied with appropriate recommendations. In addition, all students not previously meeting the selection criteria should be referred as was done at the 4B and 6B level. A limited number of such newly identified students may be added to the program at this level as conditions and program limitations permit.

7. All identified students participating in any phase of the program during grades 7–8–9 should be rated yearly by teachers, and any student falling below the grade of B for a semester should be given careful consideration and counseling by the guidance staff of the school, and, if necessary, referred for individual reassessment by Psychological Services.

   The results of the 8B citywide testing program should be scanned by the junior high school guidance staff for peak and low performance areas to select students for assignment to one or more classes in the program.

SENIOR HIGH SCHOOL (GRADES 10–11–12)

1. By the time students reach senior high, identification procedures will have established a well-defined group of students who can be programmed in accordance with interests, motivations, relative strengths, and relative weaknesses. This programming should be accomplished by the local guidance staff at the senior high school to which the student matriculates with special reference to the cumulative data available on each identified student.

2. New students should not be brought into the program without having met the criteria previously established at lower grade levels. Students who meet these criteria but who have not been previously identified prior to the tenth grade can be screened using the results of the 10B citywide testing program. Students who establish a score at the 95th percentile level on the ability test and establish a 90th percentile level on the achievement test are to be rated by the guidance staff in cooperation with the subject teachers and referred for individual psychological study. In addition, students who meet the 95th percentile level in any subject area, despite the fact that they do not meet the criteria of ability or overall achievement, are to be considered for placement in the special programs provided in their area of peak performance (providing they do not fall below the 75th percentile level on the group or individual ability test). Recommendations for students newly identified by such procedure at the tenth grade level will be made to the Division of Curriculum and Instruction and to the senior high school staff by the psychologist making the individual study.

3. Students previously identified as having superior ability will be routinely rated by their teachers as they progress through grades 10–11–12. All identified students who experience difficulty in specific subject areas or in personal adjustments should have the opportunity for continued counseling from the guidance staff. In situations where the guidance staff feels the student needs to be reappraised, such a student will be referred for individual study by the psychologist assigned to the high school.

4. No student will be dropped from the program at the senior high school without careful study involving the principal, the parent, the classroom teacher, the guidance staff, the school psychologist, and personnel from the Division of Curriculum and Instruction.

CHAPTER THE PROBLEM OF ENRICHMENT

13. The Enrichment Program, Shaker Heights, Ohio *

THOMAS F. BANAHAN, *Director of Elementary Education*

Understandings Basic to Determining Procedures with Gifted Children

1. School curricula are usually written for average children and often do not challenge the gifted child to work to his capacity.
2. Enrichment is usually better than acceleration.
3. A wide variety of activities enriches the child's experiences and challenges him further.
4. The gifted child needs group experiences.
5. Many opportunities to make choices increase his initiative.
6. The gifted child is capable of assuming more than the average class assignment and will enthusiastically embark upon expanding specific details that supplement the daily work.
7. High IQ and high reading ability make it possible for the gifted child to engage in a wide range of activities.
8. A gifted child is usually well-adjusted emotionally and is able to do ordinary work in an effortless fashion with superior results.
9. The gifted child must be encouraged to be patient, thoughtful, and helpful to other children without being patronizing.
10. Every child achieves at his own rate, according to his own ability, but the gifted child quickly becomes aware of appropriate goals and learns how to evaluate his achievement critically.

* From *The Enrichment Program*, Shaker Heights Schools, Ohio, pp. 5–9. Reprinted with permission.

11. A gifted child needs to become increasingly aware of his own personality development and that of others.

12. He must learn the importance of making positive contributions to groups in a democratic, responsible way.

13. Evidence of marked ability is generally recognized at the kindergarten level.

14. The gifted child, like all other children, requires the security found in love and affection. He needs challenging, creative activities and a helpful and encouraging atmosphere in which to live and grow.

15. The gifted are one of the nation's greatest resources.

Curriculum Enrichment

1. Giving children many opportunities for:
   a) Expressing feelings and emotion in art, music, dancing, and creative writing of poems, stories, and plays.
   b) Participating in dramatics.
   c) Exploring areas of interest.
   d) Reviewing interesting books that are too difficult for the average child.
   e) Creating book interpretations through drawings or miniature scenes set up in the classroom or library to stimulate others to read.
   f) Developing contributions to current events discussions.

2. Providing challenging materials.

3. Promoting the desire to help others in the classroom.

4. Providing positions of responsibility.

5. Calling attention to opportunities to write creatively and to enter general scholastic competition such as spelling, essay, art, and writing contests and to participate in science and current citizenship experiences.

6. Encouraging development of hobbies.

7. Alerting children with special talents to opportunities for further development.

8. Encouraging joy and personal satisfaction in work well-done.

Resources for Enrichment in Shaker Heights Schools

1. A well-trained staff of teachers who are aware of changing trends and who are prepared to meet children's needs. They are sincere in their efforts to help develop fine citizens.

2. School librarians and special teachers of art, music, and physical education who provide better and wider experiences in the extra-curricular program.
3. Excellent school housing, cleanliness, and orderliness that help to set high standards.
4. Well-equipped children's libraries in all elementary and secondary school buildings are constantly provided with the most recent and best reading materials.
5. Educational supplies that include many types of audio-visual aids and laboratory equipment.
6. Student governments and group activities that offer limitless opportunities for development of leadership, initiative, and citizenship.
7. Community resources that are rich in cultural opportunities.

Recommendations

Further enrichment of the program could be accomplished if there were:

1. A science teacher capable of guiding gifted children in workshop practices that require knowledge greater than that of the classroom teacher.
2. Greater use of natural resources and metropolitan parks.
3. French or Spanish instruction before the junior high level.
4. Woodworking or craft rooms available for construction work appropriate at the elementary school level.
5. Theory of music courses especially at the secondary level to meet college entrance requirements.
6. Extension of present use of local museums and civic resources.

There was universal recommendation that all classes be kept small so that the gifted child might receive more individual guidance and his teachers learn to know him as a person. One teacher's remark pictured this clearly when she said, "I have done much informal visiting with them (the gifted children), answering their questions or directing them as to where and how they can find the answers, have encouraged developing special interests and hobbies, have discussed their social and personality problems with them and with their parents. I wish I could have done much more."

14. Enrichment Provisions, Niagara Falls *

WELDON R. OLIVER, *Superintendent of Schools,*
AND
ANNE K. HORGAN

Provision for the Gifted in Niagara Falls

Someone has said if you wish to be a pioneer you must travel in a covered wagon, meaning, I presume, that the way is uncharted, the going is rough, and you must proceed slowly. I think that we in Niagara Falls have pretty well met these criteria as we do consider ourselves one of the pioneers in this area of the country. It may be recalled that the first large-scale program for academically outstanding students was reported in St. Louis, Missouri, in 1868. Acceleration or flexible promotion was the procedure used by the St. Louis School System of that time. They now use grouping and enrichment.

In organizing our program for the gifted we were influenced by Hollingworth who contended that "the problems of the gifted pertain chiefly to the period before twelve years of age, for the problems of the gifted person tend to be less numerous as he grows older, and can use his intelligence, independently, in gaining control of his life. I consider the problems of the gifted are most urgent at the elementary school level because it is in the primary and elementary school that the very intelligent child most especially needs a supplement to the standard curriculum." [1]

In September 1930, we organized our first program at Fifth Street School. Three years later the one at Cleveland Avenue School had its inception; and in this fall (1958) another combination fifth and sixth grade group was opened at Hyde Park School, and a straight fifth grade was organized at 95th Street School. We plan on having an additional fifth grade group at 95th Street School (fall of 1959). These groups are known as Informal Groups. We try to keep the teacher load at a maximum of 24 students. At the completion of the elementary school training, the

---

* From *Gifted Children,* Board of Education, Niagara Falls, N.Y., pp. 12–15. Reprinted with permission.

[1] Leta S. Hollingworth, *Gifted Children: Their Nature and Nurture* (New York: The Macmillan Company, 1926).

children go into Super A Groups at the junior high school level where the same type of program is carried on.

Our children are identified in the fourth grade and as previously indicated attend the Informal Groups during the last two years in elementary school.

Students qualify for these groups on the basis of high mental endowment as determined by several group intelligence tests and an individual psychological evaluation, high achievement level, emotional maturity, and social adaptability. In general, children who are markedly immature for their age, those who lack physical stamina or who are seriously upset emotionally, or who are low achievers do not qualify. Regarding the emotionally disturbed, I might mention that we do consider the introverted child. We feel that these children have adjusted well when placed in these groups.

Educators seem to be particularly interested in the tests we use for identification. In kindergarten all our children are given either the Gates or the Metropolitan Reading Readiness Test. Gifted children frequently attain at least the 90th percentile. In the first grade the California Pre-Primary is administered and in the third grade the California Mental Maturity Primary. (It is our experience that the verbal score on the California is of more significance than the nonverbal or total score.) In the fourth grade they are given the Henmon Nelson Group Intelligence Test. A word of warning about the Henmon Nelson. We know a positive correlation exists between speed of performance and brightness. However, we do know that occasionally the slow reacting, meticulous mentally gifted child may be penalized by the Henmon Nelson because it is a speed rather than a power test. In the latter part of September all fourth graders are given the Iowa Basic Skills. (In the fourth grade they have had the New York State Reading and Math Progress Tests.) The cutoff is the attainment of a grade equivalent of 6.0 in reading, but most of the children who qualify are reading on seventh and eighth grade levels in early fourth grade. The cutoff on the California Mental Maturity and Henmon Nelson is 130 IQ, but other factors are always taken into consideration. High reading comprehension level is a good indicator of brightness. We frequently find that students who have IQ's below 130 on the group intelligence tests but high reading levels qualify for these groups when individually appraised.

We use the S-B (L) Scale for individual psychological evaluation. Our experience has been much the same as that of Gallagher and Crowder who write, "The numerical IQ results of the WISC were considerably lower than the Binet performance and are a reflection of the way in which the two measuring instruments were constructed. It is not possible to obtain an IQ of higher than 155 on the WISC, whereas a child may obtain an

IQ of over 200 on the Binet. It is clear that many of the children were performing on the very top level of the WISC Scale and their total capacities were not measured by this test."

In general, no child qualifies for assignment to our Informal Groups unless he has attained an IQ of 140 or above on an individually administered test.

When identification has been completed, the highest ranking students are assigned to the nearest school offering an enrichment program. The parents are then invited to the psychologist's office for a personal interview where the objectives, assets, and limitations of the program are explained to them. Placement is, of course, voluntary. Parents are responsible for transportation of their children to-and-from the assigned school.

In these classes the children are held to high standards of performance, achievement, and behavior. Simply speaking, we broaden the base of the curriculum, feeling as we do that "To whom much has been given much is expected." We know they learn quickly and we strive to have them accomplish according to their abilities. They branch out on a rich program of work suitable to their ages and interests.

Among the enrichment activities we might list the following:

1. Use reference books extensively in assigned and independent research as they are taught research techniques.
2. Publish a quarterly magazine.
3. Learn parliamentary procedures that they use in their club meetings.
4. Develop individual hobbies and interests.
5. Intensive work in language and literature. Engage in imaginative prose and poetry writing.
6. Writing and producing plays.
7. Training in and shouldering of responsibility.
8. Stimulated to do critical thinking.
9. Typewriting.
10. Taking trips to museums, concerts, industrial plants, and public libraries.
11. Spend much time in becoming acquainted with and discussing world affairs.
12. Begin the study of French.
13. Reviewing books and making book reports.
14. Learn to talk well by preparing and giving talks of their own choices.
15. Receive advanced work in science, social studies, mathematics, art, dramatics, and the like.
16. Creativity and originality are stressed.

Regarding the effectiveness of our program, we have little objective data. In 1945, Minnie Jack made a comparative study of forty children who had had Informal Group training and forty who had not. They were matched on the basis of IQ ratings. Questionnaires were sent to parents and students. She found that the children who had had special training were higher achievers in high school, more made the National Honor Society, more received scholarships, and more engaged in extracurricular activities than the control group. With the exception of two or three responding, students would again choose to go into the program if again given the opportunity, and parents would choose to have their children repeat this school experience.

About five years ago there was some talk of discontinuing the groups. Immediately there was a deluge of written and verbal protests from parents, parent organizations, and former students. They also appeared at Board of Education meetings to voice their opposition to the group being discontinued.

We feel that inasmuch as there is such a very high percentage of acceptance of assignments to these groups that they have demonstrated their worthwhileness. We have very few rejections and then for some valid reason such as health or distance. In no instance has there been an objection because a parent has disagreed with the philosophy.

15. Enrichment Provisions, Los Angeles *

EVERETT CHAFFEE, *Associate Superintendent, Division of Instructional Services, Los Angeles City Schools*

Foreword

It is generally recognized that intellectually gifted pupils can learn with remarkable speed and depth and meet normal standards of achievement with relatively little effort. Therefore, extraordinary measures should be taken by educators to strengthen motivation for learning, to offer experi-

* From *Education of Intellectually Gifted Pupils in Los Angeles City Schools*, rev., May 1962, pp. 16–19. Reprinted with permission.

ences appropriate to their giftedness, and to provide for individual pacing of learning.

The following statement on enrichment for intellectually gifted pupils is directed to working groups within the Los Angeles City Schools to use as a guide for:

1. Developing courses of study and instructional guides for the gifted.
2. Establishing criteria for the selection of textbooks and library materials for the gifted.
3. Providing institute and in-service activities for teachers of the gifted at the district and local school level.
4. Conducting faculty and departmental meetings to guide, foster, and appraise the program for the gifted in the school.

Enrichment for the Intellectually Gifted

Enrichment requires a learning environment conducive to exploration and originality. An enriched educational program for intellectually gifted pupils is based on the recognition of individual differences and is planned to meet individual needs and challenge abilities. Enrichment emphasizes quality rather than quantity and adds depth and scope to learning experiences. It provides for development of the following abilities: reflective and critical thinking, problem solving, and creative thinking and expression.

Learning Environment

Enrichment requires a learning environment that:

1. Permits the gifted to progress as rapidly as each is capable of mastering concepts, content, and skills prescribed by the course outline and concurrently provides opportunity for each to pursue the subject in depth and breadth.
2. Opens up new horizons by providing a variety of materials and experiences.
3. Stimulates a desire to explore many fields of knowledge.
4. Encourages pupils to think freely, to try new ways, to originate, but to subject their thinking and creating to their own rigorous, critical analysis.
5. Develops ideals, attitudes, appreciations, and understandings that are reflected by growth in social responsibility.
6. Provides opportunities and time for reflective thinking.
7. Develops self-knowledge, a realistic understanding of abilities and limitations, an ability to set goals and evaluate achievement.

8. Provides opportunity for independent work, the development of initiative, and the ability to plan and organize.
9. Stresses efficient study habits with emphasis on self-direction.

Individual Differences

As teachers plan an enriched educational program for the gifted, it is essential to pay constant attention to the ways in which gifted pupils differ. It is generally acknowledged that:

1. No two pupils are alike and that differences between gifted pupils and other pupils are largely a matter of degree.
2. Pronounced individual differences exist among gifted pupils, and these become more evident as the pupils increase in chronological age.
3. The learning process follows a sequential order and no stage of growth is likely to be skipped; however, in gifted pupils some stage of the learning process may appear at an earlier chronological age than in other pupils.

Depth and Scope

An enriched educational program emphasizes quality rather than quantity and provides learning experiences that have depth and scope in order to elicit a high quality of pupil response. Such enriched experiences:

1. Provide a wide variety of learning opportunities.
2. Help to develop skills to a high level of accomplishment and challenge the full use of abilities.
3. Place increased emphasis on the understanding of principles and generalizations.
4. Provide opportunity to explore related areas of knowledge.
5. Encourage use of many different sources in securing information including primary sources.
6. Develop ability to recognize trends and sequences and cause-and-effect relationships.
7. Develop understanding of values implicit in events or problems.
8. Provide opportunity to delve deeply into fields of special interest.
9. Furnish intensive contacts with people and with problems demanding creative thought and critical analysis.
10. Provide opportunities for school and community service and for participation in civic activities.

11. Develop techniques of working with others toward common goals.
12. Provide opportunities to work independently in planning, executing, and evaluating.
13. Provide opportunity to utilize critical analysis and original thinking.

Reflective Thinking, Problem Solving, and Critical Thinking

These terms are used synonymously in educational literature. This type of thinking involves reconstruction of experience—combining skills, information, and thinking into a unitary process so that earlier meanings are enlarged and refined, resulting in a reconstructed conceptual pattern. An enriched program for the gifted provides ample opportunity for pupils to:

1. Associate ideas.
2. Perceive relationships.
3. Attach new meanings to previous experiences.

Problem solving involves understanding the characteristics of the kind of problem that has within it the elements of an effective learning experience. Such a problem must:

1. Challenge the mind.
2. Require reflection.
3. Involve conclusions or solutions.
4. Be real: have personal impact, be of contemporary significance, be of recurrent concern, be debatable in nature.

Problem solving involves certain formal steps that do not necessarily follow in sequence since some casual, fragmentary, intuitive thinking inevitably occurs. It is essential to:

1. State clearly the problem or question.
2. Give possible solutions, answers, or working hypotheses.
3. Gather, organize, and interpret related data.
4. Make tentative inferences and conclusions.
5. Test or verify inferences, conclusions, or hypotheses.

Creative Thinking

An enriched program for the gifted is planned to be flexible in order to afford opportunity for the pupil to:

1. Appreciate and understand the heritage from the past but not be shackled by it.

2. Value his own judgment and not be pressured by conformity.
3. Engage in thought and thoughtful action without concern for their ultimate application.
4. Evolve new ideas, concepts, and relationships from past experiences.
5. Start with the germ of an idea and pursue it through varied possibilities.
6. Recognize relationships among seemingly unrelated data.
7. Understand the value of organized experimentation.
8. Exercise intuitiveness balanced by intellectual control.
9. Discriminate between the essential and the incidental.
10. Increase sensitivity to quality.
11. Become acutely perceptive.
12. React to the creativity of others.
13. Become capable of sustained concentration and hard work.

16. *Meeting the Educational Needs of the Gifted, North Dakota* *

JANET M. SMALTZ, *Director, Division of Special Education,* AND
JAMES D. MATHISEN, *Director, Division of Guidance Services*

Some Specific Areas of Concentration

In providing for the educational needs of the gifted, three areas of concentration have been found helpful when properly coordinated. These areas are: (1) curriculum improvement, (2) guidance services, and (3) parent counseling.

The most widely acclaimed plan for gifted pupils is the *enriched curriculum.* Basic to this plan is a sufficient variety of books and reference materials in which gifted pupils can do independent reading and research. Necessary, too, is the provision for a sufficient variety of activities that not only will challenge the pupils but will provide social interaction where

* From *Guides to Special Education in North Dakota: IX. The Gifted Child,* pp. 10–13, Department of Public Instruction, Bismarck, N.D. Reprinted with permission.

bright, average, and slow-learning children can learn to play and plan together. The gifted child needs to learn to accept responsibility, to respect the potential talents of other pupils, and to tolerate the academic short-comings of his slow-learning associates. The capacity of the gifted can usually be challenged in literature dealing with science whether it be home economics or flying an airplane.

This enrichment of the curriculum may take the form of:

1. Modifying the program of studies to include more challenging subjects and more opportunity for creative work.
2. Helping pupils to work on class projects that make a contribution to class, school, and community.
3. Encouraging independent work in science, art, music, or writing.
4. Committee work.
5. Community study.

Plans should be made to identify the gifted child early so that a long term program of education may be organized. *Guidance services* are necessary if the gifted pupil is to become a well-adjusted, happy, and successful personality. Developmental guidance of the gifted child follows the general pattern of effective guidance for all children. More specifically it requires:

1. Special study of the child to recognize and understand abilities and talents.
2. Helping the child to progress in academic achievement with satisfaction.
3. Assisting the child to develop a concept of his most acceptable self and his responsibility to society for gifts.
4. Assisting the child to obtain emotional maturity.

Parent participation in the planning for the gifted is vital to the success of an effective program. Parents of such children are frequently resourceful in developing the aptitudes and interests of their children. Through conferences the parents may gain insight into their responsibilities for helping their gifted child toward social, emotional, and intellectual development. The following suggestions have been found useful in counseling the parents of gifted children:

1. Ask parents to come in for an interview in which they may talk out satisfactions and problems. The crystallization of their thinking may give them a better perspective in viewing the child and working with the school.
2. Urge fathers who are professional workers to spend more time with their gifted sons.

3. Explain to parents of preadolescent gifted children that they should have greater understanding of the problems of these children who often express adolescent behavior at an earlier age than do "normal" children.

4. Impress parents from lower social or economic classes who have bright or potentially gifted children with their responsibility for providing as stimulating a home environment as possible.

5. Suggest that parents from the professional classes do not take the success of their children for granted and set standards so high that the gap between their aspirational levels and their achievement levels results only in feelings of frustration.

6. Indicate to mothers of pre-teen-age gifted sons that greater acceptance and tolerance of their behavior may be necessary than for the behavior of their daughters of similar age.

7. Make clear to parents the importance of family cohesiveness where mutual respect and appreciation of each member are stressed, particularly where the IQ of the gifted child is higher than that of the parents or of siblings. Parents and siblings may create feelings of rejection and insecurity if they indicate to the gifted child that he is different and thus set apart from the family circle.

8. Assist parents to become active in working with other gifted children by making their hobbies, collections, or professional know-how available to children at meetings, demonstrations, or field trips.

17. Enrichment for Gifted Children in the Elementary Grades, San Diego *

RALPH DAILARD, *Superintendent of Schools*

THE BASIC plan of the San Diego Program for the Gifted has from the very beginning been that gifted pupils are offered richer experiences as a part of the instructional program of the regular classroom. Elementary principals have used cluster-grouping, acceleration, and transfer of gifted pupils to other schools where these procedures would benefit the individual children concerned.

* From *Curriculum Digest*, April-May, 1961, pp. 2–4, San Diego, Calif. Reprinted with permission. (Picture omitted.)

This fall, as an extension of this thinking and as a part of the general reorganization at the elementary level, a number of elementary schools were designated as "Instructional Study Centers." Parents of gifted pupils were invited to enroll their children in fourteen of these centers.

Consultants will devote major time to working with these pupils. This arrangement is not an attempt to segregate the gifted, for they do attend regular classes in these schools. What is accomplished is this: (1) The gifted children now have the opportunity to do group work in class with other children of similar interests and abilities. (2) Books, materials and equipment purchased expressly for the Program for the Gifted will now be available in larger numbers and for longer periods of time to the gifted pupils and their teachers in these centers. (3) There is more focusing of the gifted consultant services, for instead of having to work with many teachers who probably had only one or two gifted children in their classes, the consultants now work with a few teachers who have a larger number of such pupils.

The three elementary teacher consultants, whose time is now concentrated in the study centers, are experienced and capable teachers who have been given a special assignment assisting with the program for the gifted. These consultants suggest materials and ideas so that the teachers are helped in providing enrichment possibilities for the identified gifted and other pupils of superior ability who will be working on the same projects with the gifted.

Enrichment in the Elementary Schools

Enrichment activities for gifted pupils in the elementary schools may take many different forms. Usually, enrichment is either supplementary assignments over and above the regular class activities or the replacement of certain routine activities by something more challenging. The latter, of course, is done only after the pupil has demonstrated his mastery of this basic material.

Other less obvious enrichment activities would include the following:

1. Increasing the amount of individualized work with pupils to improve work and study skills, motivation, interest, or confidence.
2. Furthering a pupil's personal and social adjustment—planning group work to provide situations for individuals to be accepted by others; increasing the pupil's ability to work and plan cooperatively with others; furthering leadership qualities; providing "ego-boosting" situations for the shy and withdrawn; and so forth.

3. Encouraging participation in the pupil-aide program—school offices, nurse's office, library, etc.
4. Providing opportunities for the development of special interests and encouraging interests in other desirable areas.

Enriching the Reading Program

If a gifted child has mastered the basic skills of reading and is doing the regular daily assignments of his group with zest and distinction, enrichment is a comparatively simple matter. Unfortunately, this is not always the case. Sometimes discussion is halfhearted and written work is careless and incomplete. In such cases any one of a combination of factors may be responsible. Teachers analyze the situation through a study of the child's standardized reading tests, through observation of his habits and reactions during study and discussion periods, and through experimentation in their own choices of material and methods of presentation. When a diagnosis of the situation has been completed, teachers then use various enrichment procedures as seem required.

Teachers who have gifted and superior students reading a year or more above grade level, on a reading achievement test recommended by the San Diego City Schools research department, usually begin the review period in the fall with the basic text for their particular grade. Teachers may feel the need of using one difficult supplementary reader after the basic is completed, or may go directly into an accelerated reader selected from the City School's Library for this purpose.

If *all* of the children in a top reading group score one year above grade level, teachers are entitled to a set of above-grade or accelerated readers for this group. If a few of the top group fail to read at least a year above grade level, these pupils are frequently transferred to the next lower group. If only the gifted or a few of the top group qualify, teachers obtain the above-grade books as supplementary readers for these children.

Above-grade readers are available for grades two, three, four, five, and six. None are available for grade one. Children at this level are expected to use, in groups and as individuals, a great number of at-grade readers, plus much science and social studies reference material that is far above the reading level of other children in the room.

Enrichment of the reading program is further carried out through:

1. More extensive reading.
2. Questions about the reading that require more mature thinking.
3. Assignments that involve the use of advanced reference and research skills.

4. Assignments that develop literary appreciation.
5. Creative activities suggested by the reading.
6. The use of more challenging material in the recreational reading program.

Enriching Language Arts

Language development of the gifted tends to be varied and uneven. Throughout the city, their achievement ranges from far above average to somewhat below average. Many gifted children, because of native curiosity, high reading ability, and a relatively good socioeconomic background, make a good showing in oral language of the impromptu monologue type. They may be less successful in the give-and-take of conversation or discussion. Some gifted children do poorly in oral work that requires preparation and in the mechanical aspects of written language.

All gifted children have the ability to think with clarity, logic, and originality—and many do. Some, however, because of lack of inspiration or practice, express in their oral and written language only vague, hasty, and commonplace ideas.

Elementary teachers have come to realize that whatever the language pattern of a gifted child may be, he needs to begin with a challenging basic program. This basic program, however, must be adapted and paced for each individual, for only as the basic program has challenged his interest and developed a pride in good workmanship is the gifted child ready and eager to master new and more difficult skills. Unlike arithmetic, more advanced language skills can be mastered with a minimum of teacher help.

Most gifted children are able to maintain perfect scores on the weekly tests from the state speller in one or two days of study per week instead of the usual five. These children are encouraged to use the time thus freed to work on their own personal spelling lists (words gleaned from daily written work in any subject matter area) or in more creative types of language work.

If gifted pupils are working up to capacity, they will complete class assignments in from one-half to two-thirds of the time required by their classmates. This means that teachers need to provide a wide variety of spare-time activities. Possibilities in the field of language are endless. The following are only a few examples of what is done in this area:

1. Activities growing out of class work—
   a) Writing notices or memoranda.

    b) Organizing ideas developed by the group.
    c) Compiling a bibliography.
    d) Writing material for the school newspaper.
2. Activities growing out of personal interest—
    a) Writing a diary or autobiography.
    b) Recording scientific observations.
    c) Exploring the history of language.
3. Activities designed to develop needed skills—
    a) Playing a dictionary game.
    b) Matching or classifying words.
    c) Making derivatives from a given root word.
4. Activities designed to develop facility and versatility, such as writing orginal stories, poetry, plays, etc.

Success in spare-time work has been found to depend largely on teacher motivation, guidance, and evaluation. The ultimate goal, of course, is to reach the point where our gifted children write spontaneously and enthusiastically on subjects of their own choosing.

Enriching the Arithmetic Program

The gap between ability level and achievement level of gifted children tends to be greater in arithmetic than in any other subject area. This is not surprising because, by its very nature, arithmetic is a subject in which a child cannot progress on his own initiative as readily as he can in a subject such as reading.

When learning a new process, the gifted child begins with the rest of the advanced group—at the concrete level. He moves into the abstract level as soon as he is ready to do so. Enough practice to develop mastery is required; and the pupil is excused from further use of practice sheets or exercises, unless his work demonstrates further need at some future time. These pupils are then encouraged to apply the process in solving selected problems from the text or from current school or community projects.

Many teachers have found it very valuable to have an arithmetic table in their rooms. Usually found on such tables are the following:

1. Supplementary books to be used to extend mathematical concepts.
2. Games (commercial or teacher-made) to help a gifted child to develop speed and accuracy in computation comparable to his ability in reasoning.
3. Manipulative materials—gas, water, or electric meters; a speedom-

eter; gauges of various kinds; carpenter's square; and the like. Pupils are encouraged to experiment with these devices by having the teacher pose problems involving the use of the material.

When and if a gifted child has used to the full all available enrichment material provided through the gifted program and has proved by diagnostic tests that he has mastered all grade-level requirements, he may, on recommendation of teacher, principal, and teacher consultant, be permitted to use a nonstate text at the next grade level.

Enriching Social Studies–Science

Probably no subject lends itself more to the enrichment of a classroom educational program than social studies. Very capable students with careful teaching guidance, plus carefully selected social studies materials and lessons, produce results that prove of great value to all concerned.

It is important that these superior children have many opportunities to be identified with a group and that they are not always working alone on isolated activities. The following are examples of the kinds of enrichment activities provided in social studies:

1. Planning and organizing service projects, such as a tree-planting ceremony or a community survey.
2. Locating and providing community resources for the social studies unit—for example, identifying flowers and shrubs near the school for a conservation unit activity.
3. Developing additional materials for use in the classroom, such as science files or resource folders of current material.
4. Arranging special collections for display; for example, an annotated portfolio of pictures for the dairy unit or a collection of special stamps for the mail unit.
5. Doing extensive reading in assigned areas to gain special knowledge or to locate additional materials for the rest of the class.
6. Assuming leadership in guiding a committee in planning a culmination program for a social studies unit.
7. Making an extended study of maps and globes that broadens the social studies learnings.
8. Writing creative stories or accounts based upon related social studies learnings.

These are only a few examples for, as was mentioned earlier, the opportunities for enrichment in social studies–science are almost limitless.

Conclusion

When planning a program for gifted and superior children, certain criteria must be met that will motivate and challenge these pupils. In general, the student should:

1. Be encouraged to search for information beyond that which is expected of the regular class.
2. Have opportunities to have roles of leadership and responsibilities that will develop these capacities.
3. Have opportunities to explore and develop interests of his own.
4. Have opportunities to do work that is creative as well as that which is structured or assigned.
5. Be permitted to develop and use his own initiative.
6. Be provided with enriched lessons and activities that have breadth and depth to them.

18. Enrichment in Elementary Homerooms, Portland *

MELVIN W. BARNES, *Superintendent of Schools*

Meaning of the Term "Enrichment"

The term "enrichment" appears often in educational writing and is used with a wide variety of meanings. The central element in most usages of the term implies providing an opportunity for a gifted pupil to learn something over and above that which is usually offered in a classroom. As DeHaan and Kough [1] have suggested, "enrichment is the process of tailor-fitting the curriculum to the needs, interests, and abilities

* From *The Gifted Child in Portland,* pp. 31–38, Portland Public Schools, Portland, Ore. Reprinted with permission. (Picture omitted.)
[1] Robert F. DeHaan and Jack Kough, *Helping Children with Special Needs* (Chicago: Science Research Associates, 1956), p. 11.

of the gifted pupil and of adding more variety and complexity to his assignments."

The term "enrichment" is a relative term and may create some difficulties in deciding just when "enrichment" has taken place. Since "enrichment" implies doing something more than would usually be done, one must have a fairly clear idea of what is usual. Since gifted children vary in their interests, abilities, and knowledge, no particular activity or curriculum modification can be regarded as always being "enrichment." What is "enrichment" for one child may not be for another.

The term "enrichment" is not itself descriptive of any particular administrative arrangement and could be used with any administrative plan.

The phrases "homeroom enrichment" and "classroom enrichment" are usually used to designate "enrichment" in a plan where the self-contained homeroom is the administrative unit and are contrasted with such terms as "acceleration" or "ability grouping." In a homeroom, pupils of the same chronological age are assigned to classes regardless of differences in their mental ages or differences in their other abilities. In the homeroom the teacher is expected to enrich the curriculum for individuals and small groups of pupils who are gifted (advanced) in various ways.

At the time the present program was undertaken, "enrichment" in the regular classroom was to the largest number of educators in Portland the most acceptable method of providing for gifted pupils. It continued to be one of the major methods in the program.

Methods of Enrichment

UNIT TEACHING

Small group projects and individual projects provide opportunities for able, highly-motivated pupils as individuals or in groups to go beyond the regular work in the classroom.

In the unit method of teaching, a major portion of the pupil's learning experiences are organized around certain large themes or problems. This method lends itself to varied teaching techniques: individualized instruction, work in small groups, and total class projects. Content may be drawn from several subject fields related to the particular problems that are being studied.

Pupils who read well may be encouraged to read more difficult resource material. Those with unusual artistic talent, mechanical ability, scientific knowledge, mathematical ability, or musical ability may contribute according to their various strengths. All contribute to the common theme or unit.

Unit teaching does not preclude drill, practice, and memorization, but these, as often as possible, are related to the unit material.

Advanced pupils may be assigned more difficult material and may be given more freedom to be creative and original. Many opportunities arise for advanced pupils to supply leadership in planning and carrying out activities related to the unit, since committee or group work is a feature of the method.

SMALL GROUP PROJECTS

A number of pupils who have similar interests and abilities are encouraged by the teacher to choose a project that would be of interest to them but may be beyond the abilities of the rest of the class. The group may work on the project when the remainder of the class is engaged in regular work. The group may share the results of its work by reporting to the class, although this is not essential when the project selected by the group is outside the interests of most of the class.

INDIVIDUAL PROJECTS

The individual project method is similar to the small group project method except that an advanced pupil may work alone on a problem of his choice. He may be encouraged to share the results of his work with his classmates insofar as they are understood and appreciated by the other students in the class. If his classmates are not interested in the project, it is important for the teacher to show appreciation for the work he has done and to encourage him to pursue further study in the area of his interest.

Examples of Homeroom Enrichment

ENRICHMENT IN A THIRD-GRADE CLASS

There are many opportunities for gifted children to do additional work in the third grade.

One pupil found directions for making a sundial. He became tremendously interested and asked for the necessary materials to make one. The teacher assisted him in making a compass in order to draw a circle. His sundial worked, and members of the class could tell time by it after he gave a report explaining the sundial and its uses.

During a study of weather, a pupil brought a large thermometer, explained its use, and developed an individual wall chart on weather for several months, showing variations from day to day.

Pupils with exceptional ability were given an opportunity to extend number experiences beyond those designed for the grade.

In the unit studies on Portland, these pupils did more reading, more creative writing, and gained a better understanding of the growth and development of the city.

One pupil became interested in Quentin Reynold's book, *The F.B.I.*, which the teacher had procured from the district library with this child's activities specifically in mind. Almost every day while he was reading the book, he gave reports on what he had read. Since reading difficulty of the book was well beyond third-grade level, it was amazing to see how much he grasped. The boy and his teacher decided that he should write to J. Edgar Hoover. In writing his letter, he learned letter-writing skills, including use of a formal heading. One can imagine how thrilled everyone was when George received an answer from J. Edgar Hoover, himself.

Some wonderful books have been written about children in foreign lands. They give a tremendous insight into life in other lands and are interesting to pupils since they are written about children. The interest in these, inspired by the advanced children, spread rapidly throughout the room.

A classroom newspaper was an excellent means of stimulating creative writing. An editor and coeditor were responsible for choosing the best stories and deciding how the paper would be put together. The writing, choosing of good stories, and lettering of headings were done by the children.

One pupil was a very good singer. Often she started the singing at the opening of school in the morning. For this room's part in the spring festival, she made up many of the dramatic activities to go with the song.

One child was gifted in rhythms. He learned dances so quickly that he could show others how to do them.

ENRICHMENT IN A SIXTH-GRADE CLASS

Arithmetic. One outstanding pupil moved through the regular year's work at accelerated speed. He was given special arithmetic projects and worked on these during regular time for arithmetic. One project was the metric system, which he explained, using charts he had made. He also made a liter out of cardboard and gave explanations. Time was provided for presenting this information to the class.

Abacuses were made by twenty members of the class. Instruction was given on how to add. Three pupils discovered the process of subtraction and one learned multiplication and some division.

A project with the area of parallelograms as compared with the areas of triangles and rectangles was worked successfully by two boys.

Science. Advanced books were provided for three pupils working on individual science projects.

Two students made a display on simple machines. Illustrations were made for each machine, and explanations were given to the class.

Five of the class members participated in a special science class. These were the outstanding science pupils in the room, and most of their work originated from the class.

Several pupils entered exhibits in the Science Fair.

Language arts. Many opportunities for reading, writing, and speaking were made available for able pupils.

A newsletter was written occasionally by different members of the class.

One pupil wrote a story for a *Boy's Life* writing contest. This was done at home but read to the class for suggestions.

One pupil, especially interested in writing, asked for some extra projects to do. She was given the enrichment portion of the creative writing tests to use as she pleased. She made good use of these and read some of her writing to the class.

A few minutes were set aside each week for anyone who had prepared an interesting poem or story to present it to the class.

One outstanding pupil became interested in the Dewey Decimal System. The room library was turned over to her. She classified each book by both subject matter and author's call number and gave instructions to the class.

A portion of the bulletin board was reserved for a pupil especially interested in reading who also had excellent leadership qualities. Her problem was to interest others in reading. She organized bulletin board displays and a Book-of-the-Week program. After book reports were given, she had nominations for the Book of the Week. A short review of the book that was chosen was written by the pupil who had read the book. These reviews were posted in the library section of the classroom.

Social studies. Many opportunities were available through suggestions in the resource units for able pupils to gain more information about the geography and history of peoples in the Western Hemisphere, outside the United States.

One child corresponded with a pupil in Argentina and planned several interesting talks from materials and pictures she had received.

Additional reading from library materials provided greater depth of learning for bright pupils.

Maps, murals, radio programs, and models gave pupils opportunities to show what they had learned.

ENRICHMENT IN AN EIGHTH-GRADE CLASS

Social studies. One group of advanced pupils made a study of the American Constitution, which went beyond the study made by the class. The origin of law and form dating back to English and Roman government was studied. A report was prepared for the class. Charts were made showing the rights of Americans under the first ten amendments. The language and meaning of the Preamble to the Constitution were studied in detail, including word derivation and style.

Detailed studies were made of such men as Washington, Jefferson, and particularly Benjamin Franklin, as the 250th anniversary of his birth was celebrated on January 17 of this year. Excerpts from his autobiography were read by two pupils. A study of Monticello, including the architecture, the grounds, and the furnishings, as well as the horticultural developments that Jefferson himself introduced to Virginia, was made by one pupil.

Another pupil made an original cartoon showing episodes of the Boston Massacre. He also made an original cartoon consisting of several pictures showing the interesting and strange career of Citizen Genet. He had become interested enough to look up the story of Genet and subsequently put his talent to use in drawing his impressions.

The Battle of Gettysburg interested a group of boys after they had heard a record of "You Are There." They studied additional material on the battle and found many pictures and interesting narratives relating to the battle. This led to one boy's discovering the famous character of the Civil War days, Matthew Brady. His interest in photography led to a study of Brady.

In Oregon history, many adult books were read by class members. One boy read *The Astorians* by Washington Irving; several read the Pulitzer prize book *The Way West* by Guthrie; and *The Columbia* by Holbrook. One pupil read *Up the Columbia for Furs* by Dryden, and gave a detailed report of the ways of the trappers in the early Northwest. A detailed study of the founding of Portland was made by one group, and a dramatization was given, showing the naming of Portland. A pictorial map of the early waterfront of Portland was also made, and stories of early Portland people, such as Terwilliger, Corbett, and Couch were found.

Science. Several boys showed the class some experiments, using the chemistry kit that led to the study of the table of elements, atomic weights, and valences. Two microscopes were brought to school, and a committee arranged specimens for the whole class to see through the microscope and made two large drawings in charcoal to illustrate their talks. In the study of atoms, several pupils made charts to illustrate reports on the structure of the atom-neutrons, electrons, and protons. These showed how steam is formed, how a piston works, and what causes expansion. In the study of the universe, in addition to the research of the class on planets, several pupils made a study of man's conquest of space and human adaptability. A study was made of the man-made satellite sent up in 1957. A detailed drawing was made of this, and one pupil made a report on the structure and operation of the satellite. Another pupil made a barometer with a glass tube and mercury. A daily weather chart was kept for most of the year. One month a graph was made, showing the modulation of temperature and barometric reading, using a commercial barometer.

Art. One pupil who is a talented artist used his gift in many of the unit studies. He planned several murals and produced some skillful work in tempera, charcoal, chalk, and oil. He was an inspiration to all of the boys and girls in the class in artwork. Much of the class artwork was based on music, science, and social studies.

Language arts. Several pupils wrote original stories and poems based on pioneer themes. One pupil made a study of Dickens and over a period of several years read most of his works. He gave an excellent talk on Dickens, his style, works, and life.

19. Acceleration: Some Considerations *

CLIFFORD W. WILLIAMS, *Director, Special Curriculum Projects, Portland, Oregon*

THE PHONE rings. A primary school principal begins to talk about a six-year-old boy whose conversation shows the insight and vocabulary of one many years older. "This child frightens me. What can we do for him? He reads like a fourth grader, and his other skills are more or less at the same high level."

"Whatever you do, Mr. Principal, it will involve some kind of acceleration."

"But he is too young to skip and anyway he seems to enjoy the first grade so much."

"I didn't say we would put him ahead a grade, although that is a possibility. We will see if there are better ways of adapting the program to him."

An eighth-grade student is reading a biography while his classmates are working percentage problems. He says he has finished his arithmetic and has done the extra assignment. His teacher agrees. "What more can I do? I have assigned reports for him to make on arithmetic in taxation, insurance, commerce. I have helped him find material on other number systems; he helps other students much of the time. I have just run out of enrichment ideas."

"Why don't you introduce him to the next step in mathematics?"

"What good will that do? He already helps his older brother with algebra, and if I work with him he will get further out of step."

A father talks with a high school principal.

* From *Educational Leadership*, March 1961, pp. 351–55. Reprinted with permission.

"Joe apparently wants to follow the family tradition by becoming a physician. I was twenty-eight when I was able to establish my own office. Is there any way to save a year or two?"

"Joe is an honor student and would probably benefit by more difficult courses. We are considering some college-level classes for next year, or perhaps the following year, but that won't help Joe. His college may be able to save some time for him, but we can't."

Why Accelerate?

These are not theoretical cases. They existed last year and the year before, and they will be with us and most other school districts next year and the next. They point out the more obvious reasons for acceleration. Children are different; they learn at differing rates; they have different aspirations. What these brief sketches also show is that school programs, of necessity, are geared to the large majority of youngsters, and variations for individuals are difficult to make. They demonstrate something more—the myriad reasons that can be found for not accelerating.

"He is too little to skip a grade." "He will get further out of step." "We haven't started advanced classes yet."

Significant, also, are some other phrases: "This child frightens me." "I have just run out of enrichment ideas." "He would probably benefit by more difficult courses."

This also adds up to the fact that somewhere we were pushed into a position in which the adaptive function of the school had to operate within unrealistic limits. American education undoubtedly had to undergo just such pushing and tugging in order to become what it is today. In the same way, tomorrow's schools will benefit by the differing theories of today's educators.

Before the turn of the century, when comparatively few children could avail themselves of formal education, there was little need to vary the pace of instruction for children of different capacities. As the American dream— education for *all* children—became a reality, appropriate provision for those of highest and lowest abilities was an increasingly persistent and complex problem. Multiple-track plans and flexible promotion systems were instituted in the late 1800's and early 1900's. Grade-skipping came into vogue in the first two decades of the present century.

By 1920, however, the Progressive Education movement began to exert a powerful influence on schools, particularly elementary schools. Considerable light and some confusion now were shed on laws of learning and the importance of the group to the individual. Questions were raised about the wisdom of removing gifted children from their age group to put them in classes with other children. Schools began to substitute groups within classes for multiple tracks and to substitute *enrichment* for *acceleration*. Under the weight of popular opinion among professional educators, the use of ability grouping and grade-skipping diminished and almost disappeared before 1940.

One of the strange phenomena of the period of growing concern for personality development and the importance of heterogeneous grouping was the emotional charge attached to key words and concepts. Thus acceleration came to mean "unwise hurrying"; track systems were said to be for trains, not children; the word "gifted" was made synonymous with "elite." The acceptable words were "heterogeneous," "self-contained homeroom," and "enrichment."

Following World War II, the critical demands of a changing world confronted educators with the necessity for reexamining their means, the general purposes of education, and the special problems of educating the gifted. Such a reexamination was inevitable, but the rapid scientific and technological advances of a world at war brought it about much sooner than might have been expected. Following the decline of ability grouping and of multiple-track systems, the elementary school and the junior high school, to a large degree, became a series of self-contained, heterogeneous classes. Teachers, pledged "to start with each child where he is and take him as far as he can go," were charged with providing appropriate instruction for each child. This they could do fairly satisfactorily in primary grades, but older children presented a difficult problem since they ought to become more different; they ought to be more varied in their abilities and interests.

The teacher of the eighth grade is confronted with children who vary as much as seven or eight years in their knowledge, skill attainment, and capacity to learn, and who vary considerably in their interests and aspirations. It is asking a great deal to expect a teacher to provide appropriately for each child in each field, particularly in view of the fact that the teacher is himself human and has human strengths and limitations.

It is for these reasons that reexaminations were inevitable. Beginning with the Harvard Report of 1945, the public schools were sharply criticized for a program designed to meet the needs of a "somewhat colorless mean, too fast for the slow, too slow for the fast." Other critics accused the schools of fostering a "cult of mediocrity" by aiming instruction at the average and making too few gestures toward the capable.

It should be pointed out here that every observant educator must recognize the tremendous contribution of the self-contained classroom. Most criticism has not taken into account that "problems can be met through this organization that must inevitably be met if one is to have a good school." [1] What the critics have noted is that an unexplainable inflexibility of thinking has grown up around the self-contained classroom. The fault in this type of program is not that it lacks value but that some of its proponents claim that it is a panacea, solving all of the problems of all children of all ages.

An increased critical concern has resulted in some relaxation in the rigidity in educational thinking. Moreover, a wealth of studies of considerable magnitude now show that fears of acceleration, elitism, and ability grouping are largely unfounded.

A period of experimentation with administrative devices favorable to abler students has been in progress over the past ten years. Nearly all studies have been concerned with some form of acceleration in combination with enrichment. Grade-skipping is being revived as a means of giving abler children opportunities more nearly appropriate to them. Most of the newer systems, however, are based on a premise that grade-skipping is a poor form of acceleration. Consequently they attempt to achieve proper pace in education without the real or imagined disadvantages of skipping. No one holds a particular brief for this one form of acceleration, especially if other forms can be devised to accomplish the aim of appropriate instruction with a pace that allows for proper concentration of strength.

Ungraded Elementary Schools

A valid criticism of grade-skipping is that acceleration is accomplished in such a way that gaps can appear in the child's knowledge. Therefore, any plan that achieves the same end without the accompanying disadvantage is worthy of examination.

One promising practice, and in many ways the most complex, to come out of the concern for individual differences, is the ungraded, or nongraded, technique in elementary schools. In the ungraded school, children enter at the usual age. They are not assigned to grades but to a program appropriate to their ability and past learning. Usually, children of several age groups may be found together, but the groups change somewhat depending on the tasks. Normally, the program of the primary section should be completed in three years, at which time the child is promoted to the intermediate section for another three years.

An advantage of this system lies in the fact that all children do not have to follow the typical pace. A few may take four years to complete a three-

---

[1] Association for Supervision and Curriculum Development, *The Self-Contained Classroom* (Washington, D.C.: the Association, a department of the National Education Association, 1960).

year program. Others may take only two years. The determining criterion is whether or not the assigned tasks, in the program of learning, have been accomplished.

The Milwaukee, Wisconsin, system has probably the best known ungraded program. Others include Appleton, Wisconsin; University City, Missouri; Park Forest, Illinois; La Junta, Colorado; and Marysville, California.[2]

Acceleration in Specific Subjects

In schools that continue the graded system of administrative organization, various plans have been established to make it possible for students to study subjects at a more rapid pace. Subgroups in self-contained classrooms can study arithmetic at varying levels, since normally the groups are comparatively homogeneous. Several school systems have planned programs for accelerating arithmetic for abler children in this way.

Generally, the plan calls for completion of the normal eight-year program by the end of the seventh grade. To accomplish this successfully, a start must be made as early as the fifth grade, preferably sooner. The intention is to keep able children working at demanding and interesting concepts of arithmetic at a steady pace. Therefore, the first course in algebra generally follows the accelerated arithmetic plan one year earlier than usual. Such a plan for grades 3–8 is explained in Curriculum Publication M-28, Portland, Oregon, Public Schools.

Another example of specific subject acceleration that has developed rapidly in the past few years is the teaching of foreign languages in elementary schools. This has been done in a few places for many years, but the recent impetus of scientific technology and of international politics has caused rapid growth in this area. The teaching of foreign language is an example of acceleration only when it is planned in such a way that students complete the normal first-year course one or more years earlier than usual. An unorganized acquaintance with Spanish, for example, may be valuable enrichment but is not acceleration.

Between High School and College

Acceleration in this manner is also possible in other subjects—science, for example. Yet all such attempts at speeding up the study of specific subjects are wasteful unless an arrangement is made with high schools to continue the adjustment. If articulation is so poor that students who take first-year algebra, language, or science, in an eighth grade must repeat it in

[2] John I. Goodlad and Robert H. Anderson, *The Nongraded Elementary School* (New York: Harcourt, Brace & Co., 1959).

another school, acceleration does not take place and time has been wasted. Furthermore, if high schools are not prepared to carry mathematics, language, or science students through a well-planned fifth year of these courses, to offer an advanced placement class, or to graduate them a year early so they can enter college, then much of the advantage is lost.

EARLY ADMISSION

Two programs specifically aimed at accelerating high school students were started in 1951 with the encouragement of the Fund for the Advancement of Education. The Early Admission to College program, carried out by twelve colleges and universities, selected exceptionally able high-school students to enter college at the end of their sophomore or junior year of high school.

In a controlled study over a period of four years, the evidence demonstrated that well-selected younger students could out-perform equally able but older students in college. Moreover, it was shown that in social and economic adjustment the younger students were the equal of their comparison groups and of other students. Nevertheless, the Early Admission Program did not grow, in part due to the fact that colleges began to have more qualified applicants for admission from high-school graduates than they could take. This left little room for students, no matter how exceptional, who had not graduated from high school.

ADVANCED PLACEMENT PROGRAM

The other program was the Advanced Placement Program. This is a different approach to the same problem but proposes to save the student's time in college rather than in high school. This approach has grown apparently because it has given colleges important assistance in guiding students into appropriate classes. Beginning in 1953–54, with 532 students taking fewer than 1,000 tests, the program was turned over to the College Entrance Examination Board in 1955, and in 1960 more than 10,000 students took nearly 15,000 examinations.

Essentially, the Advanced Placement Program assumes that well-selected high-school students can complete satisfactorily a college-level course, and that satisfactory completion can be demonstrated by scores on examinations. The assumption is based on the thousands of students tested over the years and is apparently well-founded.[3,4]

[3] Elizabeth Paschal, *Encouraging the Excellent* (New York: The Fund for the Advancement of Education, 1960).

[4] The School and College Study of Admission with Advanced Placement, *College Admissions with Advanced Standing* (New York: The Fund for the Advancement of Education, 1954).

Advanced Placement examinations are in fact the type of tests that would be given to advanced sections of college courses. Uniformity in scoring is assured by the test-reading procedures that have been established by the CEEB. Still lacking to some degree is uniformity in the amount of credit and advanced standing allowed by colleges and universities. As the program grows, greater agreement is sure to develop.

This, then, is the place of acceleration at present. A typical program of studies is necessary to assist teachers with the large number of pupils who are enrolled. In a country in which the dream is to educate appropriately *all* of the children, some will be able to participate at a faster pace than others. Satisfactory development for these children will depend on the opportunity to push ahead, maintaining their strength through continuous exercise.

Saving a year or two for some students is probably desirable; grade-skipping will undoubtedly help some; other administrative devices certainly have a place. Yet the answer to those who ask, "Acceleration for what?" is that acceleration, in combination with effective and enthusiastic teaching, is insurance against undereducation.

20. What Are the Advantages and Disadvantages of Acceleration? *

CHARLES E. BISH, *Director, NEA Project on the Academically Talented Student*

P ASSOW [1] has formulated a list of advantages and of disadvantages to acceleration. The advantages that he stresses include the following:

1. Acceleration provides the gifted with opportunities commensurate with their ability to progress and places them in the grade corresponding to level of maturity rather than to chronological age.

* From *Administration Procedures and School Practices for the Academically Talented Student in the Secondary School* (Washington, D.C.: National Education Association), pp. 64–68. Reprinted with permission.
[1] A. Harry Passow, "Enrichment of Education for the Gifted," *Education for the Gifted,* Fifty-Seventh Yearbook, National Society for the Study of Education, ed. by Nelson B. Henry (Chicago: University of Chicago Press, 1958), p. 212.

2. Students should be allowed to acquire educational attainments in the shortest time needed. Since research shows little correlation between achievement in a given area and the time devoted to its study, gifted children should be encouraged to proceed at their own rate.
3. Indications are that a person's outstanding creative accomplishments are products of early adult life. This peak is exploited by enabling students to complete their educational preparation and to enter productive careers earlier than would be possible in a rigid system of grade progress.
4. Emotional maladjustments may result from keeping children in classes which do not challenge them. Achieving below potential ability is probably more harmful than the temporary difficulties attendant upon being placed with somewhat older students.
5. Acceleration is a form of enrichment; the time saved in mastering fundamental learnings makes possible more work in a given field, or additional work in other areas of interest.
6. The saving of a year or more enables a student to complete advanced or graduate work without having to delay marriage and independent living.
7. If able students are allowed to save a year or more in their public schooling, the consequent lowering in school years and school costs, and increased man-years of productivity will result in lower costs and significant savings for students, parents, schools, and communities.

In connection with this last point, one authority has estimated that "every year there remain in the secondary schools around 300,000 students whom a reasonable program of acceleration would have graduated. Such a reduction in enrollment would involve substantial savings, which might more than provide for the suggested special counselors for the gifted." [2]

It is clear, of course, that in today's context, wise acceleration is undertaken only in the light of advised guidance procedures, taking into account academic ability and social and physical maturity. Thus it really means moving from one level of instruction to another, after thoroughly mastering the work of the first level. The most obvious advantages need hardly be labored. Pupils are felt to be stimulated to do work of their best quality when they are not kept in a group of less able students. Furthermore, gifted children are usually advanced in maturity as well as in academic ability. In addition, there is evidence that acceleration contributes to increased social maturity; when confronted with classmates of greater maturity, accelerated students are stimulated to grow in this respect as well.

Research has shown that, upon entry into college, students who have been accelerated continue to perform as well as, and usually better than, their older classmates. At the same time they participate in extracurricular

[2] Sidney L. Pressey, "Concerning the Nature and Nurture of Genius," *Educating the Gifted*, comp. by Joseph L. French (New York: Henry Holt & Co., 1959), p. 18.

activities and give every evidence of being socially and psychologically adjusted.

The follow-up of Terman's gifted students is said to provide conclusive evidence that children with an IQ of at least 135 who are accelerated by from one to three years are usually more successful in later life than equally bright children who are held in the sequential lockstep.[3]

What Are the Possible Disadvantages of Acceleration?

Turning once again to the points listed by Passow,[4] the objections to acceleration include the following:

1. Rich learning experiences do not necessarily come from a fixed pattern of subject matter. Although the time spent on particular activities can be decreased, studies in depth and breadth also contribute an essential ingredient to the learning process.
2. There are better ways of eliminating the boredom resulting from lack of challenge than reducing time spent in class.
3. Intellectual maturity may not go hand in hand with social and emotional maturity, when younger students are placed with older ones. This may result in a denial of leadership opportunities to those whose physical or social maturity is less than that of the older students.
4. Acceleration may deny bright students the time and opportunity to think, reflect, explore, and appreciate. The pressures for rapid progress may result in a curtailment of creativity.
5. Students with like mental age but different chronological age may perform qualitatively quite differently; the more difficult work provided for the gifted child through acceleration may not necessarily yield more appropriate experiences.
6. Equal acceleration in all areas does not take into account differences in rates of maturation. A student ready for rapid progress in one area may not be ready for it in another area.
7. Acceleration tends to separate the gifted from his age peers and to emphasize differences in ability. This separation may lead to undesirable social and behavior patterns.
8. Pure skipping may leave serious gaps in the student's learnings, which, in turn, may affect his later educational attainments.

Other objections have included the fact that speeding the gifted on their way deprives the other children of the contributions the gifted could make in the classroom and at the same time deprives the accelerated student of

---

[3] Lewis M. Terman and Melita H. Oden, "Major Issues in the Education of Gifted Children," *ibid.*, p. 149.

[4] A. Harry Passow, "Enrichment of Education for the Gifted," *op. cit.*, p. 214.

the values to be gained from association with students of all types. It is sometimes argued that a child should not be taken out of the society in which he lives. While this objection may have some values in the case of placing the pupil with older age groups, it clearly does not apply when the student is kept with his chronological peers but allowed to do more advanced work.

In general terms, then, research supports the hypothesis of academic gains resulting from acceleration of gifted students. In addition, no serious detrimental effects on social and emotional adjustment have been demonstrated. This has been true for all levels of the school sequence. Thus there is no longer any question of the advisability of acceleration, even on an individual basis, for providing for gifted students. The only real question remaining is what type of acceleration is best for meeting the individual needs of each gifted child. Not all types can do all things for all students. But that the principle itself is a salutary one, in the face of the evidence presented by research, can no longer be denied.

21. What Research Says about Acceleration *

DAN C. SHANNON, *Life Member Phi Delta Kappa*

Eᴅᴜᴄᴀᴛᴏʀs are increasingly concerned about the education of gifted children. Some have attempted to enrich regular classwork. Others have accelerated the children. Many have talked about the problem of the gifted but have done nothing about it. Still others write negative articles using very fluent language. But what are the facts?

There has been a considerable volume of research done in the field of acceleration. While many educators dislike reading articles reporting research, they cannot escape the compulsion of the facts with which it deals. Just what does research say about acceleration? Let's take a good look.

A study was made by Keys and Wester among youths graduating from Oakland, California, high schools in the years 1934 and 1935. The group being studied was from one to three years younger than the control group,

* From *Phi Delta Kappan*, November, 1957, pp. 70–72. Reprinted with permission.

which was the normal age of high-school graduation. These two groups were matched by IQ, sex, father's occupation, and school class. Age was the only known variable. The findings were that the younger students took more scholarship honors, took part in more activities (even football), and were elected to more class offices. Shyness and timidity, which are terms often applied to gifted children who have been accelerated, were more common in the control group. "The few cases of serious problem behavior proved to be either bright but nonaccelerated controls or accelerated pupils of only average intelligence." [1]

This isolated research might indicate that nothing is wrong with acceleration if used correctly, and it might indicate that acceleration used incorrectly can be harmful. Since the findings from one study cannot be considered conclusive, let's look at some more.

Margaret Alltucker gathered data from Berkeley High School in Berkeley, California. She states in her conclusions "that the pedagogically accelerated student is not as great a misfit in high school as he is commonly supposed to be." [2] She warns, however, that in cases where scholastic ability and physical development are not the same, careful counseling should be given. This is one accepted feature of any sane program using acceleration. Miss Alltucker's study was reported in 1924, and there are persons who will say that children and schools thirty years ago were different. So let's look at a research project reported in 1953.

An experiment was conducted at the junior high school level. The experimental group completed a three-year junior high school in two years, while the control group completed it in the conventional length of time. It was found that the accelerated group measured slightly better in personal and social adjustment than the control group. [3]

These three research studies do not stand alone in their defense of acceleration as one practice to meet the needs of gifted children in school. Wilkins reported a study in which students were chosen by only one criterion, that they were at least one month younger than seventeen years old at the time of high-school graduation. He has drawn the conclusion that "the activities of accelerated pupils in high school . . . are beneficial and healthful." [4]

---

[1] N. Keys, "Adjustments of Under-Age Students in High School," *Psychological Bulletin*, 32:539, October 1935.

[2] Margaret M. Alltucker, "Is the Pedagogically Accelerated Student a Misfit in the Senior High School?" *School Review*, 32:193–202, March 1924.

[3] J. Justman, "Personal and Social Adjustment of Intellectually Gifted Accelerants and Non-Accelerants in Junior High School," *School Review*, 61:468–78, May 1953.

[4] W. L. Wilkins, "The Social Adjustment of Accelerated Pupils," *School Review*, 44:445–55, June 1936.

At least one doctoral dissertation has been completed on the topic of acceleration. T. L. Engle did his work at the University of Indiana and studied children in some of the larger Indiana high schools. He reports that personal adjustment is not appreciably affected by acceleration.[5]

These studies have stressed the social and personal adjustment of the gifted children who were accelerated. What effect does acceleration have upon the academic success of the child? Since we can fairly conclude that acceleration, correctly administered, does not injure the child's personality, does it do him any good? What does research have to say to this question? Again, let's turn to the files.

As is the case of many thorough research studies, several phases of a problem were probed at one time in the project carried out by Keys and Wester in the Oakland high schools. For our purposes, however, the important finding was that the younger students did better scholastically than the older, matched groups. Remember that the two groups were matched for IQ, sex, father's occupation, and school class.[6]

One might feel by now that the author has "lifted" researches that support acceleration and left in the files those that don't support it. This is not the case. It is possible, of course, that researches showing that acceleration is not useful and profitable have not been published.

It is true that not all researches have shown that the younger, accelerated group has done *better* in school than the control group of normal-age youngsters. Unzicker,[7] Wilkins,[8] and Justman [9] all conclude that there is little difference between the two groups in their achievement in high school or junior high. This is in itself significant, for if younger gifted children can maintain as good work as their older classmates, the fact strongly favors acceleration.

At this point we have seen that research has upheld acceleration on at least two points: 1. If properly used, acceleration of gifted children does not handicap them personally or socially. 2. Children who have been accelerated can maintain the quality of work done by their older classmates or even do better scholastic work at the high-school and junior-high level.

[5] T. L. Engle, "A Study of the Effects of School Acceleration Upon the Personality and School Adjustment of High-School and University Students," *Journal of Educational Psychology*, 29:523–39, October 1938.

[6] N. Keys, *op. cit.*

[7] S. P. Unzicker, "A Study of Acceleration in the Junior High School," *School Review*, 40:346–56, May 1932.

[8] W. L. Wilkins, "High-School Achievement of Accelerated Pupils," *School Review*, 44:268–73, April 1936.

[9] J. Justman, "Academic Achievement of Intellectually Gifted Accelerants and Non-Accelerants in Junior High School," *School Review*, 62:142–50, March 1954.

What Happens When They Enter College?

What happens, though, when these gifted, accelerated children leave high school and enter college? They were guided through the public schools without mishap and they did good classwork, even though they were younger than average. But when they reach college will they be able to maintain this level of accomplishment? Again, research has the answer.

Two studies were conducted at the University of Buffalo. One, by Mary Sarbaugh, reports that younger students were compared with *equally bright* older ones. She found that the younger student keeps abreast scholastically, participates in extracurricular activities, continues his education as well as older matched pairs, likes his experience in acceleration, and would repeat it if he had the chance to do it again.[10] This is a pretty good testimonial for acceleration!

They Fooled the Professors

A unique study was also conducted at the University of Buffalo by Ruth Eckert. This study came about because of a complaint of professors about the mature but bright versus the immature but bright students. The study consisted of a questionnaire asking professors to identify traits of maturity and to select, first, a bright and mature student, and, second, a bright but immature one. Cross-checks were made of the completed questionnaires. In twenty-one cases, the same student was chosen both as mature and as immature. So it was shown that the professors couldn't agree on what constitutes maturity. Out of 135 mature choices, forty-four individuals were chosen two times or more, but of the 123 immature choices only eighteen were chosen two times or more. This shows that the professors could decide who were the mature students with more accord than who were the immature students. A comparison was made between the two groups of students and it was found that the mature group was *younger* at college entrance than the immature group. The mean age was 17.3 for the mature group and 17.4 for the immature group. This difference is not statistically significant, so it was concluded that chronological age is *not* the factor determining intellectual maturity.[11]

Perhaps the foremost authority of our time on problems of gifted

[10] Mary E. Sarbaugh, "The Younger College Student," *School and Society,* 40:823–24, December 15, 1934.

[11] Ruth E. Eckert, "Intellectual Maturity," *Journal of Higher Education,* 5:478–84, December 1934.

children was Professor Terman of Stanford University. It was his opinion that acceleration should be encouraged. He arrived at this conclusion after performing a vast amount of research. He states that "children of 135 IQ or higher should be promoted sufficiently to permit college entrance by the age of 17 at latest . . . a majority in this group would be better off to enter at 16." [12]

As everyone knows, John Dewey stated that education is life. Many school people don't feel this way, though, and often claim that what might be all right for school is not good for life outside of school. The issue of acceleration is one that gets all confused in this respect. Some educators claim that acceleration puts people through their schooling too quickly. Some speak of the oak tree that grows to full maturity in twenty to thirty years and of the squash plant that ripens in one season. To rush through school would make us like the squash. Such reasoning by analogy is absurd, of course. Why should anyone want to be like an acorn? Research, again, has an answer to the question about acceleration putting students through school too quickly.

S. L. Pressey has done a tremendous amount of research at Ohio State University on the topic of acceleration and its effects on adult life. Only two of his studies will be mentioned here. Pressey made a check of the graduates of Amherst College in relation to adult success. Amherst College was selected because of its good alumni records. A rating scale, ranging from 7 to 0, was made that grouped successful persons as "internationally known," "nationally known," "locally known," "average success," "mediocre career," "unskilled worker," "failure (not self-supporting)," and "criminal or shady record." The alumni records of graduates were studied by two people who were not connected with the research study and were ranked according to the scale. If the two people made the same rating, it was accepted; if they disagreed by only one point on the scale, the lower figure was used. If there was more than one point in disagreement, a person working on the research study arbitrated the score. The following table gives a picture of the results of this research. [13]

Note how the per cent of nationally known increases as the age at graduation decreases. This suggests that acceleration in school would not be harmful in adult life. Pressey states in his report that perhaps one reason the per cent of nationally known graduates drops as the graduating age increases is that higher graduating age shortens the productive career.

[12] Lewis M. Terman and Melita H. Oden, *The Gifted Child Grows Up* (Stanford, Calif.: Stanford University Press, 1947), p. 281.

[13] S. L. Pressey, "Age of College Graduation and Success in Adult Life," *Journal of Applied Psychology*, 30:226–33, June 1946.

This line of thought was examined more thoroughly in another research by Pressey. In this study, two volumes of the *Dictionary of American Biography* and the 1942 volume of *Current Biography* were checked. It was found that the twenties are a very productive period in a person's life. This study indicates that early age in entering professional life is an argument in favor of acceleration of the gifted in school.[14]

Age of Graduation		19	20	21	22	23	24	25	26	over 26
No. of Graduates		24	114	216	235	132	59	47	37	60
After College Success	Per Cent Nationally Known	29	22	15	12	10	3	2	3	—
	Per Cent Failures	4	6	6	5	2	3	6	11	15

Marie Flesher did a follow-up study of graduates from the College of Education at the University of Ohio. She paired nineteen- and twenty-year-old graduates with older graduates of the same sex, general ability, and grade average. She thus avoided any argument that the accelerated students would have better success because they had been better students.

Younger Grads More Successful

Did they graduate too young? Were they immature? She concludes, ". . . the answer is an emphatic negative. These younger graduates outdid their elders in securing advanced degrees. A greater number of them secured teaching positions immediately after graduation. The younger women demonstrated success equal to that of their older sisters in securing mates. More of them were able to secure top salaries in the teaching professions. They impressed their school administrators more favorably as teachers. Throughout, the record of the younger graduates is as good, or better than, that of the olders." [15]

Research, cold research, is the reporting of fact as discovered by scientific probing. Many educators prefer not to listen to research. It may say things that they are not willing to listen to. This seems to be true in the area under discussion.

[14] S. L. Pressey, and Arthur Combs, "Acceleration and Age of Productivity," *Educational Research Bulletin*, 22:191–96, October 13, 1943.
[15] Marie A. Flesher, "Did They Graduate Too Young?" *Educational Research Bulletin*, 24:218–21, November 14, 1945.

Acceleration Still under Suspicion

Frank Wilson [16] discovered that fewer than half of the respondents to a questionnaire he devised favored acceleration to the extent that Professor Terman does. Wilson asked in his questionnaire if the respondents agreed with the opinion of Professor Terman as quoted earlier in this article. Wilson found that people connected with colleges and universities agreed with the Terman statement more commonly than public school people. Could this indicate that those connected with colleges and universities tend to form their opinions from research findings more readily than those connected with public schools? Hardly.

The real significance of Wilson's research is that nearly 50 per cent of all the respondents favored some acceleration. With this fact in mind when he reads articles that debunk acceleration as a means of adjusting the school's program for the gifted, one can retain his sense of balance. There are many believers in the value of acceleration, even though they may not be heard from often.

22. Educational Acceleration: Occasional Procedure or Major Issue? *

SIDNEY L. PRESSEY, *Professor Emeritus, Ohio State University*

A T LONG LAST, it is becoming generally admitted that some acceleration of some gifted youngsters is desirable. Thus a conference of representatives of the American Psychological Association, American Educational Research Association, and Association for Supervision and Curriculum Development concluded that "The research testimony as to the advantages of acceleration is weighty, consistent, and continuous over several decades."

---

[16] F. T. Wilson, "Educators' Opinions about Acceleration of Gifted Students," *School and Society*, 80:120–22, October 16, 1954.

* From *Personnel and Guidance Journal,* September, 1962, pp. 12–17. Reprinted with permission.

However, acceleration was judged not "the best method for dealing with the able," and very limited in application; "It is probable that acceleration should *not* take place with youngsters whose IQ is below 130" [italics theirs] or below about the top 5 per cent of all school children in ability (*1*, *pp. 60–62*). This paper presents considerations arguing that acceleration is certainly the most advantage-yielding and, on the whole, most sound method of dealing with talented youngsters, that the top fifth or more of all pupils might well progress faster than the usual lockstep pace, that acceleration may occur desirably anywhere from kindergarten to professional school— and presents the most rewarding of all opportunities for wise student personnel policy.

The Neglected Values of Timesaving

The chapter on evaluation and research of a recent book on education of the gifted presents elaborate schedules for appraising programs, but nowhere is there mention of the time they take. The careful design of a well-financed investigation provided excellent controls and broad appraisals but nowhere took account of timesaving, nor did the report mention that the accelerates, besides doing better than the controls, had also saved a year! There is now a nationwide effort to get more able young people to go to college; those who do so increasingly go on into graduate or professional school; of these, the ones who (for example) obtain a doctorate in a science do so at a median age of around 30. A physician who specializes gets into his career even later. Reasonable programs of acceleration would lower these ages at least two years—thus adding two years to career! A medical discovery that added two years to life would receive worldwide acclaim. An educational procedure accomplishing somewhat the same result still tends to be looked at askance.

A variety of investigations indicate that able youngsters can complete secondary school at the age of 17 or 16 instead of the usual 18, that they are then more likely to go on to college (where they do better work and are more likely to graduate than controls of the same ability but the usual entering age), that those graduating young are more likely to go on to graduate or professional school and more likely to have successful careers. Thus Terman found that most of his famous gifted group were accelerated in age of graduating from high school, and comparison of those graduating at age 17, 16, and 15 showed progressive increases from oldest group to youngest in percentages graduating from college, taking one or more years of graduate work, and (for men) in the highest classification as to vocational success—though there was relatively little difference among these three groups in childhood IQ *(13)*. The writer has obtained similar findings. A substantial number of other investigations are to the same effect *(10)*.

Why should all this be so? Obviously early graduation from high school or college leaves more time in youth for further education, for which there may remain more family funds with less likelihood of death of a parent or other reverse; and leaving school for marriage or job is less likely. Earlier beginning of career leaves more time for it. These would seem obvious but neglected timesaving advantages of acceleration. But other factors seem likely.

Educability, Creativity, Maturity

First an intriguing but seemingly completely neglected possibility. Forty years ago, Bagley showed that draftees in the First World War from the various states varied in tested "intelligence" according to the adequacy (largely the average length) of the schooling in those states. Draftees in the Second World War had had about two years more schooling than those in the first and tested as roughly that much higher in "general ability." Lorge found that boys given tests of "intelligence" in 1921 and again in 1941 showed increases in scores roughly proportional to the amount of their schooling since 1921. Several investigations have compared groups of bright pupils who completed the usual three-year junior high school program in two years with groups similar to them in initial school record and ability but taking the usual three years as to record in senior high, and found the accelerates there doing as well or better academically—and satisfactory in social adjustment. Similar results have been reported for groups doing the three years of senior high in two years as regards record in college. If at the end of its intensive two years an accelerate group and its control had been given tests of "general ability," might the accelerates have been found gaining over their controls in "intelligence"?

The writer knows of no such comparisons. But surely a junior high program includes vocabulary, concepts, and study skills of some general value that gained in two years should show on such tests as gains over the controls, if not in "intelligence" in part of what the usual "intelligence" tests measure. This might perhaps best be called "educability." At least the accelerates in the two years gained more education. There may be other gains. Thus over two-thirds of the students who, under subvention of the Ford Foundation, skipped the last year of high school (42 per cent had only ten years of public school) reported as an advantage "a much greater academic challenge in college than in high school." Parents reported gains in maturity. As a result of these and other factors not only did the "Fordies" do better in college than cases paired with them as to aptitude but who had completed high school and were about two years older, but gained more from college sophomore to senior year on the Graduate Record Examination (2).

Lehman's findings that most outstanding creative work has tended to come early in the careers of famous scientists, inventors, authors, artists, musicians are widely known (5). However, it is not generally recognized that his curves for years of optimal creativity show mostly ages of patenting an invention or publishing a report of a scientific discovery or a book, and the brilliant ideas probably came a year or more earlier. Push these curves down a couple of years and they are close to his curves for ages of winning athletic championships, and in coordination with data on ages of maximal health, capability for learning difficult material, and strong outranging interests (12, 14). Not only greatest creative potential, but also greatest health and enthusiasm to support creative effort, appears usually to come in the twenties and earlier thirties; and if full-time education extends well into these years, maximal productivity might be reduced.

Not only are the increasing numbers of college and advanced students an increasing burden on the economy for both their keep and their schooling, increasingly they are married—32 per cent of a sampling of senior men in the undergraduate colleges of The Ohio State University in the autumn quarter of 1961 and 58 per cent of graduate school men, many with children. Housing for married students is a distinctive problem of the postwar campus, and scholarship or other support for them a substantial charge on funds available for such purposes. However, in the writer's opinion it is not primarily their costs that make student marriages a threat to the prolonging of advanced training, but more broadly the desire shown by young people that they be allowed the realization of adulthood without long delay, after maturity has been reached. Adulthood means not only marriage, but the beginning of career and an independent place in the community. So earlier completion of full-time education will, the writer believes, increasingly be sought by students. That the result may be healthy educationally is well expressed in a letter from a former president of the American Psychological Association and authority on child development, now an administrator in a famous university, in answer to an inquiry about his having obtained his doctorate at the age of 23:

I cannot speak too strongly for the value of finishing up the educational process as early as possible. I am quite convinced that the greatest creativity and greatest enthusiasm for research comes before the age of 35. Certainly many of our students today are far better trained when they get a Ph.D. than I was. But in the next five years I learned probably as much factually as they do and I had the enormous advantage of already having a good leg up on my career, and the satisfaction of being an independent operator with a few small successes that unquestionably served to motivate me vitally toward a continuation of that career. I think it is almost criminal to let people stay in the social role of student any longer than is absolutely necessary. The only progress I see in people's development is that which comes from their own independent work. The longer they remain students, the longer they remain subordinate, passive, always looking up to others instead of out toward the horizon for themselves. What we need to do is get more people into their careers and let them begin to enjoy the rewards and excitements of independent endeavor.

The preceding paragraphs have argued that accelerated programs for the gifted should: (*a*) certainly give more education in a given time, but perhaps also result in more and more mature general competencies, (*b*) make more career use of the potentially most productive early adult years, (*c*) make feasible earlier realization of adult status as in beginning of career, socioeconomic independence, and marriage. If all this is desirably so, then in general those finishing an educational program young should be more successful than those finishing later. As already mentioned, Terman found those graduating from high school early most successful in later education and career. The writer gathered data indicating that those graduating young from a New England arts college and from a midwestern teachers college were vocationally more successful than those graduating at the usual age. Recently he has compiled material as to the relations of age of obtaining the doctorate to professional success. Currently, median age of obtaining the doctorate in psychology is around 31 (with only 1 per cent getting the degree at 24 or younger); however, the last 25 presidents of the American Psychological Association earned the degree at a median age of 25.7! Analogous findings were obtained for chemists, sociologists, economists, and political scientists and the presidents of their national organizations. Indeed, of the presidents of these various learned societies, 32 per cent of the psychologists, 25 per cent of the chemists, and 15 per cent of the social scientists had obtained the doctorate at the age of 24 or younger. Further, median age of obtaining the doctorate was 26.1 for a sampling of members of the American Academy of Sciences and 25.0 for Nobel Prize winners in physics and chemistry; 22 per cent of the first group and 50 per cent of the second obtained the degree at the age of 24 or younger (*7, 8*). In total, the evidence for acceleration, especially as regards career outcomes, would seem varied and impressive.

Applications, Implications

Such evidence (in contrast to the negligible good research supporting enrichment) would seem to warrant the conclusion that acceleration was the best of generally recognized methods of dealing with the gifted. And surely such benefits should not be limited to the top 5 per cent of pupils; at least the top 20 per cent should be considered for some advancement over the lockstep pace. The total of such likely desirable outcomes should make acceleration the most rewarding of all personnel procedures, and counseling looking thereto especially pleasant—and especially needed now. For acceleration recognizes ability by advancement earlier to complete more education for better vocational opportunities—sooner to meet the nation's needs with more trained manpower. And if a fifth of all high school graduates might well finish the usual 12 years of public school in 11 years or less (in the writer's judgment, a reasonable estimate on the basis of a variety of data, some shortly to be mentioned) and a fifth of all college graduates finish in three years, then the relief to crowded schools and colleges would be considerable.

But why keep the age-grade lockstep as the basic procedure, deviation from which becomes a special issue? Why not admit each child to the first grade when he is "ready"; numerous experiments have shown bright children admitted before six doing well—better than their controls when followed even through the eighth grade (15). Why not nongraded schools, in which each child may progress as he can? More might then "accelerate" than before. At slowdown and overlap places in the present ill-coordinated American educational system (perhaps around second grade, junior high, senior year of high school, and college freshman year) a large portion of all the youngsters might edge ahead. And why not "classless" colleges? Now some students enter as sophomores because of anticipatory examinations in such institutions as Harvard, and many universities permit earning of graduate credit in the senior undergraduate year. The able might, if permitted to move easily over grade-class boundaries, advance yet more rapidly. An elaborate California investigation of gifted children showed one-fourth of a group of first graders at the end of that school year reading at fourth grade level; in arithmetic they were two years advanced. The upper half of fourth and fifth grade gifted pupils was close to or beyond ninth grade level on a battery of tests of achievement (6). About a tenth of all high school seniors scored above the college senior mean on an elaborate examination supposedly covering the essentials of a college education (4). Over three-fourths of the "Fordies," who had skipped the last one or two years of high school, when college sophomores, scored above the mean for first year graduate students on the Graduate Record Examination (2).

Might social maladjustment result from any substantial acceleration, even in a nongraded school or college? Gifted youngsters have been

found to prefer the companionship of older and other gifted associates (*9*).
The California study noted the "striking and consistent early emotional
maturity" of the gifted, who "at both the junior and senior high levels
resembled college and adult populations more closely than they resembled
their own age-mates" on a personality inventory (*6, p. 4*). In fields now
less subject to age-grade rigidities—music, the graphic arts, the performing
arts, athletics—those excelling usually begin early and progress rapidly,
and different ages associate easily in their common interest. But if age-
grade rigidities be done away with *and* personnel policy is alert to the
opportunities thereby presented, might the *average* student accelerate a
little, making marked acceleration of the able less marked?

For it seems hardly too harsh to say that the total American educational
system is an ill-coordinated conglomerate, irresponsible in its readiness to
take over some of life's best years. Fifty years ago an American doctorate
regularly took three years, but now four or more; and if it is argued that
now much more need be learned, Oppenheimer's remark should be recalled
that with the present rapid changes in knowledge, soon all one learned in
schools is not so (incidentally, he obtained his doctorate at the age of 23).
The Ph.D program, imported less than a century ago from Germany
where it followed the secondary school "gymnasium," was here put after
the four-year college. So the doctorate is obtained about four years earlier
in Germany than here—four years added to career that might be a factor
in German scientific productivity. The American college was imported
over three centuries ago from England where Cambridge had had four-
year programs; that institution went to three, but not the American college,
in spite of many efforts to do so, led by such people as Harvard's President
Eliot. The American high school is largely homegrown, and may almost
completely overlap the first year of college. Not many years ago, excellent
school systems had seven elementary grades instead of eight—and research
evidence indicates that they were doing about as much educationally in the
shorter time. With guided progress aware of all this and of the brighter
student's capacity to move ahead, might the median age for the doctorate
drop to 25, for the BA to 20? And if the present "going steady" with one's
own age group was broken up, might that be socially healthy, perhaps
reducing the number of too early marriages?

Guidance might well first stress to students, parents, and teachers the
considerations outlined in this paper. Faster progress than the lockstep
may sometimes be by skipping: so by substantial advanced placement
credit a student may enter college with sophomore standing (*3*), or like
the "Fordies" skip the high school senior year; or a bright child may skip
the last year of junior high into senior high or sixth grade into junior high,

or begin primary school in the second grade if he enters already able to read. Better are smoother means: in college, accelerative honors programs, or independent study; in the public schools, rapid progress sections or nongraded structuring (perhaps aided by "teaching machines"). Wisely guided acceleration may add two or three years to the careers of able young people, not merely without educational loss but with gains in competence sometimes notable (*11*).

Summary

Belatedly, it is being recognized that research evidence in favor of acceleration is overwhelming. But old doubts persist. And the larger significance of the evidence seems not seen.

1. Fifty years ago the effort was to keep young people in school longer; now much evidence indicates that many are being kept there too long. Yet "timesaving in education" has been little mentioned since the twenties, and both school programs for the gifted and the college honors programs often ignore the issue.

2. Acceleration may not only give a student more education in a given time, but increase his functioning abilities. That greatest physical vigor *and* intellectual creativity come in the earlier adult years is now well-evidenced. That young people are increasingly insisting on less delay in adult status is evidenced by the increase in student marriages. A variety of evidence indicates that early beginning of career is associated with outstanding success therein.

3. Personnel policies fostering acceleration of able students should thus be richly rewarding. Now, years in their lives may be frittered away in ill-coordinated, slow-paced, overextended educational programs. Guided acceleration may well not only prevent such waste, but be the cutting edge of efforts toward programs better coordinated and paced for all in the schools.

References

1. ANDERSON, K. E. (ed.). *Research on the Academically Talented Student.* Washington, D.C.: National Education Association, 1961.

2. FUND FOR THE ADVANCEMENT OF EDUCATION. *They Went to College Early.* New York: The Fund, 1957.

3. JONES, E. S., and ORTNER, GLORIA K. College Credit by Examination. *Univ. Buffalo Studies,* 1954, *21* (3).

4. LEARNED, W. L., and WOOD, B. D. *The Student and His Knowledge.* New York: Carnegie Foundation for the Advancement of Teaching, 1938.

5. LEHMAN, H. C. *Age and Achievement*. Princeton, N.J.: Princeton Univ. Press, 1953.

6. MARTINSON, RUTH A. *Educational Programs for Gifted Pupils*. Sacramento: California State Department of Education, 1961.

7. McCALLUM, T. W., and TAYLOR, A. S. *Nobel Prize Winners*. Zurich: Central European Times Publishing Co., 1938.

8. NATIONAL ACADEMY OF SCIENCES. *Biographical memoirs, 27–30*, pp. 1952–56. New York: Columbia Univ. Press, 1949.

9. O'SHEA, HARRIET E. Friendship and the Intellectually Gifted Child. *Except. Child.*, 1960, *26*, 327–35.

10. PRESSEY, S. L. *Educational Acceleration: Appraisals and Basic Problems*. Columbus: Ohio State Univ. Press, 1949.

11. ———. Concerning the Nature and Nurture of Genius. *Scient. Month.*, 1955, *68*, 123–29.

12. ———, and KUHLEN, R. G. *Psychological Development through the Life Span*. New York:Harper, 1957.

13. TERMAN, L. M., and ODEN, MELITA H. *The Gifted Child Grows Up*. Stanford, Calif.: Stanford Univ. Press, 1947.

14. WELFORD, A. T. *Ageing and Human Skill*. London: Oxford Univ. Press, 1958.

15. WORCESTER, D. A. *Education of Children of Above-Average Ability*. Lincoln, Neb.: Univ. of Nebraska Press, 1956.

23. Acceleration in the Elementary Grades *

FRANCIS C. GAMELIN, *Assistant Superintendent, Robbinsdale, Minnesota*
JUNE OTTERNESS, *Principal Elementary School, Hutchinson, Minnesota, AND*
ANGELA UNTEREKER, *Counselor, St. Cloud Technical High School*

Where Do We Get Information?

Our school is considering development of a planned program of acceleration for superior students in the elementary grades. So far, however, we have not been able to find very much information on the subject. Would you be able to

* From *Minnesota Journal of Education*, September 1962, p. 26. Reprinted with permission.

provide us with factual material about acceleration as it is practiced in Minnesota schools?

ELEMENTARY SCHOOL PRINCIPAL

DEAR PRINCIPAL:

To answer your question, we sent out questionnaires to principals of elementary schools located in many parts of Minnesota. The questions and resulting answers are compiled as follows for your benefit:

1. *Do you accelerate pupils? How?*

In several cases, principals reported acceleration as meaning promotion of certain pupils to a higher grade at the end of one semester. "We have had a few cases of double promotions," said one principal, "but only when we are sure it will work out all right. Quality of work done, maturity of pupil, mental ability, tests, conferences with parents and pupils all help to decide whether a pupil will be allowed to skip a grade."

One school, with a planned program of acceleration, reported that advanced fourth, fifth, and sixth grade students meet one hour a week to enrich their curriculum. "Developmental reading and a research project are basic units of the class," reports the principal, "and the research project is preceded by a library unit emphasizing reference techniques."

2. *What are the criteria for accelerating pupils? How is this interpreted to pupils, teachers, and parents?*

It would seem that tests (including intelligence tests and achievement tests), social and emotional maturity of the child, and recommendation of the teacher are the three criteria most often used in determining whether a pupil should be accelerated.

Although response was limited to the question of *how* acceleration processes are interpreted to pupils, teachers, and parents, it appears that conferences are the most accepted method of accomplishing this.

3. *What different teaching procedures are used with accelerated students?*

Most of the principals participating in this survey indicate that their schools primarily use enrichment materials and procedures in working with accelerated students.

One principal reports that in his school superior students are allowed to work at a faster pace with no limitations on proceeding into various projects. Students are allowed to pursue projects to the extent that their abilities and interests allow. Another principal says that his teachers make a point of giving the exceptional students additional work such as book reviews, playwriting, visits to business places.

4. What other acceleration procedures would you like to try?

Notable about the answers given this question are the variety of procedures that principals report they would like to try.

One principal, for instance, said he would like to try putting upper grade students who have demonstrated a high potential in use of language into a program that would stimulate rapid growth in communication skills. Another said that he would like to emphasize the opportunity for leadership experience through committee work and student participation in school assembly direction, as well as to inaugurate foreign language study and special research project studies.

Other procedures suggested ranged from starting a core curriculum class for the accelerated, offering a special experimental curriculum that uses the newest methods being developed in mathematics, to setting up an accelerated group in first grade with a master teacher in charge to see how far a first-grader could go in reading.

Summary:

This survey reveals that Minnesota school systems are highly interested in the subject of acceleration, even though those surveyed reveal that much of the work being done in their schools is still tentative and in the experimental stages.

Not much variety of procedure was reported as being used in the teaching of accelerated students. Most often, some sort of enrichment materials are incorporated into the curriculum. In some cases, superior students are urged to do independent work.

It would seem from the replies to this survey that schools are agreed that there is a *need* for acceleration, but they also believe that they could use more guidance on *how* to bring it about.

The survey indicates necessity for more experimentation in the field of acceleration along with some way of providing the results of such experimentation to the teachers of the state.

24. Acceleration in the High School *

FRANCIS C. GAMELIN, *Assistant Superintendent, Robbinsdale, Minnesota*
JUNE OTTERNESS, *Principal Elementary School, Hutchinson, Minnesota,* AND
ANGELA UNTEREKER, *Counselor, St. Cloud Technical High School*

What about the Older Student?

In the September issue of the JOURNAL, you listed information about acceleration procedures being used in various Minnesota elementary schools. Would it be possible for our school to obtain similar information about acceleration in Minnesota high schools?

HIGH SCHOOL PRINCIPAL

DEAR PRINCIPAL:

In answer to your question, we sent out questionnaires to principals of various high schools in the state. We hope the answers, compiled in the following, will be of benefit to you.

1. *Do you accelerate students? How?*

A majority of the principals queried said their schools used some means of acceleration—usually by grouping students according to ability. Mathematics and science courses were mentioned most often as the type of program offered high-ability students.

Usually, principals from smaller school systems indicated that they were unable to offer a full program of acceleration.

Said one: "In a small school such as ours it is not possible to have a 'so-called' accelerated group. We have no more than two sections of required subjects and only one of electives. However, for the past few years we have divided these classes into two sections, a 'faster-learning' and a 'slower-learning' group in the junior high school and to some extent in the senior high school."

* From *Minnesota Journal of Education*, October 1962, p. 27. Reprinted with permission.

2. *What are the criteria for accelerating students? How is this inter-preted to students, teachers, and parents?*

As in the elementary schools, basic criteria for acceleration of students are the results of achievement and intelligence tests. Emphasis is also given to recommendations offered by individual teachers.

Answers indicate a haziness as to *how* acceleration criteria are inter-preted to students, teachers, and parents. It would seem from the limited response to this question that more interpretation is given to teachers, some to students, and little to parents.

3. *Does acceleration create any public relations problems for you?*

While most of the answers received indicate few or no public relations problems, several principals stated that there had been some touchiness on the part of parents whose children were not chosen for acceleration.

One principal also mentioned the problem of parents of accelerated students who felt that the students were being penalized if they did not receive an "A." "We tell them," said the principal, "that the student is probably getting more out of being in an accelerated class even though he gets a 'C' grade and that students may withdraw from the section if they wish. So far no one has elected to withdraw for this reason."

Still another administrator questioned the public relations effect of acceleration on students not chosen: "There are times when I'm not posi-tive that ours is a good program. I am sure it tends to divide students socially and must certainly emphasize to the poor ability student his stand-ing academically. Although many proponents argue that this is the case in life, I don't believe that it exists to this extent."

4. *How do accelerated classes differ from other classes as to content, procedures, etc.?*

An emphasis on more and better composition work, student research, individual study, deeper discussion of literary subjects, and development of reading speed and comprehension takes place in the schools practicing acceleration. Class size is generally kept down so that teachers can do more work with individual students; also, content of texts is of a higher reading level.

One principal mentioned that, in his school, content and procedure depend upon the teacher. "In some cases I suspect that content and pro-cedure vary little in comparison to what they should. However, in general, our accelerated courses have completely different objectives. For instance, research papers will never be a vehicle in the hands of a lower ability student, but he does need to know how to write simple business letters. Work load should be equal but difficulty of material should be in keeping with ability."

5. *What other acceleration techniques would you like to try?*

Individualized instruction whereby the student would consult with the teacher periodically followed by an end-of-the-course test, use of the seminar method of instruction particularly in social studies, college credit courses for high school seniors, and elimination of "nonessentials" in the math program were among techniques suggested by those queried.

Summary:

As with the elementary school systems on which we reported in the September issue of the *Journal,* most high school participation in the survey reveals a high interest in the subject of acceleration but a similar lack of knowledge about what is being done with it.

Also, while the elementary schools seemed to depend on use of enrichment materials in acceleration, the high schools indicate greater use of grouping of students according to ability. In several cases such grouping has led to problems of public relations among students themselves and, for various reasons, among the parents of students. This survey indicates a need for interpretation of acceleration selection criteria with both student and parent groups *before* acceleration programs are established.

There is a need for more experimentation in the area of acceleration in high schools along with some way of providing experiment results to Minnesota schools. "Our upper levels are equal to comparable students in any parts of the world," concludes one principal, "Why not give the high schools a chance to prove it?"

25. Programs for the Gifted: Acceleration *

HAROLD J. MAHONEY, *Chief, Bureau of Pupil Personnel and Special Educational Services, Connecticut*

LIKE SPECIAL grouping, acceleration (which includes such things as completing three years of high school mathematics in two years as well as the skipping of grades) is a highly controversial issue. Studies in human development and the current needs of society call for an objective reappraisal of beliefs.

The increased demand for a skilled labor supply requires a high level of training for many human activities. The outlook for the future, automation for instance, shows that this demand is certain to increase. Acceleration is cited by its advocates as desirable for those who are going into a profession, because for students of professions, productive work, marriage, and homemaking are likely to be long delayed. In some professions, moreover, the twenties are the most productive years.

Research can be cited to indicate that judicious acceleration does not necessarily cause social maladjustment; in fact the findings of Terman and Keys have revealed beneficial results so far as adjustment is concerned.† Acceleration is not suggested by its advocates as a wholesale solution to the problems of serving the gifted, and when used it should be accompanied by enrichment.

Many teachers and administrators are opposed to acceleration, however. Their experience leads them to believe that children develop more wholesomely when they go through school in their chronological age group. They feel concern lest children be separated from their peers and so be denied essential opportunities for social and physical development, although it should be noted that the age span in many grades is as much as four years, because of retardation.

* From *Education for Gifted Children and Youth,* pp. 26–27, State Department of Education, Hartford, Conn., 1957. Reprinted with permission.

† L. M. Terman and M. H. Oden, *The Gifted Child Grows Up,* Genetic Studies of Genius, IV (Stanford, Calif.: Stanford University Press, 1947). Noel Keys, *The Underage Student in High School and College: Educational and Social Adjustments* (Berkeley, Calif.: University of California Press, 1939).

There is another important objection to acceleration: the danger that the school may assume that grade skipping in itself will meet the needs of the gifted and thus have a tendency to forget the importance of enrichment and emphasis on development of creativity and other high-level abilities. The child who has skipped a grade has not had the equivalent of all the experiences he would have had in the omitted grade. The teacher still has a responsibility for providing for individual differences, for checking to be sure that no important facts or skills have been neglected, and for evaluating the child's special needs—needs related to the circumstances that he is both gifted and accelerated.

Those who work with children and youth may be able to harmonize their beliefs by agreeing on certain widely accepted propositions:

1. Acceleration is not the only solution to the problem of curriculum adjustment for the gifted.

2. Although most children should move along through school with their age group, there are some children whose total development level may make it appropriate for them to work with a chronologically older group.

3. Decisions regarding the placement of a child should be made only after careful study of objective data. Study should draw upon such sources as the school psychologist's reports of intellectual, social, and emotional maturity; the school health staff's records, including data on physical age from such instruments as the Wetzel Grid and hand X ray; cumulative records; teacher observations; and records of parent-teacher conferences. This type of individual study will aid in the satisfactory placement of a gifted child, which in turn ought to ensure essential developmental experiences.

26. Gifted Adolescents' Views of Growing Up *

RUTH STRANG, *Director, Reading Development Center, University of Arizona; Professor Emeritus, Teachers College, Columbia University*

THE WAY in which adolescents perceive themselves and their world determines, to a large extent, their behavior. How they feel about growing up gives important clues to their adjustment during this transition period from childhood to adulthood. Is adolescence for them a period of "storm and stress," a time of uncertainty and insecurity, or a non-eventful gradual process, or the gateway to new privileges and responsibilities?

Among any large group of adolescents all of these responses to growing up would be represented in some degree. To obtain more information about this stage of development, 1,124 pupils in grades seven to twelve inclusive were asked to write compositions during class time on the subject "How It Feels to Be Growing Up." The topic was explained in a little more detail and the students asked to sign their names.[1] The compositions gave ample evidence that the writers were giving free, frank, and sincere responses and seemed to enjoy this opportunity to write about themselves. The cooperating teachers gained many insights from reading the compositions.

* From *Exceptional Children,* October, 1956, pp. 10–12. Reprinted with permission.
[1] Acknowledgment is most gratefully made to Catherine L. Beachley, Supervisor of Guidance and Research, Washington County, Hagerstown, Md., for obtaining the interest and cooperation of the teachers in having the children write the compositions and for putting the IQ from group intelligence tests on each composition.

About half of the population studied came from urban and half from rural areas in the same county. Although a wide range of socioeconomic status was represented, the middle and lower socioeconomic groups predominated. The number of cases, according to IQ level, were distributed as follows: [2]

Grades	IQ	Number of cases
7, 8, 9	95.2 Av.	247
	120–29	121
	130 and over	35
10, 11, 12	94.9 Av.	636
	120–29	65
	130 or over	20

In some categories the relative frequency of responses of the gifted and of the average were quite similar. Other responses were made more frequently by the gifted than by the average; still others, more frequently by those with average IQ's. Some responses were made more frequently by the younger than by the older adolescents. Although these differences apply only to this particular sample, it seems probable that the greater differences would be found in other similar groups and that, when percentage differences are at least one-third greater for the gifted than for the average, or vice versa, the probability of their having arisen from a chance variability of the sample studied would be extremely low. In the interpretation of these data, comparisons for those categories where the relative frequencies of responses are below 10 per cent have been omitted.

Similarity of Responses

Some feelings about growing up were expressed with similar frequency by average and by gifted students.*

Feelings of dissatisfaction with changes in body growth, functioning, and status were mentioned by about a fourth of each group. Such changes are common to both gifted and average adolescents and are emphasized in

[2] In this article "the gifted" or "the bright students" will refer to students with IQ's of 120 or above on a group intelligence test. "Average" will refer to the group with an average IQ of 95. The compositions were read by Dr. Warren Roome, responses categorized, and percentage of responses calculated for each type of response. In the tables, both numbers and percentages are given because the percentages based on the small number of cases in some categories may be misleading.

* Table 1, "Similarity between Average and Gifted Students with Respect to the Frequencies of Certain Response Categories," and Table 2, "Differences between Average and Gifted Students with Respect to the Frequencies of Certain Response Categories," have been omitted in reprinting.—EDITOR'S NOTE.

books on adolescent psychology. It is not surprising that adolescents should be aware of and concerned about unevenness in growth, individual differences in rate of growth, and attitudes toward themselves arising from these physical and physiological changes.

However, as may be seen in Table 2 (which has been omitted), the gifted expressed *satisfaction* with their body growth and status much more frequently than the average students. These feelings of satisfaction may be attributed to the general superiority of the gifted in physical development and health. The gifted expressed only slightly more concern with clothes, makeup, and other details of personal appearance than those of average intelligence.

Certain references to family relations were common to both average and gifted adolescents. With respect to sibling relations the entire group mentioned both satisfactions and problems. Some enjoyed their younger brothers and sisters and spoke of good relations with older siblings. Almost as many found younger children in the family a trial, a nuisance, or a cause for jealousy, and felt some resentment toward older brothers or sisters. Intelligence does not insure happy family relations. However, roughly half of both groups [data omitted]—but a larger percentage of the gifted—expressed satisfaction concerning relations with parents. This apparently good relation is reinforced by the fact that less than 10 per cent mentioned problems of mother-father-child relationships, such as parental differences with respect to discipline or differences in their feelings toward the two parents. Although so many of the gifted (58 per cent in the junior high school and 49 per cent in the senior high school) made comments that indicated satisfactory relations with parents, almost one-fifth of the gifted group in the senior high school, as contrasted with 6 per cent of the senior high average IQ group, also mentioned conflicts or lack of closeness or rapport with parents. Good relations with parents may be more difficult for the gifted to achieve in the lower socioeconomic groups than in the middle or upper classes. Still, it is significant that such a large percentage of the gifted, during the years when emancipation from the family is a major goal, seem to be accomplishing this developmental task without excessive emotional wear and tear.

Desire for a particular vocation was mentioned by about one-third of both groups. Slightly fewer—one-fifth to one-fourth [data in omitted table] —expressed feelings or other indications of indecision about their vocation. The indecision of the gifted may stem partly from the wide range of vocational choices open to them. They may also realize that a decision concerning their vocation need not be made in junior or senior high school. If they take the educational program designed to develop their potentialities, they will be prepared to make a decision regarding vocation when the time comes.

Approximately one-third of both the average and the gifted gave indications of self-acceptance. One might expect greater self-acceptance among the gifted. This was not indicated by the compositions. Other studies, too, have suggested that gifted students often have feelings of inferiority. Sometimes they compare themselves with the lives of great men and women about whom they read, rather than with their peers.

Nor are the gifted much less *concerned with scholastic success or grades* than are students of average intelligence. About one-fifth of both groups expressed concern with school success or grades. They are also not entirely satisfied with their school experiences: about one-tenth of the total sample expressed dissatisfaction. Actually many gifted children become bored and disillusioned with school. Their attitudes toward school and achievement will depend a great deal on the morale of the school, the attitude of other students toward them, and the challenges offered by the curriculum and methods of instruction. The pressure of ambitious parents or the indifference of other parents to the education of their gifted children will likewise influence the adolescent's school achievement.

Differences in Responses

In certain respects there were differences between the average and the bright students studied.

The students of average intelligence mentioned more frequently than the gifted *increasing independence and self-direction* as an advantage of growing up. Possibly those with lower intelligence have been more irked by restrictions and, being more dissatisfied with their present status, they look forward to any change. Somewhat allied to this desire for freedom is the wish to own or operate a car—a desire that was expressed by twice as many average as bright students.

At the same time, less able students seem much more *aware of increasing responsibilities*. One possible explanation is that students of average and below-average intelligence are closer to the time when they will leave school and go to work than are the gifted who are planning to continue in school; therefore responsibilities loom larger to them. Another possible explanation is that the bright students, feeling capable of carrying responsibilities, are not anxious enough to write about them.

In interpreting these tables, the relative number of responses given by the average and by the gifted should be considered. The bright students wrote more freely; they gave a larger total number of responses—6.8

categorized responses per composition as compared with 5.9 responses given by the average group.

In the junior high school the bright students more frequently referred to *financial security* and money problems than did the average. In the senior high school the percentage was about the same.

Very marked was the gifted student's *social concern for world peace.* Such precocious interest in more remote and abstract matters, including morality and religion, is characteristic of the gifted.

Contrary to popular opinion (but not to the results of research), the bright students frequently expressed *satisfaction in relations with their peers.* Social giftedness is often associated with verbal ability. However, some mentioned their desire for greater acceptance with their peers and almost half were concerned with boy-girl relations.

The most striking difference on the junior-high-school level was in *enjoyment of voluntary reading.* In these years, when voluntary reading is at its peak, 42 per cent of the bright students as contrasted with 13 per cent of the average made some reference to the enjoyment of reading. But in senior high school the difference in voluntary reading was far less marked—23 per cent by the average as compared with 31 per cent by the gifted. The decrease in interest in voluntary reading of the gifted may be attributable to competition with other adolescent interests, more time devoted to required reading with college entrance in mind, reluctance to be considered a bookworm by age-mates, lack of intellectual stimulation in the home, and other reasons.

Age Differences among the Gifted

Some additional age differences in responses are suggested in Table 3. For categories in Table 3, the frequency for one age level was actually one-third-or-more greater than the frequency at the other age level.

Interest in sports is much more frequently mentioned by the gifted in junior high school than in senior high school. Perhaps this is because other kinds of activities introduced during senior-high-school years, such as school publications and departmental clubs, interest them more than sports. Sometimes, too, the bright child, though equally able to learn athletic skills, learns them relatively more slowly than he does verbal tasks and consequently becomes impatient with his progress.

In *family relations* also some age differences were noted in the groups studied. During junior-high-school years the gifted mentioned concern about their family's problems and welfare more often than they did later. The older brighter students seemed to find less satisfaction in their relations with brothers and sisters than those of junior-high-school age. Among the explanations of this difference is their increasing attention to boy-girl relations, which may crowd out other interests and also put brothers and sisters in the nuisance class. Many individual factors, of course, enter into sibling relations. According to their responses, both age groups have about the same proportion of problems with brothers and sisters. Approximately one-fifth to one-fourth of the gifted expressed a desire for marriage and children. In the gifted group there was only a slight increase from the junior to senior high school for the bright students, whereas for the average students the frequency of mention in this category increased from 16 per cent at the junior-high to 33 per cent at the senior-high-school level. This difference between the two intelligence levels may be related to the generally greater precocity of the gifted group: they read earlier, are earlier concerned with religion and with moral values, and also seem to be somewhat more mature socially.

TABLE 3

DIFFERENCES BETWEEN GIFTED STUDENTS AT THE JUNIOR AND SENIOR
HIGH-SCHOOL LEVELS WITH RESPECT TO THE FREQUENCY OF
CERTAIN RESPONSE CATEGORIES

CATEGORY OF RESPONSE	156 JUNIOR-HIGH STUDENTS (IQ 120 or greater)		85 SENIOR-HIGH STUDENTS (IQ 120 or greater)	
	Number of Responses	Per Cent of Relative Frequency	Number of Responses	Per Cent of Relative Frequency
Interest in sports	39	25	7	8
Concern for family's welfare	26	17	6	7
Satisfaction with sibling relations	46	29	15	18
Lack of closeness or rapport with parents	13	8	16	19
Concern with social behavior, making friends	41	26	13	15
Desire for greater peer acceptance	14	9	12	14
Problems about money	19	12	7	8
Concern with military service	5	3	11	13
Concern with morality and religion	25	16	24	28
Enjoyment of voluntary reading	66	42	26	31

With parents, too, the bright student's relations seem to be better during junior-high-school years than later. More than twice as many of the senior-high-school gifted students mentioned lack of closeness or rapport with parents. Part of this feeling is a natural and desirable accompaniment of gaining independence from the family, but antagonism and misunderstanding underlie some of it. They expressed an awareness of differences between parents in standards and methods of discipline and showed a preference for one parent. However, the numbers in these categories are small and the dominant finding is the fact that about half of the gifted senior-high-school students and still more of the junior-high-school youngsters made some reference to satisfying relations with their parents.

Concern with social behavior, with making friends and getting along with people in general, was mentioned by about one-fourth of the bright junior-high-school students. This percentage was almost twice as large as that for the average IQ's. But fewer of the gifted in the senior than in the junior high school mentioned this aspect of adolescent adjustment. Perhaps the brighter students had learned to make a better social adjustment; perhaps the senior high school provided social activities that appealed to them; perhaps they have become more absorbed in intellectual pursuits. Perhaps their concern took the form of desire for greater peer acceptance, which a number of both age groups mentioned. There are many possible reasons, some highly individual and stemming from early childhood experiences.

Problems about money were mentioned by relatively few of the gifted in their compositions about growing up, and there was a decrease in frequency of mention from the junior to the senior high school. Possibly these students had found ways to meet their increasing need for money, or they may have come from socioeconomic backgrounds where money was not a problem.

Concern with morality and religion showed a marked increase among the gifted from junior to senior high school. It may be of significance that the increase was larger for the average group than for the gifted—from 9 per cent to 23 per cent, while the corresponding figures for the gifted were from 16 per cent to 28 per cent, reflecting the earlier interest of the gifted in such problems.

Sex Differences

A further breakdown of the data for 461 students in the eleventh grade confirmed, in general, the relations already mentioned. The responses were tabulated for:

11th-grade boys, IQ *less* than 100
11th-grade boys, IQ *more* than 100
11th-grade girls, IQ *less* than 100
11th-grade girls, IQ *more* than 100

Positive aspects of physical development and fitness seem to mean more to boys than to girls. The brighter eleventh-grade boys mentioned satisfaction with their body growth and status relatively more frequently than did the girls or the boys of average intelligence. The brighter girls expressed the most dissatisfaction.

Family relations seem to be of more concern to girls than to boys. A larger percentage of girls, especially the brighter girls, mentioned having problems with brothers and sisters. Small brothers can be very annoying to older sisters, and perhaps there are more opportunities for conflict between sisters than between brothers. It was the girls, though few in number, who more often complained of conflict or lack of closeness with parents. Girls also mentioned broken homes and concern for the welfare of their families relatively more frequently than did boys. The desire for marriage and children was expressed by 38 per cent of the girls over 100 IQ as contrasted with 18 per cent of the boys in the same classes. The relationship was practically the same for students with IQ's below 100. Girls, in general, are more "family oriented" than boys and are probably more willing to talk about it.

Careers are of concern to gifted adolescent girls, although marriage may be uppermost in their minds. It was surprising that these girls seemed to be thinking about vocations slightly more than boys. Certainly this would not have been the emphasis fifty years ago.

Satisfaction with peer relationships was expressed by slightly more gifted girls than by boys on the same level of intelligence. But, at the same time, the girls more often mentioned a desire for greater acceptance by peers and more concern with or interest in boy-girl relations and in making friends and getting along with people in general. Girls seem to be more socially oriented than boys.

With respect to indications of *self-acceptance,* the percentage of the brighter boys and girls was exactly the same—37 per cent. The girls, however, more frequently mentioned a desire to improve their personality. Possibly the boys actually wanted to improve *their* personality but did not consider it the thing to write about.

Voluntary reading showed a marked difference in frequency of mention between the brighter boys and the girls—16 per cent of the boys and 41 per cent of the girls. Both boys and girls in the upper intelligence groups complained more about homework than those below average. This may have been due to the more rigorous assignments given to students in the college-preparatory curriculum or to kinds of homework that gifted students find exceedingly boring.

The desire for world peace was mentioned slightly more frequently by the brighter girls than by the boys, but concern with military service was referred to primarily by boys. The girls also showed more concern with problems of morality and religion, as indicated by this type of response from 21 per cent of the girls as compared with 10 per cent of the boys.

Concluding Statement

This study of the spontaneous responses of junior- and senior-high-school students to the topic "How It Feels to Be Growing Up" has confirmed some of the generalizations regarding gifted adolescents. It has also contributed much more detail about the way in which they perceive the growing-up process and ways in which they are alike or different from their age-mates of lower intelligence. To read similar compositions written by one's own groups of adolescents would give teachers still more insight into how it feels to be a gifted adolescent.

27. Introspections of Gifted Children *

MARCELLA R. BONSALL, *Consultant, Division of Research and Guidance, Los Angeles County Schools*

INTEREST in educating gifted children has produced many administrative devices, curriculum implementations, methodological procedures, and guidance adaptations. Most plans were developed from, and are limited by, the accumulation of psychological principles and descriptions of characteristics of gifted children. These plans strongly suggest generalizations applicable to groups of gifted students, such as advanced courses and increased participation in extracurricular activities.

Generalized plans allow little or no emphasis to be placed on the individual student's own development. One common practice is the assignment of an "independent study project" to a gifted student, regardless of his

* From *California Journal of Educational Research*, XI, No. 4 (September, 1960), 159-66. Reprinted with permission.

interest and curiosity in the topic assigned, simply because it will benefit classmates. Such devices foster procrastination and boredom. Frequently the "broadening socially useful experience" is accomplished by delegating a gifted student—sometimes for a semester, or a school career—to a routine school job, such as front office helper or cashier in the cafeteria, where a high level of efficiency is attained in two or three weeks' time. These tasks force the gifted student to stand still for the rest of the semester. When educational plans fail to account for each gifted student's growth, these plans will, in part, defeat the purpose for which they are designed.

Gifted students face similar problems in adolescence as do "normal" students. Although identical descriptive terms can be used for both groups, gifted students are more keenly aware of and feel more intensely about these needs, and yet it is frequently assumed that they can and will work out their personal problems unaided. When school plans are at variance with what individual gifted students think and feel about themselves, they quickly become inadequate.

The identification of personal concerns might well aid school people in more effectively individualizing the general educational plans specifically geared for gifted students. It was the purpose of this exploratory study to attempt to locate personality needs of satisfactorily achieving, well-adjusted gifted high school students through the use of personal documents. In other words, this study searched for answers to the following questions: What are some of the personality needs of gifted students? What kinds of solutions to personal problems are gifted students seeking? Are gifted students attempting to solve personal problems unaided by adults? What are the more pressing personal problems with which gifted students need help?

Procedure Followed

The topical autobiographical letter, which is ego-centered, was employed for this study. Whether written either from the nomothetic or the ideographic approach, personal documents are useful as "self-revealing records that intentionally or unintentionally yield information regarding the structure, dynamics, and functions of the author's mental life" (1). Through this technique the intensity of feeling and the crucial importance of problems, which are ordinarily not available, are brought to light.

Forty-five gifted high school students in the eleventh grade in each of three metropolitan high schools met with the examiner in three groups of fifteen. These students had IQ's at or above 130 on the L form of the Stanford-Binet, and placed at or above the national 85th percentile on the ITED. All were taking college preparatory courses, had earned better than average grades, and were participating in one or more major extracurricular activity. The students were considered by the principals, the vice-principals, and the counselors to be well-adjusted teen-agers.

The students were informed that a study was being made on the personalities of teen-agers. Letters from teen-agers who could and would write on what they considered to be personal concerns were being voluntarily sought. The original letters would be kept strictly confidential. The only limitation, which they were to keep in mind while writing, was that each writer should restrict his comments to his own concerns. To insure anonymity further, a stamped envelope with the home address of the examiner was furnished.

Twenty-seven eleventh-grade gifted students voluntarily returned responses. The chronological age spread for fourteen boys was from 15.5 to 16.1, while that of thirteen girls was 14.8 to 16.0 The letters varied in length from two to five pages. Seven students signed their names to their letters; one added, "if you have any suggestions to my problem and have time I would appreciate it." Approximately half of them started their letters with what they considered to be their poor traits, while the others started with what they considered their favorable attributes.

Responses Categorized

The contents of the letters suggested the following categorical arrangement:

Social- or Other-directed Concerns	Self-directed Concerns
Parental Concerns	Vocational Concerns
Peer Concerns	Religious Concerns
Social Concerns	Physical Concerns
	Intellectual Concerns
	Temperament Concerns

The majority of the letters used an ideographic approach spilling over with ego-centered individuality. A few were written from a nomothetic approach accounting for individuality more or less in terms of objective norms.

An example of the ideographic approach is as follows: [1]

If my personality is what I feel and what I do then I have a very confused personality. I am never quite the same from one day to the next. One day I feel very satisfied and confident and the next day I feel I am not accomplishing anything and am terribly uncertain and lost.

[1] All quoted responses have been reproduced verbatim.

An example of the nomothetic approach is as follows:

Personality is the sum total of any human being. In order to obtain even a brief glimpse into the mannerisms and characteristics and complexities which comprise an individual, a complete but concise statement of principles, beliefs, opinions, ideas, and ideals is necessary. Please do not think me egotistical or overcritical of others in this analysis of myself and my environment.

PARENTAL CONCERNS

Several students considered their home lives and their relationships with parents to be very good ones. A boy said, *"My mother gripes me but I suppose that's natural for one my age. I love her anyway."* One girl whose relationships were poor had this to say:

I've never really depended upon anyone to help me with my problems, especially my mother. I have never been close to my mother or my stepfather, whom I've had since I was six. My girl friend knows more about me and my problems and what I feel than my mother. Mother has never taken the time out to try to understand me. Now I just never bother to tell her anything.

PEER CONCERNS

Among those who had similar concerns about peer relationships, they mentioned liking people and having many friends but they were anxious about their "shyness and self-consciousness" and being "too easily embarrassed." All mentioned these conditions were not as satisfactory at the elementary and junior high level as at the senior high level. Eight "still felt different and somewhat inferior" yet they "got along well and seem to be tolerated."

All had learned to "talk to people" and to "make friends easily" but found themselves at times "feeling uncomfortable."

One girl had this comment to make:

Popularity and personality seem to walk hand-in-hand. Away from my home where I know people don't know that I am smart I seem to be popular. The people that I meet tell me that my personality is a good one. But despite the fact that I overcame one problem away from home I gain another. Most people think that I am three years older than I am. I don't act older than I am but I find this is quite a problem in getting boy friends. Everything is fine until the matter of age comes around. If I could only lie, my problem wouldn't be as great but I pride myself on my honesty.

SOCIAL CONCERNS

Almost all students were interested in the more abstract and the more far-reaching results of human wants, needs, and values rather than the immediate time and closeness in space of people. It was not that they neglected or overlooked the immediate situations but rather that their concerns are far-reaching and appear to be extended and to include long-term goals and eventualities. The nearness aspects were "attempting to see both sides," valuing as important the traits of "courtesy and graciousness even though considered by some as sissy," "loyalty," "trustworthiness," and "consideration of others' feelings regardless of age."

The future aspect mentioned most frequently pertained to recognition as "worthy persons," becoming a "good citizen," and working toward "having little or no racial or religious prejudices." The latter type of comments were qualified by mention of having friends who were from different ethnic groups.

A quotation that follows is included in order that the feeling-tone of attitudes and the scope of concerns may be illustrated.

In one English class we were asked to tell of what we'd wish for if we had one wish. Instead of wishing I'd lose 50 or 60 pounds I wished for world peace, happiness, and prosperity; freedom from want, greed, and ignorance. You see I am fairly people-loving and I'd like to help that wish come true. I want to help the unfortunate. I don't think I'm medically inclined. I can't help my fellow man that way, but I'd love to be able to help somehow—but how? (girl)

Only a few wrote of vocational concerns. Because each was unique no summary was made. One quotation is included here.

I have several goals in life, but one of them is particularly important. This is accumulating a tremendous amount of wealth. Not so much for the money itself but the enjoyment and pleasures in obtaining it by successfully carrying out a well-calculated risk. I could never discipline myself to enter into a professional field, for I would certainly be limited (wealth and endeavors). By endeavors I mean that because I have found it impossible for me to contain a true and lasting interest in any one field it will be necessary for me to be free when desired. As money covers all fields it should be quite sufficient in pleasing my whims. Though this is definitely an age of specialists I will no doubt succeed, for there must be an organizing force. Marriage is necessary but will undoubtedly not hinder my progress.

RELIGIOUS CONCERNS

Two girls and one boy expressed strong attachments to religious beliefs as sources of satisfaction. The following two held reservations. One said, *"Even though I have a very strong set of ideas and ideals concerning God, my mind is constantly being put in a turmoil by the additions of new facts and pressures."* One girl wrote, *"I don't believe absolutely positively, indubitably in God. I even doubt He exists."*

One girl sighted disbelief in the existence of God.

My strongest belief has to do with religion. As far as I am concerned a God whom everyone worships is nothing more than a figment of men's imagination. I consider it as being beyond the capabilities of men's minds to really know whether or not God exists. Organized religion I think is one of the greatest evils of society. Any time one group broadly proclaims that its doctrine is the only way to salvation, conflicts are bound to arise. (girl)

PHYSICAL CONCERNS

Four boys expressed strong likings for sports and mentioned that they "were fairly good at them." All four said they received the "most satisfaction from accomplishments" in this area. One girl was concerned about not having a good figure while another girl had guilt feelings for "not eating the proper foods, or getting the proper rest." Two girls mentioned concerns about emotionally induced illnesses. One said, *"I excite myself easily. I think I talk myself into headaches."*

One boy talked of an inferiority complex and the means he was using to overcome it. For instance, he said:

I believe I have a slight inferiority complex but nothing too serious that I won't be able to handle. This was caused by a lack of coordination and ability in many sports. My appearance, when I was younger, was quite heavy and I became used to being kidded about goofing up a play in sports, whether malicious or not. I learned to accept my inability. During the past year I have been trying to offset this by going out for more sports and building myself up so that I can break even with other kids. As far as my appearance goes I am learning to accept the fact that we can't all be handsome and I can develop a good social personality that will make up for this.

One girl had a particular problem. This is the way she stated it:

I always feel self-conscious because of my large nose. It has always bothered me. When we are around boys I always stay behind because I think if I start kidding around they will get the idea I am flirting and that idea is absolutely ridiculous because I am not pretty. However, I am not a complete washout with boys. I am going out with one now that just graduated. He is real nice. So I guess I am not that ugly, but this one thing has always been a barrier to me, probably mentally more than anything else.

INTELLECTUAL CONCERNS

The intellectual aspects of personality that these students said they enjoyed were: being intellectual; enjoying competition; enjoying school; learning something new and different; being able to perform well scholastically; having ability to reason, to form, and to keep opinions; possessing good memories; being curious and having many interests. The disturbing factors were: being bored unless interested; coasting along and yet getting good grades; talking too much; having to slow down pace; being pressured to perform more; and finding themselves lost in thought "even when in a group." The factor most frequently mentioned and appearing universal for this group was procrastination, not only in the sense of feeling guilty but also in the sense of not stretching to the possible heights of intellect and imagination.

The following examples will illustrate the itemized factors.

I like being intelligent but wish people wouldn't consider me a brain. I am an average teen-age girl liking clothes, records, boys, movie stars, and the like. However, it seems that many people don't realize this. I realize I am persistent and even stubborn at times but I think persistence and stubbornness are good traits to have. (girl)

I do everything on the basis of competition. I always am very proud of myself if I can be tops in a certain category. If I have the best school assignment, or if I get the most points in the class I have reached my peak of performance. Even though I achieve this peak a few times I never seem to be satisfied with it, and know that I could have done better. After I finish a notebook, for example, and even though I might get an A on it, I find fault with it and am partially not satisfied with it. There is that margin of fault with it which I will examine and will become again partially unhappy over my performance. I always strive to overcome this margin of fault, which results in better and more efficient work. I am trying now to overcome this complex of perfectionism. I have partially succeeded but the seed of discomfort is still there. Another unsatisfactory fault of mine is laziness. I never used to be quite so lazy as I am now. I have to drive myself a lot harder to do my homework than I used to. Last semester, for example, it took me almost 15 weeks to get back to the old grind. I am very angry at myself when the clock strikes 7:00 and I have not even started my homework and yet I think I am intelligent as the next fellow and sometimes even more so. I think I am more of an adult, have accomplished more mentally, and am as dependable and as reliable—or more so—than the next man. I am especially proud when I discover a new fact and use it in conversation for schoolwork, but if I do not use it the tables are turned. (boy)

TEMPERAMENT CONCERNS

The temperament concerns appeared to fall into two categories, one of satisfaction and one of dissatisfaction. The satisfactory characteristics were: joy in living; working to overcome faults; satisfaction when a goal is achieved; liking people and making friends easily; having strong will powers and determinations; attempts at being responsible and attaining humility; enjoying curiosity and desiring to learn; enjoying competition; and other factors mentioned previously.

Those of dissatisfaction seemed to be: feeling inferior; loneliness; feeling different from others intellectually; often being self-conscious, shy and becoming easily embarrassed; not liking responsibilities; being selfish and inconsiderate; being conceited at times; having quick tempers and at times being unreasonable; listening to and relating gossip and being mixed-up "like other teen-agers."

The examples that follow are offered in order to show similarities and also to show the uniqueness in individuality:

> *A phase of life I like very much is competition on the athletic field or in a grueling debate. It affords me one of my greatest pleasures in life. Speaking of life—I love it! People, cities, deserts, oceans, mountains, trees, animals, etc., all give it that extra touch.* (boy)

> *I believe I have a slight inferiority complex. My feelings of inferiority seems to come and go in relationship to my sad and happy moods and possibly as a result of some incidents or remarks made. At times I am very self-conscious although I know there is no reason for it. It just makes things worse. I am also inclined to be conceited even though I really have no reason to be. As far as my opinions go I am not really extreme about anything, or so I think. I might be considered conservative. I like people and try to make friends with all people. There is one drawback: I am inclined to be bossy and want my way. Of course this doesn't always go; I have to think of others.* (boy)

> *Even though I think like an adult I don't act like one many times. Sometimes I talk too much even though I know I do. Sometimes I joke too much or become belligerent or sassy even though I know it is wrong. After I do stop I become angry with myself for acting like a child. I realize that no one considers me a full-grown adult but I am very pleased when I find someone who treats me as such and again I am angry when someone treats me as a child which I don't consider myself to be. I am striving to not only think like an adult but to act as one also. This doesn't seem to be progressing very rapidly, but it is progressing.* (boy)

> *I want to wake up tomorrow, for I dream that tomorrow I will find myself. I know not why I am unhappy, dissatisfied with my surroundings. I cannot perceive why I am created, what duty I am to perform. Life is incomprehensible to me. I do not know what I am or what I believe. A desire to know myself keeps me searching.* (girl)

Future Research Indicated

Merely the surface has been scratched in identifying personal problems of well-adjusted, satisfactorily achieving, gifted students. The questions postulated were barely answered; however, direction for research and kinds of help needed for gifted students are indicated. These are some of the questions with which future research must be concerned:

1. Through the use of personal documents is it possible to locate potential and/or submerged personality concerns of well-adjusted gifted students that might block discovery of more natural endowments sooner in life, thereby decreasing frustrations?

2. Is evidence apparent that well-adjusted gifted students are seeking satisfying and lasting solutions to their personality problems depending almost entirely on self-direction?

3. Is evidence apparent that they are attempting to gain self-control without loss of self-esteem?

4. Are well-adjusted gifted students being pressured into "paying high prices" for acceptance and popularity among peers?

5. Are well-adjusted gifted students gaining status among peers at the expense of failing to uncover unique aspects of personality and perhaps retarding future productiveness?

6. Is there evidence that well-adjusted gifted students attempt to remove obstacles and overcome certain faults in order to be more effective in leadership activities?

7. What is the effect on well-adjusted gifted students who have keen sensitivity to desires of classmates, but lack confidence in themselves?

8. Is there evidence that the concerns are great enough to hamper well-adjusted gifted students seriously from achieving optimal growth and limit future accomplishments?

9. Do feelings of guilt and frustration about the tendency to procrastinate spring from tasks that do not challenge and stretch the intellect and the imagination enough or in ways to satisfy the desires of well-adjusted gifted students?

10. In socialization processes have enough thought and consideration been given to helping well-adjusted gifted students develop feelings of belongingness and worth, or are they pressured to help others under the assumption this method will bring about, by some magic twist, these necessary feelings?

11. Are they being helped to establish satisfactory relations of self to society and to find answers to "Who am I," and "What am I?"

12. Can these students be helped enough to dare to be themselves and to develop outstanding ego strength, which is the common denominator of gifted, highly productive adults?

13. Can the school apply the concepts of enrichment and acceleration

in the effective areas, as well as in the intellectual areas, in order that well-adjusted gifted students' talents become more spontaneous and more creative?

References

1. ALLPORT, GORDON W. "The Use of Personal Documents in Psychological Science," New York: *Social Science Research Council, Bulletin 49*, 1942.
2. DEMENT, ALICE. "Good Students Want Counseling, Too," *Journal of Counseling Psychology*, April, 1957: 124–28.
3. GALLAGHER, JAMES J., and CROWDER, THORA. "The Adjustment of Gifted Children in the Regular Classrooms," *Exceptional Children*, May, 1957: 353–63, 369, 398.
4. STRANG, RUTH. *Guideposts for Gifted Children Themselves*. Columbia University, Teachers College, Bureau of Publications, 1958.

28. *Adjustment Problems of the Gifted* [*][1]

EDITH H. GROTBERG, *Associate Professor of Psychology, Northern Illinois University*

S CIENTIFIC approaches to the study of the gifted, which followed the development and use of mental tests, yielded results inconsistent with beliefs held forty or fifty years earlier. The early works of Terman (10), Witty (12), and Hollingworth (4, 5) dispelled the beliefs that the gifted are "the products of supernatural causes of human behavior," and that "intellectual precocity is pathological" (10). Indeed, Terman, Witty, and Hollingworth found the gifted to be physically superior, attractive, and generally well-adjusted.

* Reprinted from the April, 1962, issue of *Education*, pp. 472–76. Copyright 1962 by The Bobbs-Merrill Company, Inc., Indianapolis, Ind. Numbers in parentheses refer to references.
[1] The gifted are identified here mainly by a high IQ. Currently these gifted are called the verbally gifted, since the IQ tests used are highly correlated with verbal ability.

Although these authors recognized that adjustment problems existed among the gifted, relatively little effort was made to investigate problem behavior until recently. It should be recalled, however, that Hollingworth (4) found that pupils of IQ's 180 plus had more adjustment problems than pupils whose IQ's fell between 130 and 180.

Recently a number of studies have appeared that tend to substantiate the findings of the early research endeavors as far as the generally superior adjustment of the gifted is concerned. But recent studies have attempted to determine the factors correlated with maladjustment.

Some of these studies have dealt with identifying the characteristics of underachievers, i.e., verbally gifted students who are not earning grades commensurate with IQ or test score expectancy. Haggard (3) found that by third grade, high achievers responded to socialization pressures and accepted adult values readily. They cooperated, had good work habits, and maintained satisfactory relationships with parents, peers, and teachers. They were also highly competitive.

Gowan (2) reported that the underachiever experienced parental rejection and hostility frequently. Roesslein (8) found among high school male underachievers a pattern involving oversolicitous parents and resultant feelings of inadequacy. Armstrong (1), who studied the adjustment of underachievers in the ninth and eleventh grades, found that they were more influenced by the desires of others rather than their own wishes and were regarded by their teachers as uncooperative, undependable, and poor in judgment.

Further, O'Leary (7) found the underachievers in the ninth grade to have poor work habits. Patterns of maladjustment found among underachievers at the college level by Wedemeyer (11) and Horrall (6) were similar to those noted in the elementary and high school pupils. And Shaw and Brown (9) found a high degree of hostility and hypercritical attitudes among underachieving college students.

Institutionalized Gifted

Clearly the verbally gifted have adjustment problems, although their incidence is lower than that found in less intelligent individuals. A frequently used method for identifying the maladjusted gifted, as we have already indicated, has been in association with underachievement in elementary, high school, and college.

Another method of identifying the problems of the maladjusted gifted is to study gifted adults who have been institutionalized and whose conditions have been diagnosed. These individuals are to a large extent the underachievers or failures as adults. An examination of their records reveals a number of factors that should be of interest to educators. The remainder of this article is based on a study of institutionalized gifted in the Elgin, Illinois, State Hospital. This study was made by the writer in 1961.

Test Groups and Tests

Forty gifted and forty nongifted institutionalized patients comprised the experimental and control groups. Each group contained twenty male and twenty female patients. Psychological tests, consisting of a Wechsler-Bellevue or Adult Intelligence Scale, the Rorschach Test, a Thematic Apperception Test, and a Sentence Completion Examination, were given to ascertain the characteristics that differentiated the gifted population from the nongifted population.

The gifted population was selected on the basis of high IQ. An IQ of 120 was set as the base, and the range was from 120 to 137. An IQ between 80 and 110 was used to designate the nongifted population.

A Summary of Characteristics

A summary of the findings concerning the characteristics of the gifted as compared to the nongifted institutionalized population is organized around (1) age, (2) education, (3) occupation, (4) psychological controls, and (5) general diagnosis, frequency of paranoid tendencies, and incidence of obsessive-compulsive features.

1. *Age:* The institutionalized gifted and nongifted had a median age of 33.5 to 34 years. The age differences are not significant. The gifted enter mental hospitals with the same relative frequency as the nongifted. Another way of stating this fact is that the percentage of gifted in mental hospitals is the same as the percentage of gifted in the total population. Mental hospital populations represent the total population in terms of IQ distribution. The adjustment advantage of the gifted in childhood and youth apparently is lost in adulthood.

2. *Education:* The gifted have obtained on the average from three to five years more education than the nongifted. The gifted male has continued his higher education more frequently and for more advanced degrees than the gifted female. Nine of the twenty gifted males were college graduates; two of these had master's degrees; three had doctor's degrees. Four gifted females, by contrast, were college grad-

uates; two of these had master's degrees; none had a doctor's degree. Apparently the male is encouraged to pursue higher education more frequently and for more advanced degrees than the female.

3. *Occupation:* In spite of more education, the gifted female attained no higher occupational status than the nongifted population. The gifted male holds the occupations associated with higher education, such as physician, teacher, publisher, pilot, and engineer.

4. *Psychological Controls:* The F score of the Rorschach was used to determine the degree of control that the patients indicated as they interact with their environment. No significant differences in control were found between the gifted and nongifted populations. Further, the gifted demonstrated no greater control than that which would be expected by chance.

5. *Diagnosis:* The most frequently occurring diagnosis for the gifted male and the nongifted population was schizophrenia or schizophrenic reaction. No significant differences existed. The gifted female was significantly more psychoneurotic than the nongifted male (.01 level of significance) and the gifted male (.05 level of significance).

Statistically significant differences in incidence of paranoid tendencies did not appear between the gifted and the nongifted. However, the gifted male showed the highest frequency of such characteristics. Over half of the gifted males could be so designated.

The gifted male also showed the highest incidence of obsessive-compulsive tendencies, although differences were not statistically significant.

Feelings and Attitudes

Factors that may further contribute to an understanding of differences between the gifted and nongifted institutionalized population are organized around (1) feelings of superiority, (2) perceptions of failure, (3) attitudes toward work, and (4) attitudes toward parental pressures in terms of parental expectations.

1. *Feelings of superiority:* At times, the gifted male tended to perceive himself as superior to others. The gifted female and the nongifted populations did not perceive themselves so often in this way. The feelings of superiority of the gifted male were significantly higher than the gifted female.

2. *Perceptions of failure:* Half of the gifted female population perceived themselves as failures while three-fourths of the gifted males so perceived themselves. The gifted female resembled more closely

the nongifted population. The gifted male felt significantly more of a failure than the nongifted population. He felt more of a failure than the gifted female, but the difference was not significant.

3. *Attitudes toward work:* Negative attitudes toward work were held most frequently by both male and female gifted, while positive attitudes were held most frequently by the nongifted. The gifted female had more negative attitudes toward work than the gifted male. She also had the least positive attitudes toward work. All of the relationships were significant at the .01 level.

4. *Attitudes toward parental pressures:* More male and female gifted resisted parental pressures than nongifted, but the gifted submitted to parental pressure with about the same frequency as the nongifted. The gifted showed a similar frequency of ambivalence toward parental pressures as the nongifted. Both the male and female gifted showed a higher frequency of striving beyond parental standards than the nongifted. All of the relationships were significant at the .01 or .05 levels.

Discussion of Findings

The discussion is organized around two focuses: (1) the characteristics and perceptions that distinguish the institutionalized gifted from the institutionalized nongifted, and (2) educational implications of the findings.

The institutionalized gifted resembled the age groups of the institutionalized nongifted and have developed no higher set of controls to ward off or postpone a psychotic or psychoneurotic disorder. The adjustment advantage found among gifted children and youth is apparently lost in adulthood.

The institutionalized gifted was better educated than the nongifted. The gifted male continued higher education more frequently than the gifted female at a rate of more than 2 to 1. The gifted male also continued higher education for more advanced degrees than the gifted female. Gifted males held the better occupational positions and had the highest socioeconomic status. Gifted females attained no higher socioeconomic status than the nongifted.

The institutionalized gifted male tended to become schizophrenic and to display paranoid or obsessive-compulsive features. He was more likely to project the blame for his failure onto others. He was not so likely to assume responsibility for his own failures. The gifted female more frequently developed psychoneurotic disorders.

The gifted male was more frequently aware of his superiority and also of his own sense of failure. Neither the gifted male nor female had marked positive attitudes toward work; indeed their attitudes were highly negative. Both the gifted male and female tended to reject pressure in terms of parental expectations. Yet as a group, they submitted to parental pressures about as frequently as did the nongifted population. However, they more frequently attempted to surpass the expectations and achievements of their parents.

Implications

Assuming that growth and development are continuous, and that adult adjustments are to a large extent contingent upon earlier experiences, a number of implications for education may be derived from the findings on institutionalized gifted. These findings may be suggested by the following questions:

1. What are the schools doing to determine and influence the gifted student's attitude toward work?
2. How does the school help gifted students deal with failure?
3. What are schools doing to help the gifted student develop a self-concept and ideal consonant with his promise?
4. How do the schools work with parents to foster achievement of a high order?
5. Are teachers and parents working together in efforts to stimulate more gifted girls to continue their education and make greater contribution in accord with their promise?

The institutionalized gifted have poor attitudes toward work. Is it possible that too many gifted meet school requirements without much effort? Perhaps these students acquire knowledge and information with a minimum of effort and therefore do not find it necessary to develop positive attitudes and desirable work habits.

The institutionalized gifted, especially the male, experience pervasive feelings of failure. Has academic work been so easy in the elementary school and high school that the gifted seldom experience failure and therefore do not learn to deal with it constructively? Does the gifted male's pattern of blaming others for his failures need to be examined and altered?

The institutionalized gifted male appears to feel superior to others. Have the schools contributed to the feelings of superiority on the part of the male? Similarly, have schools attempted to help girls develop a realistic appreciation of their abilities?

The institutionalized gifted report excessive conflict with their parents.

Is the school helping parents to formulate realistic expectations for their gifted children? Are teachers helping the gifted relate effectively to those in authority?

The institutionalized gifted male is better educated and is higher in the occupational hierarchy than is the female. Do present programs for the gifted provide sufficient incentive for the full development of gifted girls?

Answers to these questions seem to be worthy of consideration by schools in their efforts to provide more adequately for gifted pupils.

References

1. ARMSTRONG, MARION E. *A Comparison of the Interests and Social Adjustments of Underachievers and Normal Achievers at the Secondary School Level.* Ph.D. dissertation; Storrs, Conn.: University of Connecticut, 1955. Abstract in *Dissertation Abstracts* 15, 1955, pp. 1349–50.

2. GOWAN, JOHN C. "The Underachieving Gifted Child—A Problem for Everyone," *Exceptional Children,* XXI (April, 1955), 247–49, 270–71.

3. HAGGARD, ERNEST A. "Socialization, Personality, and Academic Achievement in Gifted Children," *School Review,* LXV (December, 1957), 388–414.

4. HOLLINGWORTH, L. S. *Children Above 180 IQ.* Yonkers, N.Y.: World Book Company, 1942.

5. ———. *Gifted Children: Their Nature and Nurture.* New York: Macmillan, 1926.

6. HORRALL, BERNICE M. "Academic Performance and Personality Adjustments of Highly Intelligent College Students," *Genetic Psychology Monographs,* LV (February, 1957), 3–83.

7. O'LEARY, MAURICE J. *The Measurement and Evaluation of the Work Habits of Overachievers and Underachievers to Determine the Relationship of These Habits to Achievement.* Ph.D. dissertation; Boston: Boston University, 1955. Abstract in *Dissertation Abstracts* 15, 1955, pp. 2104–5.

8. ROESSLEIN, CHARLES G. *Differential Patterns of Intelligence Traits between High Achieving and Low Achieving High School Boys.* Washington, D.C.: Catholic University of America Press, 1953.

9. SHAW, MERVILLE C., II and BROWN, DONALD J. "Scholastic Underachievement of Bright College Students," *Personnel and Guidance Journal,* XXXVI (November, 1957), 195–99.

10. TERMAN, L. M., and ODEN, M. *Mental and Physical Traits of a Thousand Gifted Students,* Vol. I of *Genetic Studies of Genius.* Stanford, Calif.: Stanford University Press, 1925.

11. WEDEMEYER, CHARLES A. "Gifted Achievers and Non-Achievers," *Journal of Higher Education,* XXIV (January, 1953), 25–30.

12. WITTY, PAUL. *A Study of One Hundred Gifted Children,* University of Kansas Bulletin in Education, Vol. II, No. 7. Lawrence, Kansas: University of Kansas Press, 1930.

29. Adolescent Reactions to Academic Brilliance *

ABRAHAM J. TANNENBAUM, *Associate Dean, Graduate School of Education, Yeshiva University*

THE OBJECTIVES of this study were pursued by (1) studying the ratings of the eight stimulus characters; (2) comparing the reactions to individual and combinations of characteristics; (3) locating the traits distinctively associated and unassociated with each character; (4) measuring the degree of association between background factors and the ratings of the characters; and (5) comparing male and female respondents' reactions to the characters and characteristics. . . .

Summary of Outcomes and Conclusions

A number of important insights into adolescents' attitudes toward academic brilliance were revealed through the present survey:

1. The adolescents surveyed rated academic brilliance per se about equal to average ability as a personal attribute.

2. The adolescents rated academic brilliance as far less acceptable than average ability in the case where its possessor also devotes a greater-than-average amount of time to schoolwork and lacks interest in sports.

3. Studiousness per se was rated a less acceptable attribute than nonstudiousness in all but one of the communities surveyed.

4. Athletic-mindedness was regarded as far more desirable than its absence.

5. Female adolescents tended to favor nonstudiousness and athletic-mindedness more than did the males.

* From *Adolescent Attitudes toward Academic Brilliance*, pp. 35, 68, Bureau of Publications, Teachers College, Columbia University, New York, 1962. Reprinted with permission.

6. The attitudes expressed toward each of the fictitious characters were not influenced by the respondents' intelligence levels nor by the extent of their parents' education.

Insofar as verbal stereotypes reflect face-to-face relations, these results suggest that academic brilliance in-and-of itself is not a stigma in the adolescent world. However, when it is combined with relatively unacceptable attributes, it can penalize its possessor severely. The nonstudious athlete may demonstrate outstanding brainpower without fearing social derogation by peers; but a display of brilliance by one who is studious and indifferent to sports constitutes a definite status risk. The implied impression is that the brilliant student is an exceptionally prominent target for teen-age pressures to conform to certain behaviors and values. If so, there is danger of his deliberately masking his talent in order to relieve these pressures.

30. Occupational Adjustments of the Mentally Gifted *

WALTER B. BARBE, *Professor of Special Education, Kent State University*

MANY STUDIES have been made concerning the gifted child. But little attention has been given to the study of former gifted children once they have reached maturity. Reports of eminent people, who were in most instances precocious in childhood, yield little information: these are always reports of the successful in terms of position or moneymaking ability.

It is the purpose of this paper to discuss the job satisfactions of the gifted—both those who are eminently successful as well as those who, perhaps, are satisfied with their jobs even though, in certain respects, they are not high achievers and may not have reached the occupational level that was expected of them.

Any report on the gifted would be incomplete without reference to

* From *Vocational Guidance Quarterly,* Winter, 1956–57, pp. 74–76. Reprinted with permission.

Lewis Terman's monumental study (4) of 1,500 gifted children over a period covering more than twenty-five years. The report of most interest to those concerned with the occupational achievements of gifted individuals will be the twenty-five year follow-up study (5) *The Gifted Child Grows Up.* It is from this work of Lewis Terman that the modern concept of the gifted individual has been drawn.

Only a few years ago the individual who was blessed with better than average mental ability was labeled, "odd," "freak," or faced the old wives' tales "early ripe, early rot" or "insanity and genius go hand in hand." Fortunately, such ideas are now recognized as superstitious; and mental precocity, while it still is not always accepted and is rarely understood, is not now treated as some type of ailment.

Superior Traits Cited

Before any consideration of the occupational adjustments of gifted individuals, it is desirable to list those characteristics that describe mentally superior individuals. Terman and Oden (5) include such factors as quick understanding, curiosity, extensive information, retentive memory, large vocabulary, early interest and ability in reading, more imagination, and keen sense of humor. While it is true that average individuals also have many of these characteristics, it is probably the degree to which they are possessed that distinguishes the gifted.

Bristow (2) lists as characteristics of the mentally superior such factors as alertness, quickness, broad attention-span, high degree of insight into problems, and ability to generalize. This list was extended still further by Carroll (3) who included early development of self-criticism, initiative, independence in thinking, ability to see relationships, make associations, adapt abstract principles to concrete situations, observe and remember details, desire to know, desire to excel, originality, and power to learn.

Adjustment Problems Arise

In discussing the job satisfactions of gifted individuals, questions arise that can be only partially answered. Identifying these problems is an essential first step.

Do gifted high school students benefit from vocational guidance?
One of the major characteristics of mentally superior individuals is their wide range of interest. Since this is coupled with superior mental ability, a vocational counselor is faced with a major problem. It essentially means that the individual may succeed in many occupations in a wide range of

areas. Instead of the gifted being able to take care of himself merely because he is gifted, he is actually faced with an even greater problem than the average whose interests and abilities are narrower.

In advising gifted individuals it is necessary for the counselor to indicate the individual's potentialities rather than limit him to what appears to be the dominant interest at a particular time.

In a study (1) made by the writer of the graduates of special classes for gifted children in Cleveland, Ohio, Public Schools, one of the most frequently mentioned changes in the high school was the addition of more vocational counseling. This probably means more of an exploratory type of counseling rather than directive counseling aimed at choosing a vocation.

Do all students with high IQ's go to college? While it would be expected that those students with high IQ's would be the ones who would attend college, research studies have indicated that many such students do not attend college.

In a study of gifted children in Cleveland it was found that almost all of the men at least started in college, but only a little over 60 per cent of the women did so. This would seem to point out the need in this particular community for more attention to stressing the importance of advanced training for women. Perhaps the large preponderance of foreign-born parents would be an explanation for this, since it has been found among foreign-born groups that little importance is placed on advanced schooling for women. In other studies of the gifted, it has been found that a larger percentage of the women attended college.

While not all students with high IQ's should go to college, it would be expected that most of them should do so. The problem of whether gifted women should attend college remains unanswered. It would certainly seem logical, however, that many of those who do attend college should come from the gifted group.

Do all gifted individuals enter professional-level occupations? It is apparent from all studies of gifted individuals that the majority of them eventually work up to the professional level of occupation. There are those, however, who do not.

There appears to be little evidence, however, that the gifted individuals in occupations other than at the professional level are not as well satisfied as those at the higher level. There is evidence that each occupational level, from unskilled to the professional, contains some gifted individuals.

Are gifted individuals satisfied with their occupations? Gifted individuals are more sensitive to stimuli from their environment. Because they do respond to stimuli, this could have a tendency to make them less satisfied with their vocations. However, in every study of the gifted there has been clear-cut evidence that they are better satisfied than the average. This does not mean, of course, that all gifted individuals are happy in their work; there are many who are not. Some of the problems that gifted individuals face in obtaining job satisfaction may be stated as follows:

1. The difficulty of reconciling slow progress toward a goal. Because of the superior intellect of the gifted, they sometimes resent the necessity of beginning at the bottom. This, added to the "promotion on the basis of longevity" rule, may tend to make them dissatisfied. In spite of such rules, however, most gifted individuals are able to progress rapidly.

2. The difficulty of reconciling the desire to obtain personal success with the desire to have money or to be of service. The very essence of mental superiority is sensitivity. This sensitivity frequently carries with it a strong desire to be of service to mankind. This desire is frequently in conflict with the desire to be successful in terms of monetary values. Because gifted individuals frequently can succeed in any number of fields, they must choose the area in which a balance is maintained between these diversified ambitions.

Should gifted individuals go into teaching? Of utmost importance to the future development of gifted individuals is the extent to which gifted adults enter the teaching profession. The number of gifted students choosing teaching as a profession is alarmingly low.

There undoubtedly are many reasons for this. Some major reasons may be: (1) dissatisfaction with those in positions of authority, (2) lack of recognition for outstanding achievement, (3) lockstep promotion based on seniority, and (4) low financial return.

If the potentialities of gifted individuals are to be fully realized, it is essential that the best possible education be provided for them. The only hope for this is through the recruitment of more teachers from among the ranks of the gifted.

Talents Must Be Developed

In a democratic society that is dependent upon the intelligence of its people for continued existence, it is essential that the talents of individuals be used to the utmost. This can be achieved through good education and effective guidance.

Merely because an individual is gifted is not reason enough to expect him to be able to take care of himself unaided. Only if the gifted are happy in their occupations can we expect them to produce to their fullest extent. It is our responsibility to identify and understand the gifted and make any necessary provisions that will promote their better adjustment to life.

References

1. BARBE, WALTER B. "A Follow-up Study of the Graduates of Special Classes for Gifted Children." Unpublished Ph.D. Dissertation, Northwestern University, 1953.
2. BRISTOW, WILLIAM H., *et al.* "Identifying Gifted Children." *The Gifted Child.* Witty, Paul A. (ed.). Boston: D. C. Heath and Co., 1951.
3. CARROLL, HERBERT. *Genius in the Making.* New York: McGraw-Hill Book Co., Inc., 1940.
4. TERMAN, LEWIS M. (ed.). *Genetic Studies of Genius,* Vols. I–IV. Stanford, Calif.: Stanford University Press.
5. ———, and ODEN, MELITA H. *The Gifted Child Grows Up.* Stanford, Calif.: Stanford University Press, 1947.

31. Isolation as a Characteristic of Highly Gifted Children *

PAUL M. SHELDON, *Professor of Sociology and Anthropology, Occidental College, Los Angeles*

THE TENDENCY of highly intelligent children to become isolated has been suggested by Hollingworth,[1] Terman, and others. Several years ago,[2] an intensive exploratory study of children who had achieved an IQ of 170 or higher on the Stanford-Binet Scale was made at New York University's Counseling Center for Gifted Children. The subjects comprised all of the children in this category under the age of twelve [3] who could be located

* From *Journal of Educational Sociology,* January, 1959, pp. 215–21. Reprinted with permission.

[1] Leta S. Hollingworth, *Children Above 180 IQ* (Yonkers, N.Y.: World Book Co., 1942), pp. 262–64.

[2] This study was made from 1947–51, but the results have been withheld for ethical and legal reasons. The existence of the aggregate of subjects was well known and some of the individuals were identifiable.

[3] Children 12 years of age and older in this intelligence range cannot be measured adequately on standardized tests. They tend to "go through the ceiling."

in the New York area. Sources of information included the files of the Center, the records of the New York City Board of Education Psychological Clinic, and the records of the large elementary school that admitted students on the basis of high intelligence test scores. Twenty-eight subjects were involved. It was possible to study 24 of them intensively.

Answers were sought to these two questions:

1. To what extent do these children *feel* themselves to be isolated?
2. To what extent do their peers and adult observers consider them to be isolated?

Instruments used for this purpose included the Rorschach Technique of Personality Diagnosis; psychiatric interviews; sociometric studies; the California Test of Personality; the Haggerty-Olson-Wickman Behavior Rating Scale; and statements and observations by teachers, parents, and trained interviewers.

1. Feelings of Isolation as Interpreted by Rorschach Analysts and Psychiatrists

FINDINGS FROM RORSCHACH EXAMINATIONS

The Rorschach cards were administered to each of the 28 subjects, and their reactions were recorded. Exploratory interviews were held after each examination.

The overall impression obtained from the subjects' responses was that, with two exceptions, these children indicated a high degree of constriction. The examiner found only two subjects whose responses were creative, original, and free. Twenty respondents fell into a middle range that was described as normal, but with indications of confusion, pressure, feelings of inadequacy, lack of confidence, or loneliness.[4]

Two of the subjects who made the best impression on teachers and other observers gave Rorschach responses indicating severe internal cost for exterior social conformity.

Six of the subjects presented neurotic or schizoid patterns.

TABLE 1

RORSCHACH FINDINGS

Free, Original, Healthy, Creative	Feelings of Inferiority or of Peculiarity, or Constrictive	Neurotic in Need of Therapy
2	20	6

N = 28

[4] On the California Test of Personality, twelve of the respondents gave answers that placed them in the lowest quartile in feelings of personal freedom.

RESULTS OF EXPLORATORY PSYCHIATRIC INTERVIEWS

Psychiatric interviews were arranged for 21 of the 28 subjects. These were conducted by two staff psychiatrists at Bellevue Hospital, one of whom was the director of the children's psychiatric ward.

The findings indicated that six of the subjects were "comfortably adjusted." These include the two subjects found by the Rorschach examinations to be most healthy; and four whom the Rorschach findings indicated as being normal but having problems.

Eleven were found to be within the normal range, i.e., having some feelings of inferiority, neglect, loneliness, anxiety, and rejection, but having sufficient internal resources to handle their problems.

Four could be diagnosed as being neurotic or in need of psychiatric help. These four were among those whose Rorschach responses indicated severe disturbances. Although the Rorschach examination included more subjects, the findings of the two examinations were generally consistent.

TABLE 2

PSYCHIATRIAC FINDINGS

Comfortably Adjusted	Normal but with Pressures	Neurotic
6	11	4

N = 21

The psychiatrists and the Rorschach examiner indicated that the causes of disturbances in these subjects were not necessarily related to their high intelligence.

Of the 28 subjects, 15 knew their approximate intelligence level. Six of these seemed to get some constructive satisfaction from the knowledge and to use it in their vocational planning.

SUMMARY OF SUBJECTIVE FINDINGS

The description of a self-definition of isolation is difficult to agree on. For the purposes of this study, it was decided that, when a subject spoke of, or the preponderance of the material indicated that he felt himself to be isolated, rejected by parents, teachers, and peers, or that he was odd, peculiar, constantly lonely, or queer, he could be said to feel isolated.

The evidence from interviews with subjects, Rorschach and psychiatric interviews, and answers on pencil and paper tests indicated that, of the 28 subjects, fifteen felt themselves to be isolated.

2. *Attitudes and Opinions of Others*

SOLITARY PLAY

The nature of a child's play has frequently been used as an index of isolation. Summary of data obtained from subjects, parents, teachers, and other observers indicated that, among the present aggregate, 21 of the subjects nearly always played alone; six. often; one, seldom.

TABLE 3
SOLITARY PLAY

Nearly Always Plays Alone	Often Plays Alone	Seldom Plays Alone
21	6	1

N = 28

IMAGINARY COMPANIONS

In the course of extended family interviews, all parents were asked about imaginary companions. Hollingworth had pointed out earlier [5] that "the imaginary playmate as a solution of the problem of loneliness is fairly frequent."

Of the 28 subjects, only three were described as having had imaginary human playmates; two had had imaginary dogs. None of these had siblings near their own age, or dogs; nor was there evidence of a close relationship with any adult.

TABLE 4
IMAGINARY COMPANIONS

Imaginary Companions	None Mentioned
5	23

N = 28

SOCIOMETRY

Twelve of the subjects were included in a sociometric investigation (that was being carried on concurrently with this study) to test the amount of social interaction, both in acceptance and rejection, within public school classes. Sociometric findings are based on student responses to questions concerning students whom they would choose or reject as companions in three school activities.

Of the twelve subjects included, three were placed in the lowest quartile; four were in the second quartile; five were in the third quartile; and none in the top quartile. The significance of this data is colored by the fact that

[5] *Op. cit.*, p. 263.

all but two of the subjects attended the segregated elementary school where the lowest IQ in each class tended to be between 130 and 140.

TABLE 5
SOCIOMETRIC RATING IN CLASSROOM BY QUARTILES

Low	Second	Third	Top
3	4	5	0

N = 12 (Students in HCES—material taken from another study. Data not available on other subjects.)

HAGGERTY-OLSON-WICKMAN BEHAVIOR RATING SCALES

The authors of these scales do not suggest norms, but provide a checklist of traits by which teachers can describe their pupils. The list is divided into two scales: Behavior Problem Record and Behavior Rating Scale.

On this two-part scale, three of the subjects were given 0, meaning that, in the opinion of the teachers, they had no acute behavior problems. Fifteen were rated as being socially unpopular with the other students; eleven as "disinterested in school work"; ten as having occasional temper tantrums; and eleven "overactive." There was an overlap, since several of these traits might be found in a single child.

TABLE 6
BEHAVIOR RATING SCALES

Unpopular	Disinterested	Temper Tantrums	Overactive	No Rating
15	11	10	11	2

N = 27
Total Responses = 49 (Several traits were assigned to a single child.)

TEACHER INTERVIEWS

In addition to the Haggerty-Olson-Wickman Scales, personal interviews were held by field workers with the teachers of 24 subjects. One purpose of these interviews was to get the teachers' judgments regarding the attitudes of other children toward the subjects.

The teachers reported that six of the subjects were disliked; that two of the six were unpopular but not isolated; the classmates were willing to include fourteen of the subjects in their activities; and that four were well liked by their classmates. There was a strong overlap but not complete correlation with the findings of the psychiatric and Rorschach examinations.

TABLE 7
TEACHER OPINIONS ON POPULARITY OF SUBJECTS

Disliked	Accepted	Well-Liked
6	14	4

N = 24

The field workers also inquired into the attitudes of the teachers themselves toward the subjects. Only four were actively disliked by their teachers. Nine were casually accepted; and eleven were well-liked. The four subjects disliked were among the six found by the Rorschach examinations to exhibit neurotic patterns.

TABLE 8

TEACHERS' REACTIONS TO SUBJECTS

	Disliked	Accepted	Well-Liked
	4	9	11
N = 24			

ATTITUDES OF PEERS

On the basis of sociometric studies, classroom observation by field workers, interviews with teachers and students, and the Haggerty-Olson-Wickman Scales, it was found that, of the 28 subjects, three were popular with their classmates; nineteen were accepted; and six were rejected by their classmates and by other children. There was a positive correlation between rejection by classmates and the Rorschach findings of neurotic patterns.

TABLE 9

ATTITUDES OF PEERS

	Rejected	Accepted	Popular
	6	19	3
N = 28			

SUMMARY

An unexpected finding was the high evidence (in more than half of the subjects) of apparently deep-seated feelings of inadequacy and lack of confidence.

Results of the investigation indicate a need to revise the theory of isolation as a necessary function of high intelligence. Of the 28 subjects studied, six were comfortably adjusted by psychiatric judgment; three were popular with their peers in unsegregated schools; two gave Rorschach responses indicating a high degree of spontaneity, creativity, freedom of association, and freedom of interplay. One adolescent had been markedly gregarious from early childhood. While the early childhood play of three-quarters of the subjects was nearly always solitary, the significance of this finding was minimized by a number of factors, such as the pattern of New York urban living. Social contacts tended to increase as the children became older.

While fifteen indicated personal feelings of isolation or rejection, in only six cases was this feeling borne out by the objective judgment of peers, teachers, and other observers.

It may be concluded that:

1. High intelligence in and of itself is not a sufficient cause for subjective or objective isolation, although it may be one contributing factor.

2. Further research is needed into the discrepancy between isolation as felt by the subject in defining his own role and the opinions held of him by his peers. With the exception of strongly neurotic or schizoid subjects, classmates appeared ready to include these superdeviates in their activities

3. It may be that the isolation previously considered to be a characteristic of highly gifted children is not a necessary component of their intellectual level, but rather is due to factors in the dynamics of roles played in the family and the school. Since so little research has been done in this field, and since the present study indicated a consistent pattern of pressure, there appears to be a need for further investigation to determine whether the pattern of isolation is an evidence of difficulties associated with but not necessarily a part of high intelligence.

At the time of this study, New York City had not had a complete program of individual testing of all school children, so this is to be considered as an exploratory study, with no claim to being a random sample. Since many of the subjects were found through clinics or counseling centers, there is perhaps a tendency for the sample to be weighted with subjects who had emotional problems.

Terman found among the 81 highly gifted children whom he originally studied in 1922–23 a minimum of problems in the field of personality and mental health. Since his findings were based largely on the subjective judgments of parents, medical examiners, and teachers, and since it is possible that the marked discrepancy in findings could to some extent be attributed to class and ethnic differences between the two samples, a study of a group of comparable subjects in California is indicated.

32. How Do Cleveland's Major Work Children Develop? *

WILLIAM B. LEVENSON, *Superintendent of Schools*

Introductory Comments to 32. Cleveland's Plan for Gifted Children

Major Work classes were first organized in Cleveland in the year 1923. The learners include high ability individuals from all grades—first grade through senior high school. This program is so devised as to encourage all who are accepted to utilize their abilities to the fullest. They are encouraged not only to develop their mental potential but also to learn to live happily and successfully with others. One aim of the program is the achieving of leadership in an area of individual competence.

The report that follows is an evaluation of the program that for these many years has been fostering independence of thought and action, developing self-confidence and moral stamina, and stimulating a greater appreciation of life values in physical, social, scholastic, and professional areas.

LDC

Physically Superior

The following excerpts from Dr. Barbe's Summary of his chapter on Health Status give a superior bill of health to these students:

The belief that the gifted child is below average in physical characteristics has been proved to be false by Terman and Oden. The health status of these subjects as adults reveals that they are not the poor health specimens that they were once thought to be.

The status of their health was reported as good by 92.3 per cent of the subjects, as fair by 7 per cent, and as poor by only .7 of 1 per cent. These ratings of general health indicate slightly better health than the rating of subjects in Terman and Oden's study. . . .

The median height of the male subjects in this study was 70.7 inches with a range from 5 feet 5 inches to 6 feet 6 inches. The median height of the

* From *Major Work Program, Thirty Years After,* Cleveland Public Schools, Cleveland, Ohio, 1960, pp. 21–26. Reprinted with permission.

female subjects was 65.2 inches, with a range from 5 feet to 6 feet 3 inches. This would indicate that the gifted male subject is about 3 inches taller than the average American male, and the gifted female is about 2.7 inches taller than the average American female.

The median weight of the male subjects in this study was 167.7 pounds with a range from 120 pounds to 285 pounds. The median weight of the female subjects was 125.4 pounds with a range from 90 pounds to 175 pounds. This would indicate that the gifted male subject weighs about 16 pounds more than the average American male, but the gifted female subject weighs about 4.6 pounds less than the average American female.

Almost 44 per cent of the male subjects and 50 per cent of the female subjects wear glasses. . . .

The types of things about which the subjects worried revealed a normal pattern. Concern over financial problems was mentioned most frequently.

The data obtained from the subjects indicate that their health status is very superior. Both the men and women are taller than average, and the men weigh more than the average American male. The incidence of defects is extremely small. . . .[1]

Socially Well-Adjusted

Dr. Barbe summarizes as follows on the social adjustments of the students included in the study:

The interests and adjustments of adults, identified in childhood as gifted, are as superior as the interests and adjustments of gifted children. The picture does not indicate an adult who is so different that he cannot adjust to adult life, but, instead, indicates an adult who has a wide variety of interests and participates in activities with other adults to a great extent.

The leisure-time activity in which the largest number of men spent the most time was sports, while for women it was reading. . . .

Over 60 per cent of the group, both males and females, report their social adjustment as being better than average. Less than 5 per cent rate their social adjustment as being below average, and only two men and no women rate their social adjustment as poor.[2]

The marital adjustment of the subject appears to be very good. . . . The men rated their marital adjustment as being slightly better than did the women. Over 70 per cent rated their marital adjustment as above average.

Over half of the subjects in Group I [3] are members of some community organization. The percentages are lower in the other groups [4] because of the

[1] Walter B. Barbe, "A Follow-up Study of Graduates of Special Classes for Gifted Children," pp. 150–51.
[2] *Ibid.*, p. 170.
[3] Group I—Graduates from 1938 through 1941.
[4] Groups II, III, IV—Graduates from 1942 through 1952.

youth of the subjects. Two-fifths of the subjects attend church either often or regularly. About 10 per cent never attend. There appears to be a drop in church attendance after graduation from high school, which is maintained until the subjects are out of college, at which time church attendance again increases.

In attempting to determine if there had been a single determining influence on the lives of the subjects, they were asked for this information. Of those who answered this question, 102 were men and 117 were women. About one-third of the men and two-fifths of the women stated that a person had been a determining influence on their lives. A single book played a small part, while philosophy in some form was mentioned by 20 per cent of the men and about 14 per cent of the women.

It is apparent from the data that the interests of the gifted are varied. They are not retiring, but prefer activities which include others. Reading, although it is placed high on the list of preferred activities, is second to sports and is followed closely by various types of activities which have been classified as "socializing." The social adjustments of these individuals are certainly superior as demonstrated by their liking for, and participation in, numerous community and school activities.[5]

Scholastically Superior

Dr. Barbe points out that since all of the subjects in the present study are of superior intelligence and were identified as gifted early in childhood, there are many reasons why they would plan to attend college. The fact that they were part of a special education program that placed a high value upon learning undoubtedly contributed to the realization on the part of these individuals of the value of advanced education. Their achievements and adjustments should have been good because these individuals had been provided with challenging experiences for many years in the Major Work Program.

These further excerpts from Dr. Barbe's chapter on Educational Achievements and Adjustments show superior scholastic attainments:

An extraordinarily high percentage of the male subjects (91.3) attended college, while a much smaller percentage of the females did (63.3).

The amount of education beyond high school reported by the largest number of subjects was four years.

Two hundred and two (44.3 per cent) of the subjects have college degrees. The largest group of these, 32.2 per cent, hold the bachelor's degree.

Of those who did not attend college, the reason given by nearly half was lack of funds.

For those whose college career was permanently interrupted, marriage was given as the reason by about one-third and lack of funds by one-fifth.

[5] Walter B. Barbe, *op. cit.*, pp. 170, 172.

Of those who attended college, two out of every five received financial assistance in the form of scholarships or assistantships. . . .

About 67 per cent of those who went to college reported being in the upper quarter of their class. This indicates very superior academic achievement.

Membership in Phi Beta Kappa was over 10 per cent in Groups I and II,[6] while membership in other scholastic honorary groups was over 40 per cent.

Nearly half of the subjects who attended college were members of a social fraternity. . . .[7]

Dr. Barbe summarizes as follows:

Attendance at college is exceptionally high for the male subjects but somewhat low for the females. Financial difficulties were reported as the reason for not attending by nearly half of those who did not go to college. The scholastic success of the subjects in college is apparent. Socially, they appeared to participate in many activities. . . .[8]

Professionally Inclined

In a Pilot Study made by the Bureau of Educational Research of the Cleveland Public Schools, the most significant finding was the unusual variety of occupations and professions engaged in by the graduates. The men chose the following occupations in the order listed: teacher, engineer, minister or rabbi, physician, salesman, attorney, architect, accountant. For women, the occupation that was listed most often was homemaker. After that the choices were in this order: teacher, secretary, medical doctor, nurse, bookkeeper, engineer.

At the time of Dr. Barbe's study 231 of the subjects were working full time. Three-fourths of the men had professional or managerial positions. About 15 per cent were in clerical or sales work. The women who were working did clerical or sales work in sixty-one of the cases, and had professional or managerial positions in thirty-six cases out of a hundred.

Forty-four per cent of the subjects are members of professional groups. It is apparent that far more of the subjects, both males and females, are in the professional category than is typical of the general population. (Less than 15 per cent of the total population are in the professional category.) Even though the subjects had been in their positions only a short time, their incomes are higher than the average in the country, and they appear to be well satisfied with their present employment.

[6] Group I, graduates from 1938 through 1941; Group II, graduates from 1942 through 1945.
[7] Walter B. Barbe, *op. cit.*, pp. 120–21.
[8] *Ibid.*, p. 121.

Happily Married

In the recent Pilot Study, the indications are that over 80 per cent of those who were graduated from high school in the years 1938 through 1952 are married. Dr. Barbe's study in 1953 of the same fifteen years found about half of the subjects married. Almost all of these people rated their marital adjustment as average or better, while six out of ten evaluated it as excellent. The incidence of divorce is less than 1 per cent, so it would seem that the gifted in this study are successful in their marriages.

No one married anyone with less than a high school education. About half married people with college degrees. The trend has been consistent over the fifteen-year period toward spouses with college degrees.

CHAPTER VI
GUIDANCE OF THE
ACADEMICALLY ABLE
STUDENT

33. Guidance of the Gifted *

PAUL WITTY, *Professor of Education, Northwestern University*

UNTIL RECENTLY, "gifted" children were generally neglected in our schools. This neglect was traceable in part to misconceptions concerning their nature and their needs. It was believed by many people that typically the gifted child was peculiar, eccentric, and ill-balanced socially. In fact, some writers held that eccentricity and genius were inseparable characteristics. Others asserted that since the gifted child was well equipped to take care of himself, he needed little help or guidance in school.

The falsity of the aforementioned views was clearly shown by the genetic studies of L. M. Terman and his associates who have traced the development of more than 1,500 gifted persons for more than 25 years. When first identified, the children were about ten years old on the average. At that time, the typical child in this group was found to be a rather well-rounded child—neither a physical weakling nor a social misfit.

In every investigation, rapidity of learning proved to be a characteristic of the gifted child. His mastery of language was typically remarkable; and his attainment in school subjects was similarly phenomenal. In two or three studies, it was found that by the time the gifted pupil was ten years of age, he had, on the average, knowledges of pupils in grades two or three grades above his own. Yet he was seldom accelerated or offered an enriched program of study. Almost without exception, studies made during

* From *Personnel and Guidance Journal*, November, 1954, pp. 136–39. Reprinted with permission.

161

the period 1900–1945 showed that schools were making little special provision for gifted children. As one writer stated:

> The gifted, the potential leaders, discoverers, and creators . . . are usually left to develop their own skills in their own way and in terms of personal initiative alone.[1]

The need for more adequate stimulation and guidance of the gifted throughout high school and college was suggested by other studies. One of pertinence here was reported by C. Gilbert Wrenn. This investigator cited a follow-up of the top 16 per cent of Minnesota high school graduates.[2] Nine years after high school graduation, 45 per cent of this group had received baccalaureate degrees, and 8 per cent had earned advanced degrees. At the same time, however, only 4 per cent of the pupils whose IQ's were estimated to be at or above 125 had received degrees beyond the baccalaureate. Such facts have led to a concern on the part of educators for identifying and encouraging the gifted in large numbers to prepare for positions of leadership in science, education, and other fields wherein training beyond the baccalaureate degree is essential. There is also a growing concern for giving financial aid to enable the gifted to carry on advanced work in school. It has been pointed out that in many states half of the estimated number of gifted high school graduates fail to go to college.

Increasingly, educators are recognizing the close relationship between the amount of education a pupil receives and the economic status of the pupil's parents. The authors of the book, *Who Shall Be Educated?* show the significance of economic factors in determining whether a pupil goes to college.[3] It is clear from such studies that subsidies, scholarships, and fellowships are needed by many gifted high school and college students to continue their education. Encouragement and guidance are also required by gifted students in college in order that they will develop fully.[4]

Recent Educational Provisions for the Gifted

An awakening interest in the gifted has been observed in many schools during the past two or three years. This condition is attributable in part to

---

[1] C. C. Miles, *Manual of Child Psychology*, ed. by L. Carmichael (New York: John Wiley & Sons, Inc., 1946), p. 931; rev. 1954, p. 1028.

[2] C. G. Wrenn, *The Educational Record*, XXX (January, 1949), 20–22.

[3] W. L. Warner, R. J. Havighurst, and M. B. Loeb, *Who Shall Be Educated? The Challenge of Unequal Opportunity* (New York: Harper & Bros., 1944).

[4] Paul Witty and Samuel W. Bloom, "Science Provisions for the Gifted," *Exceptional Children*, XX (March, 1954), 244–50, 262.

the widespread dissemination of facts contained in the book, *The Gifted Child*.[5] It is traceable also to the influence of the recommendations found in the monograph, *The Education of the Gifted,* published by the Educational Policies Commission of the National Education Association.[6]

In 1951, outstanding programs for the education of gifted children were described by Albert I. Oliver in *The Nation's Schools*.[7] Endeavors cited by him included the work of the Robert E. Lee Junior High School in Baltimore, a school set aside for the education of the gifted; the opportunity classes in the Allentown (Pa.) schools; the special classes in Public School 208 in Brooklyn; the workshop groups in the Colfax Elementary School of Pittsburgh; the special English class in Lower Merion (Pa.); the extensive curricula for the gifted high school pupils in the Monroe High School of Rochester (N.Y.); the senior seminar in the Swarthmore (Pa.) High School.

Oliver reported also the work of the Philadelphia Suburban Study Council, which was organized in the fall of 1948. This group investigated the needs of the gifted and experimented with enrichment programs and evaluation procedures. In 1950, the University of Pennsylvania published a report of this work in the monograph entitled *Programs for the Gifted.*

Additional successful programs for the education of gifted children were described by Grace I. Loomis in 1951. These included such well-known efforts as the major work classes in Cleveland and the opportunity classes of Los Angeles. Included also were descriptions of the Speyer School of New York City; The Hunter College Elementary School in New York City; the hobby clubs of Appleton (Wis.); the program in Baltimore; the work of an "enrichment teacher" in Birmingham (Ala.); and an enrichment plan in Brockton (Mass.).[8]

Another plan of recent origin has been followed successfully in the high school of Modesto (Calif.). The 20 most highly gifted pupils in the 11th and 12th grades are given a two-hour a day enriched course. In these classes, both group and individual instruction is provided. During the remainder of the day the pupils are enrolled in regular classes.[9] Interest is especially keen at present in departments of science and mathematics in

[5] Paul Witty (ed.), *The Gifted Child* (Boston: D. C. Heath & Co., 1951).

[6] Educational Policies Commission of the National Education Association of the United States and the American Association of School Administrators, *The Education of the Gifted* (Washington, D.C.: National Education Association, 1950).

[7] A. I. Oliver, *The Nation's Schools,* XLVIII (November, 1951), 44–46.

[8] Grace I. Loomis, *Curriculum Bulletin,* December 12, 1951. Ed. by H. B. Wood, professor of education, School of Education, University of Oregon.

[9] N. B. Scharer, *The Bulletin of the National Association of Secondary School Principals,* Part I, Vol. XXXVI, March, 1952.

attracting gifted pupils. James W. Gebhart voices this concern about the importance of full utilization of our assets:

Living in an age when survival seems to be mathematically in direct proportion to scientific achievement, we should take stock of our intellectual assets and act accordingly.[10]

Gebhart advocates the adoption of a "long range program that would require years of study and possibly the establishment of several experimental schools." Such schools should, he says, be supported by the state.

Harry A. Cunningham, too, expresses concern over the "manpower bottleneck in scientific research." He fears that this shortage is likely to become much more serious in the next ten years unless we immediately do some long-range planning. He suggests the establishment of schools of science either on a citywide or a statewide basis. An outstanding school of this type is the High School of Science in the Bronx.[11]

High School Programs for the Gifted

Appropriate guidance given early in the career of the superior high school pupil can do much to lead him to want to make full use of his ability. Participation in activities associated with Science Fairs, the Science Talent Search, The National Science Teacher Association Achievement Awards, and contests sponsored by scientific and engineering societies serves to engender interest on the part of many gifted pupils. However, many others are not given this stimulation and fail to become interested in the development of their abilities.

The conservation of talent requires the cooperation of the entire school staff. Some efforts are being made to achieve this goal. For example, in the San Francisco schools a student with a specific gift or talent is directed early in his career to a teacher in the field of his special ability. As a part of the guidance program, he is encouraged to read published accounts about science careers for high school students.

An adequate program of guidance for the gifted requires not only the cooperation of all the staff members within the school, but it also involves the associated efforts of parents of community agencies to provide additional incentives and opportunities. In these efforts, the first problem is the identification of the especially capable student.

With the advent of the intelligence test, children of IQ 130 and higher

---

[10] J. W. Gebhart, *School Science and Mathematics,* Vol. LII, May, 1952.

[11] H. A. Cunningham, Department of Biology, Kent State University, *School Science and Mathematics,* LII (May, 1952), 373–80. See also E. F. Peckman, *School Science and Mathematics,* Vol. LII, February, 1952.

were referred to as gifted. In the early studies of the distribution of intelligence, it was found that these children constituted about 1 per cent of the entire school population. Several writers have recently advanced a broader interpretation that would include a larger number of pupils. One group suggested that pupils with IQ 137 and above be considered as highly gifted, and that moderately gifted students be identified by IQ ratings 120–37. Such a practice would include 10 per cent of high school students in the moderately and highly gifted group.[12]

Various other proposals have been made from time to time. And practices in schools vary widely in the designation of the gifted. Hollinshead [13] voices a warning of importance:

We ought not to let ourselves get so bemused with the importance of developing genius or near genius that we neglect in any sense those just below them in ability, for those just below have an almost equally important contribution to make, mostly in the direction of developing, explaining, and diffusing the thought of those who are in the very top rank.

In the March, 1954, issue of *Exceptional Children,* the writer, in collaboration with Samuel Bloom, described the methods of selection used in some outstanding science programs for capable students in the high schools of New York City, Indianapolis, Forest Hills, New York, Baltimore, North Phoenix, Arizona, Los Angeles, Oak Park and Evanston, Illinois.[14] The provisions now being made for exceptionally capable pupils in these cities is indeed heartening. These schools and others initiating similar programs are participating in a great movement in behalf of gifted pupils. The combined effect of this renewed interest and endeavor promises to enrich the lives of many superior students and at the same time to contribute to the advancement of society through the development of capable leaders in science and other fields.

Despite these efforts, the gifted pupil is still neglected in many schools. The guidance worker or counselor has an important role to play in correcting this condition and in helping to conserve talent. He can aid materially:

1. By assisting in the identification of pupils having distinctive ability in the elementary and secondary school and in college.

2. By working with teachers and administrators in planning stimulating curricula for such pupils.

---

[12] See *The Gifted Child, op. cit.,* chaps. 2, 10.

[13] B. S. Hollinshead, *Who Should Go to College?* (New York: The Columbia University Press, 1952).

[14] Paul Witty and Samuel Bloom, *op. cit.*

3. By seeking appropriate scholarships and financial assistance for them.

4. By directing students to appropriate reading materials to help them plan careers that will call forth the best use of their abilities.

5. By working with parents and teachers in efforts to understand and meet the special problems of the gifted.

6. By directing gifted pupils to community resources that will enrich interests.

In these and other ways, the guidance worker can make a distinct contribution in conserving and utilizing fully our country's greatest resource—its gifted children and youth.

34. The Gifted: What Will They Become? *

HERBERT J. KLAUSMEIER, *Professor of Education, University of Wisconsin*

TEST all four- and five-year-old children. Allow the potential high achievers to start the first grade a year earlier than most children and two years earlier than the slow developers."

"Identify the potentially gifted children in the first grade and put them together in a separate class or separate school for special instruction thereafter."

"Follow the European pattern of identifying the university-bound children at age ten to twelve and set up special schools and instruction for them."

"Accelerate the gifted so that they may enter college at age sixteen."

"Make sure that every gifted child has at least four years of high-school mathematics, or science, or Latin, or whatever else the promoting individual or group desires most."

"Do away with general education in high school and go back to the liberal arts; increasing numbers of high school graduates are going to college; the gifted need a liberal education."

* From *Phi Delta Kappan*, December, 1956, pp. 112–16. Reprinted with permission.

How shall the public, tax-supported schools, responsible for providing good education to all children of all parents, respond to the many current pressures to identify and make special arrangements for gifted children? The most important question to be answered by the schools, by parents interested in education of gifted children, and by those organized groups who wish the public schools to get more gifted students ready to meet certain college or career requirements is: "What kinds of individuals would we like gifted and talented children to be as a result of our educational efforts?" This broad question needs further defining in the areas of intellectual achievements, social competence, and moral values.

1. *Intellectual Achievements.* (a) Do we want the gifted high-school graduate to be very highly specialized in one or two areas such as mathematics, science, English, art, foreign language, and business education? (b) Do we want a nonspecialized individual with some competence in several subject-matter areas and in several expressive areas? For example, do we want the gifted graduate to have two years of work in several areas such as mathematics, science, language, English, and social studies and also some experiences in music, art, dramatics, homemaking, business education, agriculture, shop? (c) Do we desire the gifted graduate to have quite high specialization in one or even two areas and also competence in several others?

2. *Social Competence.* (a) Do we want the gifted high-school graduate to avoid others so that he may use his talents exclusively in individual efforts? (b) Do we want the gifted student to be skilled only in working and living with others of similarly high achievement? (c) Do we want the gifted person to find satisfactions in independent work and in communicating and living with others of many levels of competence and many areas of interest?

3. *Moral Values.* (a) Do we wish the gifted person to be unconcerned with the effects of his efforts on self and others? For example, do we want a person so strongly motivated for high achievement that he ruins his own health in the process or is unconcerned with producing a "monster" product or idea that destroys the happiness or endangers the welfare of others? (b) Should the gifted high-school graduate use his talents for personal gain only, taking advantage of those of lesser abilities to achieve economic, social, or political mastery over them? (c) Do we desire the gifted youth to use his talents in caring for his own needs and to be concerned with improving conditions for effective living for himself and others?

The writer proposes that we should strive to identify and develop individuals who, upon high-school graduation, will have rather high specialization in at least one area in which their particular talents lie, will find satisfactions in living with others of varying talents and interests, and will use their talents to improve conditions for themselves and others. None of the practices listed in the opening paragraphs will reach this goal for all the potential highachievers in all schools, and some will prevent its fulfillment. The nine proposals that follow are applicable to many situations, are in line with achieving the stated goal, and pertain to education from kindergarten through high school.

Proposal Number One. Develop a systematic, continuous program for the identification and development of any talent any child may possess.

Only the amateur proposes that he can reliably identify in the elementary grades every child who will make an outstanding contribution to society as an adult. Psychologists and educators, working together with high-school students, recognize that many factors that they cannot control lead to one student with a Stanford-Binet IQ of 115 and high motivation achieving at a higher level than another with an IQ of 140 and low motivation or an emotional problem. The best minds in our universities have not yet found an efficient way of predicting which entering Ph.D. candidates will complete the requirements and which will fail—much less of predicting who will contribute significantly and who will not after the degree is awarded.

Faced with an increasing demand for creative, gifted individuals, the schools must make certain that they do not eliminate future high-achieving adults from specially-provided school programs. Instead of limiting the special provisions to the 1 per cent with Stanford-Binet IQ's above 140, or the 2 per cent with IQ's above 132, or even the 16 per cent with IQ's above 116, we would do well to provide every child with the opportunity to express himself creatively. As part of the process of identification and development of talent, especially in the first nine years of school, we probably need much more emphasis on instruction in the expressive areas—music, art, dance, creative writing, dramatics—and in various areas of organized knowledge such as science and literature, so that reasonable opportunities are present to ascertain the areas in which the child's talents may lie (or may be developed) and so that the child and his parents may become aware of it. Were this done on a more widespread basis, many above-average but not outstanding students would possibly find an area of interest that could be developed to a very high level prior to high school graduation. And those few towering intellects of genius proportion could advance in this environment as rapidly and as broadly as their curiosity and energy impel them.

The number of individuals who achieve high in any society at a given time is determined not only by what is in the individuals, but also by society's opportunities and demands for high achievement. The experiences of World War II demonstrated that many young men and women of varying talents, when presented with the opportunity and the demand to achieve, responded well. Apparently the Russians are now providing more opportunities and are developing more talented individuals. Much research yet remains to be completed before children who have the potentiality for making significant contributions to society as adults can be identified without error. Much research needs to be done to determine how our society can increase the opportunities for creative, significant contributions. While this research is in progress, upgrading the quality of education for all children, and especially those with academic or other talents, is the most reasonable way for making sure that the really gifted are adequately provided for and that the best in all children is developed to meet society's demands.

Proposal Number Two. Admit all children to kindergarten or first grade at about the same chronological age, giving all of them opportunity to profit from such attendance, and making certain that as much attention is given to identifying and providing for the potential high achievers as to the physically handicapped, mentally retarded, slow learners, and average children.

Even if we could reliably identify the future high-achieving adults among the present four-, five-, and six-year-old children (which we cannot), the practice of admitting some to first grade at five, others at six, and still others at age seven, would likely lead to widespread dissatisfactions among children and parents. For within a family of several children we might have one entering first grade at age five while another waits until age seven. And among neighboring families the same entrance ages might occur. Only in very large cities and other communities where parents care little about the education of children residing in their close vicinity is it possible to have differential entrance ages to the first grade without incurring parental disapproval of the policy. Even where the policy is practiced, we should recognize that many slower-maturing six- and even seven-year-olds may eventually achieve higher than some of the faster-maturing five-year-olds.

Proposal Number Three. Place children throughout the elementary grades, in classes that have both a range and variety of talents, and group within the class or individualize instruction within the class to meet the needs of all.

Some segregating of the potential high achievers in the intermediate grades for some portion of the instruction—such as in reading, arithmetic, music, art, dramatics, student council, and library work—may prove beneficial. Some sectioning into special classes for part of the instruction in those larger schools where only one or two outstanding pupils in each class are found might also prove beneficial, but segregating the potential high achievers for all instruction into a special class or a special elementary school deprives these children during the formative years of learning how to understand and live pleasantly with those of lower talents. While it is possible in poorly-taught classrooms for the fast learner to develop snobbishness and feelings of superiority, it is also possible in the well-taught, heterogeneous classroom group for the gifted child to develop his creative powers and at the same time learn wholesome attitudes and communication skills in living with the less talented.

Proposal Number Four. Accelerate during the intermediate grades and junior high school through double promotions only those potential high achievers whose physical, social, and emotional development is in harmony with their intellectual development.

While positive correlations are found between age and such factors as height, weight, carpal development, and social and emotional development, the correlations are so low as to be practically useless when applied to individual cases. Many of our actually and potentially talented intermediate-grade and junior-high-school students are near the average in each of the areas listed. Accelerating these would be unwise except in poor schools that cannot enrich the curriculum offerings or otherwise adequately meet the intellectual needs of the high achievers.

Proposal Number Five. Encourage the potential high achievers in the high school to complete the usual requirements for four years in three years, or increase the number of subject-matter areas and emphasize depth of understanding and skills in the areas that the gifted pursue.

The latter procedure could lead to the granting of college credits upon admission to college. If we were assured that society would make higher education possible for every high-achieving graduate, rather than force thousands of them, because of financial need, to go into careers in which their talents are not challenged and developed, we would now be preparing more fast-maturing high-school students for college entrance in three years. The principle of having the gifted student complete the usual requirements for four years in three could also be applied to college education. Many gifted young adults are pursuing identical courses and at the same rate as those less gifted whose best efforts are required to make sufficiently high marks to remain in college.

Thus, if we generally favor acceleration of the gifted students, ample opportunity is present for acceleration at the senior-high-school and college levels with little if any need for it in those elementary and junior high schools that have material resources and adequately prepared teachers to provide for the gifted children. Assuredly, the closer the individual is to full physical maturity and the closer he is to becoming intellectually, economically, and socially independent, the more reliably can his potential achievements be appraised and the more responsibility can and should he assume for making his own decisions concerning career and speed of reaching it.

Proposal Number Six. Continue to emphasize general education for effective citizenship for all youth of high school age; and as the size and resources of the high school allow, offer various curriculum patterns that provide for a degree of specialization for the academically gifted and for those with talents in such areas as visual art, music, dramatics, creative writing, applied arts, and other career areas.

Specialization of instruction in high school necessarily involves some grouping of children according to areas of interest and must be done to meet the possible career goals of the gifted. Classes are needed, however, in social studies, core, or other areas in which children of all performance levels learn the attitudes and skills needed for living effectively with others of various abilities and interests. As the general high school in the larger community and the vocational high school in the larger city have assumed responsibility for preparing some less gifted students for gainful employment immediately following graduation, so should we make certain that potential high achievers are provided with opportunities to get the most from their education, including some specialization toward a career that will involve college education.

Proposal Number Seven. Reexamine the requirements placed upon the high-school graduate for being admitted to the various careers attainable through college education.

It is possible that denying college students admission to programs of higher education leading to certain careers may actually be keeping many potential high achievers from entering these careers. While some youth know the career they wish to pursue as early as age thirteen or fourteen, others are very uncertain even as college freshmen and sophomores. These latter individuals frequently decide upon a challenging career only to find that because of "lacks" in their high-school preparation they cannot enter the necessary program. In some cases, their only opportunity is to get the required courses through evening high-school work, correspondence, or transfer to another college. It is tempting for the gifted student not to do any of these but to make a career selection to which he can be admitted "as is."

Proposal Number Eight. Utilize community resources fully.

Many schools and classrooms are more crowded today than they were five years ago, and we have not secured nearly enough talented and gifted persons to pursue teaching as a career. It is not uncommon to find a teacher attempting to provide instruction in English each day to as many as 180 adolescents in five separate classes. The nonathletes in high school often get their physical exercise (it really cannot be called physical education) in groups as large as 100. Parents are still expected to pay for the private music, art, and dance lessons the child needs to develop his talents—the school lacks space, time, and teachers. We yet find many persons trying to teach adolescents mathematics and science who themselves have poor backgrounds in the areas. Instruction in foreign languages is often offered by persons who cannot speak the language well.

The principal cause of this educational neglect of the talented and gifted children lies squarely within our total society, which persistently refuses to provide adequate support for education at all levels—kindergarten through higher education. We apparently are committed to defend ourselves with military might developed and maintained through high individual federal income taxes, while defying the localities and states to find sufficient remaining tax resources to provide good education for children and youth. This condition has existed for many years and probably will continue. Therefore, parents and school people may well look toward every available resource in the community to aid in the education of the gifted and talented. Community recreation programs that offer crafts; YMCA and YWCA programs in which art, science, and physical talents may be developed; the museum, art gallery, music hall, and science exhibit that may spark a dormant interest; some special commercial television programs for children and youth; some educational television programs; the retired professional or business man with an interest in his field and in children; the various special-interest groups that develop in school and carry on out-of-school activities; the education programs for children and youth carried on by the college or university in the fine arts, in languages, and the like— any of these that may exist within the community are useful in the identification and development of talent. Children, teachers, and parents should be aware of them and utilize them. Efficient utilization will mean many hours of work for a teacher or other school person in addition to his regular duties; the rewards—intellectual, moral, and social—are worth such effort.

Proposal Number Nine. Inform society fully of the loss of the gifted that is occurring at present after high-school graduation.

Many gifted youth do not have the money to continue higher education; many go into occupations before or after high-school graduation in which their talent is lost, with no attempt made by employers to identify or develop them; many young men enter military service and do not then or later develop their potentialities fully; many academically gifted young adults find the first two years of college work so unchallenging that they leave. The loss of the gifted is probably much higher after than during the twelve years of elementary and high school.

Careful attention directed toward identifying the motivations that society generally provides for the gifted should also prove fruitful. Who is awarded recognition and economic gains, as revealed by our mass media of communication—newspapers, popular magazines, television, and radio? Millions of youth and young adults observe prowess in athletics, the ability to make large audiences chuckle or guffaw, and managerial knack receiving the ovation from all sides. Relatively little incentive is provided for our children and youth to apply their potentialities in other areas where creativeness is desperately needed, such as in government, the fine arts, the professions, industry, and organized labor. Only occasionally is a Dr. Jonas Salk lionized; the man-of-the-year is usually selected from management. The brilliant discoverer of Vitamin D is relatively unknown to the typical high-school student, but everyone knows the first- and even the third-string quarterback. The creator of an expressive dance is obscure, while the physically attractive and sometimes intelligent Miss Mainstreet receives wide publicity and is well paid to advertise some wonder product on the television screen; the poet's audience is counted in hundreds while the rock-and-roll singer reaches the millions.

Summary

In summary, it must be said that there is no one best way to identify, motivate, and provide for the gifted child. We do not want all gifted children to be alike; we need many kinds of gifted individuals, and we need to develop any useful talent that any child may possess. The better way of providing for the gifted depends in part upon the nature of the individual child, his family, the school he attends, and the community in which he resides. None of the varying solutions practiced in New York City, or Cleveland, or Portland, or in the private schools may work well in a smaller city, in suburbia, or in the rural public school. Educational solutions for the gifted are complex, involving many persons rather than a few. But any proposed solution needs the careful consideration of the persons with the most responsibility for the gifted—parents and school people— and should generally start with attempting to answer the question: "What kinds of individuals would we like the gifted children to be as a result of our educational efforts?"

References

COMMITTEE ON EXCEPTIONAL CHILDREN AND EXCHANGE REPORTERS. *How to Educate the Gifted Child.* New York: Metropolitan School Study Council, 1956.

COOMBS, PHILIP H. "Lessons from Recent Experiments in Articulation and Acceleration," *Current Issues in Higher Education.* Washington, D.C.: National Education Association, 1954.

CUTTS, NORMA E., and MOSELEY, NICHOLAS. *Bright Children: A Guide for Parents.* New York: G. P. Putnam's Sons, 1953.

HAVIGHURST, ROBERT J., *et al. Are the Community and School Failing the Unusual Child?* Chicago: University of Chicago Press, 1952.

————, *et al. A Survey of the Education of Gifted Children.* Chicago: University of Chicago Press, 1955.

HILDRETH, GERTRUDE, *et al. Educating Gifted Children at Hunter College Elementary School.* New York: Harper & Bros., 1952.

JEWETT, ARNO, *et al. Teaching Rapid and Slow Learners in High Schools.* Washington, D. C.: Government Printing Office, 1954.

KLAUSMEIER, HERBERT J. *Principles and Practices of Secondary School Teaching.* Harper & Bros., 1953.

————, *et al. Teaching in the Elementary School.* Harper & Bros., 1956.

SCHEIFELE, MARIAN. *The Gifted Child in the Regular Classroom.* New York: Bureau of Publications, Teachers College, Columbia University, 1953.

TERMAN, LEWIS M., and ODEN, MELITA. *The Gifted Child Grows Up.* Stanford: Stanford University Press, 1947.

WITTY, PAUL (ed.). *The Gifted Child.* Boston: D. C. Heath & Co., 1951.

The recent thinking of Professor Herbert J. Klausmeier on "Effects of Accelerating Bright Older Elementary Pupils: A Follow Up" can be found in the *Journal of Educational Psychology,* June, 1963. In his "Discussion," Klausmeier reports:

A principal objection to acceleration is that essential subject matter content is skipped, resulting in lower educational achievement of accelerated students.

This objection was shown to be invalid in this and other experiments. In Table 3 are presented methods of acceleration which do not involve any skipping of content, the school level at which experimentation has been done, and indication of the reference in which the results are reported as favorable in terms of the educational achievements of the accelerates.

Other objections to acceleration revolve about the personal, social, and emotional adjustment of the accelerates. In Tables 1 and 2 [not included here] of this article, substantial evidence is presented that accelerating bright older pupils, after attending school in the morning for 5 weeks during the summer, produces no undesirable effects on their personal, social, or emotional adjustment. The same conclusion was drawn in the other experiments cited in Table 3.

TABLE 3

MEANS OF ACCELERATING PUPILS WITHOUT SKIPPING OF SUBJECT CONTENT

Method	Level of schooling	Investigator
Being admitted early to kindergarten or first grade	Preschool	Hobson, 1948 Birch, 1954 Worcester, 1956
Completing six semesters of the non-graded primary school in four or five semesters	Primary school	Klausmeier, 1962
Attending summer session, mastering content of next higher grade, going into higher grade in fall	Elementary school	Klausmeier and Ripple, 1962
Condensing or compressing content into shorter time periods, e.g., 3 years of English into 2 years	Junior high school	Justman, 1954a Justman, 1954b Klausmeier, 1962
Taking advanced college placement courses in the senior year of high school	Senior high school	Meister, 1956 Barnette, 1957
Taking additional classes and summer session attendance	College	Flesher and Pressey, 1955

Since acceleration by one or two semesters without skipping may be accomplished at any school level with desirable results, it appears unwise to force bright students to spend 12 years in completing high school and 16 years in completing the requirements for the baccalaureate degree. Terman (1954) favored gifted students entering college not older than age 17. In terms of present shortages of teachers and other educated talent, an appropriate national educational goal might be to have all bright students complete the baccalaureate degree at least by their twenty-first birthday and the most able and rapidly maturing by age 20. Since we have compulsory public education of pupils of all abilities, excellent nurture of the superior abilities of the top 5 per cent or more is improved when appropriate subject content and emergent abilities are brought into harmony through acceleration.[1]

[1] Herbert J. Klausmeier, "Effects of Accelerating Bright Older Elementary Pupils: A Follow Up," *Journal of Educational Psychology* (June, 1963), pp. 170–71. Reprinted with permission.

35. Guidance of the Gifted *

RUTH A. MARTINSON, *Professor of Education, Long Beach State College, Long Beach, California*

THE PUPIL personnel worker in the school system serves as a professional intermediary who works with teachers and others toward the ideal of appropriate educational planning for every gifted child. He begins his efforts when the child enters kindergarten; actually, his efforts never end, since the process of interpretation, planning and implementation, and evaluation of program effectiveness transcends the limits of school attendance. He directs his energies toward the goal of a meaningful, productive educational experience for the child from the first day he enters school until he is graduated. He works with all persons concerned, including the child as well as adults, toward that goal.

Identification of the Gifted

The first task, and the one for which the pupil personnel worker is uniquely trained, is that of proper identification. Proper identification means complete study of the gifted child, aimed toward as complete an understanding of his talents, skills, interests, and needs as possible. Without such knowledge as a basis for educational planning, the teacher is in a position comparable to that of a surgeon who initiates an operation without adequate diagnosis. To the surgeon, such procedures would be unthinkable.

Individual study is especially important in the case of the gifted, since it is on the basis of information derived from such study that the teacher gains an appreciation of the complex being with whom he is to work. Within the gifted category is found a greater variety of diverse educational needs than within any other grouping.

Group measures and teachers' or administrators' nominations, as well as data of many types from cumulative records, serve a useful function in

* Reprinted from the February, 1962, issue of *Education*, pp. 342–46. Copyright 1962 by The Bobbs-Merrill Co., Inc., Indianapolis, Ind.

the selection of children for further study and identification. All such data should be employed in the screening process to insure as comprehensive and accurate an identification program as possible. The employment of varied means in a search for pupils of high ability is important because it has been amply demonstrated that single screening devices, of whatever sort, fail to locate many gifted children.

Hazards in the use of group intelligence tests exclusively have been illustrated in several studies. Pegnato found vast discrepancies between group and individual measures. Over half of his 84 identified gifted junior high school students were penalized 20 or more points on a group measure, and nearly 20 per cent lost at least thirty points on the group test (3).

In another study, Walton found that ten of 94 identified gifted kindergarten children had group test IQ's ranging from 100 to 109, and another 12 per cent of the total group ranged from 110 to 119 (5).

In the California State Department of Education Study, group IQ's ranged downward as low as 100 for individuals whose individual Binets were 130 or more (2).

Even when an individual measure is used, the meaning of intelligence test performance requires interpretation. The IQ by itself is relatively meaningless. When the teacher becomes aware of the qualities and variations in performance on items involving comprehension and understandings of abstractions, when he learns of the unusual logic applied to the solution of problems, when he sees evidence of the superior verbal facility of the gifted, or of other abilities that the gifted may possess, then he is better able to use test results meaningfully. The IQ then progresses from a concept that implies a uniformly accelerated quantity of material to the concept of planning on the basis of individual abilities.

Lewis Terman pointed out many years ago that teachers are less accurate in the identification of their brightest pupils than they are in the identification of the oldest (4). Accuracy of identification is a problem, at least with young gifted children, even when listings of characteristics are used for guides (5). In the Walton study, kindergarten teachers who used the list of identifying characteristics developed by Kough and DeHaan failed to mention even once 43.6 per cent of kindergarten children who subsequently were found to have Binet IQ's of 130 or more (1).

The purpose of any identification program should be the location of all children with unique educational needs. The discrepancies that are found between many screening devices and final results in identification have several implications for the pupil personnel worker:

1. He should encourage school personnel to employ all means for the location of potentially gifted children, including group measures

of intelligence and achievement, personnel referrals, informal interest surveys, and the like.

2. He should train personnel in the proper administration and use of group measures.

3. He should develop a systematic, continuous identification program so that the educational needs of gifted children may be met throughout their school experience rather than on a partial basis.

Gifted Children Complicated

The gifted child, by virtue of his giftedness, is a complicated being. He is an individual who in total general development has progressed beyond his peers in many areas. Data gathered systematically from parents show conclusively that the gifted child, before he enters school, has acquired information, special interests, and academic skills far beyond his years (2, 4). In an adequate educational environment, these differences tend to become magnified rather than diminished as the child grows older.

The more extensive the study, the more apparent the unique qualities of excellence become. Personality measures, for example, have shown that junior high school students with Binet IQ's of 130 and beyond possess psychological maturity very similar to that of gifted high school students and of the general college population (2).

The acquisition of individual study material is a necessary concomitant to educational planning. Teachers need assistance in the understanding of the qualities of gifted children. They need to realize, from the evidence of individual study, that special and sometimes so-called unorthodox plans are required so that the child may progress at rates and in ways proper for him. The information within a continuing individual study, carefully interpreted, can be used by the pupil personnel worker toward this end.

When grouping is employed, need for the interpretation of pupil variability occurs on a somewhat different basis. The term "homogeneous," if applied literally, can nullify the values of grouping. Any "homogeneous" group of gifted children presents a greater diversity of educational needs to the teacher than any regular classroom group, as successful teachers of the gifted frequently testify. This diversity must be considered carefully in the planning of educational experiences of value.

Interpreting Gifted Children

Interpretation of the characteristics of gifted children should deal not only with their skills, educational backgrounds, personal and social qualities, but also with some of the characteristics that may prove baffling and frustrating to the teacher who works with them.

Gifted children are not always easy to have in the classroom. Some of their characteristics, such as their oftdemonstrated intensity of interest in obscure problems, their independence of logic, their incisiveness and tendency to criticize both themselves and others, their many questions, and even their unusual vocabulary development, may create needs for interpretation to the teacher. Underachievement, poor work habits, or personal difficulties in some gifted individuals may add to the teacher's frustrations.

The teacher needs help in learning to accept gifted children and to help them in working effectively with others. Counselors and teachers have attained notable success with students who have had histories of misbehavior or nonachievement. Such success is not easily attained, but educational planning for the gifted should include the occasional individual who may be described simultaneously by his teachers as a nonproductive, nonconforming person who is the brightest, most original person in the group, as well as toward the high-achieving, accepting child who is a classroom joy. Programs planned only for the latter may indeed provide for those who need special planning least.

Pupil personnel workers at the secondary level can help to eradicate two problems that more often ruin programs than any others—work load and grades. Unless someone helps teachers to coordinate their planning for the gifted, burdens may become unrealistically heavy, and students may express the wish that they had not been included in special programs.

As one student put it, the problem is one of "achieving harmony among our instructors." The harmony must be directed not only toward assessment of total requirements, but toward assessment of the quality and value of requirements.

The tendency of gifted students to immerse themselves in the study of a topic requires that they be given assistance in the planning of boundaries for their activities within the day and total week. They need help in budgeting time properly so that they have time for recreation and activities.

Grading the Gifted

Grades pose a problem especially for students who are grouped with others of high ability. Grades represent the avenue to college entrance and qualification for scholarships. Since gifted students are those who are particularly concerned about advanced professional education, evaluation for them should be based upon the evaluation of their entire age group, and not upon comparisons within a special group. The grades given should reflect the actual quality of achievement, rather than quantity of production.

Teachers often need help to understand that the majority of gifted students would obtain A's in heterogeneous groups with little effort; the same opportunity to obtain A's should occur in special classes where they operate at an advanced level.

Planning for the Gifted

In addition to working with teachers during the course of the academic year, the pupil personnel worker has the obligation for continuity of planning from year to year. This requires reinterpretation of achievements, interests, and special skills to additional teachers, and additional efforts in teacher education.

It may also mean planning with administrators so that special adjustments may be made for the gifted child, and so that, when he has completed everything that the school has to offer, he may be permitted to go on to higher education, despite the fact that he may be a little younger than the minimum age for graduation.

The advantage in continuous planning is twofold: (1) It enables the child to pursue his education in meaningful fashion, and (2) it enables the adults who work with him to profit from their increased understanding of individual differences.

Work with Parents

Parents of any children want close contact with pupil personnel workers who can interpret their children's abilities and needs to them. The same is true of the parents of the gifted. These parents often desire an interpretation of abilities, discussion of a balance in work and activities, planning for the future, homework, and parental contributions to the education of the gifted. The latter consideration is of special importance, since the parents themselves may be bright, well-educated individuals who, with guidance, can provide many opportunities for the child.

Vocational Guidance

Specific vocational guidance responsibilities are assumed primarily by the secondary pupil personnel worker, although vocational guidance in the areas of understandings and appreciations of the occupational world begins in the primary grades. At the secondary level, the gifted student plans more specifically on the basis of his abilities and interests. Interpretation of abilities is important, for many gifted students have little or no concept of their potential. Some, indeed, feel that they are "dumb" and react with surprise to the notion that they might qualify for scholarships or college entrance.

The problems of appropriate scholarships, appropriate colleges, and tentative vocational plans require skillful, expert advice, since the gifted student typically has many conflicting possibilities open to him. At this point the well-trained pupil personnel worker may exert a profound influence on the entire future life and contribution of the gifted student.

Evaluation

Since the pupil personnel worker most often is the person within the school system who possesses some research skills, and since he is concerned with a continuing program of high effectiveness, he is often assigned the responsibility for evaluation of educational programs for the gifted. His efforts serve to indicate the strengths and weaknesses in planning, and form a basis for staff improvements of programs.

The evaluation process adds to individual study data, develops continuing data on individuals and on groups of children, involves parents, teachers, and pupils, and provides a basis for community support and understanding. Ideally the personnel worker's studies include not only comprehensive evaluations during the time of school attendance, but also follow-up studies that determine what graduates are doing five or ten years from graduation, and what their views of their educational experience are when they are seen in retrospect.

Responsibilities that include interpretation of child needs from the time of identification to the time of final evaluation are difficult and time-consuming. Within this frame of reference, the pupil personnel worker endeavors to extend horizons, to interpret information, to improve the educational process, to help teachers and others develop a challenging educational atmosphere for the gifted, and to evaluate the results of all efforts. The task, which is one of individualized education, is great, and endless. The satisfactions and contributions to the individual and to society are without bounds.

References

1. KOUGH, JACK, and DeHAAN, ROBERT. *Teachers' Guidance Handbook, Part I. Identifying Children Who Need Help.* Chicago: Science Research Associates, 1955.

2. MARTINSON, RUTH A. *Educational Programs for Gifted Pupils.* Sacramento, Calif.: State Department of Education, 1960.

3. PEGNATO, C. V. *An Evaluation of Various Initial Methods of Selecting Intellectually Gifted Children at the Junior High School Level.* Unpublished Ph.D. dissertation; University Park, Pa.: Pennsylvania State University, June, 1955.

4. TERMAN, LEWIS M. *Genetic Studies of Genius,* Vol. I. Stanford, Calif.: Stanford University Press, 1925.

5. WALTON, GENEVE. *Identification of Intellectually Gifted Children in the Public School Kindergarten.* Unpublished Ph.D. dissertation; Los Angeles: University of California at Los Angeles, June, 1961.

36. Counseling Needs of Gifted High School Students *

LESTER BEALS, *Oregon State University,* AND
PATRICIA SIMMONS, *Director of Research and Statistics, Orange County Schools, Santa Ana, California*

M ANY STUDIES have been made of the characteristics of the gifted student and the type of school program needed. Comparatively little study, on the other hand, has been made of the counseling needs of these students as related to vocational and personal decisions. Studies so far have been more concerned with the curricular needs of the gifted student than with his personal needs, with his academic potential rather than with his leadership potential. In a sense, it would seem that our public concern has been that of directing the gifted student into careers valuable in our national defense or our economic well-being. Perhaps more emphasis should be given to guiding the gifted toward making diversified contributions to society. Counseling has generally followed the premise that society will benefit most as each person achieves self-realization.

America needs people who will contribute solutions to problems of

* From *Personnel and Guidance Journal,* April 1962, pp. 712–16. Reprinted with permission.

science and technology and to civic, social, and moral problems. The able person is often able to be both a scientist and an educational statesman, a physician and a humanitarian, or an artist and a physicist, a Conant or a Schweitzer, for example. There are a multitude of people in America today who could make a much larger social contribution if they had been given better guidance. Ernest Ligon has done much study along these lines. He says in *A Greater Generation* (*1*) that there are a million and a half people today who are more highly endowed intellectually than Lincoln or Washington! The question seems, then, why are there not more people with a sense of social responsibility and dedication? Counseling may play an important role in helping develop this social conscience.

The Present Study

A study was undertaken in Orange County, California, under the sponsorship of the County School Office with the cooperation of the high schools and financed by Title V of the National Defense Education Act.[1] The purpose was to determine the counseling needs and the kind of counseling being given a selected group of gifted high school students. This study required, initially, that the group to be studied be defined and described.

To select the students called gifted, scores on the California Test of Mental Maturity were used. All eighth or ninth grade students are given this test as preenrollment to high school in the various school districts of Orange County. A minimum score of 140 on either the Language or NonLanguage sections of the CTMM was set to define the lower limits of the group to be studied.

An analysis of the test scores for the four years prior to the study yielded the names of 310 students from 30 schools who became the sample studied. The test had been administered during the eighth grade, and some diminution of the sample occurred. Complete information was secured on 247 students placed in grades 9 through 12.

After identification, student achievement was examined. Student achievement was considered to be revealed by scores on standardized achievement tests and scholastic grades earned. Student participation in leadership activities and clubs was also examined. Furthermore, study was made to discover the kind of future planning that these students were doing, their life goals and values, and the extent to which they were guided in achieving

[1] Project V-71, "A Study of a Selected Group of High Academic Potential Students in Orange County High Schools," Office of the County Superintendent of Schools, 1104 West Eighth Street, Santa Ana, Calif., June, 1960.

these goals. Hence, parents, teachers, and counselors needed to be contacted. Terman and others had earlier shown that the "gifted" students are not the stereotype so popularly pictured and that they tend in fact to be very well adjusted (2).

During the summer of 1959, letters were sent to all student participants. Interviews followed. The interviews were structured to ensure securing the same basic information from each student. These informal interviews were conducted in each student's school and varied in length from 25 to 35 minutes.

Later, a three-page questionnaire was sent to the parents of the students participating in the study. Information requested included parental opinions regarding the counseling received by their son or daughter, the extent of parental involvement in the decision-making by the student, and ways in which the home and school might work together better.

Finally, a brief opinionnaire was sent to all high school counselors regarding the students involved in the study. The opinionnaire supplemented informal interviews made with the counselors prior to the student interview.

Findings

An analysis of all scholastic grades earned indicated that about 70 per cent of these students were making a 3.00 point or above grade-point average on a 4.00 scale, or a B. Another 20 per cent were making between a C and a B average. The rest, about 10 per cent, were making less than a C, including one student making less than a D average. Many of these students are in accelerated groups. It would appear that the majority were doing quite well academically. An analysis of the students making less than a C average indicated that many had personal problems or were not highly motivated.

On the average, girls earned higher grades than boys. Boys, on the other hand, had higher intelligence scores. The grades of both boys and girls tended to improve a bit as they progressed in school. A study of the relationship of intelligence scores to grade-point averages using the Pierson Product Moment Formula was made, but yielded very low correlations, especially on the Non-Language section of the CTMM and grade correlations. The correlation for the Language score on the CTMM and grade-point average was 0.340; the relation between the Non-Language section of the CTMM and grades was 0.028. The publishers of the CTMM collaborated these findings as this is a truncated sample drawn from the upper portion of the normal distribution range. A correlation with grades is influenced by the fact that each person in the sample seems to have the potential of an "A" student.

Much information was secured from the interviews. Additional information was secured from the student questionnaire, which was combined with the material from the interviews. A study of this information, in general, reveals that these students come from homes economically and socially in the middle or upper middle class. Nearly 90 per cent of the students are living with both their natural father and mother. Students from unbroken homes tend to make better grades than those from broken homes. In view of the fact that Orange County is a changing and rapidly growing county, it is interesting to note that 65 per cent of the students have lived in the County or in the adjoining Los Angeles County all of their lives. Ten per cent come from other regions of California, while the other 25 per cent have migrated to California.

The occupations of fathers and mothers, when placed in job classification given in the *Dictionary of Occupational Titles,* reveal a high percentage of highly trained personnel. Fifty-two per cent of the parents were employed in managerial or professional positions; 13 per cent clerical and sales; 9 per cent skilled workers; 7 per cent in service occupations; the remainder are scattered among other major groups. The 52 per cent engaged in managerial and professional occupations is very considerably higher than the national proportion of 10 per cent in these occupations. It may be assumed that children whose fathers are in professional and managerial occupations may have greater opportunities at home to practice academic skills and understandings that will enable them to succeed better in a typical academic high school.

A large percentage of the mothers, 65 per cent, are not employed outside the home. Of the mothers employed, most are in professional, managerial, clerical, or sales occupations.

All of the students plan to finish high school, and approximately 96 per cent plan to go to some kind of a college. About half of them do not have a specific college in mind. A named college is more frequently given by these students who are about to be graduated. About half of all these participants stated that they were encouraged by their counselors to consider college. Most have also been encouraged by their parents.

In terms of present and future educational planning, a large majority, or 63 per cent, said that their parents gave them the most help; 17 per cent say counselors; and 11 per cent mentioned teachers.

Vocational objectives for 80 per cent of these students tend to be in the professional and managerial areas. The most popular vocational choices were: mathematics, science, teaching on all levels, engineering, medicine, and law. Again, parents seem to have supplied the primary information and incentive to these young people.

An analysis of vocational choices in terms of test scores, grades, and stated interests tends to indicate realistic planning. A majority of these students seem to have made their vocational decisions on the basis of personal interests and aptitudes without parental pressures. During the student interview and on the parent questionnaire, little evidence existed that parents coerce their offspring relative to specific occupations.

When questioned relative to their counselor, the students answers revealed great variance, depending for the most part on the kind and length of time that a counseling program had been operating in the school plus the length of time the student had been in school. A large number knew that there was someone to whom they could go for help; this might be the counselor, vice-principal, or dean. A large number indicated that they see their counselor twice a year; presumably these visits are for program planning. A large number said they feel free to talk with a counselor or a dean about an educational or vocational problem; however, they did not say they felt as free in discussing their personal problems. It may be that these students have fewer personal problems than other students or that they go to their parents for such help. In interview, students stated that they received nearly as much educational and occupational information from teachers as from counselors.

In addition, the interviws revealed that the participants take an active part in community and school events. Nearly all of them, boys and girls alike, are interested and active in sports. While not many of this group were represented on the first team of a major sport, most of them had attained skill and participated in minor sports. Further these students said that they took part in some kind of an interest club. They also were actively engaged in community groups, e.g., church organizations, Scouts, YMCA, YWCA, and recreation groups. Their interests seemed to be most varied.

Very few of the participants had important leadership positions. There were a few student body officers or organization officers among these students. For the most part these able students did not take leadership roles. They were responsible participants but not very active in leadership roles. The lack of leadership responsibilities raises questions. Could it be that this kind of a student does not want to take the time to prepare for leadership positions?

The students, for the most part, indicated that their counseling had not included guidance in the selection of activities. Parents stated that they felt this is an area of need in the counseling program.

An attempt was made during the interviews to determine the basic life motivation or philosophy of the individual. Certain questions and discussions gave some clue. A summary of the data from this part of the interview indicates that three-fourths seem to lack a well-defined philosophy. For example, when asked this question, "What do you hope to get out of life?," a majority stated that they did not know. Many young people seemed to be groping for more definite life goals and values to which they might tie their educational and vocational plans. A small number, however, reflected in a very mature fashion and had definite life goals or plans for attaining these goals.

A large majority of the parents were found to be college educated and many hold advanced degrees. Since much of the educational and occupational guidance comes from parents, the parental education level becomes significant. The parents said also that they wanted to work more closely with the school in providing information and guidance. Parents said they would like to have more information on standardized tests. Parents further stated that although they felt moral and spiritual guidance to be primarily their responsibility, they did appreciate all the help that the school could give them in reinforcing such guidance. A large number of parents expressed an opinion that counselors and teachers should give more guidance in aiding young people to develop a life philosophy and in establishing the values needed in a democratic society.

Implications

The high schools in the County have a variety of counseling programs, and multiple services are offered. Most of the large high schools tend to have a staff of well-trained, experienced counselors. The counseling program is organized so that each student has some individual counseling. In addition to counseling, the counselors spend some time working with teachers and administrators. Most of the counselors surveyed said that these students should be counseled as are all students. However, counselors said they would like to give more time to the parents. Counseling programs seem to lack time for much parent conferencing. Some counselors indicated that they felt that they should spend more time with teachers in order to provide the teacher with information and understandings. While counselors say that they believe guidance in the moral and spiritual areas are important, they are not sure how to offer such service. Counselors said they have so many clerical duties to perform that they do not have the time to do what they feel should be done.

It seems clear that academic underachievers among the able students should be identified as early as possible. The reasons for the lack of top achievement by these students needs to be analyzed carefully. A diagnosis might be possible early in the elementary school. If such an early diagnosis could be made, perhaps corrective action could be taken. Assistance needs to be given to the underachiever from the time a diagnosis is made until his schooling ends. In some cases financial assistance to the student and his family may be necessary.

It appears that counselors need to guide students so that they also achieve outside of class activities. Counseling may be in order so that the able student might be helped to enter and achieve in those activities that would seem best to fit his needs and interests.

The data indicated that counselors and teachers should work much more closely with the home. The parents of the gifted exercise much influence in both educational and vocational decisions. Such decision-making implies that counselors are important assistants to the parents. Nearly all parents indicated that they wanted to work much more closely with the counselors in matters related to the progress of their sons and daughters. Counselors, teachers, and administrators, therefore, should spend more of their time with parents. Counselors might profitably spend one-fourth to one-third of their time in individual and group contacts with parents. Perhaps time could be used during the summer for counseling with parents and students. What has been said in terms of working with these parents may well be applied to all parents.

The findings seem to point to the teachers' role of providing educational and vocational information to students. Therefore, counselors may well spend more time in providing information of many kinds to teachers, who in turn could pass it along to their students. Such information might well include the educational and vocational requirements of the various occupations, college admission requirements, training facilities available, and employment opportunities. Teachers need to be given more information about the student, along with interpretation of this information. Guiding all students, including the gifted, can be much more effective if a team approach is used with the teacher, counselor, and parents working together to help the student. Such teamwork may mean that counselors through periodic group meetings, written reports, and materials provide parents and teachers with the information each needs to help each student.

This study revealed that counselors needed more time to spend with students in exploring life goals and values in terms of their own needs and that of the democratic society in which the school operates. Perhaps too much of the counselor's time is spent in program-making and other clerical chores that could be done in part by others.

Juniors and seniors receive additional counselor time when they request help in checking admissions requirements for college and securing scholarship information. These are important services; but could such services be simplified?

All students have a social contribution they can make. The gifted need to be encouraged and helped to make social and civic achievements in keeping with their abilities. Many social scientists do not accept the premise of Plato's *Republic*. At the same time, many of these leaders would agree that America and the world must look to intelligent leadership for a solution to the problems of the world. Needed are people who see the social significance of their actions and who have more concern for others than these leaders do themselves. Needed today are people who are willing to dedicate their lives to serving humanity and themselves well.

References

1. LIGON, ERNEST M. *A Greater Generation.* New York: Macmillan, 1948.
2. TERMAN, LEWIS M. *Genetic Studies of Genius, the Gifted Child Grows Up.* Palo Alto, Calif.: Stanford University Press, 1947.

37. Guidance of the Academically Talented, Philadelphia *

ALLEN H. WETTER, *Superintendent of Schools*

Guidance of the Academically Talented

Adequate guidance of gifted students and their parents is time-consuming and complex. Identification, an important aspect of guidance for the gifted, requires special attention. Other aspects of guidance are course selection, rostering, follow-up, evaluation, help with personal psychological problems, counseling for post-high-school education, advice on application for admission to higher institutions, and processing transcripts, College

* From *The Academically Talented in the Philadelphia Public Schools: Progress Report*, pp. 62–65, Philadelphia Public Schools, 1961. Reprinted with permission.

Board, and scholarship applications. In schools where a guidance program is provided for the gifted, time for it is now gained at the expense of other important services to the average or slow-learning pupil.

1. Individually the counselor cites various gifted children to members of the staff and makes suggestions as to ways in which their abilities can be used to special advantage. This is especially true when a particularly intelligent child is not functioning at top level because of some emotional or other type of problem.
2. Special attention is paid to reviewing with students the results of C. E. E. B., S. A. T., and National Merit Scholarship Examinations to determine individual strengths and weaknesses, and to decide what further review or enrichment should be provided.
3. There is follow-up of graduates to determine the relationship between enriched programs and success in college.

Every teacher has a list of better-than-average pupils who have been identified by valid means. Thus, the designated pupils in each class, within the regular work as provided for in the course of study, are stimulated to increase their activities by challenging, additional material. Parents of these pupils are advised at the conclusion of each report period as to actual achievement. If the better-than-average child is not working at capacity, parents and pupils cooperate in attempting to solve the problem. For the faculty, this takes the form of a mentor system. Names of nonachievers are submitted to all teachers; and, according to needs and interests, faculty members volunteer as mentors or sponsors for these pupils.

Experimentation in providing for the better-than-average pupil is continuous here. A permanent faculty committee meets periodically to plan, process, execute, and evaluate the various facets of the program. Departmental, inter-departmental, and extracurricular activities are constantly geared to accelerate these efforts. This term there will be a special 9A—9B group in English and social studies, a tutoring plan for scholarship candidates, and active participation in worthwhile competitive writing, art, and scientific contests.

Seniors who have satisfactorily completed the work of the advanced curriculum are eligible to take the Advanced Placement Tests of the College Board, and will be recommended by the school for advanced credit at the college of their choice.

Advanced courses in our school begin in the 10A term and extend through 12B. In 9B, a group of very able pupils will be selected to take our advanced curriculum. These pupils will be counseled to discuss the advanced courses with their parents, with the option to accept or reject the invitation to take advanced work. Any pupil electing to take the advanced curriculum may rest assured that (1) he will not be required to continue in it if the pace is beyond his ability; (2) he will not be graded to his disadvantage in comparison with pupils in standard courses, either with regard to Barnwell honors, or rank in class, or in scholarship competition.

COLLEGE GUIDANCE

Recognizing that it is increasingly important for the student to choose and gain admission to a suitable college, the Board of Public Education plans to appoint an additional counselor to each high school who will serve as chairman of college guidance at all grade levels.

A college guidance program handled by four specially interested and trained faculty members lines up gifted students as early as 9A. They aim to make certain that no pupil, scholastically capable of going to college, is left unaware of the opportunties that are ahead of him if he performs at the highest level and works toward good scholarship from 9A through 12th grade. Colleges of his choice are discussed, their requirements made known, and parents informed of the everincreasing opportunities for college attendance.

The director of college guidance compiles a case history for each gifted senior. By maintaining an extensive library of college catalogues and brochures for pupil use, by planning for and accompanying groups to the various career conferences in the area, by providing the individual with all scholarship information applying to his needs, by conducting or arranging for scholarship examinations when necessary, the person responsible for college guidance aims to direct each talented individual into that field of endeavor and that seat of learning where he can make the best use of his gift. Interviews with representatives of the colleges are arranged. Students whose scholastic records make them potential scholarship material are collectively and individually advised and prepared for the tests and application forms relating to admission to college.

Evaluation

This remains one of the major unsolved problems.

Assuming that rapid learners can be accurately identified and grouped; that they can be properly motivated, guided, and taught; on what policy shall teachers' judgments (grades) rest? Shall the academically talented pupil be measured on the same literal and numerical scale as his less gifted schoolmates? Is a failing grade or a low passing grade appropriate for him? Has he a right to expect nothing lower than an *A* or *B;* an 85, 90, or 95? Having placed him in competition with others of similar abilities, shall teachers expect him to be content with the same *A* or 90 that is awarded to average learners for educational achievements that differ in both quantity and quality? There is no uniform policy among the schools, although agreement upon criteria to be used in establishing rank in the senior class has been reached, and is a related problem.

BASIC GRADE

In Philadelphia, as elsewhere in the United States, the most common way of compensating the academically talented student for work that is both greater in quantity and superior in quality to that done in average classes is to set a basic grade that may not be earned by other students, unless there is no Honors class in a given subject. Some schools set the line at 92 or 93, with a possible mark for A. T.'s that may go up to 98. In some schools where all *A's* are required for listing on the Academic Honor Roll, an 85 in an advanced class is considered the equivalent of an *A* in a regular class. Usually no mark below *B* is given to a member of an Honors class.

38. Guidance for the Gifted Underachiever in High School *

HELEN G. STERN, *Counselor-Coordinator, Nyack (New York) High School*

GUIDANCE for the underachiever with superior ability at the secondary level cuts across the whole fabric of secondary education, involves all of guidance and counseling theory and practice, builds on an emerging body of research findings and implications related to the gifted child and the academically talented, and focuses essentially on the nature and treatment of underachievement.

Scholastic difficulties at the secondary level may first be evident in academic subjects, such as mathematics or foreign language. A student with these difficulties may be rebelling against teacher standards and daily assignments. An underachiever is often identified in junior or senior high school because he seems to lack the proper motivation to become a high-achieving student.

In some instances, the home climate may have precipitated academic underachievement. Families with an absent or weak father, homes where

* From *The NEA Journal*, November, 1962, pp. 24-26. Reprinted with permission.

education is not valued, homes with a history of frequent moves—all may be providing environmental influences that contribute to underachievement.

In other cases, the climate of the school itself may have fostered lowered academic achievement. Rather than underscoring the value of education, some school climates seem to develop patterns of anti-intellectualism or to superimpose attitudes against the worthwhileness of education during and beyond the secondary school years.

In still others, overemphasis on conformity to teacher standards that may have little to do with academic excellence creates attitudes in some students that lead to underachievement. On the other hand, the high school underachiever may be a youth whose own personal dynamics reflect basic psychological, physical, or sociological influences that lead to the development of academic underattainment.

In order to assist the underachiever properly during his junior and senior high school experiences, special guidance and counseling procedures are needed. Of course, basically, effective guidance and counseling of under-achievers of superior ability depend upon a strong ongoing program of guidance for everyone.

An effective guidance program for all students implies that the secondary school offers complete educational, vocational, and personal-social guidance and counseling services for every boy and girl. Active programs for all gifted students—achievers as well as underachievers—implies that there is leadership and support by the administration, interest and involvement of the community, utilization of specialized resources, differentiated curricula, ability grouping, referral procedures to specialists where indicated, and the participation of trained and selected staffs, with special attention to teachers working with underachievers.

The teacher's role in working with gifted underachievers cannot be overemphasized. Accepting the underachiever as an individual, treating him fairly but firmly, holding him to his best and not his least efforts, enhancing his learning skills, broadening the base of his knowledge and understandings, and providing a healthy model for him to identify with and emulate are all actions that fall within the domain of the teacher.

Reports by underachievers themselves point up the necessity of the proper attitude on the part of teachers. Teachers who seem to reject gifted underachievers contribute to lowered ambition and motivation. Underachievers state that teachers who are sarcastic, overly critical, overly demanding, rigid, and officious are not helpful. Teachers who judge students as persons only on the basis of performance in their subjects are likewise to a degree ineffectual.

In a special experiment for teaching and guiding gifted underachievers made by Goldberg in 1959, students were interviewed concerning their perceptions of themselves and their school experiences. In the words of the report:

Many of the responses to questions about school success, difficulties, abilities, and other topics were answered in terms of their teachers. Doing well in a subject was usually related to a "good teacher," doing poorly to an unsympathetic or unfair teacher. Their willingness to work in a subject also depended on their perception of the interest of the teacher. The students wanted teachers who merit "respect," and who can "control the class," who "give you an interest in the subject," and are "cheerful" and "understand the student."

In the same study there is a brief summary of some of the current findings:

. . . for those students for whom it is possible to effect improvement, two factors appear to be crucial: (1) identification with a teacher who is consistently interested and supportive, who views each student as an individual and accepts him as a bright and able person with a need for special help; and (2) assistance in mastering the skills of learning that many of the underachievers failed to acquire in the earlier grades.

The teacher has a vital contribution to make, too, during staff conferences, which are usually conducted under the supervision of the school counselor or guidance director. The principal, vice-principal, remedial reading or study skills teacher, school psychologist, and other appropriate specialists are often involved in these conferences.

During such case conferences, the teacher has valuable information to report on the day-to-day personal and academic behavior of the underachiever, including all of his attitudes and relationships.

The teacher has more than a reporter's role in conferences, however. Teachers should be apprised of the observations, evaluations, and recommendations of other specialists, so that later they can return to the classroom to implement these suggestions. The guidance staff should support the teacher in his renewed efforts.

Teachers, administrators, and couselors must work on a cooperative basis to identify properly and correctly group gifted underachievers on an individualized basis. School counselors or guidance directors, specializing in guidance of the gifted, have a significant role to carry out in implementing the differentiated course content recommended by curriculum and related specialists. One is struck by a kind of leitmotiv that recurs in almost all of the pamphlets produced in cooperation with the National Education Association in providing for the academically talented. This is the role of the counselor in locating and nurturing special talents in the various subject matter and aesthetic areas.

Counselors can serve as a type of academic "talent scout" and report their observations and recommendations to the various teachers. This discovered talent can then be encouraged toward development and fulfillment in high school and beyond.

The school counselor or guidance director, of course, has a basic role in developing counseling relationships with underachievers of superior ability. The counselor can make his contribution in many ways, but perhaps the single most important service he can render the gifted underachiever is to convey an attitude of faith and belief in him, a kind of empathic tie that the student senses and knows he can rely on.

Educational counseling of underachievers with superior ability takes on special significance at the secondary level in view of the vital choices and decisions that must be made during these years. In many school systems, students must make a commitment while they are in the eighth grade to a high school course of study that will determine the content of both their immediate and long-range educational programs.

Where this is true, the counselor has the dual responsibility of helping the school system understand the impact of such an early commitment on students, and of helping students to make the wisest choices available at that moment. In all this, the effective counselor works with and through the faculty.

For the usual type of gifted underachiever—the one who tests extremely high on all kinds of measures but whose daily work results in a low scholastic average—it seems evident that the difficulty is with academic conformity and performance rather than lack of basic skill or actual acquisition of knowledge. Items appearing on scholastic aptitude tests are academically oriented. Since a gifted underachiever usually scores high, this indicates that considerable learning is taking place.

The difficulty seems to reside in the underachiever's attitudes toward actual daily attainment, his lack of pride in doing a job well, his refusal to meet teacher requirements, and his inability to postpone immediate satisfactions for more long-range goals.

The counselor must interpret and treat these attitudes as crucial to later academic and professional achievement.

Depending on the amount of his training, competency, and experience, the school counselor will frequently be able to assist gifted underachievers directly in working through individual personal adjustments. The nature of such personal adjustment counseling will be determined by the kinds of problems the underachiever brings to the counselor.

School counselors must be alert to the personal needs of gifted underachievers, and make a proper referral in those cases where additional specialist help is indicated. If underachievers manifest deep-seated personality problems, counselors probably should recommend psychotherapy. Arrangements can be made through the school psychologists or directly with the community psychiatric services.

An important specialized service that the school counselor provides to the underachiever is college admissions counseling. The underachiever with superior ability is a particularly difficult youngster to place in college, primarily because of his record of poor achievement. Because the single best predictor of success in college is rank in class, the school counselor finds it imperative to interpret the underachievement properly in each case. The problem here is not to select several colleges for a final choice but to find a college that is willing to take a chance on the applicant.

For example, following is a record that is typical of many gifted underachievers: intelligence quotient of 135 or higher; College Board scores on both the Scholastic Aptitude Test and achievements in the 700's; Differential Aptitude Test scores on verbal, numerical, and abstract aptitudes at the 90th percentile and higher; results on other college aptitude tests at about the 95th percentile rank; and a cumulative high school average of about 76 or 77, which places him in the lowest quarter of the class. In short, the youngster has a superlative test record, and a barely passing high school record.

In a spot check of several leading colleges and universities throughout the New England and Middle Atlantic States, the writer inquired of numerous admissions officers what their action would be on such a set of credentials. These universities ranged in admissions practices from quite flexible to quite selective, in SAT medians from the 400's to the 700's, and in small liberal arts programs to large all-encompassing combination curricula. Some of the replies from the admissions officers include:

We wouldn't touch a kid like that with a ten-foot pole. He's loafed all through high school. Why should he suddenly change in college?

Well, there is such a thing as a late bloomer. Maybe in the right course he'll really produce. We might take a chance.

A boy like that is obviously emotionally disturbed. We don't have the psychiatric facilities.

It's bad enough to try to help such a person. He won't help himself, and what's more, he'll drag others down with him.

I think we owe it to the students and to their families to take a close look at their potential. I would be willing to take a risk on such a student on your strong recommendation.

Perhaps the most effective way of placing underachievers in college is to continue service to them on an individualized, highly qualitative basis. The underachiever requires considerable professional attention and interpretation, and probably nowhere in the educational sequence is there a greater need for closer articulation, mutual understanding, and cohesive approaches than in the process of counseling for college placement.

There are, of course, other important considerations such as research, motivation, and qualifications of staff, for example, which might well be explored.

Effective guidance services require the professional dedication and cooperation of counseling specialists, the administration, and assigned faculty. By such involvement, secondary schools have the opportunity of assisting gifted underachievers toward heightened attainment and fulfillment, thus making fuller contributions of their talent to society.

39. Study of Underachieving Gifted *

A. HARRY PASSOW, *Teachers College, Columbia University,* AND
MIRIAM L. GOLDBERG, *Teachers College, Columbia University*

THE "GIFTED underachiever"—i.e., the student whose scholastic performance is far below that predicted on the basis of measured intelligence and aptitude—has been one of the continuing concerns of the Horace Mann-Lincoln Institute's Talented Youth Project.[1] Since 1954, studies of attitudes toward self and toward school of gifted high achievers and underachievers have been conducted cooperatively with Evanston (Illinois) Township High School. These studies have shed light on differences in self perceptions and attitudes of variously achieving high-ability students and have suggested the need for experimenting further with special school provisions for underachievers.

An opportunity to conduct such experimentation came in the spring of 1956. The administrative and supervisory staff of DeWitt Clinton High School (New York City) became concerned with the fact that about half of the entering high-ability tenth grade students over a three year period were underachievers. This staff invited members of the Talented Youth Project to study cooperatively ways of helping such students perform at a level more in line with their potential.

A number of exploratory sessions resulted in the designing of a study

---

* From *Educational Leadership,* November, 1958, pp. 121–25. Reprinted with permission.
[1] For an earlier account see A. Harry Passow, "Planning for Talented Youth: A Research Project," *Educational Leadership,* XIII (January, 1956), 249-51.

aimed at examining the academic, personal, and social characteristics of underachievers and at assessing the effects of programming a group of such students with a single teacher for homeroom activity and one subject class. The arrangement was intended to test the hypothesis that if underachieving students could share their common problems and identify with and receive support from a teacher, their attitudes and scholastic performance would improve.

In June 1956, 102 entering tenth grade students with junior high school IQ's of 120 or higher (Pintner or Henmon-Nelson) and ninth year grade mark averages below 80 were retested on the California Test of Mental Maturity. Seventy students with IQ's of 120 or higher on both the junior high test and the CTMM were selected for the study and paired on the basis of IQ, reading scores, and ninth grade marks. One of each pair was placed in a "study" group and the other in a control group. A third group of comparable IQ but high achievement (ninth grade averages of 85 or above) was identified.

In September 1956, the study group was assigned to a social studies teacher who also served as homeroom officer. The students were informed that they were specially selected and placed in a "special class" because of their high potential and need for raising the level of their school performance. Dr. Jane Beasley of the Project staff interviewed 26 of the underachievers (15 from the study group and 11 from the control group) and 4 of the high achievers. In addition, data were gathered on self-attitudes, attitudes toward school, family patterns, problem areas, academic aspiration levels, and vocational choices. The parents of involved students met with staff members, learned the purpose of the study, and filled out questionnaires that dealt with some of the same areas as did the student forms.

Iowa Tests of Educational Development, administered in October 1956, indicated that achievement on such measures is more closely related to intelligence than to school grades. The two groups of underachievers' scores did not differ significantly from the high achievers on any part of the test. However, the composite ITED scores of the control group were significantly higher than those of the study group, even though both groups were alike on all junior high school measures.

The attitude and personality measures provided a revealing picture of bright young adolescents and indicated some significant differences between the high and low achievers among them. There were no differences in their own appraisals of most of their abilities and characteristics, in their occupational aspirations (most preferred professional careers), in the kind or intensity of interests. Families were similar in occupational status, parental educational level, number of working mothers, and family size. Disruption of the normal family pattern through the absence of the father by death or divorce was much more frequent among the underachievers. Grade expectation was quite different among the high and low achievers with the latter expecting to pass but not anticipating very high grades.

The tape-recorded interviews supplemented the paper and pencil data and presented a picture of the underachievers as recognizing that they are bright and potentially capable of outstanding academic achievement, but showing a strong resistance against making the necessary effort. The interviews pointed up great differences among the underachievers and suggested that each must be studied as an individual with his own motivations, his own rationalizations, his own system of defenses.

Because of the fused homeroom and social studies period, the guidance activities did not have to be terminated at the end of one period. Sometimes the social studies period was curtailed in order to conclude discussion on a particular problem raised in the homeroom. Since the group remained together in class as well as homeroom, social studies achievement meant recognition and status among one's peers. The boys in the study group seemed to want to do well not only for themselves but also for the teacher.

At the end of the first semester, the grades of the study group indicated some improvement, but, contrary to expectation, as a group they showed less improvement than did the controls. The differences were largely accounted for by the intitial differences on the ITED. However, an analysis of the final grades at the end of the second semester showed that the study group improved in all subjects, except social studies where they remained the same (possibly a reflection of the teacher's reluctance to be too lenient in grading his special class), while the control group went down in all subjects. The differences were most striking in mathematics, science, and total average. The study group made up its first semester deficit and, in all subjects but English, equaled or exceeded the final marks of the controls.

For the eleventh year, the study group remained together as a homeroom section with the same teacher but, for social studies, were assigned to a woman teacher who had been very successful with honors students. The evaluation at the end of the first semester of that year showed that the new arrangement for the special class had not proved satisfactory. The boys and the teacher were in conflict throughout the semester. The teacher, expecting high quality performance, was unable to accept the erratic, tardy, and often slipshod work of the students. The techniques, which she had found successful with honors classes over the years, seemed completely ineffectual in this situation. For the second semester, the group was programmed with another social studies teacher, in this instance a man again. Evaluation at the end of the eleventh grade by the teacher corroborated the impressions of the two previous teachers that the group lacked emotional stability and control. On homework of a factual nature, the assignments were done on time. Homework that required independent thought and organization of materials was subject to delay, stalling, and nonperformance. Aware of the danger of strong rebuke and nonacceptance on the one hand, and of allowing the students to "get away" with inadequate performance on the other, the teacher followed a middle course— accepting late assignments, allowing students to rework poorly done assignments, and requiring that they incorporate suggestions for improvement. Several class periods were devoted to practical demonstrations on how to do an assignment. The teacher paid attention to each student and tried to understand him in terms of the particular problems and weaknesses presented. In short, the teacher tried to create a warm and accepting climate, allowing leeway in performance standards and consistently showing an interest in the individual problems of the students. He concentrated on teaching the group much-needed study skills. On a midsemester economics test in April 1958, the study group performed somewhat above the average for all academic students.

Even though at the end of the tenth year, the study group showed greater improvement than did the controls, there were "improvers" and "nonimprovers" in both groups. Twenty-one improvers were compared with an equal number of nonimprovers. The two groups differed significantly with respect to the ITED composite and correctness of writing scores (the improvers were higher) and on self-attitudes inventory (nonimprovers showed a greater discrepancy between their perception of abilities and their wished-for abilities status). Since this latter score is viewed as an index of adjustment, the discrepancy suggests that nonimprovers see their ability to perform in various areas as too far from what they would like it to be to warrant making an effort to improve. There were differences in other areas as well but these did not reach statistical significance. For example, the incidence of divorce was greater among the parents of the nonimprovers; fewer had reached a decision on vocational goals and, where they did state a preference, it was less often above the level of their father's present occupation; fewer were only or oldest children; fewer had older siblings in college who could act as achievement models for them. These observed tendencies will be used as hypotheses for further study.

At the end of two years of experimentation with the study described in the aforementioned and with other approaches, these tentative conclusions have been reached:

1. Academic underachievement appears to be a symptom of a variety of more basic personal and social problems. The depth, seriousness, and duration of the underlying problem determine the extent and kind of help a student needs. Some high school students may be beyond profiting from the kind of direct help that the school can provide. The criteria for making a prognosis on the basis of the kinds of information collected have not been arrived at as yet.

2. For those underachieving students who did improve, two factors seem crucial: first, they were able to identify with a teacher who is consistently supportive and interested, who views each student as an individual, and accepts his need for special help; and, second, they received assistance in mastering the skills of learning that many underachievers have failed to acquire in the earlier grades.

3. It seems advisable to separate the teaching and guidance functions for these students so that the person who is working closely and personally with them will not be the same one who has to grade or evaluate them.

4. Grouping these students in a subject class may not be wise since they tend to give each other negative support that often cannot be adequately handled within the context of the class.

In view of the foregoing conclusions, the plan for 1958–59, in addition to continuing follow-ups of the existing groups, involves setting up special groups of underachievers, who would be together for a daily continuous homeroom and study hour. This would provide opportunity for intensive group and individual guidance as well as instruction in work study skills without involving the teacher in the role of evaluator. In June 1958, 87 students with IQ of 125 or higher and ninth year grades below 80 per cent were identified and divided into three matched groups of 29 each. Intelligence, age, membership in Special Progress classes in junior high school, and equivalent reading and arithmetic scores were considered in the matching. Two groups have been designated as special sections with carefully selected homeroom teachers; the third group is distributed among the remaining homeroom sections and serves as a control group. These special groups will be kept intact with the same teacher for the three years of high school. Any student who, after the first year, attains honor roll status (87 or higher) will be permitted to use some of the study period time for one of the school service activities. The two basic purposes of the study—acquiring greater insight into the nature of underachievement and possible modifications for overcoming it—continue to be explored.

40. Overachieving and Underachieving Gifted High School Girls *

MARGARET M. GREENE, *Guidance Counselor, Sayville, New York*

IT IS THE purpose of this study to determine and describe certain factors in the home and family background, the patterns of value, and personality organization of a group of intellectually gifted girls who have been designated as overachievers and underachievers (at Hunter College High School).

Interest in the problem developed from the investigator's experience in working as a guidance counselor with these students. In counseling many of the girls, whose measured academic potential would suggest prediction of high academic achievement, varied levels of scholastic success were observed. The degree of their success was not always commensurate with their scores on tests of scholastic aptitude. In individual cases, factors other than scholastic aptitude were obtained that suggested a possible influence upon the level of achievement attained.

Specifically, then, the problem may be stated as follows: What factors in home and family background, value patterns, and personality organization contribute to underachievement and overachievement in a group of intellectually gifted girls? . . .

Conclusions

As a result of personal experience with the subjects and from a familiarity with the literature regarding achievement of gifted students, the investigator hypothesized that it would be possible to classify subjects into three groups—those who achieved at their level of expectancy as predicted by a measure of scholastic aptitude, those who achieved above their level of

* From Margaret M. Greene, "A Study of Certain Characteristics of Overachievers and Underachievers in a High School for Intellectually Gifted Girls" (Unpublished Ph.D. dissertation, St. John's University, Jamaica, N.Y., 1962), pp. 3–4, 110–13. Reprinted with permission.

expectancy, and those who achieved below their level of expectancy. Subjects were so classified and the three groups were designated as at-level achievers, overachievers, and underachievers. . . .

Significant differences in scores obtained on the personality inventories suggest the following conclusions:

1. Overachievers, as the term is used in this dissertation, and at-level achievers do not differ in those personality characteristics measured in this study. This conclusion further substantiates the prior one that there is no difference in the two groups here identified as overachievers and at-level achievers.

2. Underachievers show a tendency to place greater value upon relationships with people than upon ideas than do either of the other groups of achievers.

3. Underachievers show greater disregard for social mores and conventions than do overachievers or at-level achievers.

4. Underachievers appear to have less deep emotional responses than do overachievers.

5. Underachievers seem to possess less ability to profit from experience than do overachievers.

6. Underachievers tend to take on more activity than they can cope with and tend to lose interest in the projects they initiate more than do overachievers.

7. At-level achievers show a greater tendency toward paranoia and a withdrawal from social contact with others than do underachievers.

One major conclusion may be drawn regarding the home and family background of subjects of the investigation. The data of this study support the findings of earlier research in the area of the gifted child. As earlier studies have shown, this group of intellectually gifted girls have homes that usually are not broken by death or divorce, where there are often two children, where there is a high level of education of parents, frequently college-graduate fathers, and where there is a tendency for the occupational level of the father to place at the upper end of the occupational scale. The choice of future occupation for subjects of this study reflects high aspirations, with college planned for the great majority, and occupation chosen in a professional field, as do reports of previous investigations.

In general, gifted underachievers differ significantly from gifted achievers in certain personality characteristics. As a group, underachievers show a tendency to place greater value upon relationships with people than upon ideas, show greater disregard for social mores and conventions, seem to possess less ability to profit from experiences, tend to take on more activities than they can cope with, and tend to lose interest in the projects that they initiate.

41. Underachievement of the Gifted That Hurts Most *

FRANK T. WILSON, *Professor Emeritus, Hunter College*

M ANY public-minded people, including educators, are lamenting the "underachieving" of children in schools and colleges, particularly on the part of the more able pupils. Whether this concern will produce new insights and lead to brighter days for gifted children, or end with little more than fury of words, remains to be seen. The former outcome is not hopeless by any means, however, but its eventuality will be more likely and will appear earlier, perhaps, if general understanding of the problems of educating gifted individuals in the democratic tradition is clarified in various respects.

It is true enough and in stark reality alarming that large proportions of able youth do not go to college, and thereby fail to receive the training that alone, for most of them, will make possible their potential self-realization and valuable contributions to the nation. Only a small fraction of these able school leavers will make reasonable success of their lives in terms of their potential capabilities. Among the able who do enter college only about one-third will graduate, and of these scarce a tenth will complete graduate work qualifying them for professional and other careers requiring highly specialized performance. As compared with the well-authenticated reports of what the story is in Russia, this fact of American educational life gives no exaggerated cause for thinking persons to ponder.

Reflection, however, makes one realize that this is not the whole of the matter. Almost any teacher will attest to the well-nigh incredible fact that, in elementary and high schools, many if not most of the unusually able

* From *The Educational Forum*, November, 1960, pp. 21–25. Reprinted with permission.

students despite their routine "straight" A grades achieve at a level reasonably close to their potential only occasionally. Furthermore, there seems no doubt but that the death toll of many highly able college freshmen is in large part related to their inability to perform in college with enough zeal and skill as students to meet standards suddenly required of them. In the lower schools they floated easily to their A's, but in college floating doesn't always work, and some are not able to function in unfamiliar arduous situations, while others don't like to work. This is serious business, which people are justified in condemning.

Unpleasant as these facts may be regarding scholastic underachieving by able students, this situation does not merit our only serious concern. More bitter in our mouths is a third exhibit: the delinquent, the racketeer, and criminal crowd that boast the leadership of skill, intelligence, resourcefulness, disciplined personalities, and unholy creativity. A glance at daily papers, a hasty attendance to five minutes newcasts review day by day the exploits of able persons gone wrong. The devil, as we all were taught, is indeed able and ingenious. It is doubtless true that over the centuries evil, in some places, has been reduced, but enough still abounds to worry most of us. And to many a devoted social worker, to many a teacher, and to many a parent it seems clear that young people have beeen recruited into the kingdom of evil by force of circumstance, rather than by a devil or by an inherent sinful nature. Circumstances might have been made different in most cases, we believe.

These dismal facts are not in any degree eliminated by the brighter side of the picture, bright though that side may be. Most, though not all, follow-up studies of gifted individuals read like success stories of Americana, and many of them truly are such. The records show that these in a large majority of cases have entered and performed in professional and business careers with sound achievement. They have become active leaders in their fields, doing highly valuable research, writing books, making other creative productions, and have resisted corrosion of ethical and moral virtues. Many of them have advanced rapidly to positions of importance. Some of them become public servants in appointive or elective positions, contributing nobly to the welfare of the body politic. Their careers testify to the inherent possibilities for all gifted individuals to render that godly "service which is perfect freedom," according to the book of common prayer.

What then is the underachieving that hurts most? I propose that what hurts the largest number and the most deeply is the failure of present-day education to develop skill and zeal in the fundamentals of democratic living. When compared with the reported success of Russian education, in which Communist ideology is arduously cultivated from preschool through the whole educational career of pupils and on through adulthood, one might justifiably shudder with misgivings at the prospects for democracy. We don't like this Russian ideology and we don't believe in teaching democracy a la coercion or misrepresentation. But we also should quail if the underachievement in commitment to the ideals of democratic living is as great as some signs portend.

Specifically, how complete is devotion throughout our country to the "Bill of Rights"? How informed and active are professionally trained people in encouraging concern for honest and responsible government? How functionally dedicated are the press and other mass media of communication to true freedom of the press? How pure is academic freedom? How skillful are the majority of college graduates in carrying on thinking and discussion in democratic fashion? Do individuals in positions of authority eschew authoritarianism, and how able are they to develop maximum return from mutual give and take of ideas? Are position, prestige, material gain more highly treasured than sharing for the benefit of all, cooperating to improve circumstances that grind down the lives of many? For which—personal profit or the commonweal—will most people give up convenience, material reward, or comfortable living? These are hard questions to have to answer and yet they touch the soul of democratic behavior.

How well or poorly democratic idealism is being made effective in the minds, hearts, and purposes of future citizens of America when they are children in our schools may be estimated at several crucial places in our educational programs.

1. How veritable in making teacher ready to develop the democratic way of life is the preparation of students in colleges and universities that undertake teacher education? There seems little reason to believe that great results are achieved in this respect in many teacher education programs. Concern is apt to be limited to the acquirement of academic learning, for the attainment of elementary and often sterile understandings of child nature, for mastery of some of the skills in managing the book learning of pupils, and for the control of their conduct. Courses or experiences that arouse teachers-to-be to devotion to living democratically with children seem of quite minor importance in many of these institutions.

2. If typical practices are observed in representative schools, one can only be depressed that so much of so many pupils' emotions and wills are dominated by pressures coming from without them. The authoritarian symbols of birch rod and dunce cap seem only to have been exchanged for other devices of like effect. Instead of the rod, a clear line of control (often

kindly but usually authoritarian) runs from teacher to principal to superintendent to boards of education. For the dunce cap there are low or failing grades for poor achievement, for "attitudes," "adjustment," "cleanliness," et cetera, et cetera! The net effect of almost fifty years of looking afresh at education following the war to make the world safe for democracy is not convincingly cheerful.

3. Our citizenry seems to have little prime concern for an educational program centered around the purpose of leading youth to a functional understanding of living democratically in a populous world society. It appears much more preoccupied with strivings for material gains and creature pleasures. Roads and automobiles, cigarettes, liquor, entertainments, violence, and sex seem of first importance in endeavors to find joy and delight day by day or night after night, with lame hopes that missiles and space control will take care of threats to security. A half-aware guilt about what is happening to children in midcentury America is placated, one is inclined to deduce, by providing palatial type buildings—then encouraging teachers to police children therein and teach them disagreeable lessons about matters vaguely related to their good, or in a few extreme instances, letting pupils respond to whims and idle fancies much of their time. But even such building pride seems lately to be giving way in many communities that are repeatedly voting down bond issues for needed new construction.

This gloomy picture, fortunately, is not universal, and it is in the hundreds of instances of another sort that hope lies that our country may rise to the opportunity of leading, with other free peoples, the cause of democratic idealism. In these more promising instances, homes, schools, and communities are achieving reasonably close to the potential of democratic ways of life. It is worth while noting some particular ways by which this is being accomplished.

First, in these sorts of places there is solid belief in democracy and understanding of how it works. Sacrifices are made for it, real sacrifices of material sort, such as payment of high taxes and the denials of some pleasures, prestige, and conveniences. For example, some communities compensate teachers sufficiently to insure cultural experiences and professional improvement for them, which clarify and reenforce understandings of and skill in developing human virtues. The sort and number of specialists necessary are provided in schools to enrich educational opportunities abundantly. Buildings, plant, equipment, and supplies (the teachers' tools) are likewise adequately provided so that the best services known can be rendered by the professional staffs that use them. The educational philosophy of having children learn to live and to be devoted to democratic principles, as opposed to authoritarian practices, is approved and cultivated in these schools and communities. Parents and other citizens contribute much of their time and thought, at the cost of personal convenience and gain, in assisting school people in providing enriching experiences that help children develop understandings and appreciations of good human relationships. In other less favored communities there also will sometimes be found individual schools and individual teachers within schools where, despite less auspicious circumstances, much of the same direction of the educational program is apparent.

A few features of the beliefs and practices that are functioning in this manner in individual classrooms are also worth noting. The climate of the room is friendly and favorable to constructive growth. Children feel free to take responsibilities for managing themselves with sympathetic, trusting, and trusted teachers to help. Many decisions, some of quite trivial matters, others of wider importance, are made by children individually on their own, others by groups, still others by all. Teachers participate, but rarely as mere authoritarians. There is much sharing in experiences—planning, producing, enjoying, and evaluating. Consideration of special needs of others is constantly in the thinking of all, and the worth of each child is cultivated. The class as a part of the school and the school as part of the community are accepted as a matter of course. From such natural expectancies it is likely that each child will come to think of my class, my school, my community, my world, and thus to develop growing responsibilities toward all.

Philosophical and psychological theory support this kind of educational program as the realistic way to develop commitment to democratic ideals. The weight of evidence shows that most pupils achieve well in such learning situations, and that gifted children in particular tend to respond to them with ease, enthusiasm, and success. As one teacher exclaimed, "It's a natural for them!" The rival ideology and techniques of modern communism—authoritarianism and the crystallizing of prejudiced emotional attitudes—are the utter antithesis of both our beliefs and our practices in well conceived education for democracy. Those who cry, "Wolf!" though they have reason for alarm, are misled in their demands for another kind of action to save the beloved object of the dreams of us all. Not by might nor by magic can the ideal of enduring democratic peace be attained.

Here is the underachievement that hurts America—blindness to see or unwillingness to accept the simply stated truth that *democratic living must be learned, and to act energetically upon that truth.* This, of course, is a complicated lesson to learn, requiring much homework. Parents must share in this homework from babyhood days of their children, and the community similarly must vigorously support these learnings when children are pupils and thereafter as long as they, as adults, live. All must partici- pate in arranging, enjoying, and treasuring experiences that elucidate the nature, high purposes, and everyday ways of living together in broadening meaningfulness of common human endeavors.

Who are the underachievers in these fundamental respects? Some—or many (?)—of our most gifted, sad to admit. But also all teachers and citizens who put other things first in place of liberty, equality, and fraternity, trusting foolishly that something other, perchance, will make us and our fast-shrinking globe safe for democracy.

42. The Gifted Underachiever *

C. C. TRILLINGHAM, *County Superintendent of Schools,* AND

MARCELLA R. BONSALL, *Consultant, Division of Research and Guidance Programs for the Gifted*

OF ALL THE children with problems, none concerns the schools more than the gifted underachiever. Here is unfulfilled potential. Here, in a time when there is greatest need for every person to do as well as he is able, are valuable human resources being indifferently developed.

For the most part, the situation is not dramatized by actual failure on the part of gifted students. Rather they drift along, content to do average work, accepting their own mediocre performance as suited to their capabil- ities. The comment is often made that most gifted are underachievers to some extent, and it has been estimated that 15 to 25 per cent of the gifted in most schools are performing at a level significantly lower than their place- ment on the aptitude scale would indicate.[1] John Gowan reports that in one California high school where 7 per cent of the students had IQ's of 130 or above, 42 per cent of these supposedly gifted youngsters were under-

* From *Four Aspects of Educating More Capable Learners,* Los Angeles County Superintendent of Schools Office, 1960, pp. 3–4. Reprinted with permission.
[1] NEA, *Identification and Education of the Academically Talented Student* (Wash- ington, D. C.: The Association, 1958).

achievers.[2] He goes on to comment that "where the percentage (of underachievement) runs much higher than 15 per cent, there may be problems of morale, antisocial trends, or other factors in the school that should receive special attention."

Of course, discussions of the underachiever are based on the assumption that school grades are an accurate measure of his performance. Under numerous circumstances, however, it has been shown that the underachiever has learned more than his classroom grades indicate and attains higher scores on standardized achievement tests than he receives from his teachers. But when he obtains mediocre grades year after year in various subjects from many different teachers, it is clear that some serious problem is limiting his performance—or, at least, his ability to communicate and work comfortably with others.

In fact, as underachievers are studied, it becomes obvious that they are youngsters with a varied assortment of problems, so that the causes for underachievement differ greatly from one individual to another. A look at some of these major causes and at the behavior of pupils handicapped by them is in order.

Underachievers with Personal Problems

In 1957, freshman underachievers at Chico State College were studied in some detail.[3] Students were chosen whose scores had been in the top 25 per cent on the college entrance examinations but whose grade points were below the mean of the freshman class as a whole at the end of the first semester. Any who were not of normal college entering age or who had previously attempted college work were excluded. The group was matched with a control group consisting of freshmen whose performance matched their potential in that both the entrance examination and their class grades indicated they were in the top 25 per cent, and the two groups were compared with the following results:

1. The achievers ranged from 17 years, six months in age to 19 years, seven months; the underachievers ranged from 18 years, three months to 19 years, seven months.
2. The achievers brought 17.72 recommended units from high school, while underachievers brought 14.75 units.
3. On standardized achievement tests covering subjects in which they had

[2] John Gowan, "Dynamics of the Underachievement of Gifted Students," *Exceptional Children*, XXIV, No. 3 (November, 1957), 98–101.

[3] Merville C. Shaw and Donald L. Brown, "Scholastic Underachievement of Bright College Students," *Personnel and Guidance Journal*, XXXVI (November, 1957), 195–99.

been enrolled that semester, the two groups did not show significant differences.

4. So far as courses carried during the freshman year were concerned, three-fourths of the achievers were carrying more than a normal load, while less than half of the underachievers carried more than the usual number of units. Moreover, there were twice as many underachievers carrying a less than average load as there were achievers.

5. Underachievers tended to be more critical of people and to feel that they had been shortchanged on the good things of life when they were living with their parents.

6. Achievers came from larger population centers than underachievers, and their parents had had more education.

Conclusions reached as a result of the research were:

1. The underachievement of this group was "related to the basic personality matrix and was not a surface phenomenon."

2. In terms of actual learning, these students were achieving, even though class grades were low.

3. Lack of achievement may be related to personality characteristics —hostility, masochistic tendencies, and the like.

4. Underachievement is closely related to the family and the social environment.

5. Possibly students in smaller communities have a different value system from that of students in larger areas, a difference in values that affects the goals, purposes, and self-image of the high-ability individual.

Since the Chico State study bears out frequent reports that underachievement relates to certain personality characteristics, to problems in the family, and to socioeconomic factors, the question quickly arises, "What can be done to help these students with problems of this sort?"

Garden Junior High School in Coatesville, Pennsylvania studied the effects of individual counseling on underachievers in the eighth grade.[4] Forty students who were underachieving more than 13.48 months were matched with a control group of students whose achievement equaled their potential. Each underachiever was given three interviews. In the first, he looked at his record and indicated whether he would like to improve it. In the second, he recorded much personal data and learned about the discussion that was to take place in the third interview so that he might think about it in advance. During this third interview he was to give his own opinion concerning causes for his underachievement and suggest a

[4] S. Reed Calhoun, "The Effect of Counseling on a Group of Underachievers," *School Review*, LXIV (October, 1956), 312-15.

plan for improving his record. Counseling was nonprescriptive, and counselors felt that pupils' assessments of their difficulties and their plans for action were pretty good. It was found, however, that teachers had to take the initiative in getting these underachievers to put their plans for improvement into operation.

Outcomes of this junior high school experiment were interesting:

1. On standarized achievement tests, the forty underachievers had made no progress beyond what might be expected within the semester's span.
2. School marks went up, however.
3. Teacher ratings of the forty pupils also went up so far as *interest* and *industry* were concerned.
4. Student concepts of their own potential, as revealed in interviews, were extremely vague.
5. Goals also were vague, and parents tended to agree with their children as to the degree of satisfaction or dissatisfaction they felt concerning the mediocre level of achievement.

In 1956, with the help of the Horace Mann-Lincoln Institute of School Experimentation, Evanston Township High School conducted a survey of student attitudes toward self and the school.[5] The information obtained was divided into four areas:

(1) *personal* characteristics in which were included such items as "appearance" and "sense of humor," (2) *self-reliance,* which referred to "making decisions" and "carrying out responsibility," (3) *special talents,* which included such items as social or athletic or artistic ability, (4) *intellectual qualities,* which included "solving problems" and "thinking clearly."

The next steps consisted of analyzing responses in terms of four groups (1) students of high ability and high achievement, (2) underachieving students of high ability, (3) high-achieving students of average ability (overachievers), (4) low-achieving students of low ability.

In this survey, underachievers of high ability perceived themselves in much the same way as the high achievers did in two categories: *personal characteristics* and *special talents.* But in *intellectual qualities* and *self-reliance* they appraised themselves as less able. They were less satisfied with their school situation than were either the high achievers or a random sampling of the total school population, and they desired more opportunities for participation in school and community organizations—in which

[5] Jean Fair, "A Comprehensive High School Studies Learning," *Educational Leadership,* XVI, No. 6 (March, 1959), 351–54.

they had smaller roles than the high achievers. They saw their parents as less than satisfied with their accomplishments and as sources of pressure toward better achievement. In one way or another, these were youngsters at odds with their world.

With these underachievers, various procedures were tried:

1. Placing them in honors classes where they were surrounded by high achievers.
2. Assigning them to friendly teachers who would take an interest in them as persons without exerting pressure to achieve, and who would stress flexible learning situations.
3. Asking the teacher to be impersonal, to exert pressure toward achievement and to maintain a quite structured curriculum.
4. Asking the teacher to be friendly but to exert pressure and to maintain a structured situation.

Since none of these situations brought greater achievement or better self-concepts, some different approach seemed to be in order.

Therefore, several series of six weeks' sessions of group therapy were set up under the label of discussion groups, and almost all of these underachievers joined the groups though they were counseled that their enrollment was voluntary. Their parents also had two discussion sessions of their own. Exploration of emotional problems and clarification of self-concepts have had major emphasis. Though it is too soon to analyze results, the procedure seems to have considerable promise.

. . . .

43. The Underachieving Gifted Child: A Problem for Everyone *

J. C. GOWAN, *Assistant Professor of Education, Los Angeles State College*

O NE OF THE greatest social wastes in our culture is that presented by the gifted child or young person who either can not or will not work up to his ability. Moreover, this situation often leads to undesirable social or

* From *Exceptional Children*, April, 1955, pp. 247–49, 270. Reprinted with permission.

personal behavior as an outward indication of the power within that is seeking some outlet. Counseling and rehabilitating these young people presents a challenging and important problem for teachers and personnel workers.

Definitions and Population

The present study uses *gifted child* to mean a youngster two or more standard deviations from the mean in general intelligence, within approximately the top 2 per cent of the population, equivalent to an intelligence quotient above 129 on the Stanford Binet. Recognizing that practically all gifted children are underachievers to some extent, we define *underachievement* in general as performance that places the individual 30 percentiles or more below his ability standing in the same group. Applying this concept to gifted children, we shall call them *underachievers* when they fall in the middle third in scholastic rank, and *severe underachievers* when they fall in the lowest third.

Some of the best work in surveying the problems of gifted underachievers has been done by teachers, counselors, supervisors, and principals in the field. All of the research referred to in this article presents unpublished projects undertaken by experienced school personnel in the writer's classes as listed in the bibliography that follows.

First, let us see what percentage of gifted children are underachievers as represented by the previous definitions. Alter (1) found that in a high socioeconomic area, one suburban high school enrolling 1,162 students had 74 or 7 per cent of students with intelligence quotients of 130 or more on the California Test of Mental Maturity. Among the 45 of these who were in senior high school, 19 (or 42 per cent) were underachievers, and 3 (or 6 per cent) were severe underachievers. In similar research in an independent boarding school enrolling 485 boys of whom 57 (or 12 per cent) showed 130 IQ or above on the Terman-McNemar, the writer found that only 5 of the 57 (or 9 per cent) were underachievers and none to be severe underachievers. This lower number of underachievers probably reflects greater 24-hour control as well as differential attrition factors. Wilbar (5) discovered that in a representative suburban high school, 31 (or 9 per cent) of the students had intelligence quotients of over 130 on the California Test of Mental Maturity, and of these 5 (or 16 per cent) were underachievers and 1 (or 3 per cent) was a severe underachiever.

It seems evident that, while the percentage of underachievers and severe underachievers is a function of the program of the school, its location, the control it has over its students, and student interests, there are in all cases significant numbers of underachievers among the highly gifted. These students merit special attention.

Studies of Underachievers

Robert (4) found that of 587 cases of maladjusted youngsters handled by a clinic in a large metropolitan area, 38 (or 6.5 per cent) had intelligence quotients of 130 or above on the Stanford-Binet almost evenly divided between boys and girls. The majority of these children liked school and their problems centered around the home situation. Those who were school problems stated their reasons as follows:

Not interested.

Didn't like the teacher.

Work was too easy.

Didn't have any friends and couldn't make any.

Liked to stay home with mother. (4:4)

Only one child was proud of her school record, and only one had been accelerated. All indicated that they could do better work if they tried.

The major disturbances characteristic of the group (some children, of course, had more than one) were noted in clinic records as follows:

27 felt insecure.

17 had poor social adjustment.

15 had enuresis.

14 were intolerant of parental authority.

13 were fearful.

7 were jealous.

9 had no identification with parents.

6 were poor sleepers.

5 were nail biters.

5 were poor eaters.

9 had miscellaneous behavior disturbances.

(4:5)

The basic causes for the children's behavior as diagnosed by the clinic staff were:

1. Disagreement between the parents, and of the parents with their parents, over methods of rearing the child.

2. Transference of problems of parents to the child.

3. Overanxiety or overprotectiveness on the part of parent.

4. Fears of parents regarding child's health or safety.

5. Divorces or separations of parents.

6. Parents' failure to prepare child for the birth of a new baby.

Landstrom and Natvig (3) conducted a provocative survey of four groups of 25 students each in a metropolitan senior high school. All were scored on the California Test of Mental Maturity. Group I consisted of gifted students who were high achievers with IQ's ranging from 125 to 150 with a median of 131. Group II consisted of gifted students who were underachievers ranging similarly from 125 to 150 in IQ with a median of 130. Group III consisted of overachieving students who were not gifted, whose school marks matched those for Group I but whose IQ's ranged from 86 to 112 with a median at 103. General biographical data including material concerning home relationships were then secured from each individual.

TABLE 1

HOME BACKGROUND AND EXTRACURRICULAR ACTIVITIES OF HIGH SCHOOL
STUDENTS BY CATEGORIES OF ABILITY AND ACHIEVEMENT

	I Gifted Achievers	II Gifted Non-achievers	III Over-achievers	IV Average Controls
Number in group	25	25	25	25
Scholarship grades	A	C	A	C
Median IQ	131	130	107	103
Number of boys	12	19*	3‡	6
Number of parents deceased	1	3	5	0
Father in professions	11	8	5	5
Mother a housewife	12	13	17	20
Parents divorced	2	3	4	6
Family attends church	14	6*	15	10
Foreign language in home	11	12	6	8
Favorite subject, Mathematics	13	7*	1‡	0
High school major is Mathematics	16	15	4‡	1
Skipped grades	15	10	4	4
Hours per week homework	8.4†	5.5	11.0	6.9
Number with time for other work	21	11*	16	14
Private lessons, training	20	12*	16	14
Total number of awards	50†	20	42	20
Activities or offices	134†	65	145	50
Number with 100 books or more	15	6*	6	7
Part-time job	13	7	9	15
Vocational choice, profession	25	21	13‡	5
Preference for working with people	20	16	18	21
Preference for working near family	19	10*	11	11

The minimal difference between columns to make the activity discriminate at the 5 per cent level is seven.

* Indicates a difference between columns I and II significant at the 5 per cent level.

† Means the response is in uits as given, but the significance of the difference was not computed.

‡ Indicates a difference between both columns I and II and column III at the 5 per cent level.

Table I indicated that the gifted achievers and underachievers in this study differed significantly (at the 5 per cent level of confidence or better) in that the underachievers were predominantly boys, had parents who took little part in church activities, had fewer books in their homes, had less often received private lessons, and expressed a desire in choosing a vocation for working away from the parental family. In general, the pattern that emerges is one of indifference and rejection on the part of the parent, or at least of behavior that is significantly more often interpreted in this manner by the underachiever. In addition, it is interesting to note that while the underachiever does less studying, he also has less time for other activities. Clearly, one of his problems is handling his time. He seems to lack ability to handle himself well in social interaction and to make easy adjustments to the societal structure.

In an earlier study (2) the writer found that when a secondary school population of 485 boys was analyzed for underachievement and overachievement as previously defined, 16 per cent of the *total* group were underachievers and 11 per cent were overachievers. The overachievers asserted much more leadership than did the underachievers. The underachievers were significantly less sociable as measured by the sociability scale of the Bernreuter. The conclusion was that the genesis of underachievement lay in self-sufficiency, and that, in general, underachievement in academic work and underachievement in leadership tended to appear together and to be connected with high unsociability ratings.

Research Findings

Summing up the experience of these and other researchers, it may be said that counseling gifted underachievers offers a number of problems:

1. The gifted underachiever tends to be *self-sufficient* and unsociable. He is, therefore, harder to reach and harder to interest in social activities. He learns less from exposure to the normal socializing effects of his peers because he has less contact with them.

2. The gifted underachiever has identified less with his parents, who themselves seem to be less active than parents of overachievers and less supporting of him and of his increased needs.

3. Because the gifted underachiever is less sociable, and because most teachers are overachievers, he tends to find fewer surrogate parental models among his teachers. This added lack of identification with an adult model makes his behavior still more difficult to influence.

4. The gifted underachiever seems to have fewer salable skills, either

to offer for part-time jobs, to bolster his economic situation, or to gain eligibility for college scholarship.

Employment is limited because he participates less and hence is less well-adjusted; college is lost because of his poor scholastic showing. As a result it is harder for him to become independent of an unsatisfactory family situation, harder for him to gain a sense of worth and participation through his job, and harder for him to keep going in college. The combination tends to push him out of school into an economic market where he has only marginal skills and into situations where he derives little if any job satisfaction.

Suggestions for Counselors

The following suggestions are offered for working with gifted under-achievers.

1. Make a survey of the percentage of underachievers in your school. If it runs much higher than 15 per cent, there may be problems of morale, antisocial trends, or other factors in the school that should receive special attention.

2. Since gifted underachievers are usually boys by a ratio of two to one, make an effort to assign counselors who are most capable of reaching them; a male counselor may often be more effective than a woman with such boys.

3. Give attention to building up the gifted underachiever in the area where he has a real chance of outstanding success, whether this is athletics, music, a hobby, or an academic course. The real enduring interest of some strong adult model figure with whom the young person can easily relate should be secured.

4. Give attention to the anxieties that plague boys at this period. These stresses may include economic dependence on a hostile home figure, ignorance about sex, worry about the draft, concern with how a mediocre record can be brought up to college standards, anxiety over the rejecting attitudes of a fussy stick-to-the-rules type of teacher, and many others. If the manifold social roles that the adolescent male is called upon to play in our culture can be gradually and easily assumed, much anxiety and frustration can be prevented. Above all, the boy should sense that the counselor *has time for him*. He should be encouraged to go on with college plans.

5. Try to find membership roles for the gifted underachiever in clubs, activities, and student leadership. He should be engaged in responsibilities that will enlarge his social ability as much as possible.

6. Because this type of young person feels insecure and is likely to lack a real peer group, attempt group therapy with a number of gifted under-achievers if at all feasible. This may at least lead to confidences and possibly friendships among these people, leading ultimately to improved social adjustment. It may also help to establish stronger worthwhile personal attitudes.

Summary

This article has attempted to bring together some recent unpublished research in the special problems of the gifted underachiever. Because of the nature of the needs of this type of young person, the material has been organized around a counseling situation; and suggestions for such counseling that have been indicated by experience are listed. It would seem that no other group in high school is potentially capable of making greater personal and social gains than this one as a response to wise and sympathetic guidance.

References

1. ALTER, H. M. "A Study of High School Students with Scores of 130 and Above on the California Test of Mental Maturity." Unpublished paper, 1953.
2. GOWAN, J. C. "The Analysis of Leadership in a Military School." Unpublished Ed. D. dissertation; Los Angeles: University of California, 1952.
3. LANDSTROM, F. M., and NATVIG, A. M. "Biographical Study of Gifted Achievers and Non-Achievers Compared with Over-Achievers and Central Groups." Unpublished paper, 1954.
4. ROBERT, LUCILLE. "Findings from Clinical Reports on the Behavior Problems of Gifted Children." Unpublished paper, 1952.
5. WILBAR, MILDRED. "High School Evaluation Study of the Program for Gifted Students." Unpublished paper, 1954.

44. Motivating the Gifted Underachiever *

WILLARD ABRAHAM, *Coordinator, Special Education, Arizona State University*

THE underachievement of many gifted children is serious. Working with it is neither easy nor inexpensive. It is a detailed, difficult, costly process, but well worth the effort. The choice is a relatively simple one to express. Do it, and help meet society's major ills with the skilled personnel capable of working toward those goals; or ignore it, and delay solution of our medical, social, and other problems, lose the major contributions of potentially qualified personnel to their nation and community, and condone the frustrations of many who for their entire lives operate on a plane below their own capabilities.

The symptoms of poor study habits, the pattern of underachievement, the greater frequency of boys than girls in this category, the overlapping reasons—such as broken and disturbed homes, poor physical health, family mobility, parental rejection, immaturity and others—all these lead to a framework for listing some recommendations and ideas to help solve the problems of lack of motivation or underachievement. The seven that follow dig deeply into the issue, and there are, of course, others.

The Place of Inspiration

The child who is bright and fast, but moving at a slow pace academically, needs outside interest, enthusiasm, and support. Though some may consider this point to be naïve or unrealistic, it must be stated and recognized for its real worth: The key to unlock a drive toward an achievement commensurate with one's abilities may come from the inspiration provided by some adult.

This one-to-one relationship, whether it comes from a teacher, guidance person, parent, school administrator, neighbor, or sibling, may provide the one bit of stimulation that had been missing. It may be the bit needed to

* Reprinted from the April, 1962, issue of *Education*, pp. 468–71. Copyright 1962 by The Bobbs-Merrill Co., Inc., Indianapolis, Ind.

help the child realize he is important or smart or capable. Such inspiration may be expensive (if provided by a professional person working with many young people), but the American dream of educating all children to their capacities is costly as well as worthy. Few thoughtful people could conclude otherwise.

Need for Definiteness

Terminology in the field of education is frequently rather vague, indecisive, and indirect. Too often phrases such as "taking the child where he is," "individual differences," "educating all children to their capacities," and "the whole child" have been used without the specificity needed for their full understanding and implementation.

In some areas of education, such lack of definiteness may not matter. But in the area of exceptional children, where identification, teaching techniques, educational materials, and class and school organization are almost forced to become detailed and specific, such indefinite approaches are not acceptable. A realistic appraisal that recognizes where the gifted "slow learner" is in his personal and academic development may help him to reach the goals of which he is capable. The teacher and counselor involved in the process may thus be able to motivate him on the basis of their factual knowledge about him.

Time for an Earthy Approach

What encourages us to battle the problems of overweight, a faulty golf game, making ends meet financially, or playing bridge better than the neighbors with whom we've been competing for years? The stimulant varies from one problem to another, and from one individual to another.

Similarly, although the sheer enjoyment of reading, solving problems, or performing scientific experiments may motivate some bright children to perform to their capacities, a more "basic" (and some persons will insist, a less desirable) approach may be successful with others. The individual teacher must decide whether the end is worth the means employed. Here are several examples:

1. *Earnings.*   Figures have been used many times that indicate that the lifetime earnings of the average college graduate is $100,000 or more in excess of the average high school graduate.
2. *Grades.*   It is not enough to place bright youngsters in "honors" or other special class settings and hope that such placement will be sufficient motivation for all of them. To expect an "A" or its equivalent in a special

class to mean the same thing as an "A" in a regular class assumes that grades have lost the meaning that has unfortunately been so strongly attached to them for many years.

Successful methods have been used in numerous school systems to weight grades so that on the transcript a heavier credit is recognized for similar grades obtained in special classes or courses. Another approach has been to assure the student of a top grade as long as he performs adequately in the enriched setting. A third is to footnote the type of class on transcripts so that colleges and universities to which they are sent can recognize the distinction.

3. *Guidance in terms of change.* When it comes to vocations of the present and future, the status quo is bound to be wrong. Although the U. S. Bureau of Labor Statistics and other public, professional, and private sources can be helpful, no one can be sure what tomorrow will bring in occupational changes, despite the existence of trends expertly analyzed.

For this point to take on real meaning, all that we need to ask is: How much did we know twenty or twenty-five years ago about the tremendous recent changes and demands of science, engineering, and even the full field of teaching? We cannot know with certainty now which fields will be in short supply that far in advance. Neither can we know, on the basis of recent experiences, what new fields will exist of which we at present are not even aware. One of the world's oldest religions has as one of its statements the admonition to "limit not thy children to thine own ideas. They are born in a different time."

The Factor of Freedom

Our attitudes toward bright children, based on freedom, acceptance, and understanding, are a matter of degree and their relationship to the individual child and his problems. Too often in recent years, however, many of us have fallen into a trap of loading burdens on children in direct proportion to their ability to learn. This approach implies a double standard for children and adults—for children a longer schoolday and school year, less television, and more homework, and for adults a shorter workday and workyear, as much television as they desire, and more freedom for leisure activities.

As a result of these inconsistencies, children sometimes develop various doubts and fears. They wonder about the "fairness" of the double standard they see applied. They both fear and anticipate adulthood. And they have serious doubts about the purposefulness of the educational activities to which they are exposed.

A recent educational film on gifted children mistakenly concludes that a ten-year-old child with an IQ of 130 "thinks and acts" like a thirteen-year-old. It concludes further that a ten-year-old with an IQ of 170 or 180 "thinks and acts" like a seventeen- or eighteen-year-old, and that a ten-year-old with an IQ of 200 "thinks and acts" like a twenty-year-old! Interpretations such as this make it difficult for a child who is bright to enjoy the one childhood to which he is entitled. The learning process is slowed for him because expectations and pressures are all wrong. If there is any appropriate time for having fun, being different, exercising creativity, and experimenting within "reasonable limits" with knowledge and life, it is childhood. To treat intellect too seriously may stifle or discourage its normal growth.

A Fallacy

Sometimes we assume that slowness exists because of lack of enthusiasm for higher education. To try to motivate bright young people toward more education may be totally fallacious. The goals may be entirely out of line with their real aims.

For example, we err, if we feel that the brightest pupils must obtain top academic degrees. Such academic accomplishments may be unnecessary for the most capable and creative, especially in engineering and business. A goal one or two steps below the top may be the most effective background for competent performance in those fields.

Those who need high degrees may be using them as security and as a step toward advancement. The more creative individuals feel no need for them because they recognize that their own abilities, combined with a more limited formal education, will help them reach vocational goals with greater ease and satisfaction. Creative individuals may appear to be slow if judged by standardized intelligence tests, but it may be that the tests are wrong because they fail to measure some of the less discernible factors of intelligence.

Deprivation and Motivation

Deprivation may be one of the most unusual and effective techniques for motivating the gifted "slow learner." This idea may have little attraction in a time when it is assumed that all children profit from an environment based on enrichment and success at every turn.

But the question arises, do *all* children profit from such an environment? Recently a brainstorming session of professional psychologists and educators discussed the education of gifted children. "If we could have the most ideal circumstances, materials, and teaching," they asked themselves, "what would we want for bright children?"

They compiled a list that was lengthy, expensive, and ideal. Then they began to wonder. Would such an environment oppress and suffocate the children's talents? How would Van Gogh and others like him have performed in such an environment? Is there not a possibility that their contributions would have been limited by the abundance they found around them?

A final answer is still to be found. But certainly deprivation has spurred the creation of many a masterpiece.

Early Identification

We have saved till the last one of the most important factors related to the motivation of gifted "slow learners," early identification. Slow learners must be discovered early before mediocre learning habits have become established beyond correction. The secondary school should not wait for slow learners to appear on their own doorsteps, but should cooperate closely with the elementary schools in studying records and planning appropriate programs and materials.

A child's brightness appears early through vocabulary, performance, and other signs. To ignore these signs is to encourage slovenly academic habits and a slower rate of progress than the child's intelligence warrants. It is easier to note and capitalize on a child's brightness when he is young than it is to correct problems of slow learning after he has had several years of school.

Conclusion

We have discussed seven approaches to the motivation of the gifted underachiever or slow learner. More than anything else, our discussion points up the need for an individualized approach. As the famous comedian Danny Kaye has said, "You can't bring health and happiness to a million children by signing a paper or waving a wand. It has to be done child by child."

To the "health and happiness" of bright children we might also add "achievement of their unfulfilled capacities."

45. Underachievement of Gifted Students *

CHARLES E. BISH, *Director, NEA Project on the Academically Talented Student*

Underachievement of Gifted Students

If gifted students were fully motivated, underachievement would largely disappear. Most manifestations of underachievement are directly related to inadequate motivation.

THE DESIRE NOT TO BE CONSPICUOUS

The school's guidance efforts must reinforce those of teachers and administrators in breaking down resistance to excelling obviously, and in counteracting the negative attitude of peers and community toward academic ability and achievement.

POOR WORK HABITS

Sometimes a child who was poorly motivated or bored because of lack of challenge early in his school career suddenly conceives an interest in scholastic achievement and a desire to excel. However, if his earlier experience has left him with poor work habits, he may be unable to work efficiently and to achieve to capacity.

A teacher who becomes aware that poor work habits are impeding achievement may be able to help improve them. If guidance personnel are made aware of the obstacle, they may be able to contribute materially to its removal. When a child with clearly identified ability plus adequate motivation is achieving at less than capacity, poor work habits should be suspected. Here again, teaching and guidance go hand in hand.

LAZINESS

Gifted children who are not adequately challenged quickly learn that they can accomplish the work with much less effort than the average stu-

* From *Administration Procedures and School Practices for the Academically Talented Student in the Secondary School* (Washington, D.C.: National Education Association), pp. 104–8. Reprinted with permission.

dent. This leaves them with time to pursue their own interests, daydream, or merely loaf. It also leaves them with habits of laziness that in later school years may make them unwilling to do the extra work necessary for significant achievement.

Laziness also often stems from the conviction that it is sufficient merely to pass—certainly enough to be first in the class. The student fails to see the challenge of his school work in terms of the best of which he is capable.

The guidance department, then, should work with the teachers to inspire the able student to measure his achievement against his own abilities, and not merely against the achievement of his classmates. When this lesson is learned, laziness will be conquered. The later the lesson comes, however, the more difficult it will be. An effective program will therefore recognize laziness early and work to replace it with a drive toward maximum achievement.

PREOCCUPATION WITH GRADES

Some students are so obsessed with the importance of grades that they try to avoid courses that they feel may jeopardize their record. This preoccupation is an outgrowth of the emphasis that some schools and many parents place upon grades. In an extremely competitive atmosphere, where a grade is made to seem the ultimate goal of a course, the student may easily come to regard it as all-important, not necessarily understanding that the real issue is not whether he receives an "A," but whether his performance is at the level of his abilities. This problem is especially acute when grading is done "on a curve," since it may be relatively easy for a gifted student to excel in comparison with the other students, even when not working to capacity. It is further complicated if the parents are unduly grade conscious.

This preoccupation has been reflected in schools that offer honors courses for exceptionally able students. Some who clearly qualify are sometimes unwilling to enroll in the courses for fear of failing to get an "A" in the face of the stronger competition. This problem will largely be solved by not grading "on the curve," and by transfer of underachievers to classes demanding less creativity, problem solving, and critical thinking. Effective guidance by both teachers and specialists can help overcome a preoccupation with what should be a secondary aspect of the educational program.

EMOTIONAL PROBLEMS

Many underachievers fail to realize their potential because of emotional problems that prevent them from devoting their full attention and energies to their education. These are not always easy to identify. Their existence should be suspected in any case of underachievment; an alert and sensitive teacher can sometimes isolate the underlying problem.

When the problem area has been identified, guidance personnel can try to help resolve the difficulty. This may frequently involve work with the parents.

Nason [1] studied achievement in superior pupils by comparisons between those with low achievement and those with high achievement. He identified a pattern of circumstances seemingly related to high achievement and made up of the following factors: future educational plans of the pupils, level of academic expectation of parent for pupil, future vocational plans (particularly of boys), parental attitude toward future vocational plans of the pupil, personal adjustment scores of the pupil, and indication by the pupil of the presence of inspiration or a source of inspiration or encouragement toward success. He found that in cases of low achievement one or more elements of the pattern were missing.

He concluded further that low achievement seems to be associated rather with a lack of positive influences than with the presence of negative ones; pupils with high achievement were sometimes found to face negative influences as strong as those faced by low achievers.

He also observed that superior pupils with high achievement tended to have more satisfactory status with their peers than did those with low achievement.

Among other things, Nason makes the following recommendations bearing upon guidance:

1. That the pattern of circumstances including personal adjustment, social adjustment, and future academic and vocational plans be used as a frame of reference in the counseling and guidance of high-school pupils of superior ability.
2. That special provisions for superior pupils be based upon individual needs as determined by an analysis of the patterns of circumstances associated with them.
3. That records maintained for superior pupils include a record of the pupil's progress toward personal adjustment, social adjustment, future academic plans, and vocational plans, and his concepts of parental attitudes toward his plans for the future.
4. That superior pupils be counseled regarding future vocational plans as early as possible.
5. That counselors guide teachers involved in programs for superior pupils on the special provisions most appropriate in each individual case.

[1] Leslie J. Nason, *Academic Achievement of Gifted High School Students* (Los Angeles: University of Southern California Press, 1958), p. 92.

6. That counselors give more attention to the self-concepts of superior pupils and to the pupil's own ideas as to his environment and future.

7. The consideration be given to counseling and guidance which will aid poorly adjusted pupils to achieve adequate personal and social adjustment. Satisfactory academic achievement at the high-school level should not be considered sufficient when poor personal or social adjustment indicates a possible lack of success at a later date.

Cutts and Moseley [2] have advanced three generalizations concerning achievement. First, high achievers are more likely to have made a definite career choice, and thus are working toward something. Second, they are more likely to be accelerated by a year or two; this has two consequences —they feel they have a reputation to live up to, and they meet a more appropriate challenge. And third, they are more likely to have somewhat studious parents who set an example of intellectual activity.

Kurtz and Swenson [3] have also identified a number of factors common to underachievement in general. Among them they cite unfavorable home conditions with little exchange of affection. Children from such circumstances are not anxious to please their parents; the parents, in turn, do not have high expectations of them. Neither do their friends have high standards for school achievement or favorable attitudes toward school. In fact, some underachievers have no close friends at all.

Such an underachiever is less than happy in school. He is changeable, unstable, burdened with an inferiority complex. Frequently he has emotional conflicts. In general, he prefers to work with his hands rather than engage in so-called book learning; there is a general disinclination for academic activity.

A failure to seek "deferred goals" is also a characteristic of underachievers. Their educational and vocational aims are those that can be attained quickly.

[2] Norma E. Cutts and Nicholas Moseley, *Bright Children: A Guide for Parents* (New York: G. P. Putnam's Sons, 1953), p. 134.

[3] John J. Kurtz and Esther Swenson, "Factors Related to Overachievement and Underachievement in School," *Educating the Gifted,* ed. by Joseph L. French (New York: Henry Holt & Co., 1959), p. 402–11.

The inclusion of a chapter dealing with the creative individual is not done with the purpose of suggesting in any way that the creative thinking aspect is associated only with gifted students. Much evidence is appearing to indicate that creative learners need not be among the gifted students. We hope to indicate, however, that talented individuals have the capacity for creative thinking and should be sufficiently motivated to give full expression to their creative potential.

46. The Evaluation of Creativity *

MARCELLA R. BONSALL, *Consultant, Research and Guidance*

CREATIVITY has many meanings for many people. Some people place major emphasis on an original production or a unique end result— that which is visible, touchable, audible to others—something that can be judged for its beauty or ugliness, its usefulness or uselessness in terms of criteria that are predetermined. In other words, persons favoring this definition of creativity see a new product as that which must be acceptable to others and, quite frequently, they expect it to be repeatable. This definition often appears to fit and to be used to judge adult productions. The evaluation is in terms of a social criterion, and it is external. Lay people, in general, embrace this definition.

* From *Programs for the Gifted*, Los Angeles County Schools, Division of Research and Guidance. Reprinted with permission.

Educators and psychologists prefer to think of creativity not as a product alone, or an end result, but they see the process as including much more. To these persons, creativity is a process, a bringing into being, a discovery, an act. They affirm creativity as a personal process that is an involved, time-consuming, frequently uncomfortable period of an absorbing application of effort after which emerges an unpredictable but novel solution for the individual concerned. This idea is expanded further by Carl Rogers who states that the process does not spring from a mere accumulation of knowledge and technique. Rather, it is a result of stubbornness in the pursuit of an aim and it is accompanied by a wealth of associations that are logical and intuitive. It leads the individual into new areas of perceptions. Rogers is thus saying that there is not just one creative process but a variety of creative processes. Therefore, some authorities state it cannot be said, "This is a creative person." It should be said, "This is a creative act."

Rollo May succinctly summarized this point of view preferred by educators and psychologists when he wrote: "Creativity is encounter of the intensely conscious human being with his world." Evaluation here dictates the use of a psychological criterion, frequently used with children, in which the emphasis is placed on the novelty and satisfaction of the idea or the object to the individual who produced it. In this setting, the evaluation is internal.

Both the definitions of lay and professional people have at least one facet in common—that of newness. The first definition emphasizes the use of a social criterion, which is external, for evaluation of the new for society. Although this evaluation seldom includes the use of a psychological criterion, it need not be excluded. The second idea of creativity emphasizes the use of a psychological criterion, which is within the individual who produced it, for evaluation of the newness of an object or an idea. Here, too, a social criterion may be included (and often is) in a school situation where in a modified form it is used by educators when a student's work is evaluated in relation to the work of other students.

To evaluate the creativity of students, basic assumptions need to be stated—assumptions that are the results of logical thinking, exploratory investigations, and more recently, confirming investigations. Some of these assumptions are:

Abilities involved in being creative are universal and are manifested in some way and to some extent by almost everybody.

Creativity can and does operate at all age levels.

Some of the creative abilities can be identified and assessed.

Creative abilities can be fostered, developed, and trained.

There are very few, if any, established objective standards for evaluating the worth of creative productions. Until such standards of evaluation are available, it is possible for educators to establish a school climate and to formulate objectives that will contribute to the development of creativity. A partial list of guideposts that may prove useful for this project is offered here.

Unless a person is relatively free from serious problems of adjustment, his creative functioning is likely to be impaired.

Realization that intelligence tests per se do not measure creativity.

Realization that creativity applies to areas other than music and art.

Realization that emphasis is needed both on the identification of creative potential and the "how to" of developing this potential under different circumstances.

Identification of and recognition given to teachers who divert from the usual and are comfortable in the presence of learners who display creativity.

Realization that skills, information, and rich experiences are the texture —the "mulch"—the "stuff"—from which creativity develops.

Focus on the search for answers, the process of the search, rather than on right answers.

Dare children to be themselves through providing a classroom atmosphere free from premature and external evaluation of the creator and his product.

Willingness of teachers to keep "hands off," not to judge, and not to teach always with a large "T."

Thus, the certain criterion of the worth of a creative act or product at this point in human knowledge resides within the individual who himself was the creator. Yet there is much that the school can do to respect the essential assumptions underlying creative endeavor and to create a climate within which young people may increasingly experience truly creative experiences.

47. The Creative Individual: A New Portrait in Giftedness *

CALVIN W. TAYLOR, *Professor of Psychology, University of Utah*

A MAJOR problem facing educators is to speed up the application in education of research findings from pertinent fields. Basic research results with implications for education should be communicated so that these findings can be tested in the educational setting and incoporated if relevant and effective.[1] In this paper, I will attempt to transmit some of the research findings on creativity to date.

My research interests have been in the relatively unsolved area of seeking the creative more than in the traditional area of seeking the gifted. The word "gifted," as typically used, is closely tied to the current intelligence tests, but quite different tests are usually being used in a search for the creative. As I describe this approach to others, they usually expand their meaning of the word "gifted" to include the creative. Nonetheless, some points should be made by contrasting intelligence, as measured by the traditional type of IQ tests, with creative talent.

The traditional intelligence tests cover only a very few of the fifty or more dimensions or characteristics of the mind discovered to date. Consequently, there may be several types of intellectually gifted other than the IQ type, even though the IQ type may be closely tied to current academic activities and to the grades that measure success in the academic world.

Several Types of Gifted

In focusing on other areas of giftedness, one should be forewarned that there may be several different types of creativity. In addition, there are

* From *Educational Leadership,* October, 1960, pp. 7–12. Reprinted with permission.
[1] In a current cooperative research project with the U.S. Office of Education, we are searching for relevant research findings from psychology and other fields that have implications for education.

probably several other types of gifted, relatively separate from the IQ type and the creative types. Other types may be found in each of the areas of planning, communication, and evaluation or decision making activities. A similar paper could be written, at least tentatively, on each of these other types of gifted. Likewise, in certain of these areas, such as the communication abilities area, where we uncovered a sizable number of different dimensions in each subarea of reading, writing, speaking, and listening, there may also be several different types of giftedness.

In transmitting new research findings on the intellect, difficulties arise because forty or more new intellectual characteristics have been discovered that have been excluded from the so-called intelligence tests. The current tendency is to classify these new characteristics downward into a lesser category called "special abilities," even though they really parallel those that were earlier incorporated into the so-called intelligence tests. The human characteristics that psychologists have been able to measure first are not necessarily the only important characteristics. Some of the remaining characteristics that had been postponed for later measurement may often be extremely important characteristics. We had just not known any way in which to measure them earlier.

To me it is highly inconsistent to conceive of the mind as being represented by a single score or even by only a handful of scores or dimensions that are present in our current intelligence tests. The brain that underlies the mind is far, far too complex to hope that all of its intellectual activities can be represented by only a single score or by only a handful of dimensions. It is an insult to the brain and human mind to allow this oversimplified viewpoint to survive.

Emerging evidence from several sources suggests that many important high-level abilities are not only missing in our searches for talent but are also being largely ignored in the education and development of our youth. Let us be flexible and toy for a moment with our present situation. If a creativity index had been established first in our schools, we might now be putting forth the same type of arguments to make room to add an intelligence type of index if it had been largely ignored to date.

Results to date indicate that creative talent is not measured well by the use of IQ tests. In our three Utah conference reports on creativity there are several indications that creativity scores and IQ scores are, at most, only lowly related. The nature of traditional intelligence tests does not directly involve the ability to create new ideas or new things. The abilities needed in sensing problems, in being flexible, and in producing new and original ideas tend to be *unrelated* or to have only low relations with the types of tests entering into current measures of intelligence.

Perhaps one reason why our society does not give much moral and tangible support to education is that persons leave the academic world and find, to some degree at least, that intellectual characteristics in which they are highly trained are not called for in the world of work as much as they expected. Contrarily, other intellectual characteristics in which they have had little training may be crucial characteristics in their part of the world of work.

Some indirect evidence that key people in school systems are not necessarily seeking for or encouraging creativity is found in the report by Frank Jex at the 1959 Utah conference. A group of high school science teachers were tested with a "creativity" battery when they enrolled for a year of graduate study. Their creativity scores were correlated with their principals' or supervisors' ratings of their overall teaching ability, as judged during the previous year. The correlation was —.38. This result suggests that teachers with certain creativity characteristics may be looked upon with some disfavor in certain educational settings. A study is needed to determine whether those teachers develop creativity traits in their students more than other teachers do.

Utah Creativity Conferences

My remarks on creative characteristics will be based largely on research reported in the three (1955, 1957, and 1959) University of Utah research conferences on the Identification of Creative Scientific Talent. In the three conferences, 37 different nationally-selected participants presented a total of nearly 50 reports, covering various subareas such as criteria of creativity, predictors of creativity, education and training of creativity, and working environments that affect creativity. NSF supported these conferences.

The main research approach to date has been to study creativity in full bloom in adults with the hope of tracing these characteristics back to their earlier budding stage. Many leads are available from this approach that could be tried on children. An alternate approach, which may be at least equally promising, is to study creativity "in its more natural state" in children before it may be curtailed, distorted, and even blotted out by various features in our world.

Ghiselin suggests that the measure of the creativeness of a product of the mind should be *the extent to which it restructures our universe of understanding.* Lacklen indicates that the Space Agency judges the creativeness of the contributions of scientists by determining *the extent of the area of science that each contribution underlies,* so that the more basic a contribution, the wider its effects. In a study of creativity on the job, Sprecher was interested in both the novelty and the value of the ideas and other products produced by scientists. In our studies of scientists on the job, after obtaining judgments of products, judgments of processes, and overall ratings of creativity, we found at least five separate types of contributions that, to some degree, could be called creative.

In research on the identification of creative talent, a broad approach has been emphasized, somewhat in contrast to the identification of the so-called gifted by means of a single (IQ) score. A broad coverage of intellectual, motivational, biographical, sociometric, and other personality characteristics will now be presented to illustrate the nature of creative talent and of current attempts to identify it.

Intellectual Traits in Creativity

From the research results of many workers, Guilford has evolved and listed the following intellectual characteristics as most likely to be valid measures of creative talent: originality, redefinition, adaptive flexibility, spontaneous flexibility, fluency of associations, fluency of expressions, fluency of ideas, fluency of words, elaboration, and probably some evaluation factors.

Speaking more broadly, some components of memory, cognition, evaluation, and especially convergent production and divergent production are involved in creative work. The divergent production area, largely overlooked to date in psychological measurement, is probably the most important in creative talent since it includes production of ideas in quantity and in quality, originality, flexibility, sensitivities, and redefinition abilities. Pictorial fluency may be an example of a characteristic needed more in creative work in art than in science.

Ability to sense problems is another intellectual characteristic usually included in creativity. It may also lead to motivational features. The capacity to be puzzled may be a very important characteristic. A rejection of superficial explanations and an ability *to know when you don't know* may be important in making original contributions.

Our verbal revision test is at least analogous to the manipulation, restructuring, and reworking of ideas found both in the earlier and later stages of the creative process. It is probably also related to the ability and tendency to strive for more comprehensive answers or solutions or products, another feature found in studies of creativity. Unfortunately, too few occasions in our academic programs require such strivings for higher quality or for more original and workable products.

Two response-set factors, which we have found, may measure characteristics functioning in creativity. The first one is called *"broadly diffused attention."* This type of attention has often been a part of the description of the crucial moments preceding the insight stage of the creative process. The second response-set factor is described as a *"resistance to idea reduction."* The opposite pole of willingness to reduce ideas may be valuable in creating broad new generalizations.

Other tests or test ideas that may have validity include the abilities to form and test hunches (hypotheses), to foresee consequences, to infer causes, to evaluate revisions in a product, and to be able to toss one's ideas into the arena of ideas. Our finding of a verbal originality factor leads us to hope for an analogous measure of *nonverbal originality*. Another hunch, expressed by Shockley, is that we should test how many ideas each student can manipulate at one time.

In summary, there are many relatively new and separate intellectual components in creativity. I have a hunch that many of the components of curiosity and of motivation are also intellectual in nature.

Motivational and Personality Traits

In this motivation area the great need is for good measuring instruments that will demonstrate the widespread conviction that motivation is a strong component of creativity. From our communication abilities research, we feel that the ability to sense ambiguities, plus effective questioning ability, are a part of curiosity. Bloom has indicated that science students who truly become involved in research work and in the research role during graduate training, tend to become productive researchers afterwards. If the creative are to be found somewhere among the productive, then in science our problem will be reduced by finding those students who truly become involved in research problems during their academic careers. Analogous situations entailing student involvement could also be sought in nonscientific fields.

Other motivational characteristics suggested are intellectual persistence, liking to think, liking to manipulate and toy with ideas, need for recognition for achievement, need for variety, need for autonomy, preference for complex order and for challenges therein, tolerance of ambiguity, resistance to closing up and crystallizing things prematurely coupled with a strong need for ultimate closure, need for mastery of a problem, insatiability for intellectual ordering, and a need to improve upon currently accepted systems. High energy with vast output through disciplined work habits is usually found.

McClelland suggests that the creative person may be willing to take a calculated risk larger (though not unrealistically large) than others and that his judgment of the chance of success is actually greater than the average judgment from other persons. The creative individual presumably does not want to deal in a sheer gamble situation but rather to engage only where his own efforts may make a difference in the odds.

Younger persons with creative talent according to Getzels' findings, have a much greater interest in unconventional careers than do their fellow students. They sense that their views are not the predominant ones of what success in adult life is. They are also more willing to be non-conforming and to be in the small minority.

From personality evidence to date, creative persons are more devoted to autonomy, more self sufficient, more independent in judgment (contrary to group agreement, if needed, to be accurate), more open to the irrational in themselves, more stable, more capable of taking greater risks in the hope for greater gains, more feminine in interests and characteristics (especially in awareness of one's impulses), more dominant and self assertive, more complex as a person, more self accepting, more resourceful and adventurous, more radical (Bohemian), more controlling of their own behavior by self concept, and possibly more emotionally sensitive, and more introverted but bold.

Nearly every time that even a brief biographical inventory has been tried on creative scientists, it has been found to have promising validity in the initial sample studied. Our research team is currently studying samples of scientists locally, in the air force and in the Space Agency, with this biographical approach. This approach gets at work habits, attitudes, interests, values, family and academic history, and several personality characteristics.

Some Final Comments

Clues for spotting creative talent may be obtained by watching the reactions of others around a person. If some persons in a group appear excited, disturbed, or threatened, *perhaps* there is a creative person around whose ideas and work are being at least vaguely sensed as threatening the present scheme of things. Group behaviors that try to reduce this threat include a developing of *sanctions against* the person and an overorganizing and building of other controls into their world, as found by Torrance. On this point the creative persons may most appreciate the necessity of a few very good rules in an organization. Contrarily, they may be most sensitive to unnecessary organizational controls or other rules that are built in by administrators or other people. The creatives may be those who try to work their way out of such needless restrictions.

As one Utah conference participant reflected upon those *rare* persons whose work had truly reshaped the world, he observed that nearly all of these individuals had eventually done their work outside of an existing organization. They were neither supervisor nor supervised. Organizations that are effective either in transmitting or implementing ideas should not automatically be assumed to be the types of organizations best suited for creative work.

Another major concern in creativity is with restrictions, inhibitions, and deterrents within a person as contrasted with freedom within him. These restrictions, often self-imposed or built in through the influence of others, can thus reduce the freedom and potentialities of a person and may even block his efforts that would otherwise lead to creative performance.

Until shown otherwise, I believe that quite different psychological processes are involved when we learn existing knowledge and systems than when we produce new ideas, new knowledge, and new systems. Education may teach people to recite the past and repeat past performances more often than to prepare them to develop new things or even to be ready for new developments by others. Too often, strong fears rather than positive abilities emerge when opportunities arise to take a new step forward, to pioneer at the frontiers. The sheer amount of education is probably not a good basis for identifying those ready to take a new step.

We should identify and develop people who can learn the past without worshiping it, who can mentally toy with and manipulate man's knowledge and ideas and products of the past, who can use the past as a springboard for future developments, and who can find and use new leads to improve upon the past. In other words, maybe our task is to identify and develop more minds that are "tomorrow minds" than "yesterday minds."

References

1. TAYLOR, CALVIN W. (ed.). *The Identification of Creative Scientific Talent.* Essentially verbatim report of the 1955 University of Utah national research conference. Salt Lake City: University of Utah Press, 1956. 268 pp.

2. ———. *The Identification of Creative Scientific Talent.* Essentially verbatim report of the 1957 University of Utah national research conference. Salt Lake City: University of Utah Press, 1958. 255 pp.

3. ———. *The Identification of Creative Scientific Talent.* Essentially verbatim report of the 1959 University of Utah national research conference. Salt Lake City: University of Utah Press, 1959. 334 pp.

4. ———, SMITH, WILLIAM R., GHISELIN, BREWSTER, SHEETS, BOYD V., and COCHRAN, JOHN R. *Communication Abilities in Military Situations.* Technical Report WADC—TR-58-92. Wright-Patterson Air Force Base, Ohio: Pers. Lab., Wright Air Development Center, 1958.

48. Problems of Highly Creative Children *

E. PAUL TORRANCE,   *Director, Bureau of Educational Research, University of Minnesota*

I NESCAPABLY, the individual who thinks of a new idea is in the very beginning a minority of one. Even when matters of demonstrable fact are involved, as in the Asch experiments, there are very few people who can tolerate being a minority of one. Since creativity involves independence of mind, nonconformity to group pressures, or breaking out of the mold, it is inevitable that highly creative children experience some unusual problems of adjustment. Thus, the highly creative child must either repress his creativity or learn to cope with the tensions that arise from being frequently a minority of one. Repression of creative needs may lead to actual personality breakdown. Their expression frequently leads to loneliness, conflicts, and other problems of adjustment. Educators of gifted children need to understand both types of problems.

1. Sanctions against Divergency

In one of our studies, we have asked approximately 5,000 children in grades three through six to write imaginative stories concerning animals or persons with some divergent characteristic. These have given us many insights concerning the way children see the operation of their society's sanctions against being different. The following story by a sixth-grade girl illustrates many of these sanctions:

Far into the jungle of Africa lived a flying monkey named Pepper. Pepper was a well-educated monkey and very cute . . . Pepper was unusual too. He

* From *The Gifted Child Quarterly,* Summer, 1961, pp. 31–34. Reprinted with permission.

was not like all of the other flying monkeys. You see, Pepper didn't eat bananas like everybody else. He wanted to be different. He ate peppers!

No one ever went out of the jungle so Pepper, being different, decided to go to America! . . . When the people saw him, they began to laugh and then others began to scream. Then out of nowhere a man from a zoo came and took Pepper by surprise. . . .

"Now Pepper was sad. He didn't like the cage they put him in. He made a vow that if he ever got out he would never be different again and ten minutes later he saw some bent bars big enough to fly through. All of a sudden he flew out and in two days was back in the jungle. He kept his promise too. He was never different again. He was a good little flying monkey.

I suppose *he ate his bananas!*

About two-thirds of the stories about flying monkeys tell similar tales of conformity or of destruction. Some cultures, however, are more indulgent of divergency than others. Stories written by gifted children in special classes are far more hopeful in outlook than those of gifted children in regular classes. In about 70 per cent of the stories of pupils in classes for high achieving children, the flying monkey is in some way able to persist in his flying. The stories written by children in a small Oklahoma town composed of Indians, whites, and a few Negroes also reflect this tolerance of divergency. In 74 per cent of their stories, the flying monkey succeeds.

2. Creative Children May Not Be Well-Rounded

The highly creative child is likely to have lagged in some phase of his development. Many investigators in a variety of fields have been disappointed to find that outstanding individuals in the field under study are not well-rounded, "all-American" boys. Verbal abilities frequently will be below some of their other abilities. Perhaps the most inventive and imaginative child we have tested is a boy who has had unusual difficulty in learning to read, yet his store of information and his ability to use it imaginatively in solving problems and developing ideas is fantastic.

This problem is particularly acute at the fourth-grade level. In a number of cases, fourth graders identified by our tests as highly creative have been reevaluated by teachers. Teachers then discover that these children are far more knowledgeable and thoughtful than they had imagined. One examiner after testing orally a certain fourth-grade boy remarked: "This boy impresses me as the kind of individual who will become a top executive who can dictate to five secretaries at the same time without becoming confused." The boy's responses gave evidence of high inventive level, flexibility, and originality. This boy, however, has a serious reading disability and ranked near the bottom of his class on the written test of creative thinking.

Because verbal skills are highly valued in our society, tremendous pressures are placed on children to be "well-rounded" in this respect. The relentlessness of these pressures is symbolized in the following story by a sixth-grade girl:

Quack! Quack! They were after him again—the Ladies Duck Aid Society, with their hair up in pin curls and their screaming, fat ducklings swimming and holding onto their skirts. They never failed. Alas! It was getting too much for little Glob-Blob. Every day there would be quacking and screaming of ducklings while poor Glob-Blob would run as fast as he could to get away from the vicious ducks.

The reason for this was because poor Glob-Blob could not quack. So every day the Ladies Duck Aid Society would chase Glob-Blob, for they said it was for the good of the ducks, and it was not only right but they were doing a good turn.

It was lucky for Glob-Blob that the ducks were fat and flabby, for if they were limber, I will not mention what would happen. But one day, these lazy ducks did reduce, and when chasing Glob-Blob dealt him a good many hard blows. And the next day, poor Glob-Blob was at last doomed. The vicious quackers had come and the chase was on. Glob-Blob was failing. It is a shame that so noble a duck should be doomed, but "That's life," said Glob-Blob to himself as, slowly but surely, failing, he dropped to the ground. The quackers, very pleased with themselves, sat down for a chat.

But I shall always remember Glob-Blob and his death. So I shall let him finish his journey, where there will be no more quackers and chasers, and where at last, he may have passionless peace forever.

Many children must consider their counselors, teachers, and parents as "quackers and chasers" when we work so hard to make them become "better-rounded personalities." They might contribute far more to society and be far happier and more successful by capitalizing upon their unique strengths rather than spending fruitless energy trying hopelessly to compensate for some divergent characteristic or behavior. I would not, of course, deny that it is necessary for some of our highly creative youngsters to achieve basic skills necessary for success in their chosen areas of specialization.

3. Creative Children Prefer to Learn on Their Own

Many creative children prefer to learn on their own, and schools have been slow in providing such opportunities. Last year we conducted an exciting study in which we found that children would do a great deal of writing on their own, if properly motivated. In another it was found that gifted children in a split-shift school showed more growth in language development, science, and social studies than under a full-day schedule. Only in spelling was there significantly less growth among the split-shift children (seventh graders).

Since we have generally assumed that children do not learn on their own, we have seldom provided them with opportunities to do so. I have seen learning situations "accidentally" left "open" a sufficient number of times to have become quite excited about what would happen, if we should do so more frequently. The following story by an Oklahoma sixth grader, symbolizes this situation:

> Once there were some monkeys sitting in a group. They were all alike except three monkeys. They were very different because they could fly.
> One day some men from a park zoo were looking for some monkeys because theirs had died. They came upon the three that flew. So they took them in a cage. The cage didn't have a top to it. They were in the sun one day and the monkey said to the other, "I wish we could get out of here."
> "Then, why don't we fly out of here?" said the other.
> They started to fly out. When they got about half a mile, some men came to feed them. When they couldn't find the three monkeys, they saw them flying away. One of them said, "If we would have put them in a cage with a top, we would have had a real good thing here in the zoo."

One function of the school counselor might be to help highly creative children recognize or discover the "openings" in their cages to which they might be blinded.

4. Creative Children Like to Attempt Difficult Tasks

Frequently highly creative children strongly desire to move far ahead of their classmates in some areas. They always make us afraid that they are not "ready." Fortunately, however, educators of gifted children are rapidly revising many of their concepts about what can be taught at various levels of education. This terrifies many. The following recent headlines reflect such a fear:

"Caution Urged in Changing Primary into High Schools"
"Can We Rush Primary Education?"
"Don't Turn Grade Schools into High Schools, Educators Warn at Parley"
"Reading for Kindergarten, Language Too Soon Attacked."
Some of the panic may have been eased by a recent report of the

Educational Policies Commission of the NEA and the American Association of School Administrators (*Contemporary Issues in Elementary Education, 1960*).

A very frequent theme in our imaginative stories is related to this problem. The young animal or fowl asks, "When can I roar? When can I crow? When can I quack? When can I fly?" Almost always, the answer is, "When you are a little older." We are always afraid that the young one might not be ready to learn and that he would be forever scarred by even the most temporary failure.

A common experience in the lives of many highly outstanding individuals has been their ability to cope with failure and frustration. Certainly, almost all highly creative scientists, inventors, artists, and writers attempt tasks that are too difficult for them. Had they not attempted such tasks, it is quite unlikely that their great ideas would have been born.

5. Creative Children Are Searching for a Purpose

It has been said of most outstanding creative achievers that they seemed to be possessed by a purpose and to be "men of destiny." Creative children need some purpose that is worthy of the enthusiastic devotion they seem capable of giving. Some of this need is symbolized in the following story by a sixth-grade boy.

There once was a South American monkey that didn't know what he was, who he was, or why he was even alive. He decided that he didn't know even the way to figure it out, so he thought he would make up a reason.

He had seen many airplanes fly overhead. He had seen many ferocious animals, many nice animals, and many machines. He had always thought that it would be nice to fly, so he pretended he was an airplane.

He had also heard that buzzing sound of the engines, so he called himself "Buzz." He also decided that he was a real fast flyer so that this was the reason he was alive.

Now we all know that monkeys can't fly, but he didn't know this. Why he didn't even know that he was a monkey, so he kept trying and trying— and you know what? He flew!

Perhaps this has some implications not only concerning the need for helping children discover their potentialities but for helping them achieve their self-concepts creatively rather than by authority.

6. Creative Children Search for Their Uniqueness

Counselors and teachers may become irritated with creative children who seem to create problems for themselves by trying consciously to be different—searching for their uniqueness. Barron maintains that creative individuals reject the demands of their society to surrender their individuality because "they want to own themselves totally and because they perceive a shortsightedness in the claim of society that all its members should adapt themselves to a norm for a given time and place."

One way in which the creative individual searches for his uniqueness is through his vocational choice. Getzels and Jackson, for example, found that their highly creative compared with their highly intelligent subjects gave a greater number of different occupations and more "unusual" or rare occupations. Their attitudes toward adult success were also different, the high creatives being less concerned with conventional standards.

7. The Psychological Estrangement of Creative Children

In no group thus far studied have we failed to find relatively clear evidence of the operation of pressures against the most creative members of the group, though they are far more severe in some classes than in others.

When we select the most creative members of each sex in each classroom and match them for sex and Intelligence Quotient with other children in the same classroom, three characteristics stand out as differentiating the highly creative children from the less creative ones. First, there is a tendency for them to gain a reputation for having wild or silly ideas. Their teachers and their peers agree on this. Second, their work is characterized by its productivity of ideas "off the beaten track." This explains one of the difficulties of teachers and peers in evaluating their ideas and perhaps why they show up no better than they do on traditional intelligence tests. Their ideas simply do not conform to the standardized dimensions, the behavioral norms, on which responses are judged. Third, they are characterized by humor and playfulness. All of these characteristics help explain both the estrangement and the creativity.

. . . .

49. Freedom of Choice and Creative Activity *

HAROLD H. PUNKE, *Professor of Education, Auburn University*

THE GROWING importance of communism, particularly in science and international politics, challenges ideals that are often proclaimed as basic in the American conception of democracy. One such ideal concerns the freedom of choice open to individuals and the relationship of that freedom to creative mentality. Many Americans consider it axiomatic that free mind is creative and that regimented mind is not. Failure to analyze concepts and differentiate circumstances or degrees, regarding both freedom and creativeness, results in confusion and error.

1. *Nature of creativity.* In attempting to define creativity, as man's adding something new to what already exists, one should recognize its extensive scope. A three-year-old playing with blocks creates designs and develops neuromuscular skills that are new *to him.* But probably nothing in his experience is new to mankind. Throughout life most people frequently have new experience that is creative for them individually. But civilization grows through experiences that are primarily creative for the race. This is the creativeness implied when one compares creativity under democracy and under communism. What conditions favor such creativity?

Creativity occurs within the individual organism—although group life influences the functioning of such organisms. Since creativeness involves a reorganization of experience, an extensive background is important to supply material for reorganizing. A fertile imagination does not emerge from a vacuum. Freedom from tension becomes important in one's ability to reorganize his experience. The reorganization is the crux of hypothesis formation, and chance seems to play a role concerning which of the available impressions from experience actually become associated. Freedom from tension increases availability, but it does not guarantee creative associations. Avoiding crises is one way to prevent tensions. Dealing with minor problems, before they become crises, is important. Recreation,

* From *The Educational Forum*, May, 1962, pp. 439–45. Reprinted with permission.

perhaps drugs, and other means of securing relaxation may be significant. Confidence in one's ability to create may increase alertness and objectivity in evaluating hypotheses that arise. Confidence may also stimulate one to look for, or actively seek, possible associations among data from experience—that is, stimulate him to form more hypotheses than he would otherwise form. These statements about confidence imply a feeling in one that effort in the direction indicated will produce varied results to be evaluated, some of which may be fruitful. The procedure suggested is essentially experimenting to increase one's output of hypotheses. It resembles the experimental approach in chemistry or economics.

2. *What does choice mean?* Choice assumes alternatives. Only where there is a fork in the road is choice possible—or necessary. Scope of choice depends on number of alternatives. But seldom are existing alternatives equally open. Various pressures and obstacles accompany alternatives, and influence their relative availability. Choice usually implies conscious volition in determining which alternative to pursue. But the current setting, plus one's earlier conditioning, determine the framework within which his volition operates.

The different types of social structure—i.e., democratic or communistic, as related to personal volition in determining among alternatives, become largely a matter of the form and duration of pressures and obstacles. Alternatives as to fields of study in a university may thus be accompanied by bait in the form of scholarships or by allocations enforced with bayonets. The two procedures differ more in technique than in objective. Using bait is more subtle. By enabling the individual to think that his ideas are important in determining among alternatives, there is room for considerable ego satisfaction—especially among naïve persons. This could be significant for motivation. But there is considerable motivational potential in contemplating what might follow being shown a bayonet. In both cases, the aim is to secure adherence to group objectives.

Indoctrination is not new—concerning government, religion, home life, or other institutionalized clusters of values. Early clergymen who allegedly proclaimed: "Give me the child up to the age of six, and I will build up the church," lived and spoke as amateurs. They worked mainly before the days of general literacy and mass printing; before radio, television, and tape recordings; before high-powered advertising, rock-and-roll, or more comprehensive forms of brainwashing. These devices and techniques are not directed primarily at children of preschool age. Thought control, and the manufacture of personality and values as a basis for exercising "choice," is becoming a science.

3. *Role of discipline in choice and in creativity.* The techniques im-

plied in foregoing paragraphs constitute forms of physical and mental discipline. The discipline influences choice. Some educators emphasize discipline from within rather than from without. One might ask if there can be any discipline from within until after there has been discipline from without. Before a child walks he has numerous stimuli from without. Some of these come from persons, some from the nonhuman environment. Through reactions to these stimuli, habits are established. Habits and other behavior reflect values—according to whether the result of action seems pleasing or good. After accumulating considerable experience of the type implied, the individual foresees the consequences of different reactions to situations that confront him. Henceforth the individual's background enables him to "choose," in a socially acceptable way, among alternatives that appear. That is, after a substantial period of discipline from without, he becomes sufficiently indoctrinated and habituated to exercise "self-discipline." In some respects the procedure resembles toilet training. After close and persistent supervision during early life, a child becomes sufficiently attentive and habituated that he can solo in regard to the process.

Although one cannot become disciplined in mind or body wholly upon his own initiative, personal initiative and responsibility should become increasingly important as a child matures. Mental discipline implies a capacity for persistent application to some things and rejection of the appeal made by others. Thus discipline is essential in exercising choice. It is also essential in creativity. Developing sufficient experience to have a rich base for speculative imagination usually demands courage and persistence—regarding skepticism as to outcomes, distracting appeals from friends or the nonhuman environment, physical fatigue, and perhaps competing moral obligations. Persistence may include successive efforts, through carefully varied experiments, to reach desired goals. A disciplined mind is essential to analysis and evaluation of experience.

4. *Relativity in choice and creativeness.* The idea that choice and creativeness are matters of degree, should appear from preceding comment. With respect to choice, a question then arises concerning freedom for whom and under what conditions. With respect to creativeness, a comparable question relates to how much—and, as judged by whom. A background of knowledge and discipline in thinking are necessary for one to recognize where his own interests lie. American democracy assumes that each individual desires to promote his personal interests. To implement the desire, he must know what his interests are and how to proceed regarding them. A person who does not have knowledge concerning alternatives, and techniques for evaluating the knowledge, does not have

freedom of choice. His determination upon one of the alternatives is essentially "blind" chance—or outside pressure. Few people are wholly devoid of knowledge about situations that confront them. Possessing such knowledge is a matter of degree—and so is the exercise of choice.

Where several alternatives exist, freedom of opportunity to choose is always accompanied by a tyranny of necessity to do so. This is because a person's action can follow only one route, but he cannot merely delay and follow none. He must follow one. The paths of dictators are substantially cleared by multitudes of persons who feel that the burden of necessity more than offsets the freedom of opportunity. At this point lies the crux of the political struggle between freedom and dictatorship. The point gyrates somewhat, but the difference between freedom and dictation is always one of degree.

American emphasis on personal choice often neglects the idea of public duty and responsibility. One manifestation of individual responsibility toward the group, appears in the status of respect that exists for law and order—as these are determined by group action. This is discipline of the individual by the group—largely from without. A totalitarian society emphasizes duty, with the individual's importance determined largely by his usefulness in performing duty—as indicated by the group. But it should be clear that, in any society, rights and duties are socially determined. The same is essentially true of opportunities. From the standpoint of choice, a practical fact in any society is that the individual experiences some combination of learning to get what he likes with learning to like what he gets.

An earlier paragraph incidentally noted the relative nature of creativity, by reference to what is new to a child and new to the race. Creativeness is relative in another respect. The importance attached to a contribution that is new to the race depends on social appraisal. Whether the appraisal is high or low depends on social conditions when the contribution appears. In wartime, inventions that improve weapons are highly valued. At other times, discoveries on how to improve health or learning capacity may be valued rather high. Social value is a reflection of current social usefulness. Hence the direction in which the creativeness of a people will be oriented is relative.

5. *Choice and Creativity in Russia and the United States.* Many Americans compare this country and Russia on scope of personal choice and its implications for creativity. Responses attuned to value patterns that are not critically examined, generally lead to the conclusion that regimented mind cannot be as creative as free mind. The conclusion often reflects exaggeration of the extent to which American mind is free or

Russian mind regimented. Members of either camp can be so steeped in their own propaganda that they are unable to conceive of doubt about any part of it.

A thoughtful person need not be a communist to recognize the limitations on free mind in America that accompany McCarthyism; religious and racial discrimination; censorships; indifference to educational possibilities; preoccupation with spectator athletics, "resort" pleasures, and popular songs pleading for a return to infantile bliss; failure to develop adequate health programs; continued limitation on political representation of the people in many regions, etc. And one does not have to be RED to sense degrees of regimentation concerning different levels of civic, professional, or industrial responsibility in Russia, or differences in regimentation among different areas of the culture. Thus one might expect less regimentation of high-level personnel in chemistry than in economics. But when we are confronted with realities of current Russian creativity, we often buttress our illusions by saying that "eventually" the values of free mind will show up in our favor. We should recognize the role of nostalgia in such statements.

The basic point concerns areas of freedom in relation to one's competence to do creative work and his willingness to devote himself to it. No one person does creative work in many areas of a complex culture, but in one or a few specialized areas. The important thing is extensive freedom in the area concerned. It is easy to imagine numerous Russian scientists having greater freedom to study, experiment, or associate with other scientists than a McCarthy-ridden America allowed its scientists— and perhaps having more adequate facilities and assisting personnel. Freedom for creative work in chemistry or pharmacology does not depend greatly on freedom to do such things as make stump speeches on religion. A creative person probably derives his greatest satisfactions from the special field to which he devotes the major portion of his time and energy. Probably the greatest freedom for him is freedom to work in that field and to associate with others who do so.

A substantial part of the satisfaction that comes from devoting or dedicating oneself to a field or a "cause," results from one's sensing that his personality expands to permeate the entire field. Religious, patriotic, and other workers have emphasized the participation in a "larger life" that often accompanies extensive devotion to socially approved activities that extend or focus well beyond the physical self. The greater the extension, the greater the number of other persons affected. For dedicated scientists, teachers, statesmen, religious workers, or others, the extension may be such that the individual seems to forget about his own physical well-being, as pursuit of his work appears oriented to benefit the group—even all mankind. Dedication often demands that one oppose, or at least learn to work within, the major framework of the current social order in which he lives. This pertains to every society, current and historic. Creative leadership tries to make it easier for dedicated persons to work for the general welfare.

In any country, freedom to get satisfaction from one's work varies from one vocation to another. Sociopolitical difficulties that Americans have faced concerning research or experimentation in such fields as birth control, hypnosis, genetic inheritance among humans, socialized medicine, public ownership of means of production, consolidation of counties or similar units of local government, crime and delinquency, or federal aid for general education illustrate the point. Moreover, in a society like that of the United States or Russia, most persons must engage in some vocation; each must do some work for which society is willing and able to pay him. Earlier comment mentioned differences between the two countries regarding pressures and inducements by which one gets into a vocation. Social change and vocational mobility influence how long he stays in the vocation upon which he first embarks. But after one is in a particular vocation, much of his life satisfaction usually comes from that vocation— with decreasing regard to how he got into it. Promotions, bonuses, insurances, fringe benefits, or improvement in the place where one works may increase the satisfactions. So may creative imagination applied to the skills and processes that his job entails.

With the range in developmental potential that characterizes human beings, it may be naïve to assume that people the world over find their major satisfactions through the aspects of freedom that have been emphasized in this country. Frontier life and the drive for private material wealth have helped cause the intellectual to be ignored in America. The attitude still prevails regarding some of the arts and social philosophy. Also regarding creativeness in some racial and ethnic groups, and regarding the individual genius whose creativeness is not tied to a current fad.

In America there is still considerable freedom for anybody to pose as an expert in any field, in contrast with respecting competence that has been earned by long and persistent work in a particular field. So, laymen pressurize outstanding scientists to pose as experts in religion, economics, or government. Americans rightly emphasize freedom to vote. But to evaluate the importance of that freedom, in many cases, one must view it as freedom to vote for candidates produced by a gerrymandering politics or a rigged caucus—with the significance of one's vote severely reduced through failure of legislative apportionment, an electoral college, the committee structure of legislative bodies, etc. The implications of radio time in the American social system, relative to the whole electoral process, are also important.

There is a marked difference between equal freedom for everybody in every area of human interest and greater freedom for persons in the fields of their principal interest and service to mankind. Intellectual freedom in accordance with one's type of work and level of competence seems as important for his creativeness as good experimental or other equipment. But freedom and inducement to be amateur and mediocre in several fields does not produce creativeness in any field. Such freedom usually results in dissipation of time, energy, and other resources. The Jack-of-all-trades finds his major usefulness in a pretechnical society. The creative person in a complex culture is one who undergoes rigid discipline in some area of socially useful activity, and thus earns "freedom through competence" respecting that area.

Creativeness as viewed in this discussion indicates "superior" achievement, but there is some vagueness about what superior means. The amount of creativeness that a people manifest may depend considerably on the percentage of the population who are encouraged to think they can be creative in a significant way and who have opportunity for developing the capacity to be so. But there is no reason to expect large masses of people to be "superior." No society can provide superior opportunity for all of its members. Such opportunity is provided for a rather small per cent, on some basis of selection—private income, scholarships, political affiliation, religion, sex, ancestry, etc. Selection in relation to opportunity provided is among the tools that a society uses to determine the direction of cultural growth. Likewise, no society can expect everybody to have superior genetic qualifications or superior dedication. Many factors thus exist in degrees. So does creativeness—as noted earlier.

It seems quite possible for Russia to develop extensive creativeness in numerous directions, without stress on some types of freedom that Americans claim to emphasize. In this country we should not delude ourselves by assuming that our conception of freedom is all inclusive, that freedom is unchanging in balance and proportion among its ramifications, that we have whatever is worth while in it, and that peoples with a different conception of freedom and its role in life will indeed "see the light" eventually and accept our view.

50. Creativity in the Elementary Classroom *

RUTH STRANG, *Director, Reading Development Center, University of Arizona; Professor Emeritus, Teachers College, Columbia University*

TEACHERS are concerned with creativity both as a product and as a process. They watch for drawings, paintings, handicrafts, poems, stories, dramatizations, or ideas that have the stamp of originality. But they are also concerned with creativity as a process, and welcome any idea or action that is new to the child and represents, for him, a creative experience.

To foster both creative expression and creative experience in the classroom, a teacher must recognize, delight in, and encourage all signs of creativity.

The class group itself should be receptive to spontaneous expressions of individuality. Any moves in the right direction should be reinforced by the availability of materials and tools that invite exploration and make it possible to turn out a successful product. Finally, both the creative process and its products should be appraised and evaluated against standards of excellence appropriate to each individual student.

The role of the teacher is to recognize, appreciate, and release the creativity of every student, in whatever form or degree. Too often, as children go through school they lose their curiosity and sense of wonder. They become less spontaneous and less inventive in their expression. To paraphrase Wordsworth, "And custom lies upon them with a weight, heavy as frost, and deep almost as life."

Look, Listen, Enjoy

The face of a teacher who is attuned to fresh and vivid expressions will show his delight when a child sees a new relationship or an unusual aspect of a situation, or when he uses a particularly felicitous word or phrase.

* From *The NEA Journal*, March 1961, pp. 20–22. Reprinted with permission. (Pictures omitted.)

This is what makes teaching exciting. I still remember the comment of a nine-year-old boy when he saw a statue representing the Alma Mater of a large university. "Oh," he said, "it's the Statue of Liberty sitting down."

As the teacher listens to students' conversations and discussions about things in which they are emotionally involved, he notes original ideas and vivid phrases and sentences. Sometimes the student will catch the teacher's spontaneous smile of appreciation; sometimes the teacher will commend him privately after class. This personal contact sharpens the student's awareness that he has been "speaking poetry" or making a discovery in the realm of ideas.

When a teacher sees evidence that a student is wholeheartedly absorbed in an activity, he tries, if possible, not to interrupt it. Such concentration should be encouraged. A rigid schedule with frequent class changes is often frustrating to a child who finds satisfaction in sustained effort on an absorbing project.

In recalling their happier school experiences, students repeatedly refer to special projects that they suggested and were allowed to work on with a minimum of interference. For example, one boy began to write a history of the world and continued to work on this project for several years. His effort was reinforced by the teacher's interest and enthusiasm.

A boy in the seventh grade developed an intense interest in conservation. He became an expert on it. The teacher, too, became interested. When the class came to this topic in social studies, she turned the pupils over to the boy, who did an excellent job of teaching and even prepared the test on this unit. By sharing the boy's special interest and finding a worthy use for it, the teacher established a personal relation with him and was able to help him improve his other subjects, which he had been neglecting.

The teacher often overlooks the creative ability of the quiet, docile child. One teacher had a boy in whom she had not recognized any special ability until one day he asked a searching question. Once the teacher was alert to this analytical potentiality, she noted and encouraged other instances of the boy's exceptional ability in the realm of ideas. A career in science stemmed from this initial recognition and appreciation of special talent.

Set the Stage

Creativity is fostered not only by the teacher's enthusiasm but also by favorable interaction among the class members. Creative expression, however, involves the individual's private world, which he may be reluctant to reveal.

A permissive atmosphere that encourages the shy and withdrawn adolescent to participate in and profit by group expression can result from certain simple procedures. In a creative writing class, for instance, no student should be required to read his manuscript before the group unless he wants to. Instead, he may hand in his composition privately, and it may be read anonymously by some other student.

Once a manuscript has been read aloud, classmates make comments that give the author recognition of his strong points and insight into his weak ones. Even suggestions for major rewriting may be less disheartening when they are given by the group rather than by the teacher.

In the primary grades, a similar group atmosphere can stimulate the children to dictate their thoughts and feelings about a windy autumn day or about their personal thankfulness on Thanksgiving Day. If the teacher writes each child's thought as he expresses it, later the class can combine and rearrange the statements to make a poem or story.

The showing of a picture carefully chosen by the teacher is another simple way to stimulate a variety of creative activity. Children may wish to discuss such points as the picture's pleasing use of color, or to make up a little play leading up to, or following, the action depicted in the scene.

Creative expressions of many kinds can come from class activities such as these:

1. Writing and illustrating a book for little children.
2. Composing songs, plays, or stories for special occasions.
3. Making stage sets for their original plays.
4. Personalizing a problem in any subject (by using the *You Are There* technique in social studies, for example) and working out solutions.
5. Analyzing two poems and giving reasons for preferring one or the other.
6. Listening to records and interpreting the music in dances or pantomimes.

Any other experience will serve if it captures interest and arouses feelings. Timing is important—one must catch the magic moment.

Encouragement and Approval

The teacher should select for special recognition only those writings, drawings, and discoveries that have the mark of originality and sensitive perception. These need not be—and perhaps should not be—finished products. But they should clearly show the creative spark. Only in this way can the students themselves learn to distinguish between the exceptional and the mediocre.

While giving recognition to the exceptional product, a teacher need not discourage children who have not yet attained this authenticity of unique expression. They, too, produce things worthy of approval.

Teachers are also concerned with creativity as an experience. The idea or thing created may seem ordinary to adults, but, if it represents a discovery for the child, it is a creative experience well worth cultivating.

In the second and third grades of the Agnes Russell Center at Columbia one of the teachers, Virginia Heflin, gave children opportunity for experimenting in the development of number concepts. Providing each of them with twenty-eight counters, she asked them to see how many equal groups they could make out of them. They discovered that they could make two groups of fourteen or fourteen groups of two, or seven groups of four; that eighteen could be thought of as fourteen and four or as nine and nine.

A similar approach was used in other activities. Miss Heflin was careful not to say "No" when the children did not give the answer she was expecting. She did not give approval only to the children who did things her way or only to drawings that were in accord with her standards. She shared the youngsters' satisfaction in experiences that were for them new and wonderful.

As the time to leave school approached, Miss Heflin's class made a large mural, showing the places to which each child was going, and wrote verses about going away:

> *Here we are in the room,*
> *The year has gone zum, zum, zum!*
> *The ones that have to leave in June*
> *Will be going very soon.*
> *Who is that lucky little guy,*
> *Who doesn't leave until July?*

The teacher who wishes to elicit creative responses from all the children must know how to reinforce the exceptional element in an imperfect and unfinished product: "You saw something in that tree that nobody else has seen," or "I would never have thought of using that word; it's just right."

Indifference or ridicule or harsh criticism inhibits a sensitive person. This does not mean that the teacher should never criticize, for a good product can usually be made better.

Artists and writers go through the drudgery of perfecting their paintings and poems. A child, too, will welcome kindly and constructive criticism, especially when he recognizes that he lacks the technique necessary to communicate his ideas. The teacher's criticism also serves as a model for the child's own appraisal of his products.

Materials, Know-How, and Quietude

Creative ideas spring from careful thinking and deep feeling; from the stimulation of a book or a film; from the handling of materials and tools.

Creative activity is inhibited by a confusing conglomeration of experiences and by constant clatter and chatter. Television and radio leave children little time to put their fleeting thoughts into words. Some solitude is necessary to bring individuality to the surface and to allow the creative spirit to try its wings.

51. Developing Creativity in Children *

ROBERT C. WILSON, *Associate Professor of Psychology and Statistics, Portland State College, Portland, Oregon*

B Y THE time we get children in high school, their creativity has been killed. They all want to be told what to do."

"I feel that I ought to do more to make my pupils creative, but I don't know how to do it."

These are typical remarks of secondary and elementary school teachers. They feel that schools destroy children's creativity and that they, as teachers, have an obligation to attempt to develop it. What can teachers do?

First of all, what is creativity? One might define it as the process by which something new is produced—an idea or an object, including a new form or arrangement of old elements. The new creation may contribute to the solution of some problem, or it may be the production of an aesthetic effect or the clarification of a concept. Indeed it may be any intellectual, emotional, or social problem with which an individual in our society is interested or concerned. The creative solution is aimed primarily at solv-

* Reprinted from the September, 1960, issue of *Education*, pp. 19–23. Copyright 1960 by The Bobbs-Merrill Co., Inc., Indianapolis, Ind.

ing a problem that concerns the person engaged in the process. It may or may not solve a problem for someone other than the creator.

It is realized that the foregoing is not a complete definition, but further connotations of the term "creativity" will appear in the remainder of the article. This definition stresses the purposes of the creator and the problem he is trying to solve rather than the purposes and problems of some social group. It also stresses the wide range of problems of daily living, the solutions of which may require creativity.

Creativity in the Classroom

One study of the primary abilities in creative thinking revealed several abilities that seem to be important in creativity in science, engineering, and invention (4). Another study carried on in the Department of Art Education at The Pennsylvania State University found similar abilities to be important for creativity in art (1). These two studies have led to the following suggestions for encouraging "new ideas" in the classroom (3). The validity of the suggested methods has not been established in any systematic research studies. Such merit as they may have rests upon their content validity and the reports of teachers who have employed them.

Brainstorming

Alex Osborn (2) has described a procedure for group thinking sessions designed to provide an atmosphere permissive of new ideas. This procedure, dubbed "brainstorming," can be used effectively in the classroom.

The purpose of brainstorming is to obtain as many ideas as possible in relation to a given problem. There are four simple rules that must be followed:

1. *Judgment is ruled out.* Criticism of ideas must be withheld until later.

2. *Freewheeling is welcomed.* The wilder the idea, the better; it is easier to tame down than to think up.

3. *Quantity is wanted.* The greater the number of ideas, the more likelihood of finding a successful solution.

4. *Combinations and improvements are sought.* In addition to contributing ideas of their own, participants should suggest how ideas of others can be combined into still another idea.

A problem may be written on the board, and the pupils may be asked to suggest as many ideas as possible, with the teacher listing these ideas on the board. No idea is rejected; every idea is accepted. Each idea stimulates others. At times, the ideas will tumble out so fast that the teacher will have difficulty keeping up.

Only after the ideas have been written down does evaluation take place. The class goes over the list, selecting those ideas that seem most likely to work; modifying some ideas into workable form; and rejecting those ideas that seem unworkable. Next, those ideas that seem workable may be tried out.

Brainstorming may be used with school and classroom problems such as the following: (*a*) "What can we do to make our schoolroom more interesting and comfortable?"; (*b*) "How can we make the line in the lunchroom move more rapidly?"; and (*c*) "What questions would be most interesting to study in this unit?"

On the other hand, brainstorming may be used with personal problems. For example: "What can each of us do to make our home more happy?" or "How can we earn extra money?"

Another possibility involves brainstorming first a list of problems and then a list of suggested solutions for each of the more important problems. For example, "Let's list as many problems as we can that sixth graders must face." Then, in regard to each problem, "Let's list as many ways as we can for solving this problem."

Sensitivity to Problems

A primary mental ability that seems to be important in creative thinking is sensitivity to problems. To solve a problem creatively, one must be aware of the existence of the problem. This ability involves approaching problem situations with such questions as, "What is the problem here?"; "Is the apparent problem the real problem?"; "What would happen if such and such were changed?"; and "How can this situation be improved?"

We are unaware of certain types of problems, because we do not observe the world around us. We are unaware of other types of problems, because we make unconscious assumptions. We take things for granted about our world and its problems. Many creative acts have had their beginnings because someone questioned an assumption that previously had been taken for granted.

Pupils may be encouraged to make better use of their senses by observation trips. For example, they may be asked to walk around the building; on their return, they may be asked to list the things they saw. Then they may repeat the trip, looking for things they overlooked the first time; after the second trip, they can make a second list.

Other trips can be made to look for objects colored red, for round objects, or for things that one wouldn't see during another season of the year. The children may be asked to look for unrecognized problems or for things that need to be improved.

Pupils may be encouraged to question some of the things that they take for granted and to consider what things might be like if some basic assumptions in their lives were different. Questions of the "What-would-happen-if————" or "What-would-it-be-like-if————" variety may serve to develop sensitivity to problems. The following are a few examples:

What would happen if (*a*) everyone in the world were suddenly to become deaf; (*b*) everyone always told the truth about everything; (*c*) we had only three fingers; (*d*) we all lived by the Golden Rule; (*e*) we knew when we would die; (*f*) the air all over the world became radioactive?

Ideational Fluency

A satisfactory solution to a problem is most easily found when one is choosing from a large number of ideas. Individual and group activities, which have as their aim getting as many ideas as possible, are probably helpful in encouraging a second primary mental ability, ideational fluency. Brainstorming is one such activity.

The following list contains some suggestions for helping individual pupils to increase their flow of ideas. The time limits are arbitrary and may be changed to suit the group.

1. List on a piece of paper all the uses you can think of for a brick. You will have five minutes.

2. List as many things as you can think of that are square in shape. You will have five minutes.

3. When students have trouble thinking of ideas to write about in a report or theme, suggest that they first list all the things that might possibly be related to the topic. If pupils do this, uncritically, for fifteen or twenty minutes, they usually will come up with an abundance of ideas from which they may choose.

4. List all the ways you can think of in which you might entertain yourself if you had an evening to spend alone at home.

5. Fluency in creative writing may be encouraged by allowing fifteen or twenty minutes each morning for pupils to write whatever they wish to write. At first, some children may have difficulty in getting started. It may be well to suggest that they write about something that happened yesterday (real or imaginary) or about something that they saw on the way to school.

The teacher may look over the work of four or five pupils each day. It should be emphasized that, during this particular writing exercise, spelling, punctuation, and grammar are not the concern. The important thing is for the children to write anything they feel like writing. Free and fluent development of an idea is the aim.

Encouraging Originality

A third important primary mental ability is originality, the ability to have unusual, uncommon, or clever ideas and to see relationships between things that are only remotely connected.

Classroom activities in this area may encourage a deliberate effort to give uncommon or unusual responses, to look for a different or new way of doing something. The following are some suggested activities:

1. In presenting reports, as in connection with a social studies unit, the pupils may be instructed to use any method other than the obvious ones of reading to or telling the class. Pupils may decide to use dramatizations, quiz sessions, opaque projectors, tape recorders, interview techniques, etc. —the possibilities are innumerable.

2. An adaptation of the first technique is "selling a book." Instead of presenting a book report, a pupil may be told that his problem is to put himself in the position of a salesman. He may use any technique he wishes in an effort to arouse the interest of the class in reading the book.

3. Let the pupils pretend that they are going to write a poem about spring (or any season of the year). "Everyone will have an opportunity to go to the window and look outside for four minutes. When you come back to your seats, you will list all the things you saw that you would not see on a rainy day. If you list something that no one else lists, your score on that idea will be *ten*. If only two or three people in the room put down the same idea, your score will be *five*. If four or five people list the same idea, your score will be *three*. If more than five people list it, your score will be *one*. You will note that the closer you observe and the more uncommon your responses, the higher your score will be."

This activity may be followed by a discussion of creative thinking and the function of unusual or uncommon ideas.

Strong Interests Needed

Studies of the childhood backgrounds of eminent scientists indicate one thing that many of them had in common: They possessed strong interests at an early age, and they have carried these interests into their adult lives so that they have worked at their jobs with persistent intensity and single-minded devotion. For these men, time spent on other activities usually is spent reluctantly and, then, chiefly because of outside pressure. Most of these scientists are happiest when they are working; moreover, they achieve their greatest personal satisfactions through their work.

Many teachers and parents are concerned lest a child will not develop into a well-rounded individual. The evidence seems to indicate that to be a highly productive or creative adult, one cannot be well rounded. One must devote a very great amount of time to one area of interest. In other words, one must be somewhat lopsided.

Teachers, therefore, who feel that creativity is important should not try to force pupils to be well rounded, nor should they force children to play down their strong interest. On the contrary, it would seem that one way to develop creativity might be to encourage pupils to develop some strong interests. The capacity to have a strong interest in something may be an important prerequisite to creativity.

Figuring Things Out

Another interesting finding is that the capacity for intense concentration on a problem accompanies the development of an understanding of the concept of research. That is, at some point in his school career, the more creative individual becomes aware of the possibility of finding things out, firsthand, for himself.

The implication is that creativity may be promoted by situations in which the pupil is encouraged to work out his own solutions to problems. The teacher's task is to provide materials for students to work with; to provide sufficient time for them to manipulate ideas and toy with the elements of a solution; and to provide for problems that do not have pat answers. Obviously, it is not easy to furnish these things for a class of thirty pupils in an already crowded curriculum, which may require that pupils shift to a new subject every forty or fifty minutes.

It is, of course, much easier to tell a student what to do, what to read, and what to think than it is to set up a situation in which he must figure out these things for himself. Perhaps not all students can learn to work on their own. Nevertheless, it seems evident that we, as teachers, have an obligation to encourage them to try.

References

1. Lowenfeld, V. "Current Research on Creativity," *NEA Journal,* XLVII (1958), 538–40.

2. OSBORN, A. F. *Applied Imagination.* New York: Charles Scribner's Sons, 1953.

3. WILSON, R. C. "Creativity," in *Education for the Gifted,* Fifty-seventh Yearbook, Part II, of the National Society for the Study of Education, ed. R. J. Havighurst. Chicago: University of Chicago Press (Distributor), 1958, pp. 108–26.

4. ———, *et al.* "A Factor-Analytic Study of Creative Thinking," *Psychometrika,* XIX (1954), 297–311.

52. Creativity in the Classroom, Canton *

IRENE McKEE, *Teacher Belle Stone School, Canton, Ohio*

Creativity Is a Way of Thinking

Creativity involves: self reliance, independent thought, motive power, inner drive or desire, ability to continue in face of difficulties, patience, persistence; working without constant direction, supervision, or praise; knowing how to fail intelligently (Research is 99.9 per cent failure); studying and using what is already known; appreciation of the contributions of others; critical attitude toward own work; recognizing what is good and what needs improvement.

Developing Creative Ways of Working and Thinking

Children are developing creative ways of working and thinking when they:

1. Begin work without being told.
2. Find answers to many of their own questions.
3. Look at own work with critical eye and make revisions.
4. After finishing one task, decide what to do next and do it.

* From a special report on *Creativity in the Classroom,* Canton, Ohio. Reprinted with permission.

5. Have courage of own convictions (backed by proof and reasons) even though it means standing alone.
6. Look for and develop constructive differences rather than sameness; express individuality.
7. Consider many ideas and solutions, never sure there is just one right answer.
8. Do not give up easily; are willing to check and correct many times until a high standard is reached.

Creativity of Children Difficult to Identify

The best-dressed, most artistically decorated classroom does not always prove that its students are creative. The "creation" may have been largely teacher-planned and produced. A fluently given oral talk or a well-organized cleverly written composition may easily fool even a very discerning teacher when in reality much of the effect has been parent engineered. However, these situations may well be used as an introduction or springboard for creativity on the part of children themselves if everyone concerned is willing to identify and accept rather crude beginnings. Anyone versed in identification realizes that creativity like any other skill requires practice and that first clumsy attempts are steps to learning. These attempts are identified as creative, are accepted, and are criticized *constructively*.

Creativity Increases with Practice

IN THE CLASSROOM

Assignments that provide opportunity for creativity:

Each child chooses a different way of reporting what he has learned.
Write other titles for story, chapter, or topic.
Express an emotion in many ways—voice, facial expression, actions, posture, words, picture (art), music.
Round robin story; one child begins and each child adds.
Show picture to class; child imagines situation and in limited time writes his idea.
Give phrase; child lists as many events or plots as he can in allotted time. Examples of phrases: "How wonderful!"—"Having Trouble?"—"I hardly know where to begin."

We work each day the creative way:
Group selects topic; works out display for classroom or bulletin board and puts it up.

Each child chooses or is assigned a different topic. He locates information, takes notes, organizes material, writes about topic, and makes illustration or chart. This is all done at school.
Work an arithmetic problem in all the different ways possible. Discuss merits of various methods.
Find out how different children solve problems mentally. Compare and practice ways others suggest.

Write letters to pen pals throughout the United States.

Assign questions in social studies. Make sure that some answers may: necessitate search beyond text and encyclopedia; depend on reading map, picture, graph, or chart; require arithmetic computation; be controversial; be matter of opinion; depend on reasoning; be found in newspapers or magazines.

Biographies afford excellent examples of creative thinking in action. How was each person creative and what characteristics helped him to succeed?

Make a special study of one scientific topic. Give demonstration and share extra information with class. Explain value of this principle to our lives.

Every day a different child plans opening exercises and is chairman for the day.

Other creative activities used in our classroom are oral, written, drawn, pantomimed, or sung. They may be fanciful, factual, or fictional, and include: original stories, poems, newpapers, plays, essays, songs, puppet shows, assemblies, models, murals, riddles, posters, letters, news, stories behind the news, rhythmic interpretations; evaluation of books, films, radio or television programs, biographies; quiz programs; vocabulary games.

"I Wonder" Assignments

Students often wonder about items not covered in the textbook. These topics are jotted down for future investigation. Twice a week for homework, information is located and read. Reports are then written with the book or magazine closed. Brief oral reports, without notes, are shared with class. This aids both written and oral expression.

Graphs

Make graphs using information about class. Besides being able to make and read a graph, it is important to know what the graph does not show and also what possibilities it suggests for further investigation.

The following is an example of how one child outlined how to interpret a graph on the number of library books read by his classmates:

I. What does this graph tell
   A. How many books read by each person
   B. When books were read
   C. How many persons in class
   D. Who read books

II. What this graph does not tell
   A. Who is very best reader
   B. What type of book is read
   C. Speed of reader
   D. Who will receive best grade
   E. Comprehension of reader

III. Some probabilities of reading this graph
   A. Which students like or don't like to read
   B. Students with many books read may be better readers than others
   C. Which students are anxious to learn new things

53. Challenges for Talent Search and for Education *

CALVIN W. TAYLOR, *Professor of Psychology, University of Utah*

Challenges for Talent Search

After we have learned at least crudely how to identify new types of talent such as creative talent, the question emerges as to what will be done in education and elsewhere to recognize, develop, and utilize such new talents, and what might be done to design environments for human beings so that

* From "Educational and Architectural Implications of Some Creativity Findings," excerpts from address delivered at the A.A. Cleveland Conference, June 25, 1962, Washington State University, Pullman, Wash., pp. 8, 9, 13, 14 of a mimeographed copy. Reprinted with permission.

these talents will have a greater chance of being identified and encouraged to grow and flourish.

My next point is that *current widely available measures and educational tasks are inadequate both for identifying and developing potential to be creative.*

School grades. If school grades were efficient predictors of creative performance, the identification of persons with more potential to be creative from those with less would be a simple problem. We would largely have it already solved. Although certain school grades have been found to have a little bit of validity for the prediction of creative performance, there is some indication that school grades in general have little or no validity for this purpose. There is an article in *Business Week* (pp. 77–78, February 24, 1962) that states good scholars are not always best. This article cites three studies—actually there are more than three, because we have some too—and in these three studies there is absolutely no relationship between performance in school, as measured by school grades, and later scientific research work. One of these studies is presented in my report at our 1957 creativity conference. These results raise very serious questions both about the nature of education and about the measures (the grades) we get out of our educational programs. A more noticeable portion of school activities may have to change in nature so that creative performances and behaviors are demanded if grades are ever to become very useful in predicting later creative performance. My best educated guess is that quite different psychological processes are involved in learning existing knowledge, either from the teacher or from the text, than in producing new ideas, new knowledge, new systems, or even when we produce anything at all on our own—though it need not be creative. Psychologically, I think productive thinking is a different process from learning knowledge that is already available. . . .

Knowledge and creativity. Let me speculate about the relationship between the amount of knowledge possessed and creative performance. Let us consider the type of knowledge that man now possesses—knowledge with its redundancies, contaminations, irrelevancies, as well as with its pertinent and sound portions for a given purpose. If the sheer amount of knowledge were sufficient for predicting creative performance, then the problem of identifying and developing creative potential would be near solution. If so, we could merely consider each person as a "spongehead" and do everything possible to pour as much knowledge into him as possible so that he who absorbed the most knowledge would be the one who would create the most new things. But early indications are that the sheer accumulation of knowledge does not guarantee that the remaining incubation and insight stages in the creative process will occur. These later stages are different psychological processes. For example, we sense that some of the people who are walking libraries are not necessarily producing anything new of their own, but they are essentially only reproducing what man's bookshelves already contain. They, of course, can serve well as transmitters of information and as sources of man's old knowledge.

This question has been opened up fully, so that we should now try to determine the role of various kinds of knowledge in creative performance in each particular field of interest. We need to determine the relationship between creativity and prior information of various kinds. Two relevant reports were presented at our 1962 conference. One by Westcott of Vassar pertained to information and intuition. People differ quite widely in how much information they normally will require before they will make a leap to a solution, an intuitive leap. So there is an interesting area here of determining the amount of information needed before each person will make an intuitive leap. The other study by Hyman of Oregon found essentially this: Information as such may not be as important to creativity as is the manner in which one seeks and receives this information—your attitudes and response sets as you go about seeking information, whether you seek it in creative ways or in uncreative ways, how you process and store it internally, and how you utilize it later in your central processes to produce something new. It isn't information, per se, as much as it is the internal processing of this information—how you store and process and utilize it that is important. So in effect, you can find people with equal prior information but quite unequal creativeness. Such unequality can be explained largely in how individuals deal with this information rather than directly in terms of the information itself. If you seek information just to criticize it or to store it away in a critical way (and we suspect this is what is happening in our educational programs), you are not as well prepared to do as much creative work with this information at a later time as if you sought it out and stored it in more suitable ways for creativeness. . . .

Challenges for Education

Greater variety needed.   Let's look at some teacher challenges. A real question about any educational program is whether there is any transfer of training, any spread effect. Does what is learned here spread to any other situation or activity?

I am not persuaded that what is needed in education is just "more of the same." I do sense that after Sputnik many in education became excited and decided to "pour it on," doing more of the same with longer workdays, longer workweeks, and longer workyears. But studies in industry suggest that this might be going in the wrong direction. I also believe we need greater variety in education. We need to be more concerned with these other kinds of talent. Youngsters might find school to be more fascinating and interesting if they had a chance to try out all of the gear shifts of the mind, all the keys of their mind, all their talents, while they also are learning subject matter. Instead of our aiming directly for discipline in school, I suspect that it might occur as a natural by-product of greater variety for the students.

Torrance has stated in our forthcoming 1961 report that it now seems quite possible that many things can be learned creatively more economically and more effectively than by authority. Yet many of us suspect that most of our textbooks and teaching (in science at least) are designed to cultivate learning by authority only. Even laboratory experiments nearly always involve walking along old trails and repeating old experiments "by the numbers," as used in the military or widely marketed painting kits. The text and the teachers tend to focus on what is known far more than upon what is not known, which often is almost completely missing. Challenges of the unknown, therefore, are likely to be ignored.

Let me tell you a story about a person who, realizing that he had been a student for some time and was going to be a student quite a while longer, decided to become more efficient at it. He analyzed what he had to do as a student, and one of the things he found he had to do, especially while he was in the classroom, was to receive information through the ear, have it come down through the arm, go out through a pen or pencil, and make good recordings on paper without necessarily penetrating his mind. So he decided he wanted to become more efficient in this classroom task, which he clearly recognized as requiring what could be called either a high-level-memory talent or a high-level-recording talent. He worked on this talent for a while but soon decided that maybe he needed to invent a machine as man has often done to help him to extend his own abilities.

He soon realized that a machine had already been invented that might do, so he tried using this machine, a tape recorder. He brought it to class the next day, and plugged it in to work on this high-level-memory ability and also put himself to work on the same task. Afterwards, he compared and sadly found that the tape recorder had a higher level recording or memory talent than he did. It hadn't missed a thing. Not only that, but he found, as some of the "how to study" books advise, that he had written his notes in his own words and not exactly as the instructor stated it; consequently, when he regurgitated, the answers did not come out in the language of the instructor, so he lost a few points because the instructor's scoring key was in the exact language he had used to impart the topic. But the tape recorder regurgitated everything exactly in the language of the instructor. When he came to class the next day, he said, "Duplication of effort—no need of my sticking around," so he plugged in the high-level-memory-talent machine and went elsewhere to do other things that his mind was capable of doing but that the tape recorder could not do. Soon, the other students got the idea. Then finally the instructor got the idea, so that the course ended up by one tape recorder talking to a bunch of other tape recorders—real good communication—the information was being imparted and received perfectly, with no distortion, no loss, etc. And this freed the students and the teacher to do other things that their minds were capable of doing. Or to put it another way, they all went into another class-room (and I don't know how to design this one) where the other parts of their mind were practiced and put to use. The problem may be that we as teachers do not know what we would do in this next classroom to stir the creative thinking parts and other important parts of our students' minds that we haven't yet learned how to develop.

We should help students to develop their various talents while they are growing in knowledge. One of my students, William Hutchinson, is working in this area. He had worked hard in trying to have the teacher produce other kinds of thinking in their students in the classroom and found it difficult for some teachers to move away from their established means of teaching. Then the class had a short recess and went out in the hall. Suddenly he sensed that much of the kinds of thinking he was trying to cultivate in the classroom was happening rather naturally out in the hall during the break.

Self-reports have been surprisingly promising in predicting creative performance, both in our studies and in John Holland's National Merit Scholarship studies. Consequently, we wonder whether the educational program should be more of a series of situational tests where students some-how experience a wider variety of creative and other high-level intellectual and nonintellectual processes to provide them with a more full and sound basis for their self-reports. How would we design schools and schoolrooms so that students could be having a much wider variety of these kinds of ex-periences? We suspect that these numerous and varied thinking and learning experiences might have a carry-over or spread effect into the kind of situa-tions that we had in mind. If in our present classroom situations, people are primarily learning how to sit down and take notes, then the real question is to what degree, if any, does the ability to sit down and take notes spread to important work that they will later have to do in the world? If it does not, then shouldn't we have them do other kinds of things that will later show positive transfer to important kinds of work (like producing new things in science, if they are being educated in science)? So we should set the learning or thinking situation to ensure that some "spread of effects" or transfer of training will occur.

54. The Teacher of the Academically Able

LESTER D. CROW, *Professor of Education,*
Brooklyn College

I T PERHAPS is much easier to describe the kind of person the teacher of academically able learners should be than to perform effectively as such. One cannot conceive of any greater educational challenge than that of guiding the learning process of a gifted young person. Although the academically able child has made good learning progress throughout the years, he sometimes has accomplished this almost completely on his own. The superior individual often learns in spite of the teacher.

Personal Qualities

What qualifies an individual to function in the capacity of a teacher of the gifted? What traits should he possess? What techniques should be utilized? What assurance can we have that a teacher will promote further learning rather than interfere with the creative processes that exemplify the thinking of the gifted?

As do any other learners, gifted individuals need stimulation from those who attempt to lead them and direct their thinking. The teacher who hopes to succeed in motivating able learners must have extensive and intensive knowledge of the areas to be studied and learned. He himself should possess originality, imagination, and creativeness. His resourcefulness as a teacher is enhanced to the degree that a high level of intelligence is evidenced by him through his deep understanding and constructive judgments.

The teacher of the gifted must possess those personal qualities that will be admired and respected by his students. To give stimulating leadership requires that the teacher possess such personal traits as friendliness, patience, tact, enthusiasm, and a keen sense of humor. His personal influence will be more effective if he has self-confidence and is just, impartial, and open-minded. He also should be modest, adaptable, honest, and sincere. He needs to practice considerable self-control. He should be culturally and professionally qualified to assist children to learn in a teaching-learning situation. In short, he should possess: *resourcefulness, intelligence, emotional stability, considerateness, buoyancy, objectivity, drive, attractiveness, refinement, cooperativeness,* and *reliability*—the personal qualities that one can expect to find in any effective teacher.

Does the teacher himself need to be gifted in order to guide the learning of the gifted student? This probably would be an impossible goal to achieve. It would be difficult to try to staff all gifted classes with teachers having extremely high IQ's. Although good scholarship and a wide cultural background are important, it is not suggested that the teacher needs to be an expert in every area of knowledge in which a gifted individual may be interested. However, the teacher should be sufficiently resourceful to be able to give leadership to any learner who wants to explore further in any given field.

The teacher of the gifted is entitled to say occasionally "I do not know." It then is his responsibility, however, either to obtain the needed information for his students or to suggest sources that they themselves can consult. Gifted learners are ready to accept the fact that the teacher does not know everything. They do want their teacher to have the quality of understanding them as individuals. To the degree that a gifted child deviates from the average, he has great need for the display of an understanding attitude toward him.

The education of the gifted tends to be most effective in an atmosphere favorable to their special learning needs. Teachers of gifted children must be able to recognize the possession of giftedness and then to be trained sufficiently to provide the setting and conditions that make it possible for bright learners to develop their special talents to the fullest. Teachers must be prepared to deal with able students as individuals. For maximum benefit, each student needs to be motivated to extend himself as far as possible in the direction of his interests and goals.

Attention to Individual Differences

The successful teacher of gifted learners directs his energy to the end that the gifted are the focal point of his thinking and planning. He constantly is involved in identifying the needs of his charges; he helps them set and define reasonable goals. Able learners need supervision of their behavior as well as of their learning activities. These learners need to be helped to learn to live with others who are not able to progress academically as rapidly as they can. The achievement of these attitudes constitutes a great challenge to the learners themselves and becomes one of the most significant responsibilities of the teacher.

The provision for individual differences becomes more than an academic project; it is a real problem that needs to be met daily. The kinds of learning experiences that are provided for the learners or that are selected by them help create favorable mind sets and provide excellent motivation that stimulates greater activity in learning. These activities should not take on the nature of busy work but should be the kind of projects that are meaningful and worthwhile.

Since the teacher is confronted with the problem of working with gifted individuals in group situations, he must learn to direct activities that can be utilized in group situations. Here his leadership is definitely challenged. He must establish in the minds of his talented learners the portrayal of good human relations. Some of these personal qualities will show through as he carefully evaluates the progress of each learner in the achievement of his chosen goal.

The experience of teaching average children may be of value to persons who undertake the motivation of the learners with superior ability. This experience enables teachers to obtain proper perspectives and to achieve an appreciation of the manner in which able students differ from less able learners in academic pursuits. They also are helped thereby to recognize the many characteristics that all learners have in common.

The teacher who shows evidence of solid scholarship and creative ability tends to earn the confidence of the able learner. If he publishes material or otherwise demonstrates his creative talent he is likely to stimulate able students in a way that is denied another teacher who neither publishes nor exhibits ability in art or craft work, nor participates in other forms of creative production.

Teachers should take advantage of any available enriching experiences that will improve their effectiveness in working with able students. They should become active in local and national professional organizations and subscribe to as many appropriate professional journals as their funds will permit. They might engage in experimental work in which able students can take an active part.

Talented students are eager learners. They often are prepared to debate the results of their reading or listening. The teacher must be able and willing to accept such learner attitudes but should direct the discussion toward constructive conclusions. Students need opportunities to explore on their own. The skill of the teacher is shown when he knows when and how to guide the thinking in these learning situations. The able student needs intellectual discipline and help in developing good work habits. The extent to which the teacher knows the learning characteristics of able students, the better can he help them set and attain high standards of achievement.

Many gifted students are highly sensitive and are easily discouraged if rebuffed by their teachers. This is not to imply that the able student is not to be given social training along with his mental development. The good manners of gifted students are developed in the same way as they are in any other well-mannered individual. The fact that an individual has superior intelligence or is talented does not in and of itself produce a socially mature person. Social grace is a product of good social attitudes achieved in cooperative day-by-day living.

Skillful in Motivation

The teacher of the academically able needs skill in the use of any and all devices that are helpful in learning. He needs to know how to use various kinds of educational and psychological tests and to be able to interpret test results. This ability will enable him better to evaluate and motivate learning progress. He also needs an understanding of the personal development and adjustment problems of his talented learners. His training should give him competence in dealing with the adjustment problems that these students experience.

The effective teacher of academically able learners must have basic understanding and appreciation of the teaching functions that give him supportive insights. More specifically, he needs: (*a*) confidence in adapting techniques and procedures to the needs of the gifted, (*b*) appreciation and acceptance of the implications and obligations of the teacher-learner relationship, (*c*) understanding of limitations as well as potentialities of learners, (*d*) knowledge of the material he is teaching, (*e*) appreciation of the value of independent study, (*f*) a willingness to adapt new methods and techniques in the teaching-learning situation, and (*g*) ability to utilize scientific procedures in evaluating the achievement of those in his charge.

As stated by Bish and those who have participated in the NEA Project on the Academically Talented Student, the teacher of the gifted shapes up somewhat as follows:

He is creative, imaginative, informed. He is a scholar and continues to maintain a scholar's interest in his field of specialization. He is passionately committed to the subject he teaches and yet is aware of its proper place in relation to other subjects. He is the product of a good liberal education—often with an MA or its equivalent in the subject area he teaches. The teacher of the academically talented is probably himself academically talented.

He has the enthusiasm and the knowledge that will lead the student to move continuously to concepts of an increasingly higher order of complexity.

He is aware that good teaching demands fresh ideas and an ever-increasing body of knowledge. He is willing to work hard for this in summer study, special institutes, and through in-service training. He continues eagerly to explore the subject matter in independent study and research.

He must be willing and able to respond fully to the challenge of the academically talented student, seeking always to deepen the student's interest and perceptions and his own.[1]

55. The Motivation of the Gifted and Teacher Education *

FRANK T. WILSON, *Professor of Education Emeritus, Hunter College*

WHAT do teachers undertake in their classes to facilitate the motivation of their more able pupils? Do they lean heavily upon prestige factors, such as grades and praise or reprimand and give relatively incidental heed to motivation arising from the giftedness of their unusual pupils? Or do they make a substantial appeal to these children's abilities and put relatively little emphasis on prestige factors? Do teachers tend to utilize the motivating "cultural factors" in their school communities as essential leads in inducing pupils to achieve in their school work? The answers to these questions are significant for teacher education.

In order to shed light on this matter, the Metropolitan Association for the Study of the Gifted, through a special membership committee, solicited reports from interested teachers in the metropolitan area describing classroom activities that they felt were well-motivated, particularly for their more able children. Of the large number of reports received, many proved

---

[1] This material was furnished by Charles E. Bish.

* From *The Journal of Teacher Education*, June, 1961, pp. 179–83. Reprinted with permission.

to be so sketchy that they could not be used in the study, even though some were very interesting. Thirty-two were finally selected by the committee and analyzed. Three of them, somewhat condensed, were reproduced at length in the final committee report. The remaining twenty-nine were analyzed in chart form to indicate the grade and mental level of classes, the method of initiating the reported activities, and the main features of the activities as they developed. This chart comprises eight pages of the final mimeographed report. The three lengthy accounts run to twenty-four pages. The remainder of this article will be devoted to the final section of the committee's complete report.[1]

Parts I and II of "Studies in Motivation and the Education of the Gifted," have perhaps thrown some light upon certain aspects of this important, though complicated, problem. From the theoretical point of view, there seems to be support for the thesis that unusual children tend to possess strongly activating drives to achieve in areas in which their special abilities exist. Some psychologists propose that the realization of potential development for the more able has fullest promise when these drives are a major element in their developmental experiences. They believe that parents and educators should strive to seek out and nurture whatever unusual abilities children possess and capitalize on the drives that arise from such capabilities.

Drives and Interests of the Gifted

Our reports from teachers indicate that it seems to be their usual practice to take hold of these drives and interests of their unusual pupils easily and confidently. They find that such drives tend to advance projects and other activities of the class. Teachers frequently report that these children take the lead in creative productions, suggesting what to do and how to proceed, and carry other pupils along with them. In instances where many unusually able pupils work together, there seems likely to be exciting expansion and enrichment of the developing experiences. Teachers seem to feel that important satisfactions come to children from such highly motivated activities and, especially in the case of the more able, that the degree of the satisfactions are apt to be somewhat in proportion to the excellence of the achievement that takes place.

The problem of motivation and giftedness is complicated, moreover, by the multitude of cultural factors that, from earliest years, are brought to

---

[1] See Metropolitan Association for the Study of the Gifted, "Studies in Motivation of the Gifted: Part II: Practices of Classroom Teachers" (New York: the Association, 1959).

bear, consciously and unconsciously, upon children in their nurture. Sociologists and psychologists have given helpful analyses of many of these factors and have indicated some of the values and some of the ill effects that may result from them.

In our modest analysis of teachers' practices there were numerous evidences that teachers were aware of many of these factors and that they did utilize them to strengthen the outcomes of learning experiences. For example, the motivation of the group that arranged an "International Dinner" was clearly much reinforced by the approval received from the parents, who must have been intercultural in their approach to social relationships. Again, the boy who was "treading education" while awaiting the glad day when he could leave school and "swagger around . . . auctions" was jolted by the logic of his need to acquire enough English to express sales activities adequately.

However, our teacher reports also indicated that there was neither servile nor convenience utilization of extraneous factors of motivation that sometimes are used to produce effort on the part of pupils when interest is lacking. Not an instance was reported of resort to the motivations to get an "A" on an activity, to avoid disapproval at home for poor school work, or to win an enviable prestige status. These recourses in the utilization of motivation seemed to our teachers to be foreign to the outcomes they felt were important. They apparently were in agreement with Dewey's sentiments that

To make [material] interesting by extraneous inducements deserves all the bad names which have been applied to the doctrine of interest in education.[2]

Herein, perhaps, lies the heart of the problem of motivation of the gifted: How may one integrate the strong promptings of inner drives related to the unusual abilities of able children and the strong cultural factors that may be constructive in their nature, but if misused may be damaging to developing genius? This is not an easy task because the problems of motivation are truly as complicated as human life and as varied as the number of individuals living. Teacher education institutions have an opportunity to help solve this problem much more effectively than is at present the case.

Releasing Constructive Motives

No world-shaking solutions will be proposed in this report. Instead, a brief discussion will be made of the methods that teachers have found help-

[2] John Dewey, *Democracy and Education* (New York: Macmillan Co., 1916), p. 150.

ful in releasing children's constructive motives and that they believe will foster the desirable development of the abilities of unusual individuals.

1. Good teachers try to find out the nature and the degree of unusual abilities possessed by their pupils. If we may believe our colleagues in developmental psychology, this means not 1 or 2 per cent of our children, but 15 to 20 per cent, a radically different matter. Others go even further, asserting with Hughes Mearnes that "every child has a gift." Whatever the situation, unusual abilities do appear in varying degrees and preservice teachers should have some degree of insight and skill in finding and nurturing these special capabilities.

2. Parents and school people should accept these special abilities as worthy, even when the degree is not extreme, despite the present clamor to "return to the three R's" and to make many more gifted children into engineers or scientists. Difficulties are not only multiplied if we foresee 15 per cent of children as unusual in one or more respects, but they are also intensified because some of these special abilities will be strange and even frightening to some teachers. How, for instance, can all teachers be expected to accept and contribute to the development of abilities to handle snakes and lizards, to breed horses, build space platforms, fly on the flying trapeze, and more! Inevitably the acceptance of some of these abilities must be more in spirit than in exercise in the classroom, but it nevertheless can be warm, genuine, and a model of broad human interest in and approval of what other people can do. Every teacher knows how much feelings of security strengthen the development of children's personalities and, ultimately, of the achievement of most of them.

A special need for help arises when children have unique abilities not esteemed in their social group. For example, sometimes—more often than not in our culture—a boy's poetic talent is ridiculed. Unless it is supported by a teacher or another accepting adult he may develop deep psychological conflicts over the problem of whether to be loyal to his special giftedness and thereby suffer the disapproval of his peers, or to turn from his personal excellence in order to gain social approval. Students who are preparing to teach need orientation toward the significance of these matters as to both their social importance and the rights of children who possess unusual abilities for their full unique self-realization.

3. Generous provision of materials, opportunities to make use of them, and suitable experiential procedures need to be made. Books, supplies, equipment, space, program time, and encouragement to use these in ways constructive to growth are essential. Textbook teaching as the main school business is no longer defensible for these able children. Finding out, observing, comparing, analyzing, planning, evaluating—the use of the many

and varied higher-level and creative processes—must have a large place
in educative experiences if the development of individual capacities is the
main issue at stake. With 15 to 20 per cent of children growing in as many
different unusual ways, much free time for individual or small group
activities must be made available.

The task of providing and being appreciative of a wide variety of materials can scarcely be left to the ingenuity of teachers. As professional persons they must be prepared with much knowledge and skill while they are
developing competency. Almost more than anything, they must learn the
peculiar ways in which the very able utilize materials and how they progress
in their learning. There is sufficient evidence at hand to indicate that
unusual children are unusual in developmental processes as well as in
abilities. A devoted teacher who resorts to pressuring unusually able children merely to do more and better in the same old ways with the same old
materials may be jeopardizing extraordinary excellence.

4. These approaches to the growth of unusual children provide the
fertile soil from which socialized natures may be produced. From this soil
deep-lying satisfactions arise because of the successes and satisfactions that
are shared in common enterprises—some through skill in performance
and others through a superiority of mind or talents of many sorts. These
outcomes make real the hope that joint endeavor may contribute to the advantage of all beyond that which any one individual alone could achieve.

In this sort of "alive" school work there are also opportunities to help
the more able grasp and accept ethical and philosophical understandings
and insights on which the justification for democratic living has its bases.
There seems good reason to believe that the attainment of socialized living
is to a large extent the product of motivations to work and play together to
attain common and worthwhile goals. This intensely critical problem of
development also can scarcely be left to chance and to the practices and
purposes of education pertaining to "average" children. In undergraduate
teacher education every student should be helped to understand the socialization of the more able and have some skill in developing it. Much more
must also be learned by college staffs about what is involved in the problem and how to solve it constructively.

5. In schools and homes where experiences similar to those that have
been indicated previously are the regimen, there is a need for guidance
by teachers and parents that shows more insight and a sense of social purpose than is usual in authoritarian or overly permissive schools and house-
holds. Teachers who have undertaken such roles with highly gifted pupils
frequently assert that their main function is to guide rather than to instruct,
because the eagerness of thirty-five young dynamos responds powerfully
to materials, programs, and purposes. The class that dramatized "Cinder-

ella" in the "old-fashioned way," reported by one of our cooperating class-room teachers, is an instance of this self-carrying activity of gifted children. In fact, guidance of unusual children is in large degree guidance of their drives, patterned by the continuing purpose to help them engage in full and rich educational experiences, governed by their individual needs and natures. If this guidance of inner motivation is carried on day by day, and year after year, in accord with principles of individuation in vividly socialized settings, it promises reasonable attainment of potential development and lives dedicated to achievement for the well-being of all.

Improved Teacher Education Needed

Our study of teachers' practices leads us to the conclusion that, in order to secure teachers who can identify, gladly accept, provide suitable school experiences for unusual children, and perform the role of guidance counselor, there appears to be an immediate and pressing need for improved preservice teacher education programs. These programs will—in fact, must—be almost completely new ones in most of our colleges for teachers. They must be designed to acquaint teachers-to-be with the nature and nurture of children possessing unusual capabilities and to prepare every new teacher to serve gifted pupils constructively in consonance with the diversity and significance of their many varieties of giftedness.[3]

One- or two-week units on superficial points in regard to the gifted—or lightly treated topics in courses on educational psychology, principles, or methods—will not do. One of the most needed developments in this area is to gather together and work over the findings that have been made in connection with the more able. It seems likely that there is no group that has been so intensively studied as these gifted children by top-grade research investigations and by the most able analyses and discussions. These materials need evaluation and translation into programs and emerging philosophies of education for the gifted. Perhaps no greater nor more feasible contribution to the nation's schools can be undertaken than this. Teacher education institutions have a challenge and an opportunity to contribute most usefully to such undertakings.

Programs are needed that will treat the problems in regard to the gifted in sequential order, from an elementary consideration of their nature and needs to a specialized study of more complicated problems. Some of the

[3] *Editors' Note:* For a report of a survey of objectives and outlines of courses on the education of the gifted and a list of the 66 institutions reporting offering such courses, see Joseph L. French, "The Preparation of Teachers of the Gifted," *Journal of Teacher Education,* XII (March, 1961), 69–72.

advanced courses should be limited solely to the education of gifted children. Staff members especially prepared by training and experience in this particular area should be appointed to faculties and be assigned special responsibilities in developing the program. Students should have many face-to-face experiences with gifted children and should observe and participate in reasonably adequate programs for the gifted that are in operation in good schools. The program should begin early in the under-graduate years and should continue through the master's and doctor's degree levels. Advanced-degree dissertations on problems of the education of the gifted should be encouraged in all postgraduate teacher education institutions.

Workshops, conferences, study, and experimental projects dealing with this phase of school work should be continually provided in school systems in order to reeducate teachers and the public as to the importance of suitable education of gifted children and for the development of particular provisions that will assure greater success in the enterprise.

While most gifted children do "take care of themselves" up to a point, the need for suitable nurture at every stage is recognized in order to fore-stall excessive underachievement and to maximize the realization of reasonable potential. Indeed, this regimen is not unlike the constant care and culture of choice breeds and crops practiced in animal husbandry and agriculture. No sensible farmer, for instance, expends most of his energies trying to coax good-quality seed to make the best of impoverished soil. On the contrary, for his good seed the farmer prepares his best soil with care and cultivates and nourishes the crop with almost daily attention, knowing full well that the choice seed will respond miraculously to loving care. Teacher education programs also must prepare new teachers to nourish the choice seed.

The committee that helped with this study of teachers' practices was well aware of the complexity of the problem of motivation of pupils and the paucity of field and scientific studies of the problem as related to unusually able children. It therefore seems proper in this report to hope for further and greatly varied investigations in this area. Among such there might well be a study of the accounts that unusually able children give of school experiences that they have found stimulating and satisfying, with data included as to particular things that in their opinion were either constructive or unconstructive. A similar study of parents' reports on their identification of the motivational factors of their gifted children might give added information of interest and value.

56. Teaching Personnel and Gifted Learners *

CHARLES H. BOEHM, *Superintendent of Public Instruction, Harrisburg, Pennsylvania*

Introduction

A good program begins with good planning. Since the best program for able pupils is one that is locally determined, developed, and implemented, the administrator has the initial responsibility. He should lead community and faculty study of the need for the program and of the type of program and curriculum that will best serve the pupils. Community study should include a survey of community resources and attitudes. It may reveal a need for adult education on the purposes of the program. (Sometimes, to provide a really good program, the administrator must resist pressure from the well-meaning but partially informed community leader or the adamant educationist.) Faculty study includes determination of the criteria for selection of the pupils who will participate in the program; selection of the type of program organization for able children that will best serve the individual child and the school as a whole; and liaison with other schools and other educational agencies in the community.

When the program reaches the operational stage, it is the principal's responsibility to see that it functions smoothly. All too frequently, teachers, department heads, and supervisors at the secondary level develop an elective course intended to serve the needs of able pupils, and then find only two or three pupils in the class because required subjects are given at the same period.

The administrator should strive for a balanced program that provides opportunity for the optimum development of both academic and creative talent. Implementation of the program requires capable, talented teachers, well-stocked and well-maintained instructional materials centers, well-

* From *Guide to Planning for Able Pupils,* Commonwealth of Pennsylvania, Department of Public Instruction, Harrisburg, Pa., 1962, pp. 1–4. Reprinted with permission. (Picture omitted.)

supplied laboratories, and a plentiful supply of all types of consumable materials. Provision of an effective guidance program for able youth involving both classroom teachers and guidance counselors should also be of paramount concern.

Consideration: The Role of the Administrator in the Education of Able Children

THE COUNTY SUPERINTENDENT

1. Leadership—stresses the need for programs for able children.
2. Provides consultive services.
3. Acts as liaison between county office and school districts.
4. Provides liaison with colleges and other institutions of higher education.

THE SUPERINTENDENT OR SUPERVISING PRINCIPAL

1. Initiates study of need for program.
2. Secures the support of the school board.
3. Budgets adequate funds.
4. Secures consultant help.
5. Provides district articulation and coordination.
6. Provides competent faculty.
7. Provides guidance services.
8. Provides adequate materials.
9. Organizes high-quality in-service programs.
10. Helps to plan comprehensive programs of evaluation.
11. Develops philosophy favorable to the program with the principals.

THE BUILDING PRINCIPAL

1. Accepts responsibility as educational leader.
2. Participates in faculty planning.
3. Schedules program.
4. Provides liaison with community.
5. Uses sound policies for grouping pupils.
6. Insures parent-faculty understanding.
7. Participates in high-quality in-service programs.
8. Selects a key staff or faculty member, interested in the program, to provide additional momentum for project.
9. Provides effective supervision.
10. Helps to develop programs of evaluation.

Consideration: The Faculty

The expression "Only diamonds can polish diamonds" has implications for the selection of teachers for able students. Yet it may become a question of which diamond polishes the other, for a teacher who is a truly brilliant adult will be mentally far ahead of even the brightest youth. Therefore, along with superior intelligence, the patience and adaptability that are generally accepted to be attributes of a good teacher are especially necessary in the teacher of able pupils.

Probably it is well if the teacher of able children also teaches average children either for part of the day or in alternate years. Such contact helps the teacher to maintain an appreciation of how much able students vary from the norm, and conversely of how many characteristics they share with all children and youth.

The teacher must have a good knowledge of the subject area in which he works. "Learning together" between teacher and pupils can be a stimulating, rewarding experience. It can also be a waste of time, and perhaps even a learning of misinformation. The teacher must have enough personal security to say "I don't know" but, if he is to hold the respect of able youth, he must not have to say it too often. The maxim "What thou dost not know, thou canst not teach" retains its truth.

The teacher should show evidence of scholarship or creative ability. Able students are stimulated by a teacher who publishes materials, exhibits art or craftwork, plays in a symphony orchestra, participates in a little theater or dance group, or is recognized for some achievement in the community. Teachers should be given frequent opportunities for enriching experiences, and the teachers should take advantage of those that are provided. Such opportunities are of many types, not all of them large-scale or expensive. For example:

1. subscription to an educational news service that provides short reports of conferences, legislation, educational experiments, as well as other educational news, and new materials for the gifted, able, creative, and talented.
2. new books in the faculty library.
3. in-service training programs—(such as a "busman's holiday" faculty trip to observe programs for able students in another school system.)
4. attendance at state and national conferences (payment of a teacher's expenses at a conference may be school district money well spent.)
5. salary increases for advanced university work in teaching field or in closely related areas.

   6. summer workshops or seminars.
   7. observation of the able students in other programs, subjects, or classes in the school.
   8. sabbatical leave for further study.

The teacher must know when to direct the learning situation and when to let the student explore on his own. Even the best-informed teacher must be able to face challenges from able students with equanimity. Brilliant students are questing, questioning, eager, intense, and sometimes iconoclastic individuals. They do not hesitate to debate what they read or hear. They need to have guidance in evaluation, interpretation, and analysis of materials and data. Some of these students are highly sensitive and easily crushed when their questions are met with rebuffs from the teacher. Yet, it must be admitted that a highly intelligent or talented student is not by that fact a well-mannered student. In his case, to give him social grace is as important as to give him information.

The teacher must have a good knowledge of the learning characteristics of able pupils. He must exercise prudent judgment, particularly when he participates in the selection of gifted, creative, or able pupils. He must set attainable standards and goals for pupils. Faced with students of superior ability whose achievement is a challenge to the teacher, the teacher in turn is apt to raise standards continually. The teacher rationalizes these standards by believing that "students will give you what you demand" and that "stretching is good for them." Two aspects of this are true: (1) Students need to develop good work habits and skills, and (2) students need intellectual discipline.

However, there are certain detrimental effects from teachers' standards that are set too high for the student. Two probable reasons for such standards are that the teacher uses them to camouflage his own inability to meet fully the needs of the students or to insure the personal prestige that he derives from superior work by students. Able students are usually (although there are exceptions) eager to succeed. They are also apt to be competitive; in fact, they create competition among themselves within the group. While these students are mentally well-balanced, socially active and secure, and able to carry a heavy work load, more situations exist than are generally admitted where students overwork, become physically weakened, or emotionally distraught from the effort to meet unrealistic standards. Some able students are never satisfied with their own performance. Continual raising of standards may contribute to their self-dissatisfaction and emotional instability. Able students, like all other pupils, need sufficient repetition for mastery, but useless repetition, busy work, and time-consuming, poorly planned homework assignments should be eliminated.

Faculty study and planning are necessary for initiation and full implementation of any program for able children. There must be agreement concerning the necessity for the program. Sometimes a faculty studies its student body carefully and reaches a justified conclusion that no program is needed. The school, the faculty, and the students have still benefited from the study—teachers will be better aware of the ability levels of the students, and will have a better basis for future recognition of able youth. Even though no pupils may qualify under a strict definition of "able," such a study can benefit those who are relatively more able. When it is agreed that a program is necessary, there should be a faculty and administrative consensus as to the form the program should take. The program should be studied thoroughly from the view of its effect upon the academic achievement and the social adjustment of both the able and the average children in the school. Each teacher should clearly understand his part in the program or his relationship to it. Articulation of faculty understanding from elementary school through college level is of major importance.

Consideration: Guidance

Guidance for the able is sometimes hampered by the popular misconception that the able need no guidance—they can guide themselves. Simple observation will refute this—how many brilliant students have been influenced by pressure from parents and other relatives to enter certain professions because of family tradition or because of the social prestige associated with these professions. Too often such "guidance" results in an unhappy, irritable physician or clergyman, and the real losers are those whom he tries to serve.

The guidance counselor must be an alert, sympathetic, sensitive person, capable of some sympathy with a brilliant or talented child or adolescent. He must realize when guidance is necessary and when it is not. An occassional, truly gifted pupil may have so many abilities, so widely distributed, that vocational and educational guidance is very difficult, and the responsibility for helping him to make choices is very great. Specific areas in which the counselor can be very helpful include:

The pupil's program. The counselor should see that the student's program gives him an opportunity to explore all his abilities and talents. It should be a balanced program that gives him the courses necessary for college entrance or vocational placement, offers him a challenge, and when desirable offers advanced placement so that he can reach the years of professional preparation in a shorter time.

The pupil's achievement. Frequent evaluation should be made to determine whether the pupil's achievement reaches his potential as indicated by observation and by valid tests. When it does not, analysis of the possible causes, perhaps including diagnostic testing, should be made and remedial measures instituted.

The college dilemma. The counselor can do much to ease the frantic hysteria surrounding college entrance by:

1. Encouraging the school to provide a curriculum well suited to the college-bound student.
2. Having wide knowledge of college openings and scholarship opportunities.
3. Encouraging students to make their college plans early and realistically.
4. Helping parents to plan for the pupil's college program and financial needs.
5. Establishing a personal contact with the personnel of colleges attended by past students.

Vocational choice. The counselor's vocational guidance should include:

1. Career conferences at which young people may gain information concerning a profession or other vocations.
2. Occupation interest inventories with the student who is unsure of his choice.
3. Appraisal of pupil interests, capabilities, and inclinations.
4. Community liaison in job placement by stimulating the interest of business, industry, and the professions in the vocational choice of able pupils.
5. Aid to students in finding summer job opportunities that will help them in exploring their abilities.

Personal guidance. On an average, able pupils are well-adjusted, socially competent individuals. Many of them are outstanding school leaders. However, some able pupils have severe adjustment problems. They come into conflict with other pupils, parents, and teachers. Some have retiring personalities; some are not accepted by their classmates. Some have problems stemming from conflict with community mores and prejudices. For the guidance counselor, the problems are especially serious because a poorly adjusted brilliant student is usually a great loss to the school and to the community. The guidance counselor should use every technique at his command with the pupil, the school, and the family to reach an adjustment that will be of maximum benefit to the individual pupil and to the other pupils in the school. When the nature of the problem falls outside the province of the school, he should use the help available through referral to appropriate community services.

57. The Teacher of the Gifted *

WELDON R. OLIVER, *Superintendent of Schools,*
Niagara Falls, AND
ANNE K. HORGAN

WHAT ARE the characteristics of a competent teacher for gifted learners? The answer is obvious, namely, that the qualities of a good teacher of any type of pupil are needed by the good teacher of the gifted. As the gifted child possesses in greater abundance the same abilities possessed by average individuals, so it is with teachers of the gifted. Among the qualities we might mention are:

1. Good mental health. The teacher of the gifted should be a well-adjusted person and possess personal warmth and a real affection for children.
2. Superior mental endowment.
3. Intellectually curious with broad interests and a fund of general information in many areas of living; a knowledge of the past, and its implications, what is happening in the present and its implications for the future.
4. Capable of stimulating children to think critically and inspiring children to utilize their abilities to best advantage.
5. They should understand the psychology and developmental processes of the gifted and their special learning problems.
6. Must completely accept and not be threatened by the mentally highly endowed.
7. A sense of social and professional responsibility. Capable of helping

* From *Gifted Children,* Board of Education, Niagara Falls, N.Y., pp. 11–12. Reprinted with permission.

children to formulate a philosophy of life that will eventuate in relatively mature, contributing, responsible adulthood.

8. Has given evidence in a regular classroom that he or she is ingenious, creative, and imaginative.
9. Be able to help children advance toward the realization of the good of mature self-discipline.

In December 1953, we presented to the two Informal Groups then in operation in Niagara Falls a checklist of twenty characteristics that are considered attributes of a good teacher. We then asked the children to arrange them in rank order; that is, ranking the characteristic they considered the most important as number one and so on down the line.

The children in the Fifth Street Informal Group ranked *Likes Children* and *Likes Teaching* as the number one characteristic of a good teacher; the second rank placement was *Patience*.

The children in the Cleveland Avenue Group ranked *Patience* as the number one characteristic and *Fair to Every Pupil* received the second highest ranking.

58. Choice and Creativity in Teaching and Learning *

EDWARD C. WEIR, *Associate Professor of Education and Coordinator of Student Teaching in Secondary Education, University of Pittsburgh*

WE MAY define learning as the "self-incorporation of meaning into the experience of the learner." But what is the meaning of such a definition?

Among other things, it means that learning is a process of personal choice-making; it is activity in which the learner, through his own experience and out of his own motivations, decides for himself what he is to believe and what he is to do with his life. The definition also means that learning is an act of creation in which the learner brings into being new meanings for the ordering and enrichment of his own living.

*From *Phi Delta Kappan*, June, 1962, pp. 408–10. Reprinted with permission.

Teaching, then, is involvement with other human beings in the uniquely human experience of choice-making. It is involvement with other human beings in the processes through which man's unique creative powers are brought to bear upon the mysteries of existence.

To say that learning is the "*self-incorporation* of meaning" is to say that the dynamics of learning, both in its initiatory and developmental phase, lie within the organism rather than in the environment. The individual learns only that which he chooses to learn. While it is true that the environment may limit the array of alternative meanings among which the learner can choose, it is equally true that the learner is the final arbiter as to what he is to learn, and it is also true that the individual frequently can rearrange the environment so that he creates new alternatives. The choice of what is to be learned will be made by the individual in terms of how important the choice appears to him and not in accordance with how objectively important it is or how important it obviously is in the eyes of the most reasonable and authoritative people. His choice of the particular alternative that he will take into his experience and employ in regulating subsequent behavior is a function of the learner's recognition of the relationships between the alternative and his own concept of self. Those alternatives that he sees as strongly central in their relationship to his self-concept will be most effectively learned. Finally, he will tend to appropriate into his field of meanings those alternatives that serve to enhance his own self-concept.

Central in this view of learning is the idea that learning—and all human behavior for that matter—is a selective process. Or perhaps a more appropriate statement would be that learning is a *selecting* process.

The human animal is not a passive organism, waiting like a lump of clay to be molded by the accidents of environmental circumstance. The individual himself is a circumstance—the most important circumstance in his own environment. He selects from the environment those stimuli to which he is to react, and he is not only his own best judge of the appropriateness of his subsequent action, he is in the final analysis the *only* judge. No matter how wrongheaded or wronghearted his action may seem to others—to his teachers, his boss, his parents, his friends and enemies— the action that he takes is to him always the "right" action. He may modify his judgment after the event and consequently change his line of action, but it is the behaver who does the judging and makes the change—and no one else.

The application to learning is clear. We select from the environment certain elements to which we respond. We can only learn in those situations that seem to us to require action on our part. Learning, therefore, cannot be imposed upon another merely by repeatedly exposing him to stimuli that *we* select, requiring him to behave in ways that *we* know to be correct and presenting him from time to time with the results of *our* objective judgments about the quality of his behavior. The individual may learn while involved in this process, but he only does so to the extent that *his* views as to what is important, *his* discriminations with regard to appropriate behaviors, *his* subjective appraisals of the effectiveness of his own behavior happen to coincide with our own. Such complete and precise unanimity of perceptions between two or more individuals, each with his own unique complex of experiences and meanings, is a rare coincidence indeed.

What more often happens is that the learner goes through the motions of the prescribed action and presents for the teacher's observation the formulas—or at least some of the formulas—that he knows the teacher deems correct. Whereupon the teacher gives a grade or in other ways indicates her judgment as to the amount of learning that has occurred. The grade, however, is not very meaningful, for regardless of what the grade says, the learning that results from such a process of "going through the motions" can only be superficial and transitory. It is true that the learner "chooses" such a course of action, but he makes this particular choice from among other alternatives all of which he sees as being even more unpleasant and less self-enhancing. Place him in a situation where other alternatives are present and he will behave differently and learn differently. In this situation, he chooses to behave so as to give the impression of learning in order to satisfy a need that in his view will only be present as long as he is taking this subject, is with this teacher, is in school —and the learning will fade away when the need for the learning is no longer present in his field of perceptions. Furthermore, even though he "chooses" to do what the teacher tells him is best, the choice area is peripheral to his central concept of self; it is low on his own personal hierarchy of importance. As long as it remains so, the resultant learning— or at least that which the teacher or other observer has been able to detect—will remain peripheral in its effect on his behavior.

We are not saying that no significant or lasting learning occurs in instances such as the aforementioned, but rather that the learning we look for and give our greatest attention to in the kind of teaching described is seldom significant or lasting. Unobservable to our eyes, since we are not looking for it, is the extremely important learning that frequently does occur and remains to shape the direction and quality of the learner's entire life. He may learn, for example, that it is the surface things that count, not how you really are inside. Keeping up appearances, putting on a good "show," maintaining a proper front, these are the determinants of passing marks in the school of life, not what you really think and live. And, of course, if the individual does incorporate such a meaning into himself through his school experiences, the direction of his life is likely to be toward narrow ends and the quality of his living marked by preoccupation with superficiality. He will not be inclined to probe the deeper, richer meanings, the ennobling potentialities of his existence. And having made superficiality central in his own living, having inadvertently cheapened his own self-concept, he can only relate himself to others at a superficial level. He cannot share with others in the significant concerns of living, because he has nothing to share, nor can they share with him, for the deeper meanings others may have to share can have little meaning for him, little relevancy to his view of what is central in his life.

To say that learning cannot be imposed, but is a matter of choice by the learner is not to say that teaching cannot occur. Teaching, as we all know, can occur and does occur. Successful teaching—that which brings about growth in the learner and helps the learner to become what is in him to become—is of a particular kind. It seeks to help the learner to know what he is and what are his deepest wants in life. It asks of the learner, "What do these life situations mean to you? Do you sense any inconsistencies or inadequacies? What are your worries and fears, your problems, concerns and anxieties? Do these ideas or this area of human knowledge relate in any way to your life problems and goals? How can I be of help to you as you explore and expand the meaning of your universe, as you seek to identify the alternative courses of thought and action available to you? What opportunities can I provide for you to share in the thinking of others and thereby sharpen and broaden your own thinking? What support can I provide that will stimulate the development of your own unique creative powers, that will build your self-confidence in trying out new ideas in accepting both success and failure as opportunities for learning and growth, in making increasingly realistic evaluations of your own ideas and actions as you move continuously forward in your progress toward your own life goals? How can I help you to employ your own intelligence to enrich the quality of meaningfulnes in your living? *What can I do that will help you grow in your power to make effective choices?*"

The Creative Nature of Learning

Learning is not only selective, it is also creative. Our choices are not always limited to the alternatives that are—or appear to be—objectively in the environment. Man is continuously restructuring his environment so that it takes on meanings that were not there before. These innovations in the field of meaning cause the environment to take on a new configuration, so that, insofar as our behavior is concerned, we are now interacting with an environment that in some respect is different than it was before. We respond, in other words, not to the environment as it appears to others nor even solely to the environment as it objectively is. *We respond primarily to the environment we create for ourselves.* Even physical innovations occur because someone refuses to accept descriptions of environmental situations that common sense prescribes or logic dictates. Someone says, "What if it really isn't this way at all? If it were really some other way, what would happen?" He creates a new meaning, he sees the environmental situation in a new way, he finds new possibilities for action available to him, he acts accordingly, and a wheel or a theory of evolution is invented. Thus did Copernicus create a whole new universe by insisting that the obvious was not true. Thus did Kettering develop the self-starter by flouting some of the most fundamental "laws" of engineering. Thus is nuclear energy now available to us—for good or bad—because Einstein challenged an axiom.

All men, then, are innovators. Each man creates his own universe through his perceptions of it, and he behaves in ways that are consistent with the universe he creates. Rather than the environment imposing its order upon us, we impose order upon the environment. The order that the individual imposes on the environment may not make sense to anyone else; indeed it may be so out of line with reality that the individual lives in a world of delusion; nevertheless, it is the only order that makes sense to the individual. The meanings the individual creates, however disorderly they may appear to be, are always in the direction of orderliness.

Learning, then, cannot be thought of as the mere duplication of an act performed by someone else nor the copying of an idea developed by someone else. For the individual, each learning is to some extent new, fresh, and original, the personal creation of the learner. That is why genuine learning is so exhilarating an experience. That is why the world's most interesting, stimulating, and psychologically integrated people are those who live their lives as one long experience in learning, whose living is a continuing act of creation. Significant learning—that which involves the creation of deep personal meaning by the learner—is never routine nor dull. It may necessitate the most rigorous attention to routine. It may require systematic, persistent, and repeated effort of the most exhausting kind. It may be accompanied frequently by frustration and despair as our struggles to create an adequate meaning for experience meet with repeated failure. But it is never dull. The overtone is elation. Anyone who has observed or participated in a group of learners who are struggling to solve a problem that is important to them knows exactly what we mean. In such a situation—particularly as one senses that the final moment of creation is near—the atmosphere fairly crackles with excitement. These moments are, of course, the greatest joys of teaching, and the teacher who frequently experiences such moments is a successful teacher indeed.

The teacher who is sensitive to the intrinsically creative nature of the process of learning is the teacher who will say to his students, "Trust in your own creative powers, for your life can be no other than your own creation. The whole universe, through all the eons of timeless time, has conspired and is still conspiring to make in you a magnificently ironic design: you are the only creature on the face of the earth who is not just creature, but crea*tor*. As creator, you become what you were designed to become only through the act of creating yourself. Like all the living things on earth, you are form; but the essence of the *human* form inborn in you is that of becoming. You are a thought, a hope, a dream, and a passion. And the thought and the hope and the dream and the passion are yours. You are an idea that no one else has ever had.

"Here is my life that I have created. Here are my thoughts and hopes and dreams and passions. Here are the images of the universe that I have created for myself. They are no more beautiful nor good nor true than the images of your creation—unless you find them so. Take of my images —and of me—whatever stirs you or challenges you, whatever inspires you to raise your own questions and helps you to discover your own answers, whatever generates in you the quest to find out what you are and what you can become. Take of my images—and of me—whatever causes you to trust your own experience so that you can deal with experience meaningfully and productively. Take of me—your teacher—only that which you believe will help you to become the you that you want to become. Only if you make use of me in this way can I become what I want to become—your teacher."

59. Providing for the Gifted, Minneapolis *

MABLE O. MELBY, *Consultant in Curriculum*

PROVISIONS for an able learner are made through some adjustment of his learning experience. He learns more about a subject, he learns about an additional subject, or he learns about it in a different way. He has increased opportunity to take part in activities that value originality, creativity, leadership, responsibility, and critical thinking. The basic type of provision, then, for the able learner is through an adjustment of *Curriculum Content* and *Curriculum Methods*.

Curriculum adjustments for some able learners may be facilitated through group placement. The able learner may be placed in a group with whom he can work more satisfactorily, to whom he can better relate both socially and intellectually. Therefore, a second type of provision is through an adjustment in *Group Placement*, including acceleration, grouping procedures, and part-time special classes.

While it is improbable and impossible that these types of provisions operate separately in enriching the program for able learners, the two types are considered separately on the following pages.

Basic to the aforementioned two types of provisions is attention to *Resources* and *Attitudes*.

Curriculum Content—Elementary

The able learner takes part in activities that are "over and above" basic curriculum; or the able learner takes part in activities in which he assumes a different role, one which is appropriate to his abilities. Both

* From *Educating Our Gifted Children*, pp. 6–8, Minneapolis Public Schools, 1959. Reprinted with permission.

the differentiated assignment and the differentiated role can be approached in various ways.

Differentiated Assignment

The pattern of the differentiated assignment varies according to the nature of the activity, the able learner, the goal, the learning area, and difference in motivational needs.

A differentiated assignment with definable limits is an activity that has a challenge with a foreseeable scope; it has a start and a finish. For example, an able learner pursues the arithmetic assignment of measuring an area, drawing the area to scale, and computing the cost of covering the area with linoleum tile.

A differentiated assignment with less definable limits is an activity that has a start and a finish, but the challenge within the activity encourages initiative and originality. For example, the able learner accepts the responsibility of reporting in an area that requires depth of understanding and advanced reading ability; he uses several sources of information and gives his report using original and self-made aids such as graphs, pictorial presentations, organizational procedures, examples, etc.

An "open-door" challenge is an activity that is as limitless as the child's initiative, resourcefulness, interest, and time. For example, through membership in a nature club an able learner reads for information; participates in activities, such as scale drawing of bird-feeders; plans field trips; keeps records; constructs equipment, such as insect cages; makes use of community resources, such as library interest groups; and develops hobbies.

A special project is an activity that may be self-chosen within a number of suggested enrichment activities. For example, an able learner assumes leadership in the construction of an electric board, preparation of a dramatic sequence, demonstration or application of a scientific principle, or the exploration of a number system different than his own.

A special interest may be self-chosen or initiated, but guided through teacher suggestion. For example, an able learner who is particularly interested in reading biographies develops a Hall of Fame through which he classifies the biographies of leaders according to the type of contribution; sports, science, medicine, leadership, exploration, and/or government.

Differentiated Role

The pattern of the differentiated role also varies according to the nature of the activity, the able learner, the goal, the learning area, and motivational needs.

Leadership opportunity is provided to the able learner through an activity that emphasizes skills in human relationship. For example, an able learner serves as leader of the school council, the editor of the school newspaper, a contributing member of a committee, and/or patrol leader.

Contribute-according-to-ability is a plan within which the class (or group within the class) is engaged in a common activity with the possibility of the contributions varying in quality and quantity according to ability. For example, in the development of a classroom weather station, an able learner constructs and explains several instruments, including a barometer, hygrometer, and an anemometer.

Individualization within a common experience is an activity that lends itself to differentiated performance even though the activity is similar. For example, a creative writing lesson encourages a wide range of performance since the product is as different as the child who is doing the writing.

Enrichment Activities: Examples

Curriculum content, then, is adjusted for the able learner through various adaptations of the differentiated assignment or differentiated role. The following examples of such adaptations are based on classroom observation.

EXAMPLES OF ENRICHMENT ACTIVITIES

An able learner:

1. Learns and reports on the history of measurements.
2. Responds to a writing challenge with originality and expressiveness. His "writing" later appears in *Gems,* a local publication of children's writing.
3. Keeps his class informed on the latest advances in space exploration.
4. Takes his friends on an imaginary London tour; and a series of reports are thus integrated into an interesting and coordinated presentation.
5. Teaches his friends a game with winning positions dependent on binary notation.
6. Shows the comparative speed of airborne vehicles through graph presentation.
7. Previews filmstrips and films pertaining to a unit; evaluates the appropriateness of the material.
8. Constructs number problems pertaining to classroom situations.
9. Plans a time line.

10. Writes a script based on an historical event.
11. Makes scale drawings of meaningful areas—a "to be constructed" pioneer home, a terrarium, an electric board.
12. Traces the derivation of words in the English language.
13. Prepares himself and others for the Symphony Concert through sharing information about the composers, composition, and symphonic arrangements.
14. Serves the Student Council through a job analysis of responsibilities of various members of the Council.
15. Assumes leadership role in planning reports on the planets.
16. Demonstrates the use of the abacus with large numbers.
17. Constructs problems showing the use of numbers in home situations.
18. Attends the United Nations rally; shares experiences with the class.
19. Exercises leadership in editing and organizing a school newspaper.
20. Serves on the School Council.

60. School Programs for the Gifted *

JAMES J. GALLAGHER, *Professor of Education,*
University of Illinois

THE LATE humorist, Robert Benchley, was asked during his college career to write a paper on the nineteenth century Russian-American dispute over salmon fishing rights. Benchley responded that he knew little about either the Russian or American side of the argument, so he would discuss the problem from the point of view of the fish. Sometimes it pays school personnel, too, to try to see the problem from the point of view of the child rather than from the perspective of those working with the child.

The Problems Facing the Gifted Child

We have seen, already, that being a gifted child is no guarantee of escape from the wide variety of emotional difficulties, motivational problems, or

* From *What Research Says to the Teacher: The Gifted Child in the Elementary School,* Department of Classroom Teachers, American Educational Research Association of the National Education Association, Washington, D.C., 1959, pp. 19–25. Reprinted with permission.

conflict of values that beset children of this age. Even well-adjusted and well-motivated gifted children have special problems due to their high ability.

The gifted child must eventually face the problem of adjusting his intellectual skills and interests to the curriculum being offered in the classroom. Thus, he must endure systematic presentation of material that he has long since mastered. He must learn to deal with a situation where the class cannot go into interesting side issues because most of the class still has not mastered the basic concepts that the teacher considers to be part of the "must curriculum."

Another potential problem for the gifted child is his relationship with the other children. As one investigator wrote, the gifted child must learn to "suffer fools gladly." He must inhibit spontaneous and natural statements such as: "Don't you know that?" "Do I have to explain that again?" "You must be pretty dumb not to have heard of that," which can only draw the antagonistic fire of his less intellectually endowed classmates. He has to restrain himself or accept the social ostracism that such carelessly dropped statements often bring.

Another serious decision for the gifted child is to what degree he should press for presentation of his atypical or unusual ideas. Should he risk the interruption of orderly classroom procedure and sequence by suggesting that there were other causes of the Civil War besides the slavery issue? Should he risk the hoot of disbelief from his peers, and perhaps his teacher, by suggesting that some kinds of water can be wetter than other kinds?

Should he risk the teacher's disapproval by suggesting that there really is another experiment that better illustrates air pressure than the one that the teacher has so carefully prepared? Should he volunteer to read an original poem about life and death that may produce derision or uneasiness, or should he keep it to himself? If the classroom teacher is aware of the calculated risks that each gifted child runs by the flexing of his intellectual muscles, much of his puzzling behavior will become understandable.

Problems Facing the Teachers

The difficulties facing the teacher who attempts to meet the needs of the intellectually superior child are formidable indeed. The first major problem is the impressive intellectual heterogeneity in the class. This wide range of intellectual skills continues to get wider with each succeeding grade. Just as automobiles in a race, traveling at different speeds, tend to spread farther and farther apart, so children who are developing at different rates of intelligence tend to spread farther apart as their time in the school program increases.

Thus, by the fourth or fifth grade the typical teacher can expect a situation wherein a few children in the class are still puzzled by the processes of simple addition and subtraction, while others are fully capable of understanding the advanced intricacies of algebra and geometry. How can the classroom teacher meet the needs of these vastly different children?

The second major problem is the teacher's lack of important information about the children in the class. Most teachers do not have adequate access to information relating to social acceptance, motivation, or emotional problems of their pupils.

Curriculum skills make up the third major area in which there is a critical shortage. At the present time, we expect the elementary-school teacher to be a jack-of-all-trades and to possess sufficient training and background in mathematics, science, language arts, social studies, and a variety of lesser subjects to handle the questioning and inquiring minds of children, aged 6 through 14. In many instances, however, the gifted child may possess much more information than his teacher in his special-interest areas.

What Does Enrichment Mean?

One of the solutions to this multitude of problems has been to suggest that the best approach to the education of gifted children is to "enrich the curriculum." What does this mean? Enrichment can be defined as the type of activity devoted to the further development of the particular intellectual skills and talents of the gifted child. Research indicates that these major skills are:

1. The ability to associate and interrelate concepts.
2. The ability to evaluate facts and arguments critically.
3. The ability to create new ideas and originate new lines of thought.
4. The ability to reason through complex problems.
5. The ability to understand other situations, other times, and other people; to be less bound by one's own peculiar environmental surroundings.

Of course, no teacher should, or would, conclude that gifted children possess exclusively any or all of these abilities. These intellectual skills can be found in mentally average or retarded children as well, but it is the intellectually superior child who has been blessed with an abundance of them.

Unless the extra activity planned for the gifted child is directed to the advancement of the characteristics named, it deserves to be called "busy work" rather than enrichment. Thus, the assignment of extra long division problems to the gifted child, who has already finished the regular assignment, is "busy work," whereas the learning of a new method of proving the answer to long division problems would be enrichment. An assignment to search for additional facts about crop production from already used reference books is busy work whereas the task of relating crop productions to political elections would be enrichment.

Providing the Environment to Enrich

Can the regular elementary-school teacher provide the proper environment for enriching the experiences of gifted children? A number of school systems, impressed by the already heavy responsibilities imposed on the classroom teacher, have decided that additional help is necessary. The form and amount of the help differs from community to community, but the goal is the same—to establish the best environment for enriching the curriculum with a minimum amount of dislocation of the child from his normal grouping.

The total school program.   One of the rarest administrative devices for educating gifted children at the elementary level is the special school devoted entirely to the education of intellectually superior children. In these schools, children with high intellectual levels, high achievement test scores, and adequate personal adjustment are eligible for the programs. The advantages of such programs are limited class size, the opportunity to interact with other gifted children, and the availability of many specialists employed as resource persons.

As in practically all special programs for gifted children, much of the responsibility for the development of the program is in the hands of the children themselves, and life in the classroom is informal with a workshop atmosphere prevailing. Special interest groups are encouraged in art, dancing, foreign languages, photography, and music. Such a school also provides valuable opportunities for research and study. The rarity of such schools throughout the country is eloquent evidence of the resistance of other communities to this type of administrative arrangement.

The special class.   A number of communities have experimented at one time or another with the introduction of special classes for gifted children. The selection of children is usually on much the same basis as described for the special school. While the children are grouped together for the subjects that depend on intellectual ability, they often remain with the rest of their age group in music, art, and physical education.

The emphasis is on a permissive atmosphere, pupils planning nurturing the ability to interpret facts, and the cultivation of reasoning skills rather than the memorization of material. Foreign languages are also often introduced early.

Modified special class. Some schools have been impressed by the advantages of having gifted children in a separate group for part of the day, but they also try to keep them with their age peers for part of the day. Selection of students is done in a manner similar to that of the special class and special school. Characteristics of these special workshop groups of gifted children are their informality, increased pupil planning, field trips, foreign languages, and leadership development.

Itinerant teacher program. The itinerant teacher program, in most instances, represents a compromise between placing gifted children in a modified special class and keeping them in the regular classrooms. In this instance the itinerant teacher may act as a consultant in special areas to the regular teacher and also will take responsibility for meeting a few hours a week with special groups of gifted children in certain subject-matter fields. The program is an obvious attempt to meet the rapidly developing interests and skills of these children with the talents of a specialist in certain subject areas and to aid the regular classroom teacher who feels inadequate in certain subject areas.

Each of the many programs designed to educate reasonably well-adjusted gifted children more effectively differs from each other in detail since they are tailored to local conditions. Actually, the similarities between programs usually outweigh the differences. Some characteristics common to almost all the programs are:

1. Grouping of children with high intelligence for a part of the school day.
2. More responsibility given to pupils for planning of the program.
3. More emphasis on creative and interpretive activities and less time for memorization and routine practice of skills.
4. Smaller work groups.
5. More informality and less routine; less rigid time schedules.

Case-study approach. In keeping with the idea that one of the most remarkable things about gifted children is their wide range of individual differences, some school systems have started systematic individual case studies of gifted children. In this program the children are identified, one at a time, through psychological tests; they are then administered a comprehensive set of tests and interviews in an attempt to identify the particular interests and needs of each child. A committee composed of the classroom teacher, principal, psychologist, and other interested parties then meets to use the information obtained to tailor a program to the child's needs. This program may be administered by a specialist but otherwise can be operated by the regular staff of the school system. This approach seems to be most valuable for gifted children who have special problems.

To Accelerate or Not to Accelerate?

For many years the term *acceleration* has been a nasty word in the vocabulary of many school administrators and parents. The picture of the little boy in short pants in the college classroom, surrounded by tolerantly smiling upper-classmen, has become abhorrent. Such early attempts to place children with their intellectual peers without regard to their social, physical, or emotional maturity undoubtedly have left their scars. Despite these early unfortunate ventures into breaking the lockstep of the educational system, the policy of limited acceleration for gifted children has regained favor and seems to be supported by research findings.

Although the majority of acceleration procedures have been employed in secondary schools and beyond, a number of school systems have attempted to practice acceleration in their elementary schools. One method of accelerating a child has been to allow him to enter school at an earlier age than the average child. A number of investigators have noted that the strict chronological age requirement for first-graders has little or nothing to recommend it from a research or rational viewpoint. The arbitrary chronological age limits now used by school systems do not take into account either new advances in teaching or the wide range of individual intellectual differences in children with a chronological age of six.

Evaluation of early admittance programs in such widely separated states as Massachusetts, Pennsylvania, and Nebraska have shown consistently favorable results. Children admitted early, as a group, were superior or equal in all characteristics to those children admitted at the regular age. The Nebraska program found that the group that was admitted to school early was better on achievement and social acceptance at the end of primary grades than the average group, and at least the equal of the average youngster in health, coordination, leadership, and emotional adjustment.

One of the major barriers to adopting this procedure has been the administrative difficulties it creates. Early admittance would require extensive testing of children at the life age of five years and beyond, and this would be a major undertaking in school systems that lack adequate psychological services.

Other attempts at acceleration in the elementary school include grade skipping, which, although applied infrequently, is usually what laymen think about when the term *acceleration* is mentioned. It is now generally conceded that, except in unusual cases, grade skipping represents perhaps the least desirable method of acceleration. This procedure needs to be planned carefully to prevent the child from missing basic information that is taught in the grade to be skipped.

Another means of acceleration is having the primary grades arranged in an ungraded group so that sections of bright children can finish the three-year curriculum in less time and thus move ahead in the school program. Alternately, such a plan can be used to provide a vastly richer curriculum once the children have mastered the required curriculum of the primary grades. The procedure is restricted mostly to those youngsters who have good social and emotional adjustment in addition to advanced intellectual ability. The available research indicates clearly that moderate acceleration in the elementary school does no noticeable harm to the gifted child, and has shortened his academic operation by one-half to one year.

61. *Providing for the Gifted, Pittsburgh* *

CALVIN E. GROSS, *Superintendent of Schools,*[1]

AND

MARY L. MOLYNEAUX, *Principal, Henry C. Frick School*

Kindergarten—Primary Grades

SKILLS DEVELOPMENT

In the skills development area, children in the primary grades are taught in ability groups so that the more able may move along at their own speed. In addition to their own ideas, teachers make use of suggestions in the

* From *Pittsburgh Schools*, XXXII, No. 2 (1957), 79–84. Reprinted with permission.
[1] Superintendent of Schools, New York City, since April, 1963.

textbooks and teachers' guides for dramatizations, original stories, poems, and extra reading. In arithmetic, the books provide special problems for children able to solve them. The spelling book provides extra words, and the English books contain many suggestions for activities to be done by the child of special ability or interest. Many of these activities are adaptable to the unit of work being pursued by the class at the time.

THE UNIT OF WORK

The unit of work is well-adapted to meet the needs of children on all ability levels. The above-average child contributes most of the creative ideas and has the ability to assume leadership and to solve problems that arise. He is given responsibility for carrying out jobs involving the exercise of judgment and is encouraged to think critically in executing his ideas. He has the opportunity to do additional reading and can be led to generalize on the basis of his experiences.

GROUP RESPONSIBILITIES

In the kindergarten and first grade these children are given group responsibilities such as:

1. Taking children to the doctor's or principal's office, other rooms, or the school cafeteria.

2. Helping children who enter late to get materials and show them how to use them.

3. Arranging and caring for the library corner, science table, dollhouse, etc.

4. Helping with bulletin board ideas and special arrangements.

In grades two and three, group responsibilities are extended beyond the individual classroom to include responsibilities affecting the other primary grades or the whole school. For example:

1. Checking and distributing the primary book collection that goes to all rooms.

2. At special seasons of the year, reading stories to children in first-grade rooms and kindergarten.

3. Third-grade children acting as primary grade representatives to Civic Club in passing along ideas and suggestions for school betterment.

OUTSIDE ACTIVITIES

Oakland is a varied and interesting community and teachers try to make use of its opportunities as they develop their units of work or provide purely enrichment experiences. Each child derives from these activities according to his social, intellectual, and experiental background.

Trips to the post office, the supermarket, the flower shop, the Carnegie Museum and Library, or attendance at a Pittsburgh Symphony orchestra rehearsal offer much to all children especially those of above-average ability. Many young children take out cards at the library and get books not only for home reading but for school. Attendance at Saturday museum classes and free movies is encouraged, and parents frequently are made aware of these offerings so that their cooperation is secured by seeing that their children attend. Last year a teachers' committee compiled a list of activities taking place in Oakland that have benefit and enjoyment for children. This list was distributed to all teachers. It seemed to have its greatest use in recommending activities to parents of the primary-grade child on the upper intelligence level.

Middle and Upper Grades

In the middle and upper grades the activities of the primary grades are enlarged upon and extended. As new opportunities arise, children are taught to make the most of them.

SKILLS DEVELOPMENT

In the skills development area, effort is made to divide classes into ability groupings. This is working out well in reading and arithmetic in most classes. Effort will be made this year to do a more satisfactory job of grouping in spelling. Children who complete their assignments satisfactorily spend their time in extension reading or in supplementary reading in social studies; some work on some special projects.

THE UNIT OF WORK

The unit of work in the middle and upper grades is based largely upon the courses of study in social studies and science. In addition to the textbook materials, many reference books and supplementary texts are used both in the classroom and in the library. A number of children bring in books from home or from Carnegie Library to be used as reference books in class. In addition, most teachers regularly request books from the school librarian on long-term loan from Carnegie Library. These books are kept in the classroom. Teachers frequently consult with the school librarian concerning the availability of reference material on certain topics, and selected children gather material for various purposes during the regular library periods or before school in the morning. New books added to the school's collection are put on special display in the library so that teachers as well as children may know what is available.

A meeting was held recently at which the school librarian and teachers again discussed ways in which the library can enrich the classroom resources. Children with ability use these resources in preparing reports, charts, graphs, etc. They are urged to read widely, condense their facts, then apply them in the form of a report, chart, or exhibit that will be interesting and understandable to the class.

GROUP RESPONSIBILITIES

There are many responsibilities for school service that may be assumed by boys and girls of high intelligence. These are responsibilities that require ability, judgment, and dependability. They are not jobs given to these people to use their time and keep them busy. For example:

1. Savings stamps committee: Pupils take entire responsibility for sale of savings stamps in the homeroom.

2. Civic Club Minute Men: During school drives and campaigns these children prepare and give talks to self-contained classrooms.

3. Library committees: Each class has a library committee responsible for charging-out books, "carding" returned books, inspecting, and returning books to shelves. They catalogue cards, help to search for materials requested by teachers, and assist with inventory records. They act as assistants to less able children in locating reference materials.

4. Compilation of anthologies: These are used by teachers who request poetry in various subjects.

5. Research in specific areas for school use: An example is how Frick School got its name. Research led to extended use of special Carnegie Library collections, such as those in the James Anderson Room, Art Room, Pennsylvania Room.

6. Stage crew: These children are picked for their ability to help wherever needed. They learn lighting, scenery setting, setting up and operating sound system, projectors, etc.

7. Music assistants: This committee assists in sorting, mending, and storing music. Occasionally they copy music when needed.

8. Physical education assistants: Squad leaders help those who have difficulty in performance and keep the records for the group; teacher's assistants take the roll, handle equipment, etc., thereby giving the teacher more time with the class.

OUTSIDE ACTIVITIES

1. For three years a Frick child of the upper intelligence group has been a member of the special science or fine arts groups conducted by the supervisory staff of the Board of Education.

2. On a number of occasions WQED has needed a child or a small group to participate on the Television Teaching Demonstration programs: foreign-born children in our schools, a member of the Little League, etc. These children have been selected from the upper intelligence group since poise and ability to speak easily on an unrehearsed program are essential. Tape-recorded book reports done at school have been used on the Television Teaching Demonstration lessons.

3. Last year and on previous occasions, Frick School pupils have presented the Safety Program on Station WCAE. This program requires original ideas and the ability to speak well without having a prepared speech.

4. A group of above-average seventh-grade students wrote *Swimming Is Fun,* a radio script for primary grades to be presented over Station WCAE in May as a part of the Safety Story Lady series. Preliminary preparation for this class project was made by giving all children an opportunity to present ideas and suggestions. These were then turned over to a committee for writing. The class acted as critics; the committee rewrote the script; then suggested that their work be presented to the primary-grade children for criticisms. Final revisions followed suggestions given by these primary-grade children.

5. On three occasions, Frick School presented programs on KDKA-TV and several times presented programs of WQED. In all instances children helped to plan these programs as well as to participate in them.

6. Children in the upper grades who have ability and interest in science participate in the School Science Fair at Buhl Planetarium. In past years, awards have been won on occasion; last year a group of boys won honorable mention. The greatest value derived from participation is in the planning that precedes the preparation and the work that must be put into the project to carry it to a successful conclusion. We are making an effort to have these science projects an on-going part of the science program for children with ability to display as a culminating activity at the Planetarium rather than having the science show as the sole reason for preparing an exhibit in a brief period of time. Last year a group of upper-grade children, with interest and ability in science, went to the Planetarium to view the show for the purpose of creating interest in science projects.

7. An effort is made to create an interest in the children's Symphony concerts. A large number of children of the upper intelligence group, as well as others, have attended these concerts yearly and a few have won prizes in the contests conducted.

8. Children of above-average ability are recommended for the various Carnegie Museum activities each year.

9. Frequently, free tickets are donated to the school for children's plays, special programs, etc. These are distributed to children who have special interest or ability in that particular field.

10. Sometimes an entire class has an unusual opportunity to hear an outstanding program or personality. For example, last year Robert Frost requested that a live audience of children be present in the WQED studio during one of his appearances. While it is never possible to evaluate what each individual gains, comments of children afterward indicated that it had been a rich experience for them.

11. Participation in the annual Press-KQV Spelling Bee has stimulated some children to a greater interest in spelling. Last year's school winner who participated in the finals has been working with her parents and teacher ever since and is looking forward to participation again this year. She has derived great satisfaction and pleasure from this project, and she is gaining noticeably in poise and self-reliance as a result.

12. The art teacher has encouraged boys and girls to become interested in and to make entries for various art contests such as the National Soap Carving Contest sponsored by Procter and Gamble, the International Art Contest sponsored by the Junior Red Cross, the Historian's Book Cover contest sponsored by the Frick P.T.A., and the annual contests sponsored by the B'nai B'rith and the Humane Society. Awards and honorable mentions have been won in various years.

13. Students with special ability in shopwork are encouraged to enter outside contests. During this past year one boy won second prize in a bird feeding-station contest.

CREATIVE ACTIVITIES WITHIN THE SCHOOL

We realize that the child of high intelligence should have opportunity to develop his creative powers. It is an area in which our teachers are becoming increasingly aware and are planning to provide even greater opportunities. In addition to the creative projects mentioned previously pertaining to outside activities, the following should be mentioned as activities within the school:

1. Creative writing was mentioned in relation to radio and TV programs. Several teachers are working on creative writing in other ways. For example: the school librarian is developing the writing of poetry in her presentation of poetry as a form of literature. Another teacher developed an interest in creative writing as a part of her regular English work. During the year, classes had written different types of paragraphs. They decided to compile them into a booklet they called *Sketches*. Criteria for selection

were set up by the class and a student committee made the final selection of paragraphs to be included. Each child illustrated his own paragraph. A sixth-grade class wrote, directed, and presented a play for the Auditorium Club. It was one of the most interesting and well-accepted programs of the year.

2. Children talented in art frequently paint stage scenery for plays. A group last year made the Nativity scene in clay to be placed under the hall Christmas tree.

3. Boys having special ability in shopwork design and work up special projects for their home. Included in the planning is the calculation of cost. Stage scenery is a regular and on-going project for boys in the shop who have the ability to complete their assigned projects and an interest in making a contribution to the school.

62. Developing the Program in the Elementary Schools, Portland *

MELVIN W. BARNES, *Superintendent of Schools*

Developing the Program in the Elementary Schools

The Portland elementary schools, which include kindergarten through grade eight, are organized according to the homeroom plan. In the self-contained homeroom, pupils remain for all or most of the day, with a single teacher who teaches all of the subjects offered at the grade level. In Portland elementary schools, this plan has been followed except at seventh and eighth grade where pupils spend a few hours a week with special teachers for industrial arts, home economics, and generally music. In some schools pupils also have special teachers for physical education.

Provisions for additional opportunities for able, talented children were developed within the regular pattern that was used in elementary schools. Two types of programs were developed for these children—homeroom enrichment and special interest classes.

* From *The Gifted Child in Portland,* pp. 25-28, Portland Public Schools, Portland, Ore. Reprinted with permission.

Types of Programs in Elementary Schools

HOMEROOM ENRICHMENT

Homeroom enrichment was based on the premise that the general instructional program can be broadened in every classroom to take care of many special needs of able students.

. Resource units were broadened for all of the grades to provide ideas, suggestions, and materials that would make it possible for bright children to study a problem more deeply. A curriculum publication *Ideas for Classroom Teachers to Use with Gifted Children* provided many suggestions that Portland teachers had found to be useful in planning for bright children in the regular elementary classroom.

SPECIAL-INTEREST GROUPS

Special-interest groups were provided for able, highly motivated children who could profit from being with other children of high ability and interest. These were taught by a member of the teaching staff of the building who was released from a homeroom assignment for several periods each week.

Some of the subjects in which there were special interest groups were mathematics, foreign language, science, creative writing, creative rhythms, music, creative dramatics, and social leadership.

. . . .

Functions of Elementary School Personnel

THE PRINCIPAL

The principal was the key figure in the development of the school's Gifted Child Program. His attitudes conditioned strongly the attitudes and actions of the teachers on the school faculty.

The principal selected the gifted child project coordinator for the building from the teachers on the staff. The principal sometimes discussed with the administrative director of the program the qualities and traits that were desirable in a coordinator, but the final decision was made by the principal. In some schools a steering committee of representative teachers was appointed by the principal. In other schools the steering committee members were elected by the faculty.

The principal determined the framework within which the Gifted Child Program operated in the school, helped establish special interest classes, and selected the teachers to conduct such classes. He helped plan faculty orientation and training in the education of the gifted and provided time in faculty meetings and P.T.A. meetings for explaining the program. He assisted in interpreting the program to parents and the rest of the school community.

THE GIFTED CHILD PROGRAM TEACHER COORDINATOR

The principal generally selected an experienced teacher who was liked and respected by the other teachers in the building as coordinator. The activities of the coordinator varied somewhat from school to school. Those that were carried on by coordinators in most of the schools will be described.

The coordinator planned with the principal and the steering committee the overall program of the school and generally acted as chairman of the steering committee. The coordinator assumed primary responsibility for seeing that the plans were carried out after these had been determined by the steering committee with the approval of the principal.

The coordinator was responsible for seeing that identification procedures were carried out and for keeping records. He assisted teachers in the use of all tests and identification materials and helped score tests when necessary. He kept folders for all identified students, copies of all materials, and suggestions for enrichment.

Regular classroom teachers often needed help in planning and carrying out enrichment activities for pupils in their classes. One of the coordinator's duties was to help homeroom teachers find additional materials, plan specific programs for pupils, and make use of community resources.

The coordinator helped select the pupils for the special interest classes and helped to survey the teaching staff to find teachers to conduct these classes. The coordinator also helped the special interest class teachers in obtaining books and materials needed for the classes.

Once a week the coordinator met with the teacher consultant of the gifted child program who visited the building on a regular schedule. In this meeting the coordinator obtained advice on various aspects of the school's gifted child program and helped in locating needed materials.

The coordinator helped the principal plan and conduct professional meetings and in-service classes in the building on the education of the gifted. He also prepared reports, bulletins, and reading materials, and found various ways of stimulating faculty interest.

THE TEACHER STEERING COMMITTEE

The size and composition of steering committees varied from school to school. In some schools there was a teacher representative from each grade, in other schools there were representatives from each of the primary, intermediate, and upper-grade sections.

Some of the functions of the steering committee were to help the principal establish the policies of the school's program for gifted children; to determine the need for special interest classes, and to help in their establishment; to resolve conflicts that arose normally in the progress of the program; and to help the principal and coordinator plan professional meetings for the information of other members of the faculty.

The steering committee also provided an opportunity for a larger number of teachers to be involved in the development of the program within the school. This encouraged the development of a more active program.

THE SPECIAL INTEREST CLASS TEACHER

After the abilities of the pupils had been identified, a survey was made of the talents and special training of the teaching staff. On the basis of this information the principal selected teachers to conduct special interest classes in certain subjects.

A special class teacher planned and carried out the special class program, helped in selecting the pupils for the class, evaluated the performance of the pupils, and interpreted the activities of the special interest class to the homeroom teacher and to parents. The special class teacher was relieved of regular classroom duties by the coordinator or the extra teacher provided by the district.

TEST COORDINATORS

In order to facilitate identification of pupils with special talents, many schools appointed test coordinators or talent committees to assume responsibility for the tests in art, rhythms, dramatics, social leadership, music, and creative writing. These individuals assisted the regular classroom teacher in administering and scoring the talent screening exercises or in some cases took major responsibility for the administration and scoring of the exercises. These teachers were members of the regular teaching staff with special ability and knowledge of the talent.

HOMEROOM TEACHER

In a program such as the Portland program, the homeroom teacher in the elementary school carried a large measure of responsibility for the success of the program. He assisted in the identification of gifted pupils by giving tests and by personal observation. He planned and carried out enrichment activities for gifted pupils in the homeroom and served on committees active in furthering the goals of the program. He was responsible for using the results of special interest class activities in augmenting the homeroom program. Full cooperation between homeroom teachers and special interest class teachers was necessary in providing a good instructional program for individual gifted pupils.

63. The Elementary Program for the Gifted, San Diego *

RALPH DAILARD, *Superintendent of Schools*

THE SAN Diego City Schools began its experimental program for gifted children in the fall of 1949. In the beginning, when educational and social problems of the then-identified gifted were studied, it was found that "only half of the gifted were doing as well in their classes as pupils with average ability, and that approximately half of them had social adjustment problems of some severity." A voluntary committee was created to study the situation and develop a program to meet the gifted child's needs. The Board of Education approved an experimental project on a year-to-year basis.

In this program an attempt has been made to offer enrichment to very capable children in the regular classroom, either in the home school or in centers where gifted children are clustered. In several individual instances, grade level acceleration has been approved. The experimental program for gifted pupils has been evaluated annually in studies conducted by teachers and administrators. The program is subject to change and modification as a result of newer findings and generalizations that come from research and evaluation of the program. Pupils are "identified" as gifted if they score 140 or higher on an individually administered Binet L. M. Terman Intelligence Test.

In June, 1958, the Board of Education took action that made the program for gifted children a permanent part of the curriculum of the San Diego City Schools; and except for the instructional phase of the program, it is no longer considered experimental.

During 1958–59, parents of gifted pupils in the fourth, fifth, and sixth grades were notified of their children's capabilities and were invited to par-

* From *Curriculum Digest,* April-May, 1961, pp. 1–2, 8, San Diego, Calif. Reprinted with permission.

ticipate in the experiment of cluster-grouping. Under this plan, identified gifted children attend certain designated schools in their areas (called Instructional Study Centers). Clustering the pupils made for better utilization of consultant time and of materials, equipment, and books purchased for use in the gifted program. This plan was continued during 1959–60 and is no longer considered experimental. Of the 487 identified gifted pupils in grades 4–6 last year, 336 were in cluster groups in Instructional Study Centers.

Screening and Identification of Gifted Pupils

Elementary school principals are responsible for directing the program for gifted in their own schools; and they may enlist the help of psychologists, visiting teachers, supervisors, and specialists.

One of the most important phases of the program is identifying the gifted child. A city-wide screening program is used for the purpose of identifying gifted children. Intensive screening is done in the third grade and has been done on an experimental basis in some kindergartens. Binet tests are given, however, at any grade where recommendations for the intelligence test have come to the principal from teachers, psychologists, consultants, or others as a result of observations and test scores in achievement, group intelligence, and aptitude. Pupils from kindergarten through grade six have been identified by this method.

Due credit should be given to teachers of elementary grades who contribute to this rapidly expanding program for gifted children by screening likely candidates for individual testing. These teachers are always alert for clues indicating possible giftedness—and have undoubtedly used one or more of the following:

Academic Achievement: This is apparent in an extensive vocabulary, unusual reading ability, broad background of information, organized and/or abstract thinking, and ability to see relationships.
Creativity: This is apparent in art, music, rhythms, and drama. Mechanical aptitude, scientific aptitude, and use of an unusual vocabulary in creative writing are all indications of creativity.
Social Leadership: This ability is usually manifest in the child who can take charge of a group, is admired by peers, helps others, and stands up for rights of others.
Special Talents
Already-Identified Gifted Siblings: Although this is not always a guarantee of unusual ability, all siblings of children already identified as gifted merit close observation and should be tested for giftedness.

In June, 1952, approximately 125 identified gifted children were enrolled in the elementary schools. By June, 1960, this number had grown to well over 600.

Notification of Parents

Regular procedures of notification of parents that their children are gifted have been established. Parents of children in grades 3–6 identified after the school year begins and before November 1 of the school year are not notified of their child's giftedness prior to November 1.

The principal is responsible for setting up the conference with the child's parents and the school psychologist. During a *carefully structured interview,* the parents are informed of San Diego's program for gifted children and of their child's high mental ability. Parents are encouraged to request additional conferences with school personnel concerning their children, as the need arises. Occasionally, progress reports are prepared and parent meetings are held. The children themselves *are not notified* of their giftedness, nor are their classmates.

During these interviews, parents are also informed of the program at the Instructional Study Centers. Parents of gifted pupils in grades 3, 4, and 5 have the opportunity of requesting that their children be assigned to a school designated as a Study Center in September of the following school year. In the Study Centers the gifted are not segregated but are placed in "clusters" or subgroups within regular classrooms.

Gifted pupils whose parents do not request assignment to a Study Center are given the best possible placement in their own school and benefit from enrichment in the regular class. They do not receive consultant service, books, or equipment from the gifted program.

Teacher Consultants

There are three teacher consultants for the elementary gifted program who travel on a regular rotational basis to the seventeen Study Centers. Their job is primarily to be of assistance to teachers in carrying out the basic policies of the gifted program. Consultants assist the teacher with curricular and enrichment planning and in selecting library and audio-visual materials and special equipment.

On request of the principal or the teacher of a cluster group, the consultant performs such teaching or additional duties as will contribute to the best interests of the gifted. This includes preparation of lessons, introduction of new materials and teaching equipment, and the planning and carrying out of small-group field trips for special purposes.

Another important function of the consultant is to administer an achievement test to each gifted child during the school year. These test results are of help to teachers in planning for gifted children during the year and in assessing growth and achievement in basic skills.

Principals, teachers, and consultants may plan together how the identified gifted may develop potential ability to the greatest degree. Follow-up on the identified gifted child is continuous—through the grades into college and, in case of transfer, from one school to another within the district.

San Diego's Design for the Program for Gifted Children

In the present program, San Diego City Schools attempt to offer gifted students richer experiences as a part of the instructional program of the regular classroom. Experiences are provided that help develop deeper and wider insight and that go beyond the limits of regular classwork. In the past, using above-grade subject matter, which the students will learn the following year, has not been encouraged. Experiments in upgrading courses of study have been tried recently with greater frequency, particularly in such subject areas as arithmetic, reading, science, and the arts.

Three major designs have emerged from the program for gifted as it has developed during the past ten years. These are:

1. ENRICHMENT

a. *In a regular classroom at the school where the student was identified*

In order to assist teachers who have a wide range of mental abilities among the students in regular classrooms where gifted have been identified, principals usually organize these classes to include (1) slow to high average learners or (2) average to superior and gifted pupils. This grouping reduces slightly the range within the classroom and eliminates a need for the teacher to provide for extremes of ability at one end or the other of the scale. Grouping of this type is possible only where schools have two or more classrooms at each grade level.

b. *At an Instructional Study Center where gifted are clustered*

At the Instructional Study Centers are many resources and materials purchased especially for the gifted program. These books and equipment are not available to teachers of the gifted in other schools.

For example, each center has a teacher-aid, a college student enrolled in teacher training at San Diego State College who is hired to provide twelve hours of assistance each week to teachers of gifted. Typewriters and typing books are available at each Instructional Study Center. A traveling typing teacher works with the pupils on a regularly scheduled visitation basis. Other items of new equipment introduced in recent years include micro-projectors (Bioscopes), planetariums, celestial globes, individual slide rules, wall demonstration slide rules, Califone record players for listening-post activities, telescopes, filmstrip viewers, Mineralights ("black light" kits), geometric patterns, and micrometers. Russian, German, and French language records, with related manuals and dictionaries, are available to interest groups.

Hobby groups and science fairs have been organized in many Instructional Study Centers to open new areas of research and growth to gifted children. And educational trips involving small groups of gifted pupils may be undertaken whenever these trips will satisfy an enrichment need.

2. ACCELERATION

Acceleration is recognized as another means of meeting the needs of gifted children. Each gifted child is considered for possible acceleration in the light of his own needs. Grade acceleration takes place only after careful planning when it is felt that the intellectual abilities of the child are not sufficiently challenged at his present grade level.

3. ADJUSTMENT ASSIGNMENT

While the policy of the district is that of providing enrichment for gifted pupils in regular classrooms, there also have been established three adjustment classes, each of which enrolls fifteen students with superior and gifted mental ability. These adjustment classes are in line with the district's practice of providing adjustment classes for pupils in the normal range of intelligence. Pupils with social, emotional, or academic problems are admitted to these classes for more individual help. They return to their regular classes as soon as it seems advisable.

In September, 1957, the Pupil Study Center, with offices in the Education Center, was organized to provide counseling services for gifted students who have social or emotional problems that are interfering with their academic progress or their overall adjustment. Referrals for this counseling are made through the visiting teacher of the student's school, who then acts as liaison between the school and the Pupil Study Center.

More Answers Needed

While the "gifted program," as many teachers are used to thinking of it, has ceased to be experimental, it is still, and will continue to be, subject to further experimentation, change, and improvement. In 1957, for example, a study was begun of what might be called the extremely gifted—children with Binet scores of 168 or higher. On the basis of this study, experimentation is currently under way to develop a program calculated to satisfy the unique needs of these pupils.

There have been and, of course, continue to be many problems still unsolved regarding the program for the gifted. As many of us recognize and contribute to the solution of these problems, it can be expected that the results will be more individualized instruction for all of San Diego's children, whether they are identified gifted or not.

64. Language Arts Experiences for the Mentally Superior: Kindergarten through Grade 8, Pittsburgh *

CALVIN E. GROSS, *Superintendent of Schools* [1]

I. Introductory Remarks

    A. Any activity planned for the mentally superior child should be geared to his physical, social, emotional, and intellectual level.

        1. He should have the rich experiences he is ready to have.
        2. He should not be forced into experiences he is not ready for socially and emotionally.

    B. The unit plan of teaching makes it possible to meet more adequately the needs of the mentally superior child.

        1. Opportunities to read, to explore, do research, and participate in creative expression are possible.
        2. Opportunities to work individually along special interest lines can be given.
        3. Opportunities to work in committees are provided.

* From *Enriching the Program for the Mentally Superior,* Pittsburgh Public Schools, December, 1958, pp. Language Arts 2–11. Reprinted with permission.
[1] Superintendent of Schools, New York City, since April, 1963.

4. Opportunities for developing leadership are many.
5. Opportunities for developing skills of all kinds at varying levels in terms of individual needs are provided.
6. The mentally superior children can serve as chairmen of committees responsible for gathering information, organizing facts, and presenting information to the class.
7. The mentally superior child can search out and organize for class use information that is valuable to the class in the development of a unit but that is too difficult for the average child either to locate or to understand.
8. The mentally superior child can carry out independent research on a subject suggested by the unit theme but not necessarily related to it. Such a project need not be included in the class discussion, but reports can be exhibited with other materials produced during the unit study.
9. As a part of his work in connection with the class unit, a mentally superior child can develop many valuable study and research skills. He can learn to summarize conclusions reached by a committee or by the class. He can learn how to organize information for others to use. He can set up bibliographies, arrange books with bookmarks to help others in locating information, and explain to others his way of organizing material.
10. He can make outlines for class or committee discussion, and he can evaluate the use made of such outlines. He can be of help to committees by bringing to their discussions results of independent study and research.

C. In providing experiences for the mentally superior, it is wise to stress the qualitative rather than the quantitative.

1. There should be a great variety among experiences.
2. There should be a greater depth and a broader scope of activities.
3. Opportunities to apply initiative and originality should be provided.
4. Freedom to follow special interests should be given.
5. Opportunities for developing critical thinking should be provided.
6. Opportunities for drawing conclusions and making generalizations should be provided.
7. The mentally superior child in the middle and upper grades can enrich not only his own experience but that of the entire class by carrying out independent activities in editorial work. He can help other children spot errors in composition and he can help

them to improve sentence structure, etc., by serving as a special editor in a workshop type atmosphere. Children in such a permissive classroom atmosphere seek each other's suggestions and ideas while composing. The level of achievement for all can be raised by having a greater amount of individual attention for children than one teacher can give. With helping editors (the mentally superior), everyone has more help with his particular problems in language. The mentally superior children learn to be constructive in their criticism when they serve as class editors.

8. They develop skill in critical analysis by means of organizing topic sentence paragraphs and essays in which they evaluate, analyze, explain, or justify a personal opinion by using facts and figures to substantiate opinion.

D. The classroom environment plays an important part in any program for the mentally superior.

   1. Materials and creative media should be readily available.

      a. Whenever possible classrooms should include such centers of interest as a unit of work, a library table, a bulletin board for current events, a hobby corner, and/or exhibit space.

      b. The mentally superior child should have available reading material on a high interest and understanding level. The material shou'd be of two general kinds—some related to the class unit and some related to individual interests and projects.

      c. The mentally superior child should have available materials needed to carry out individual and group projects in bookmaking, letter writing, and creative work of all kinds.

   2. A teacher's interest, encouragement, and understanding along with praise of achievement are essential.

E. The cultivation of creativity and the development of skills are both essential parts of the Language Arts program for the mentally superior.

   1. Extensive opportunities should be provided for expression through creative writing.

   2. Language skills, study skills, and work habits are needed to implement the development of creativity.

   3. The mentally superior child should have ample opportunities to develop those skills in spelling, grammar, sentence structure, punctuation, and capitalization that are essential to a high level

of achievement in language at his level. If a child is able to create lovely prose and poetry because of his giftedness, he should have help in any skills necessary to complement that creative achievement.

II. Enrichment within the Language Arts Program

A. Reading

1. Grouping for instruction according to ability or interest.

   a. In every classroom, reading textbooks are allocated to each grade on different levels to take care of these varying abilities.
   b. The mentally superior child should have stimulation by means of grouping on interest levels. Children should have time to read and follow individual tastes in reading, too. They should have opportunities to talk over common interests either within a small group or with the class. Materials on all levels and on a variety of subjects should be available for individual use.

2. Using materials at various grade levels so that the mentally superior can read at a higher understanding and interest level with keener comprehension and clearer interpretation.

3. Using free time to read and explore in areas of individual interest. Supplementary material at various levels should be made available.

4. Interpreting and reacting to material read
   a. Keeping anecdotal records
   b. Making bibliographies
   c. Sharing information and enjoyment with others

5. Using many kinds of materials
   a. Factual material of all kinds
   b. Fictional materials

6. Skills in reading should be developed to a high level—skimming; work type-recreational type reading skills. The mentally superior child needs a superior command of many reading skills.

B. Oral English

1. Discussions

   a. Participating in various types of discussions
      (1) Class discussions
      (2) Panel discussions

       (3) Debates
       (4) Personal interviews
       (5) Committee discussions

    b. Participating in various capacities

       (1) As a member
       (2) As a leader

    c. Summarizing discussions and presenting summaries to the class

2. Preparation and presentation of various kinds of reports

    a. Factual reports of reading, observation, trips, experiments, etc.
    b. Aesthetic reports evaluating and interpreting concerts, plays, art experiences, etc.
    c. Reports on books, character sketches, hobbies, special interests, etc.

3. Preparation, direction, and presentation of dramatization, skits, plays, radio and television programs
4. Preparation and telling of original stories and poems
5. Retelling of stories and poems heard or read and enjoyed
6. Talking over and planning class activities

    a. Excursions
    b. Units and projects
    c. Creative writing

7. Using various means to improve speech habits

    a. Constructive criticisms by classmates
    b. Use of mechanical devices for recording and playing back oral presentations
    c. Establishment of standards of achievement

C. Written English

1. Prepare written summaries of discussions
2. Prepare written reports of various kinds

    a. Factual reports of reading, observation, experiments, trips, etc.
    b. Aesthetic reports evaluating and interpreting concerts, plays, art experiences, etc.

3. Prepare reports on books, reference work, character sketches, hobbies, special interests, etc.
4. Write dialogue for dramatizations, skits, plays, radio and television programs
5. Write summaries of personal interviews
6. Write thumbnail sketches of stories heard or read and enjoyed
7. Write summaries of class activities
8. Write captions and labels for committee, class, or individual booklets
9. Write biographies and autobiographies
10. Write original stories and poems of various kinds

   a. Some might be related to the unit
   b. Others may be purely imaginative

11. Write exposition evaluating or analyzing experiences

   a. Descriptive paragraphs
   b. Character sketches
   c. Editorials
   d. Book reports
   e. Reactions to personal experiences, art, music, etc.

12. Write news articles

   a. This has proven a particularly valuable outlet for the mentally superior child. The more able children in the third grade of Conroy School did an excellent job of gathering news for their publication, "Small Fry." They interviewed children in other grades, the teachers, the principal, and even people in the community. They organized their material and wrote their articles independently with guidance from the teacher only when needed.
   b. The collecting of facts and the writing of news articles is a worthwhile activity for all children. For the mentally superior, however, the job of getting the facts and the job of writing up the news can be particularly rewarding. (See the discussion of newspaper activities under II., F., in this outline.)

13. Write letters of all kinds

   a. Social notes
   b. Business letters

14. Prepare programs for class play, culminating activities, etc.

15. Keep personal diaries or imaginative diaries of people in history and science
16. Establish standards of achievement

D. Spelling

1. Use of basic spelling list
2. Use of supplementary lists in connection with all class activities
3. Use of individual lists in terms of needs and abilities
4. Participation in spelling bees—local, state, and national
5. Preparation of individual dictionaries
6. Establishment of high standards of achievement

E. Handwriting

1. Study the history and development of symbols and alphabets
2. Learn how to use the typewriter
3. Establish standards of achievement

F. Newspaper activities

1. Provide unusual opportunities in the literary field
2. Provide opportunities for growth in planning and organization

   a. As staff members
   b. As reporters
   c. As organizers of the dummy sheets

3. Provide opportunities for growth in business management

   a. Handling money
   b. Keeping records
   c. Carrying on campaigns to advertise and sell papers

4. Provide experiences with mechanical devices

   a. Typewriters
   b. Mimeoscopes
   c. Mimeograph machines

5. Excursions

   a. Newspaper plant

65. Suggested Activities for Gifted Children *

HELEN HAY HEYL, *Chief, Bureau of Elementary Curriculum Development, New York State Education Department*

L ISTED below are but a few of the many enrichment activities that classroom teachers have evolved and that have been used successfully in classrooms. . . . With a few exceptions, they are not, of course, suggested for development as isolated activities. They are listed only as samples of the kinds of deeper learnings that intellectually able children have pursued, beyond the activities of the rest of the class, but in relation to units of work in which the entire class was involved. It is hoped that teachers will use as many of these activities as are consistent with the curriculum framework within which they operate, and that they will seek to evolve new and varied means of enrichment. The Bureau of Elementary Curriculum Development will welcome reports from local school districts as to activities and plans that have been used and found successful.

Activities in the Area of Science

1. Build, operate, and maintain a simplified observatory and weather station, such as keeping weather records, reading weather maps, or using a can to catch and measure rainfall.
2. Study weather reports from stations throughout the country. Using their own blank maps, pupils indicate areas of high and low pressure, cold and warm fronts and learn to make actual forecasts.
3. Plan and operate a school museum.
4. Study telegraphy (simple blocks of wood, a piece of metal, wire, magnet, and a dry cell).
5. Construct a radio.

* From *Curriculum Adaptations for the Gifted,* Bureau of Elementary Curriculum Development, New York State Education Department, Albany, 1958, pp. 24–27. Reprinted with permission.

6. Make reproductions to show the development of an invention.
7. Study the production of sound from a phonograph.
8. Study the school public address system.
9. Make a xylophone.
10. Make a working model of some piece of simple machinery of interest to the child and his group and demonstrate its principle to the group.
11. Identify rocks and minerals through scratch tests, cleavage, and Geiger counter.
12. Make a soilless garden, using a sponge, gravel, moss basket, and sawdust.
13. Make a magnetic stage, using a cardboard carton in which figures pasted to bits of iron are moved by a magnet held under the figures. Explain the principles involved.
14. Prepare a primary science file in which simple experiments written on large file cards are placed according to areas of study.
15. Make a fall seed collection in which seeds are collected, classified according to mode of travel, and placed on a chart with proper headings.
16. Make a satellite demonstrator. Thread a string through a spool, tie a small stone on one end and a larger stone on the other; by holding on to the spool and whirling the smaller stone around, the larger stone will be pulled through by centrifugal force. Explain the principle involved.
17. Make a steam turbine. Attach the lid of a tin can to the top of a closed coffee can, the top of which has a few holes, and partly fill with water; place the can over heat and the steam escaping through the holes of the can will turn the wheel, illustrating the steam turbine. Explain the principle involved.
18. Make a water turbine, by having water falling from a faucet turn a simply constructed wheel with paddles. Explain the principle involved.
19. Make and explain an electromagnet.
20. Make a blinker light (constructed like a telegraph except that a light replaces the sounder).
21. Demonstrate rain by heating water, making the steam come in contact with ice and condense; observe the droplets fall from the glass tube.
22. Assemble a small electric motor with the help of a resource person.
23. Collect and analyze samples of soil.
24. Study ways of purifying water.

25. Study animal tracks.
26. Review new sample science texts.

Activities in the Area of Language Arts

1. Read or tell stories to younger children.
2. Scan and classify reading materials for the school library.
3. Interview resource persons.
4. Participate in a debate or panel discussion on a current issue (with children of higher grades if the topic is beyond the interest of the gifted child's classmates).
5. Read books on advanced levels.
6. Write scripts for radio programs.
7. Write dramatizations of historical events and stories.
8. Express orally or in written form feelings about music, paintings, etc.
9. Evaluate children's magazines (set up evaluative criteria and make a recommended list for the library).
10. Survey pupil reading habits to determine extent of magazine reading as compared to book reading.
11. Document research using bibliographies, footnotes, and quotations.
12. Analyze pictures having fine expressions of human emotion; stress joy and happiness.
13. Trace the derivation of a word.
14. Study a foreign language, after age eight, twice weekly.
15. Write plays.
16. Write unfinished stories to be completed by others.

Activities in the Area of Arithmetic

1. Draw to scale.
2. Study a problem such as the cost of building a house (involving kinds of materials, fixtures, construction, installation, and labor costs).
3. Compute the cost of traveling a given distance in early days and at present, and show the findings in chart or graph form.
4. Compile budgets for a pioneer family and present-day family of comparable size for a given period of time; compute increases in percentages.
5. Estimate answers to addition examples in new ways.
6. Discover various ways of verifying sums and differences.
7. Employ short methods in solving multiplication examples.

8. Make a time line of historical events.
9. Reduce foreign money to our values.
10. Calculate comparative costs of cash payment versus credit buying.
11. Keep a record of family buying of special sales versus regular purchases, and calculate economies effected by taking advantage of special sales.
12. Study the history of numbers.
13. Study other number systems, i.e., dyadic, duodecimal, etc.
14. Play number games (i.e., write any number you like, multiply by 2, add 18, and then divide by 2, now subtract the number with which you began; the answer will always be 9).
15. Construct riddles. (An example of a gifted fourth grade child's riddle is as follows: ¾ of Jane + ½ of us + ½ of Ann + ⅔ of rye = January.)
16. Prepare a display of banking forms, insurance forms, mortgage forms, etc., with an explanation of each.

Activities in the Area of Citizenship Education

1. Trace a series of historical events.
2. Study the origin of our food supply, laws, governments, etc., as a basis for understanding the evolution of our culture.
3. Make a map showing early travel routes in a particular area and the highways and rail and air routes now in use.
4. Compile a list of special skills used by employees in industry.
5. Make a chart showing the designs of early coins and contrast them with present-day coins.
6. Write and help produce plays and puppet shows on topics in the citizenship program.
7. Make scrapbooks, posters, paintings, murals, etc., on topics of particular interest.
8. Prepare special reports, going more deeply into topics or events than the rest of the class.
9. Do independent research into the causes and effects of selected events on topics in history and geography.
10. Prepare short biographies of the lives of famous people.

Activities in Other Areas

1. Form a chess club.
2. Observe school plant operation and maintenance.

3. Serve as head of school drives (i.e., Red Cross, March of Dimes, etc.).
4. Organize and plan a school hobby show, bookfair or folk dance festival.
5. Devise new games; give instructions and direct the game.
6. Survey community resources for field trips.
7. Study and interpret the history of classical pictures.
8. Assist in the organization of school clubs.
9. Play question-and-answer games. (The gifted make up a "panel of experts," children of average ability select questions to ask, slow children use open books and judge whether answers are correct.)
10. Study and prepare menus of different countries.
11. Help other children in his own grade or those below, under careful guidance, to see that the practice is not carried to the point of exploitation; such help may include science demonstrations, crafts, and games.

66. Criteria for Class Placement of Gifted, Oakland *

M. H. ELLIOTT, *Director of Research*

THE PROGRAM for gifted elementary school children in the Oakland Public Schools includes special classes for gifted sixth graders (program type number six as defined in Article 23, Section 199.12 (e) of Subchapter 1 of Chapter 1 of Title 5 of the California Administrative Code), and instructional groups for pupils in grades kindergarten through six (program type number one).

Two basic considerations are important: first, such special programs should be limited primarily to those who are unquestionably qualified; second, very few exceptions should be made to specific criteria and procedures. The criteria are essentially those established by the California State

* From a mimeographed document, pp. 1–4, Office of Superintendent of Schools, Oakland Public Schools, Oakland, Calif., 1962–63. Reprinted with permission.

Department of Education that defines gifted pupils as those in the top 2 per cent of the general population in intellectual ability.

A. *Basic Criteria for Admission to Special Classes for the Gifted*

    1. *Mental Ability*—IQ of 135 or above as measured by an individual test administered by a tester approved by the Research Department.

    2. *Performance*—High quality of performance as indicated by scholarship grades, achievement test scores, and other available data.

    3. *Consent*—Consent of pupil and parents for placement in the class.

B. *School Committee Approval for Admission to Special Classes for the Gifted*

    1. Each pupil admitted to special classes for the gifted must meet the three criteria presented in A. *Basic Criteria for Admission.* Pupils meeting these three criteria, however, are not automatically included. Each one must receive the approval of the school committee for placement in the program. The committee consists of the principal, the approved tester from the Research Department, the pupil's teacher, and others as appointed by the principal. In deciding upon placement, the school committee should consider the following factors:

        a. Recommendation of the guidance consultant when deemed ad-advisable.

        b. Additional factors relating to the pupil, such as:

            Emotional stability
            Social maturity
            Physical maturity and health
            Motivation and interests
            Chronological age
            Home conditions
            Activities outside the school program

    The principal and the committee should keep in mind that the purpose of this program is to provide a special and outstanding opportunity for those pupils who can and will produce an exceptional performance.

C. *Procedure for Pupils to be Placed in Center at Another School*

    1. Recommendations for placement of a pupil at a center in another school must be cleared with the principal of that school. This should be done before conferring with the parents.

2. Before requesting the Review Committee to consider applications for exceptions (IQ 130–34 on Form L, or 125–34 on Form LM), it is desirable to discuss the data on achievement level with the principal of the center school in order to determine whether the pupil would be suitably placed in the center.

3. Parents of pupils attending an elementary school out of their district shall be informed in writing that these pupils will be expected to attend the junior high school in the district of their residence.

D. *Transfers of Gifted Pupils*

1. A pupil approved for admission into the program and attending a school not having a center is eligible for a transfer to the school in which the center is located.

2. The principal of the sending elementary school should contact the receiving school, giving information on the pupil's ability and achievement. The receiving elementary school shall accept the pupil as gifted and include him in the special program.

E. *Transportation*

1. Pupils attending schools out of their district and at a distance in excess of one mile and one-half will be eligible to receive free transportation on AC Transit bus. Application for such transportation should be made by the principal of the school in which the center is located.

F. *Dropping a Pupil from a Gifted Class*

1. Once the pupil has been placed in a gifted class it is assumed that he will remain in the class as long as his achievement warrants it, without further testing.

2. When a pupil has not been achieving at the level indicated by intelligence test scores, the principal may request a retest by the Research Department, giving details on the previous test and the reason for the request. The Research Department will then decide what test to use and make arrangements for its administration.

3. When there are indications that the pupil should be dropped from a gifted class, the principal should refer the case for study to the guidance consultant.

G. *Pupils Who Have Not Been Placed in Gifted Classes*

1. It is advisable that each school committee review at least annually all cases where a pupil is qualified but has not been placed in a

gifted class. This should be done since the circumstances that resulted in the original nonplacement by the school may have changed.

H. *Grouping Gifted Pupils in Regular Classes*

1. Sixth-grade gifted pupils who do not elect to attend a center or who are unable to attend due to class size limitation will be grouped with other gifted pupils and/or pupils with high academic potential in a regular sixth-grade classroom.
2. Gifted pupils in grades kindergarten through five will likewise be grouped together for instruction to the extent possible.
3. The pupils in those gifted instructional groups will meet the same requirements as those established for pupils attending the centers, and must be officially approved by the Research Department for inclusion in the program. The composition of the class to which this group is assigned should be of such ability and achievement as to minimize the number of instructional groups. Class size should be maintained at the minimum permitted by the classification of the school within the regular allotment of teacher time.

I. *Criteria for Exceptions to Admission Requirements*

1. Exceptions may be recommended by the school committee for pupils with individual IQ's in the range of 130–34 on Form L, or 125–34 on Form LM of the Stanford-Binet Tests, when reading and arithmetic achievement, as evidenced by tests, is approximately two years above grade level.
2. In making these exceptions, the following factors should be considered carefully by the school:

    Size of classes, equipment available, etc.
    Work and study habits
    Motivation and strong persisting interests
    Social, emotional, and physical maturity
    Health
    Chronological age
    Home conditions
    Activities outside the school program

3. These requests for exceptions may be submitted to the Research Department on Form G-A2, Request for Exception. These pupils may not be placed in the program until official approval has been obtained.

4. The elementary Committee on Exceptions for the Gifted Program will include the Assistant Superintendent, Director of Elementary Education, a representative of the Research Department, and three elementary principals.

J. *Summary Outline of Procedures for Placing Pupils in Gifted Classes Meeting Basic Criteria*

1. See A. *Basic Criteria* and B. *School Committee Approval.* Check IQ with Research Department.
2. Former teachers, the guidance consultant, and the cumulative records should be consulted.
3. Any pupil with known emotional health, social adjustment, or home problems should be placed in gifted classes only after the consultation with the guidance consultant. This is particularly important in cases where the pupil is to be placed in a center in another school.
4. The school committee consisting of the principal, the approved tester, teachers acquainted with the pupils under consideration, and others as appointed by the principal, determines the pupils to be placed in the program. If the pupil is to be transferred to another elementary school, check with that school regarding class size, etc. (See Section C.)
5. The placement in the class should be discussed with the pupil and his parents after the decision for placement has been reached.
6. If the aforementioned conditions are favorable, the pupil may be placed in the class.
7. If the pupil is to be placed in a gifted class in another elementary school, issue a transfer. Transportation, if necessary, is arranged by the receiving school.

67. Guide for Teaching the Gifted: Grade Five, Wichita *

DELORE GAMMON, *Director, Elementary Curriculum*

Foreword

The *Guide for Teaching the Gifted—Grade Five* is designed to supplement the regular fifth-grade curriculum guides in all subject areas. The usual fifth-grade curriculum content will serve as a point of departure for the gifted classes. In many respects, the curriculum will be very similar to that of other fifth-grade groups.

The content of this supplementary guide is intended to enrich and expand the regular program of studies. Children may go as far beyond the fifth-grade level as seems feasible.

A very wholesome trend in elementary education today is the nationwide interest in children of exceptional ability. Never in the history of our country has the need for outstanding leadership been so keenly felt. It is generally recognized that leadership must come from the group with high potential.

Four experimental classes for fifth-grade gifted children were organized in September, 1961. The interest was not focused on the children who had unusual ability in one area such as art, mathematical aptitude, and music, nor upon the children who might fall in the genius classification. These groups need the highly specialized instruction that does not fall within the scope of the public school program. A minority group, however, with intellectual ability to go beyond the usual program of studies both in depth and breadth is the group that needs increased attention.

Teaching the gifted children in grade five is part of a vertical program beginning in the kindergarten and extending through the twelfth grade. A goal of the administration is to strengthen the articulation between elementary and secondary levels.

The guide is available for all fifth-grade teachers to use in meeting the needs of the gifted children in the regular classrooms.

* From *Guide for Teaching the Gifted: Grade Five*, Wichita Public Schools, Wichita, Kan., 1961. Reprinted with permission.

General Statement about the Program

I. The organization for instruction will be the self-contained classroom. Some special teachers will be assigned to special areas and the regular teachers will do some team teaching.

II. The program will not be prescribed but will be evolving, flexible, exploratory, and experimental.

III. The daily schedule will be considered in large blocks of time. The teacher will be expected to observe the usual time allotments for the week, however, for the various subjects.

IV. The teaching techniques will be less directive than in the regular classroom, more responsive to child behavior, but the teacher will maintain status. Individualization and differentiation in the curriculum are goals to be attained.

V. The classroom atmosphere will be conducive to democratic living and to the maximum attainment of the goals for the program.

VI. The classes will experiment with new equipment and special uses of other equipment used in the regular classroom.

VII. The approach to learning will be twofold:

A. To seek out and develop children's special interests.
B. To initiate new interests for children to explore and develop.

VIII. The gifted classes are identified by special features:

A. The class will be a highly selected, homogeneous group.
B. The group will be homogeneous with regard to:

1. Chronological age
2. Intellectual potential
3. Achievement
4. Social and emotional maturity
5. Physical fitness

C. The group will be limited in size to 20 children.
D. The teachers and principals will work closely with administrative and supervisory staff.

IX. Some characteristics of the gifted children influence in classroom techniques:

A. The children approach the learning of a new concept eagerly.
B. They are not hampered by fixed ideas but are open-minded in receiving new ideas and gaining insight.

C. They do not hesitate to ask questions. Often their questions are the result of a creative type of thinking.

D. They can think together as a group and also benefit from individual contributions to the group.

E. They are quick to understand directives from the teacher or from the printed page.

F. They are capable of helping themselves toward their special-interest goals.

G. They are resourceful in making good use of their time throughout the day.

. . . .

Social Studies

A. Summary of the subject

1. Children learn the fundamentals of government in a democracy such as that of the United States. They study the evaluation of human character traits that underlie all successful living and make for peace among nations. The major aim is to develop citizens who appreciate the American way of life and who have the understanding and skill necessary for intelligent and responsible citizenship.

2. The subject begins with the lands and people of the Western Hemisphere before the coming of the Europeans and includes the United States, Alaska, Hawaii, and Puerto Rico.

3. In social studies the development of the skills is deeper and drill activities are very creative.

4. This subject is correlated more extensively with arithmetic, science, spelling, reading, and English.

5. The pupils show great interest in most activities. They are eager both in the pursuit of individual interests and research and in the cooperative planning of groups. The pupils are very receptive to new interests presented to them.

B. Broadened concepts

1. The child is introduced to large land and water masses and political divisions of countries and their positions on the globe.

2. He understands that it takes cooperative effort at community, state, and national levels to make a democracy effective and that the people benefit from democratic living.

3. He sees evidence of the importance of research in advancing human

knowledge, which many times is built upon records of those who have preceded him.

4. He understands and realizes the contribution that courageous, dedicated lives make to the world.
5. He understands that we are simply one people among many but that the external differences are unimportant compared to the essential likenesses.
6. He understands that all peoples need spiritual help.
7. He understands that civilization results from the combined efforts of many people from physical factors (as natural resources) and from ease of transportation and communication.
8. He realizes the importance of the individual citizen in a democracy.
9. He has a better understanding of the diversity of occupations that results from geographic factors.
10. He develops a sympathetic attitude toward the position of conquered peoples.
11. He understands that the sharing of ideas with peoples of the world is important.
12. He understands that the same moral bases underlie a good life in any culture.
13. He is aware of the limitless possibilities of man's improvement in control over the barriers of time and space.
14. He understands that all people need to improve in human relationships.
15. He understands that every people from the most primitive to the most civilized must have some form of government.
16. He understands that we should feel a warm appreciation for our national heritage and recognize its symbols (e.g., the flag).
17. Through study of different countries he is led to see that people everywhere have common problems to face.
18. He shows superior ability in seeing cause-and-effect relationships very quickly.

C. Refined skills

1. The pupils locate and organize material readily and use the content effectively.
2. The basic reading skills are used and refined in the social studies program.
3. Basic social studies skills are more widely applied and refined.
   a. Understanding of social studies concepts
   b. Recognizing words new to this particular field

   c. Reading and interpreting maps, globes, pictures, and charts
   d. Using concepts of time and chronology
   e. Practicing good citizenship
  4. Special opportunities are provided for:
   a. Individual research
   b. Independent study
   c. Project development
   d. Group work

D. Suggested activities

Unit I. First People in the Americas

1. Make dioramas of Plains Indians, Eastern woodlands, Far North, Pueblos, Aztecs of Mexico, Mayas, and Incas.
2. Discuss the change of opinion on the treatment of the Indians by the settlers.
3. Make a pictograph showing the population density from the maps of regions of the United States.
4. Collect at least three different kinds of projection maps.
5. Draw the North American river system.
6. Make a scrapbook of different kinds of trees. Show a cross section of the grain of each.

Unit II. Discovering the New World

1. Have each pupil write out his own family tree to see the background of the class.
2. Collect spices and identify their sources.
3. Make a sand map of the world. Different colors represent different explorers and routes.
4. Make a chart of contemporary explorers.
5. Read "Marco Polo's Travels."
6. Carve a Viking ship.
7. Put together a model of Columbus' ship.
8. Read some of the Norse Sagas.
9. Read widely about the Crusades.
10. Read poetry about Columbus.
11. Make a time line of the explorations.
12. Play a game of "You Were There" at the discovery of America.

Unit III. Northeastern States

1. On a globe, put flags on the different areas in which Spain, Portugal, England, France, and the Netherlands made settlements.

2. Have a geological resource person tell how glaciers were formed.
3. Display models of old ships, such as the Mayflower or others of that period.
4. Discuss the Mayflower Compact and apply it to your room organization.
5. Read Stephen Vincent Benét's poems about the earliest Americans.
6. Contrast the religious beliefs of the Pilgrims and the Puritans.
7. Make a "Who's Who in the American Colonies."
8. Make a picture collection of fish found off the northeastern shores.
9. Find out how paper is made today.
10. Take a field trip to a monument works.

Unit IV. The Southeast

1. Write to a famous historical place in each southeastern state for information on places (such as Williamsburg or St. Augustine).
2. Assemble ship models of the three ships that brought settlers to Jamestown.
3. Find out the price of tobacco per pound from one of the large manufacturers.
4. Compare the Maryland Charter with the Mayflower Compact.
5. Have a panel discussion on how much religious freedom the colonists really had.
6. Make a model of a southern plantation with cereal boxes or folded construction paper for buildings, corrugated paper for cabins.
7. Make a map marking the four routes to the west over the Appalachians.

Unit V. How We Became a Nation

1. Read and discuss the Declaration of Independence.
2. Dramatize the Boston Tea Party.
3. Have a television program, "You Were There," with the script about the affair at Lexington and Concord.
4. Discuss the discord among the troops quartered at Valley Forge.
5. Write George Washington's obituary.
6. Give a book review on Theodore Roosevelt's "Winning of the West." In this case, the "west" is the northwest territory of Ohio.
7. Pretend to be members of a travel bureau taking different groups to the White House, the Smithsonian.
8. Make a map of the United States in 1861, showing the divisions of the North and South.

Unit VI. Making a Living in the Southeast

1. Make an industrial map of the South to show diversification of its industries.
2. Write to the cotton market at Memphis, Tennessee, for information and pamphlets on the price of raw cotton and to whom it is sold.
3. Make a chart of the by-products of the peanut.
4. Collect different kinds of cotton cloth such as velvet, dimity, piqué.
5. Prepare a report on thoroughbreds and horse racing.
6. Construct a bulletin board display of fish of the Southeast.

Unit VII. The North Central States

1. Have a quilting bee. Each child makes one block.
2. Make a diorama of an early pioneer scene.
3. List the machinery needed on a modern farm and its cost.
4. Use National Dairy Council farm unit.
5. Explain the differences between pasteurized, condensed, evaporated, homogenized, and raw milk.
6. Taste different kinds of cheese.
7. Make a scrapbook of pictures showing the progress of old cars to modern cars.
8. Visit a salt mine.

Unit VIII. The Southwest

1. Write to the Colt Revolver Company for their pamphlet on guns.
2. Ask a resource person to describe the Oklahoma land rush.
3. Make a collection of southwestern products in pill bottles: rice, wheat, corn, peanuts, oats, millet, milo maize, sugar, oil, bauxite, coal, lead, and zinc.
4. Bring fur samples of mink, opossum, muskrat, and raccoon.
5. Report on the King Ranch.
6. Improvise "This Week's Westerns" (Tales of the Old West), one a day for five days.

Unit IX. The Far West

1. Locate the old Spanish missions on a map of the western states.
2. Invite a resource person to show slides and tell of the National Park program.
3. Report on the Mormon religion.
4. Draw a suspension bridge and explain it.
5. Take a United States map and, with green-, yellow-, and red-headed pins, locate the national parks.

Unit X. The Northwest

1. Read Mr. Charles Johnson's diary of his trip to Oregon.
2. Listen to a record that tells of Sacajawea.
3. From *Life* magazine report more about Marcus Whitman. (See *Reader's Guide.*)
4. On a map of the United States show the Oregon, Santa Fe, and Cumberland Trails.
5. Bring flax to school.
6. Collect minerals of the Northwest: lead, zinc, copper, silver, coal.
7. Explain the different events of a rodeo and how points are counted for championships.

Unit XI. Distant Lands Under the Stars and Stripes

1. List and locate the United States possessions in the Pacific and Atlantic.
2. Compare the common mosquito with the anopheles. Learn about the conquest of yellow fever.
3. Secure information from the United States government pamphlets on our present bases located on island possessions.
4. Construct diagrams or models of the Panama Locks.

Unit XII. Americans All

1. Draw the early flags of the United States
2. Make a tape recording of children in the roles of Nathan Hale, Zebulon Pike, Alexander Bell, Elizabeth Stanton, and William Gorgas.
3. Draw the new United States flag with its fifty stars. In the middle of each star put the name of the state that it represents and the date of its entrance into the Union.

For Any Unit in Social Studies

1. Look up air or steamship routes to any area studied.
2. Write creative stories and poems about peoples of the world.
3. Use resource people to demonstrate, to discuss, to interpret their special interests and talents.
4. Make time lines to interpret such concepts as the history of airplanes.

68. Program for Gifted Children, Indianapolis *

BEN MORGAN, Supervisor, Special Education

How Are Gifted Pupils Selected?

Pupils are chosen on the basis of their intelligence, results of group tests and individual tests given by the school psychologists, recommendation of teachers and principals, and the approval of their parents. Entrance to one of the classes is purely voluntary.

Group intelligence tests are given every year to all first-, fourth-, sixth-, and eighth-grade pupils in the Indianapolis Public Schools. Pupils entering the schools here for the first time at any grade level also are tested. Pupils who have an intelligence quotient of 130 or above on the basis of the fourth-grade group tests are considered for the gifted classes.

Principals in each school in the city send results of these tests and the pupil's ability and achievement to the supervisor of special education. The supervisor then determines if the child is eligible for an individual test by a psychologist.

Parents are contacted by the principal of their child's school and by letter from the supervisor of special education. A group meeting with the parents and the supervisor may follow before a test is given. The school psychologist makes the final recommendation, on the basis of the individual tests, for enrollment in the classes. Before a pupil may be transferred to a special class, however, his parents must give their approval.

What Is Included in the Program?

The study program for gifted children in the special classes is basically the same as that in any classroom. Gifted pupils do all the work in the regular course of study, but their work is enriched and expanded at their age and social level. This program of enrichment has many advantages

* From a mimeographed document, 2 pp., Indianapolis Public Schools, Indianapolis Ind. Reprinted with permission.

over the practice of acceleration or "skipping" grades. When pupils skip, they may miss basic lesson material and may be denied their natural leadership roles because they cannot compete physically and socially with the children of the advanced grade.

The gifted child's study program is designed to increase his knowledge, power, skill, alertness, and efficiency beyond what could be done in a regular classroom. This is accomplished through additional work in literature, history, science, and social studies. Regular subject matter is expanded through teacher-pupil conferences, educational excursions into the community, special research projects, and individualized instruction.

Pupils are given freedom to explore and to experiment in academic areas in which they are especially interested. They develop their ability to think and to evaluate critically.

The study of French begins in the fifth grade and the fundamentals of typing are taught in the seventh and eighth grades. Many other special skills are developed by pupils and teachers working together.

Do Children Like the Special Class?

Comments of the children show that they enjoy the program of the special class and profit greatly from it. They find expanded curriculum more challenging than the program of the regular classroom. They are always busy, having many opportunities through research to follow up individual problems in which they are interested.

Because the program is more challenging, they enter into the various class projects with enthusiasm. Even though there is competition in the class, the pupils display a cooperative and friendly attitude toward the teacher and each other. Constructive criticism and critical thinking and evaluation are stressed.

Pupils also like the classes because they take part in the regular program of activities in the building. They are given building responsibilities and participate in all general school activities and in physical education, art, home economics, industrial arts, and music with other pupils.

Children like the classes even more when they experience, at home, the same atmosphere of understanding and cooperation they find at school. They grow in ability to appreciate themselves, their homes, their teachers, the school, other pupils, and life in general.

What Problems May a Child Have?

1. The greater distance to travel to and from school.
2. The need to have lunch away from home.

3. Adjusting to a new environment (leaving former classmates and making new friends).
4. The envy of other children and, sometimes, adults.
5. Accepting greater personal responsibility in carrying out classroom assignments.
6. The need to work harder and longer on lessons and research, both at school and at home.
7. Learning to budget time and to work alone on the larger units of study that are assigned in these classes.

What Are the Responsibilities of Parents of a Gifted Child?

The greatest responsibility of parents is to provide the physical and mental surroundings that enable the child to do his best. Included in the physical surroundings are:

1. A quiet place where the child can work without being disturbed.
2. Transportation, where necessary, to and from school.
3. An adequate lunch away from home if the child cannot come home for lunch.
4. A variety of activities with his family that will expand on his experiences at school.

Providing the other type of surroundings sometimes is not easy. Sometimes parents of gifted children tend to be highly protective, anxious, and ambitious in regard to them. This does not always work to the best interests of the child, however, especially if it continues as he grows older and tends to direct him in a way he is not inclined to go.

Overemphasizing the fact that the child is superior does him an injustice. Knowing that he is superior is good for him, and a reasonable pride in his ability and achievement helps him to develop the best attitude, generally one of humility, toward himself.

During the school year, parents have the opportunity to discuss the gifted-child program in special meetings with teachers and others connected with the program. Parents are asked, at the end of the school year, to fill out a questionnaire as an aid in continuous evaluation of the program. It contains questions about things parents liked, gains their child has made, new interests he has developed, problems that may have arisen, and suggestions for improvement.

Does the Program Help Children?

Parents who evaluate gifted-child programs repeatedly have noted the following improvements their children have made:

1. Greater tolerance and courtesy and more interest in others.
2. Development of initiative and responsibility.
3. Improvement in ability to budget time and organize work.
4. Development of self-reliance and poise.
5. Improved study habits and more concentration power.
6. Greater discrimination in selecting reading materials and television and radio programs.
7. Improvement in ability to evaluate themselves and to accept criticism.
8. Greater stability and maturity.

69. Secondary School Program for Intellectually Gifted Pupils, Los Angeles *

ROBERT E. KELLY, *Associate Superintendent,*
Division of Secondary
Education

M OTIVATION to achieve, to create, and to learn is the important factor
in the development of programs for intellectually gifted pupils at
the secondary school level. To provide the essential motivation, the
Secondary Honors Program in the Los Angeles City Schools is a multi-
track approach, and utilizes ability grouping, cluster grouping, and pupil
and subject acceleration.

Ability Grouping

Honors classes are planned for intellectually gifted pupils who should be
offered opportunities for more comprehensive study and enrichment. Such
classes may be sections of required academic subjects or advanced academic electives.

Academically enriched classes are planned for more capable pupils who
are not eligible for honors classes but who may profit by enrichment of
instruction. Such classes may be sections of required subjects or enriched
academic electives. Highly gifted pupils may be enrolled in these classes
when honors classes are not available.

* From *Education of Intellectually Gifted Pupils in Los Angeles City Schools,*
rev., May 1962, pp. 9–10. Reprinted with permission.

Cluster Grouping

When sufficient numbers have not been available for separate classes, one plan for the intellectually gifted has been to enrich the instructional program in regular classes for clusters of pupils of honors caliber.

Acceleration

Two kinds of acceleration are available for the intellectually gifted at the secondary school level—pupil acceleration and subject acceleration.

Pupil acceleration. Pupils may be accelerated one semester in junior high school and one semester in senior high school. Such acceleration is carefully planned on an individual basis to avoid the omission of essential blocks of learning and to assure the continued academic, social, and emotional adjustment of the pupil.

Subject acceleration. Provision is made for gifted pupils to enroll in accelerated sequences in mathematics and foreign language in the junior high school and to take advanced work in senior high school in certain academic subjects that will enable them to participate in one of the following programs:

1. Advanced Placement Program—College level courses are offered in the twelfth grade on the high school campus and taught by high school teachers. Pupils receive high school marks and credit for satisfactory completion of the courses. Pupils also receive college credit and/or advanced placement in college under the following conditions: (1) If they complete the courses satisfactorily, (2) If they pass the Advanced Placement examinations administered by the Educational Testing Service at the high schools in May of each year; and (3) If the college they choose to attend grants credit and/or advanced placement in recognition of the examination score.
2. Combined High School–College Program—Each high school may recommend ten twelfth-grade pupils to enroll in junior college courses, not to exceed five hours per week in the regular day classes on the college campus.
3. Combined High School–University Program (Experimental)—Selected twelfth-grade gifted pupils are permitted to enroll in a maximum of two college-level courses on the campus of the University of California at Los Angeles.

Summer School Honors Program

Honors classes are scheduled in the academic subject fields during summer school. These classes meet four hours each day for the six-week period. Each secondary school has the opportunity to recommend pupils for participation in this program.

70. High-Ability Program for High School Students, Canton *

L L O Y D M . S W A N , *Director, Department of Pupil Personnel*

Philosophy

The American way of life recognizes the worth and dignity of each individual. Every child should be given the opportunity to develop his capacities and to contribute to the program of human welfare. An effective educational program should provide for early recognition and continuous development of the gifted child.

I. Objectives

    A. Provide broad educational experiences commensurate with his abilities

    B. Develop superior work habits and study skills

    C. Develop leadership, reflective thinking, and creativity

II. Methods of Identification and Requirements for Selection

    A. Select through testing program

        1. Those who have scored 120 or more on a recent group intelligence test

        2. Those who with previous group test scores between 110 and 120 have scored higher on an individual intelligence test

* From mimeographed material. Reprinted with permission.

B. Require recommendations from subject teacher and principal on the eight-grade level and by counselor and subject teacher on the high school level, on basis of following factors

1. Achievement test scores
2. Reading ability
3. Emotional maturity
4. Classroom performance (B+ or 88 average)

C. Require written approval of the parent

III. Suggestions for Program of Instruction

A. Establish basic minimum standards in all areas of the superior program by teachers in each subject field
B. Enrich on all grade levels, present programs in English, mathematics, science, foreign languages, and social studies, when scheduling permits
C. Offer, in addition, advanced placement courses and special courses such as creative writing, analytical geometry, calculus, second-year biology, chemistry, and physics
D. Plan, with institutions of higher learning, evaluative criteria for the purpose of college entrance or advanced placement programs
E. Provide for continuous counseling with all gifted students, their parents, and teachers

1. On planning for college
2. On choosing challenging subjects

F. Accelerate on a limited individual basis to provide possible graduation in less than four years

1. Student who is socially, mentally, and emotionally well-adjusted and healthy
2. Student who has mastered the basic requirements
3. Student who has the written approval of his parents

G. Establish special classes for gifted in summer school

1. Offer courses in industrial arts and home economics at Timken High School to students in the Technical or Classical Courses
2. Organize a civics class for high-ability students who have averages of 88 and the approval of the high school principal
3. Offer conversational classes in foreign languages to students

who have completed two or more years in a specific language
with a minimum grade average of 85

4. Schedule classes in such sciences as geology and astronomy
to high-ability students with an average of 88 or more

IV. Factors to Be Considered by Administrators in Staff Selection

A. Professional qualifications

1. Possess above-average intellectual ability
2. Have certification in subject field
3. Be in good professional standing
4. Consent to take further training in teaching area, if possible
5. Have established reputation as an effective teacher

B. Personal qualifications

1. Express willingness to teach in high-ability program
2. Maintain good physical and mental health
3. Show understanding of students of high-intellectual ability
4. Possess good sense of humor
5. Command respect of students
6. Enjoy working with high school students

V. Recommendations for In-Service Education

A. Employ or appoint a city coordinator in each subject area in
order to conduct meetings, and counsel with all teachers in the
program for the exchange of ideas
B. Hold departmental meetings within buildings with principal and
advisers in attendance
C. Provide opportunities for intracity and other community visitations
D. Make grants available for summer study from other than Board
of Education
E. Select new teachers for the program in the spring in order to
hold a workshop consisting of experienced and new teachers for
interchange of ideas and for organization of the program for
the ensuing year, the workshop to be held on school time with
substitutes provided by the Board of Education

VI. Duties of the Administrators

A. Provide qualified personnel
B. Set up machinery and standards for pupil selection

C. Interpret the program to teachers and parents in respect to goals, enrichment, and acceleration

D. Provide for withdrawal when necessary, only after conference with teacher, pupil, and parent and not before the end of first grading period

E. Provide congenial physical facilities

F. Provide additional instructional materials beyond the regular needs of the classroom

G. Arrange for teachers to have fewer classes and extra assignments so they will have time to plan work; to have conferences with parents, students, and other teachers; and to mark written work carefully

H. Hold classes to a maximum of 20, especially in the field of English

I. Provide a better testing background

J. Develop a uniform, city-wide grading scale that will not penalize the students in the program

K. Visit the classes and suggest changes as the program progresses

L. Smooth out criticism of the program from uninformed sources

VII. Suggestions for Public Relations

A. Report periodically to entire teaching staff

B. Furnish to parents a bibliography on the gifted child

C. Restrict visitations to the classes

D. Hold group meetings of parents

VIII. Recommendations for Evaluation

A. Establish criteria by which the effectiveness of the program can be evaluated by parent, teacher, child, and administrator—criteria to be determined by the psychology department

B. Develop a special system of records for evaluating the child in the program, including attitudes and desire to learn

C. Arrange for a standing committee in subject area to do extensive and continuous evaluation and study of instructional program

D. Plan follow-up for postgraduates

E. Arrange for evaluation of the program by North Central Association of Colleges and Secondary Schools

71. Programs for the Gifted in Secondary Schools, Tucson *

THOMAS L. LEE, *Assistant Superintendent*

No Dramatic, Unique Programs

From the beginning, the Tucson schools have made no attempt to develop any sensational "new" approach to the teaching of the gifted. Development of such unique programs tends to draw the eye of publicity, and this in turn brings parental pressure to include certain children in the program who may not find it profitable. Teaching the gifted, as we see it, is an important part of the total educational effort, one requiring special attention—but not to the detriment of the remainder of the instructional program. It is but one facet of the total program of meeting individual needs among pupils.

Renewed Emphasis Began in 1957

Some attention was given to this problem prior to 1957, but it was in that year that first steps were taken to develop Advanced Placement courses in the high schools. System-wide committees organized along subject-matter lines explored all aspects of the program and made specific recommendations for our participation. There followed the development of course outlines in mathematics, chemistry, English, (and later, biology). University of Arizona faculty members collaborated in this work. These college-level courses are now available in our high schools. In the spring of 1962, ninety-seven Advanced Placement examinations were taken by our students.

Honors Program Developed

A definite part of the instructional program was the development of three-way sectioning in required courses. This provided for Basic (slow

---

* From a *mimeographed statement*, October, 1962. Reprinted with permission.

learners), Average (middle-range students), and Honors (top-level students). Students were enrolled in these sections on the basis of past performance, grades, achievement, and parental consent. An "open door" policy prevailed permitting students to be transferred from level to level as counselors and teachers recommended. Special attention was given to teaching methods at all levels; teaching materials were revised.

A natural consequence of the development of the college-level courses was upgrading of teaching all along the line for the more able students. The effect was felt all the way down into the junior high school. Seventh graders with high ability and interest in mathematics were permitted to enroll in a course that covered the essentials of both seventh and eighth grade arithmetic. These pupils then took beginning algebra in grade eight, moving on into the geometry, trigonometry, calculus, analytic geometry sequence in subsequent years. This made it possible to provide an excellent mathematics background for the physics student. A parallel program for the able students was initiated by teachers who had received special training in the UICSM mathematics program—one of the modern approaches. Able readers in junior high school were permitted to substitute Spanish for reading.

Grading Problems

An early tendency toward too-rigorous grading was observed. Classes composed of the select honors students were sometimes graded as if they were heterogeneous. Since the students were to receive class rank and grade-point average based on grades, the continuance of such a practice would wreck the Honors program.

It was necessary to issue an administrative directive stating that any student enrolled in an Honors course was expected to receive a grade of "1" (A); a grade of "2" (B) was to be regarded as a warning, and if improvement was not forthcoming, the student would be moved into a middle-range group. Course requirements and achievement have remained at a high level since the directive, and the only noticeable change has been in a more careful screening of students entering the Honors classes.

Special Course Development

To further meet the needs of the very able student, special seminars have been organized. A course in the humanities, a two-year sequence in world cultures, Spanish H (for native speakers), creative writing, and (now being planned) a fifth year Spanish course found their way into the curriculum. This last mentioned course was made necessary by the introduction of Spanish into the junior high school. In 1962-63, there were 140 students enrolled in third and fourth year Spanish who began their study of the language in junior high school.

Nonacademic Provision for the Gifted

Music theory and Honors music have been developed to provide courses in musicianship for advanced students. Participation in small vocal and instrumental ensembles is augmented by work in music theory and literature. Art courses emphasizing creative, original design also are available.

72. Provisions for the Gifted
in the Secondary Curriculum *

Bureau of Secondary Curriculum Development, New York State

M ANY SCHOOLS have always provided for the gifted by means of grouping, special advanced courses, individual attention, and in other ways. Likewise, the secondary curriculum bulletins published by the Department have for many years included materials designed to meet the needs of superior and talented pupils. In recent publications, a special effort has been made to give even more attention to this problem in all major curriculum areas.

English

The English curriculum for grades 7-12 makes provision for the flexibility necessary to meet pupil differences in interest and ability. A variety of elective courses and a wide reading program enable the schools to challenge the ability and interest of students generally gifted scholastically and of students with special skills in English.

* From *56 Practices for the Gifted from Secondary Schools of New York State,* pp. 25–32, The University of the State of New York, The State Education Department, Bureau of Secondary Curriculum Development, Albany, 1958. Reprinted with permission, but not copyrighted.

A supplement to the syllabus in English, entitled *English in the Senior High School,* provides many suggestions for special courses and for individualization and enrichment within courses by means of units related to that phase of English in which the pupil shows talent. At the beginning of all English courses, each student is encouraged to make a self-analysis that indicates his strengths and weaknesses. The special courses and units are then designed to meet the needs shown by this self-analysis, as well as the needs indicated by school records, by achievement testing, and by the judgment of the faculty.

In the case of gifted students, schools are encouraged to provide opportunities for each to develop his special ability in those areas of communication and literature in which he is interested. *English in the Senior High School* provides resource material on such topics as fiction, nonfiction, creative writing, speech, dramatics, radio, and television. These resource materials can be used as the basis for special courses or as enrichment material in the regular courses.

Special courses in English may be offered in grades below the 12th, but because a uniform statewide examination is permissive at this level, the 12th grade offers an especially good opportunity for enrichment. In schools with fewer than thirty seniors, the teacher may use materials in *English in the Senior High School* to develop a single general course that is sufficiently varied to provide for the senior of outstanding ability. In large schools, the teachers can develop a variety of courses to accomplish similar purposes. In many schools, these one-semester courses give students a greater choice of electives.

The teaching materials in the supplement are also useful in enriching the regular course. Units included are short and independent and can be incorporated easily into the framework of the regular course. They may be selected and combined for varying lengths of time in many different ways and with different degrees of emphasis. In such an arrangement the teacher can differentiate the activities for individuals and small groups within the class and design activities sufficiently challenging for the gifted.

Gifted students are encouraged to know the great books of world culture through extensive reading. Teachers and librarians encourage the use of the library for doing advanced work on such projects as research papers, senior essays, speeches, and special reports. Book clubs, honor reading groups, and courses in the classics or contemporary literature give students the opportunity to evaluate and review books and to make studies of specific books or authors. To encourage extensive reading, teachers and librarians aid the gifted in developing personal libraries and home reference libraries in hard-cover or paperbound editions. This undertaking involves a choosing of titles for particular interests and purposes, comparing editions, using library tools, and becoming acquainted with bookstores.

Citizenship Education

Curriculum publications in citizenship education are designed to provide a wide range in content and a variety of learning activities adaptable for use in developing the intellectual and creative talents. By making use of the *Citizenship Education Planning Guide,* a teacher can find help in developing specific teaching materials for the gifted.

The New York State syllabuses, *Citizenship Education 7-8-9* and *Citizenship Education 10-11-12,* outline the scope of courses that may be enriched to afford maximum opportunity for mature pupils to practice research techniques. Handbooks of teaching procedures for the courses in citizenship education include activities for specific topics that may challenge abstract thinking and analysis. Additional activities provide opportunities for developing leadership. Still others suggest research projects adapted to the interests and capacities of gifted pupils.

The handbook, *Teaching American History,* contains 850 learning activities. Each of the 21 topics covered includes many activities that are planned to help the teacher discover and make use of the special abilities of bright pupils. A list of these selected activities appears on pages 385-88 of the publication. To supplement this handbook, *American History Bibliography* has been published separately. This 112-page booklet contains lists of enrichment material for each of the 21 topics and various special lists designed to help talented students.

Though handbooks may not be available for all citizenship education courses in the immediate future, the procedures suggested in *Teaching American History* can serve as useful models for devising appropriate teaching procedures for the gifted in other courses.

Mathematics

The new mathematics curriculum as outlined in the syllabuses *Mathematics 7-8-9* and *Mathematics 10-11-12* provides for continuous, systematic development of mathematical knowledge and skills. The integrated sequence is better adapted for providing for such growth than was the old compartmentalized program. It is possible to provide for the needs of gifted pupils in one of two ways. The six-year sequence can be covered in five years, permitting the pupil to take a college-level course in high school. If such acceleration is not feasible, it is possible to include the study of special aspects of mathematics along with the regular courses.

In either case, it is possible to emphasize the interrelationships of the various branches of mathematics and to teach for understanding of principles.

Mathematics is required of all pupils through grade 8. The scope of content for grades 7 and 8 is combined in one outline. In planning local courses for these grades, major changes must be made in organizing the content to satisfy the needs of both slow and fast pupils.

With bright pupils, it is possible to include an extensive introduction to algebra and indirect measurement in grade 8. Where homogeneous grouping is not feasible, the class may be divided into groups and the assignments differentiated according to ability. The time spent on each unit may also be modified to permit the bright pupils to progress at their optimum rate.

Beginning with the elective courses in grade 9, a differentiated program is recommended with parallel courses in general mathematics for the less able. The gifted pupil will continue in the integrated sequence. In grade 9 the major emphasis is on the extension into the field of algebra, but the course also includes an extension of indirect measurement with an introduction to numerical trigonometry.

The new courses outlined in the syllabus *Mathematics 10-11-12* retain the essential values of the traditional courses but provide also for continued steady growth. The reduction in the number of required theorems in the 10th year course makes possible the introduction of a unit on coordinate geometry. This unit integrates algebra and geometry and results in a more varied program that challenges the bright pupils. The 11th year course through the integration of algebra, coordinate geometry, and plane trigonometry offers opportunities for continued use of skills and growth in mathematical understanding. Courses for the 12th year follow the syllabus outline for advanced algebra and solid geometry. However, some schools are introducing additional content from calculus and statistics to gear the material to the gifted students.

An experimental course in the 12th year mathematics is being offered in several schools in the state. This course introduces some topics of advanced algebra, analytic geometry, calculus, and statistics via truth tables, sets, and symbolic logic.

Science

The science curriculum for grades 7-12 makes provisions for pupils of all levels of ability. Under the guidance of an overall Science Advisory Committee, the old syllabuses for the secondary school courses have been revised and modernized and new courses have been added to meet the needs of all pupils. Special attention has been given to the program of providing for gifted students. Science syllabuses suggest appropriate modifications of content, and the accompanying handbooks contain many activities designed especially for bright pupils.

A broad but flexible program for the early secondary grades is outlined in the syllabus *Science 7-8-9*. One suggested modification for bright pupils that has proven successful in many schools is the substitution of an advanced science such as earth science for general science 9. If this is done, science should be scheduled as a major subject in both grades 7 and 8. This plan makes it possible for superior science students to take four advanced sciences beyond general science.

The General Science Handbooks, Parts 1, 2, and 3 contain over 1,500 suggestions for experiments, demonstrations, field trips, and projects. By selecting carefully various combinations of these activities and arranging them in different sequences, it is possible to serve a great variety of special abilities and interests. Many of the activities suggest additional experiments by which capable pupils can extend any one of the ten areas. These various adaptations can enrich the science program and lay the foundation for the elective courses.

The State Regents syllabuses in biology, earth science, physics, and chemistry are designed for pupils of average and above-average ability in science. Parallel courses in physical science and biological science are being developed for pupils of lower ability. This multiple-track program permits a continued emphasis on principles, theory, and quantitative treatment in the Regents courses. Since each syllabus represents only a minimum framework, many optional topics can be included in the local course for the benefit of gifted pupils.

Handbooks for teachers such as the *Physics Handbook* contain many activities that are designed as projects for the more capable students. Some of the longer projects should be substituted for the traditional laboratory "experiment" to give such students the opportunity to carry on a research-type investigation.

Foreign Languages

Current curriculum publications in the foreign language field make provisions that offer a challenge to students who are talented in languages. One objective of the study of Latin as stated in the *Syllabus in Latin* is the improvement of English. Through the study of Latin grammar, students can gain a functional view of English grammar. Through the study of Latin vocabulary, they gain a tool with which to grasp and retain the meaning of new English words.

An introductory course in Latin is provided for grades 7 and 8. The course is so designed that at its completion the pupils are prepared to enter the second year of elementary or general Latin. This introduction of Latin in grade 7 or 8 makes it possible for the abler pupils to get an early start on the subject and often awakens an interest in further language study.

The course in advanced Latin is extremely well-adapted to pupils who are talented in language. It is a two-year course designed for pupils who have superior intelligence, linguistic ability, and interest. The content of the course is appropriate for the language specialist, and high achievement is expected from the pupils. The first year's work is based on Latin prose, the second on Latin poetry.

Special suggestions are made for arranging the work so that, even in small schools, pupils have the opportunity to take the full four years of Latin. Although it is recommended that prose precede poetry, prose and poetry may be given in alternate years.

The *Modern Language Handbook* provides supplementary materials that can be used to enrich the study of French, Spanish, German, and Italian. Emphasis is placed on using these materials to provide a diversified program for slow, average, and superior students. Enrichment materials cover each country's specific history, geography, economic position, religion, government, colonial possessions, or international standing. The superior students can profit greatly from the use of the cultural background obtained from the knowledge of these materials to highlight the study of the music, the art masterpieces, the famous literature, and the cultural centers of the countries where the language is spoken.

The conversational aspect of language is emphasized. Conversational French and Spanish taught in the early secondary school build a good foundation for language study in high school. High school pupils who are talented linguistically and who have a special interest in foreign language can then prepare in two years to take the Regents examination usually taken after three years of study. The time saved enables gifted language students to continue with college-level courses in the language of their choice or to study additional languages while they are still in high school.

Physical Education, Health, and Recreation

The importance of providing all pupils with opportunities for the development of initiative, creativity, leadership, and responsibility is emphasized in the *Physical Education Syllabuses, Books III and IV,* for girls and boys in secondary schools.

These syllabuses point out the values of the early discovery of leadership potential. Among the opportunities for leadership provided by the physical education program are:

1. Teaching and directing class activities
2. Planning and directing activities clubs
3. Initiating and developing extraclass programs
4. Planning playday and sports-day programs
5. Captaining and managing sports activities
6. Officiating at games
7. Leading in recreation and athletic associations

Several sections of these syllabuses are devoted to specific suggestions for the development of leadership. Pupils who show leadership qualities are given opportunities to develop these qualities through actual practice.

Music

Although music education has concentrated in recent years on the value of music to everyone, special provisions are made for the musically talented.

The *Syllabus in Music, Grades 7-12,* describes two required courses and nine elective courses. The two required courses are general music 1 and 2 in grades 7 and 8. Special effort is made in these courses to discover musically gifted pupils and through guidance to help them begin to develop their special talents. Since all pupils are required to take these courses and the great variety of possible activities includes singing, playing musical instruments, writing simple original melodies, ear training, and dancing, children with musical talent are not often overlooked nor do they lack stimulation.

For bright pupils whose talents lie elsewhere than in music, the general education courses—general music 3 and music appreciation—are especially recommended for their cultural value.

Pupils exhibiting some form of talent in music can select from the nine electives those courses that will best develop their particular gifts. The three fundamental courses essential for almost all further work are theory 1, 2, and 3. These courses give the pupils the opportunity to develop a sense of musical values and the necessary skills for effective musical expression.

Pupils with natural vocal ability and musical sensitivity can take advanced vocal instruction in voice 1, 2, and 3 and in select choral groups. Instrumental performers can participate in concert and marching bands, orchestras, and string ensembles. They may also take advantage of the individualized instruction that is given to sections and individual members of these musical organizations.

The course in conducting is the most advanced one offered. It affords a close approach to the professional aspects of music and is designed for pupils of outstanding musical ability and leadership. These pupils learn to conduct school organizations and small ensembles in rehearsals and in public performances.

To develop further their special talents, pupils may carry on private music study under qualified teachers outside of school. Credit for this study is allowed toward a state diploma.

The *Handbook of Applied Music* contains lists of selections recommended for six levels of difficulty for many different instruments and types of voices. By using these lists, teachers can readily choose music that challenges the ability of all gifted pupils.

Art

The art curriculum for secondary schools recognizes a wide range of differences in pupils, both in interest and ability. The introductory course outlined in the syllabus *Secondary Schols Art* provides an opportunity for all pupils to explore a variety of materials, to work with different media, and to originate their own designs. As the teachers work with students over a period of time and observe them closely during these art experiences, they have an excellent opportunity to locate the pupils who have outstanding ability.

In the "studio" method, long the unique characteristic of art teaching, differences in the ability and interests of individual pupils are relatively easy to discover. Within recent years more space and time for art instruction have been provided so that gifted students may work at long-term projects that give them greater opportunity for creativity. Talented pupils are advised to take the course in basic art during grades 8 or 9. This course is concerned with the fundamentals of design and expression needed for further art study.

Following the course in basic art, pupils are offered a wide choice of courses so that they can progress in art skills and appreciation according to their particular interests and special abilities. Pupils may select from many different combinations of courses in drawing, painting, sculpture, design, illustration, graphic arts, and the crafts.

73. A Program for the Gifted at the Bronx High School of Science *

ALEXANDER TAFFEL, *Principal*

Background of the School

The Bronx High School of Science was established in 1938 by the Board of Education as a special school for students with particular interest and potential in the fields of science and mathematics. It selects its students from all parts of New York City by means of an entrance examination and an evaluation of record. In this manner, it chooses from approximately 4,000 candidates who apply yearly an entering class of 900 students having a median IQQ of 135, arithmetic and reading scores two years ahead of age level, and an impressive record of previous achievement. The register of the school consists of about 1,900 boys and 900 girls.

Philosophy of the School

Although the school is specially equipped to develop student interest in science and mathematics, its primary purpose is to give the student a well-rounded liberal arts education strong in the humanities as well as in the sciences and providing many curricular and extracurricular opportunities for development of personal and social maturity, of sports and other recreational interests, and of musical and artistic talents.

The Curriculum

The formal curriculum consists of two parts—one required and the other elective. The required courses are selected to assure a good balance between the humanities and the sciences. They include 4 years of English, 4 years of social studies, 3 years of a foreign language, 4 years of science, 3 years of mathematics, 1 year of mechanical drawing, ½ year of science

* From *The Gifted Child Quarterly*, Summer, 1961, pp. 69–70. Reprinted with permission.

laboratory techniques, and the usual requirements in art appreciation, music, and health education.

Objectives

A major goal of the school is to stimulate the initiative and independence of the student. It seeks to develop his ability to recognize and define problems and to plan a program of study and investigation for solving them. Intelligent and independent use of the library, the shop, the laboratory, and other school and community resources is encouraged and stressed.

A second major goal of the school is to identify and develop creativity, particularly in the sciences and mathematics. Too many students are mental conformists who learn thoroughly the well established content of the curriculum but who are reluctant to venture down the untrodden paths to explore new thoughts, methods, and ideas. In part, the conventional school situation is responsible for this timidity and lack of intellectual boldness because so high a premium is placed upon meeting or surpassing the expected norms of achievement in each grade as measured by CEEB and similar tests. Yet, if the school program is to stimulate creativity, it must consciously plan and make a place for it just as it provides for the mastering of content. At the Bronx High School of Science, this is done informally in the regular classes in the various subjects to an extent that depends upon the alertness of the individual teacher in recognizing the creative pupil and in launching him on a creative mission.

The Creative Science Project Program

The science project program has at its exclusive disposal four laboratories, a greenhouse, and an animal room. The students who take part in this program identify themselves by asking to be assigned to it or are identified by teachers who encourage them to apply. Each student is screened by a coordinator and, if admitted to the program, is assigned to one of the laboratories under the supervision of an assigned teacher. Here, students meet daily and explore each others' interests and ideas for the purpose of defining the problems that they would like to attempt to solve. After several weeks, each student has settled on a problem and begins to assemble the information, books, equipment, and materials needed to solve it. In addition to his regularly assigned period, the student may come to the laboratory during free periods and before and after school. From time to time, all the project pupils meet as a class to make progress reports to each other and to seek and give help and critical appraisal. These sessions broaden the experience and the outlook of all the students by giving them closer views of research areas and methods other than their own. The culmination of these research experiences includes presenting some of the findings at meetings of school clubs, assemblies, science fairs and congresses, school science publications, etc. An important outgrowth of this program has also been the establishment of contact with local research institutions who offer the students opportunities for apprenticeship to scientists in the field.

The Extracurricular Program

Particularly important in encouraging well-rounded individual development is the rich extracurricular program that includes the orchestra, three choruses, chamber music groups, dances, publications, student government, intramural athletics, varsity athletics, and a public affairs forum. It is interesting to note that, though their academic program seems heavy, the students find time for the widest variety of out of class and out of school activities. Although somewhat younger than their grade peers in other schools, they handle themselves well in interscholastic sports competition, excelling in track, swimming, and tennis. They have won the New York City tennis championship for the last four years.

Where Does the Program Lead?

What happens to these students when they leave us? All generally go on to college and higher education. An extensive survey of graduates, made several years ago, indicated that about 70 per cent of a sampling of 2,000 alumni were in or were preparing for careers associated with science or mathematics. More recent surveys confirm this trend so that it would appear that the school is successfully accomplishing one of its major missions, guiding many qualified students into the scientific and mathematical professions.

Although the school is only 22 years old and none of its graduates has been out of college more than 18 years, many of its alumni have already achieved places of distinction in the scientific and academic worlds. The current head of research for the United States Defense Department is one of our alumni as are also many heads of laboratories, professors, doctors, and research scientists. In a recent year, 0.5 per cent of all the doctorates given in the United States in the sciences and mathematics were awarded to Science graduates and 12 per cent of all the predoctoral and post-doctoral grants made by the National Science Foundation in New York State were also awarded to Science graduates. Many Science graduates are also to be found in all the other fields and professions—art, music, law, drama. Here, too, they are winning distinction.

As the school faces its future, it draws confidence from the validity of its past program but is not content to rest on its laurels. A lively program is under way for evaluating and modifying its curriculum to meet the needs of the changing times. Several experimental programs dealing with content reorganization, scheduling, and teaching methods are being contemplated. Above all, attention is being strongly focused on furthering individualization of our program and individual creativity and imagination.

74. Programs for the Gifted, Great Neck *

JOHN L. MILLER, *Superintendent*

Education of the Gifted

Alert to the needs of all pupils, the Great Neck public schools provide many opportunities for the gifted—boys and girls with superior general intelligence or those who have special talents in certain fields. These pupils are identified through day-by-day performance in their classrooms or through objective tests.

In educating the gifted, the Great Neck emphasis is on curriculum enrichment and the guidance of each individual to encourage him to carry on activities commensurate with his abilities. Enrichment opportunities are provided through many channels:

1. Having classes small enough so that each child may receive adequate individual guidance, but large enough for group participation in various learning activities and for rich experience in social living.
2. Providing classroom and other facilities to extend and enrich learning: abundant library resources; a wide range of audio-visual materials; and classroom centers of interest in art, music, and science.

* From printed material furnished by Marion E. Wiles, Executive Assistant, Great Neck Public Schools, Great Neck, N.Y. Reprinted with permission.

3. Organizing facets of the classroom program around problem situations, solutions to which will provide opportunities for wide reading and for breadth and depth of study according to individual abilities and interests.

4. Planning the school day or week so that each individual has time for independent study as well as for group work.

5. Offering a wide choice of electives at the secondary school level to provide stimulation and challenge to the gifted; examples: the *Great Issues Course, Creative Writing, World Literature, Special French,* and *Special Latin.*

6. Sponsoring student activities, such as clubs and the General Organization, which give pupils opportunities not only to enrich their own lives, but also to exercise leadership and to render service.

7. Encouraging individual pupils to use abilities and talents toward the enrichment of others—skill in playing musical instruments, storytelling, facility in speaking a second language, and development of hobbies.

8. Providing consultants (in elementary schools) whose knowledge and skill in specific fields stimulate pupils (and teachers) to higher levels of learning and expression.

9. Introducing special content and varying teaching methods as needs arise.

10. Providing appropriate guidance services—counseling, psychological, psychiatric, and medical.

Realizing the importance of adequate provisions for the gifted, staff committees continue to study needs of talented pupils, to review new techniques employed for the education of the gifted throughout the country, and to recommend new features for the improvement of the Great Neck program.

ADVANCED PLACEMENT

Young people from Great Neck have been granted Advanced Placement and/or credit on the basis of our regular curriculum for many years. In the English Department, Creative Writing, World Literature and Factual Writing; in the Social Studies Department, Great Issues in American Life and American Economic Problems are considered courses that are of an advanced nature. In addition the Advanced Placement courses of the C.E.E.B. are offered in English, Mathematics, and Science, and will be offered in Language also beginning in 1963. In 1961, forty-one Advanced Placement Examinations were written with a mean score of 3.4.

Some Great Neck Statistics

A distribution of Otis IQ's for grade 11 when tested in April 1961 based upon the descriptive classification scheme proposed by the publishers looked like this:

Classification	Per cent of General Population	Great Neck Grade 11
Very Superior	3.5	45.9
Superior	8.0	18.3
Above Average	16.0	19.6
Normal (Average)	45.0	14.2
Below Average	16.0	1.4
Inferior & Very Inferior	11.5	0.6

The American Council on Education Psychological Examination for College Freshmen was given to the entire grade 11 in December 1961. The median scores and their equivalent percentiles based on all college published norms were:

	Great Neck Medians	Percentiles All Colleges
Total Score	114.3	62
Language (L)	67.0	56
Quantitative (Q)	47.6	71

A majority of our students take the SAT in their junior year. Our mean scores on the SAT in the junior year (1961) were as follows:

Verbal	526.2	Math	537.4

Students Offered Advanced Placement Opportunities

With the inception this year of courses in Advanced Chemistry and Advanced Biology, Great Neck now offers advanced programs in three areas—mathematics, science, and English. In addition, there are plans to identify formally with the A. P. program in language after completion of our study regarding foreign language in the elementary schools and grade 7.

MATH STUDENTS SUCCEED ON TEST

In 1957, an advanced placement program in mathematics was initiated. The name "Advanced Placement" was used to designate our local accelerated program; it did not indicate that our mathematics program was committed to the national Advanced Placement Program. During 1960–61, however, the A. P. program was formally instituted. That year, the first group of students completed the sequence of accelerated courses begun in September, 1956; when they completed calculus, they were eligible, if they chose, to take the national examination.

Our own accelerated program had grown on a year-to-year basis. Although this growth had the advantage of allowing for maximum flexibility in selection and evaluative practices, it had the disadvantage of not being specifically designed for students who would take the superimposed national test. There was, therefore, some question about how well our students would fare on the national examination, which was not really a measuring stick of our own program.

That question was partially answered last year when the scores for the first group were received. In short, the results were gratifying. Twenty-six students took the mathematics Advanced Placement Program test. With 5 the highest possible rating, our students scored as follows: nine received a 5 rating; eight, 4; nine, 3.

Our present A. P. sequences call for an accelerated program beginning at grade 8; the courses, in order, are Elementary Algebra, Tenth Year Mathematics; Eleventh Year Mathematics, Twelfth Year Mathematics, and Calculus. The courses are highly flavored with a modern approach and offer maximum challenge. It should be added that the existing program is not static; the mathematics departments are currently engaged in refining both ends of the sequence—the 7th grade and 12th grade courses.

A. P. COURSES OFFERED IN SCIENCE

Both Advanced Placement Biology and Advanced Placement Chemistry were added to the curriculum this fall. As recommended by the College Entrance Examination Board, both courses are designed for students who have already completed their biology-chemistry-physics sequence and who have demonstrated superior ability in science.

A. P. Biology provides more mature presentation of content and more extensive laboratory experience than is usual in the ordinary high school biology course. It is intended to provide a typical introductory biology course such as that now taught in many colleges and universities.

A. P. Chemistry is planned to meet the general objectives of the standard first-year college chemistry course. There is a concentration of fundamental principles and a quantitative approach necessary in chemistry and related fields. The three class periods and four laboratory meetings per week stress the experimental approach to the subject.

At the end of the course, students will take the Advanced Placement Program examination. Successful completion of the test will enable a student to receive college credit for the subject and to elect more advanced courses during his freshman year at college.

ENGLISH A. P. IN SECOND YEAR

Advanced Placement in English was begun in September, 1961; a second group of students is currently enrolled in the course. Stressing close reading of texts, A. P. English offers seniors an opportunity to learn and practice critical reading techniques and to carry on individual literary research.

A study is under way to consider identifying students earlier than grade 12 for an advanced English program.

75. Educating the Gifted in Mathematics, Cleveland *

WILLIAM B. LEVENSON, *Superintendent of Schools,* AND

THE DIVISION OF MATHEMATICS

THE 1960 Report of the Committee on Academically Talented Pupils of the Cleveland Public Schools stated: "We believe that each individual should be challenged to the limit of his ability in order to develop the fullest realization of his powers. The acquisition of knowledge in a variety of fields and the development of skills should promote successful living and a worthy contribution to society. In amplifying this philosophy for the academically talented, we believe that:

1. Thorough preparation, interest, and dedication to purpose should be essential requisites of the teacher.
2. Enrichment through broadening and deepening experiences should be a principal aim.

* From *A Plan for Accelerating the Mathematics Program for the Academically Talented in Secondary Schools,* Cleveland, Ohio, 1961, pp. 5-8, 34-38. Reprinted with permission. This project was supported under a grant from the Division of Special Education, Ohio Department of Education.

3. Moderate acceleration should be considered only after thorough evaluation of the individual.
4. These pupils should have opportunities for participation and leadership in activities.
5. Special talents in the arts should be encouraged and directed, but not at the expense of basic academic knowledge and skills.
6. A continuity in the program should be maintained from the elementary grades through the high school.
7. Intensive counseling service should be encouraged to help pupils experience or seek the satisfaction of working to the limits of their abilities.
8. An atmosphere favorable to learning should be created.
9. Emphasis should be placed on methods that provide challenging experiences and promote intellectual curiosity rather than mere insistence on quantitative performance.
10. Counseling, programming, and teaching procedures should provide for individual differences among these pupils.
11. The development of academic skills and understandings should be fostered by the homogeneous grouping of pupils of superior ability.". . .

In seven schools, nine classes were organized to begin on Tuesday, September 6, 1960.

The following criteria were suggested as a basis of selection of pupil personnel:

1. A Probable Learning Rate (intelligence score on a group test) of at least 115 for pupils in the representative schools.
2. An IQ (individual test) of at least 125 for pupils in the major work classes.
3. A grade placement of at least 717 on a Stanford Intermediate Arithmetic Achievement Test given at the end of the sixth grade.
   (Note: Any pupil who has demonstrated high academic promise may be included in this program even though he does not qualify in either or both of the foregoing criterias.)
4. Recommendation of the elementary principal and teacher.
5. Superior achievement as evidenced by school marks.
6. Health information.
7. Home environment and parental consent.
8. Counselor's recommendation based on data concerning achievement, drive, motivation, and attitude contributing to an individual pupil's potential. . . .

A coordinating teacher was appointed on a full-time basis with an office at the Cleveland Board of Education Administration Building to perform the following duties:

1. Consult with principals and department chairmen in the selected schools.
2. Counsel with mathematics teachers who were teaching the experimental classes.
3. Serve as chairman of a steering committee that would:

   a. Establish criteria for the selection of pupils who are to be given the opportunity to enroll in these experimental classes for the academically talented.
   b. Decide what the content for an experimental course should be so that the pupils could complete the seventh and eighth grade course of study without sacrificing competence in mathematics.
   c. Study and evaluate test results.

4. Plan and conduct workshops.
5. Study mathematics journals, professional journals, books, and other publications for the purpose of discovering what is being done in other communities in this field of education.
6. Evaluate the experimental program in secondary school mathematics.
7. Develop plans for the additional year and one-half of mathematics that is to be taught to the academically talented pupils in the senior high. . . .

Comments

Summary of comments of the principals of the schools participating in the accelerated mathematics program.

It provides the necessary challenge for those of superior ability.

It encourages them to do better work in all of their classes.

It has caused growth on the part of the instructor.

It has pointed up the importance of high scholastic achievement in the entire school.

The teacher assigned to the class, of necessity, has to spend a great deal of time in special preparation and the use of supplemental material, and therefore should be given consideration for this additional load in the scheduling of classes. A lessening of the pupil-teacher ratio would provide more time for assisting individual pupils.

The rescheduling of pupils who drop out of the program presents a problem.

Schools with more than one accelerated class must make provision for the training of teachers who will be competent to teach these classes.

The mathematics department should define the arrangement of and the equipment for a laboratory type room and have this set up in every building that houses an accelerated class.

Summary of comments of the teachers engaged in the program in mathematics for the academically talented pupils during the first year of the program.

The accelerated course engenders teacher enthusiasm.

The program stimulates a more intensive cooperative effort on the part of teachers, pupils, parents, and members of the administration.

The program fosters high standards.

Professional growth is enhanced by the increased research and lesson planning necessary to teach such a course.

Revision of the course of study must alleviate the problem of too much content and too little time.

Parental support indicates enthusiastic acceptance of the program.

The present and potential worth of this program warrants further consideration.

Generalizations and conclusions drawn from the questionnaire answered by the pupils in the experimental program, June, 1961.

1. The majority of the pupils in this program are college-bound.
2. Engineering and science were the career choices of most of the boys while teaching, nursing, and secretarial were the preponderant choices of the girls.
3. Mathematics was always the favorite subject of the boys by a ratio of 2 to 1; the girls were evenly divided in this matter.
4. The unit most liked by the pupils was the one on geometric figures. Next in order were numeration systems and fundamental operations.
5. A 6 to 1 ratio was expressed by both boys and girls in liking this program, even though 15 did express a definite dislike.
6. With few exceptions, the pupils thought that this program would be of future value.
7. The parents of these pupils were very interested in the program and discussed it at home.

8. The majority of the pupils spent approximately 40 minutes a day on their mathematics assignments, which was more time than was formerly spent on mathematics by 90 per cent of them.
9. The report card marks indicated that this program did not adversely affect the marks made in other subjects; in fact, it had the effect of inducing better scholarship in all subjects.

Recommendations

On the basis of one years' experimentation, the Mathematics Curriculum Committee for Academically Talented Pupils suggests the following tentative recommendations:

1. Greater emphasis should be placed on mathematical structure and concept.
2. Course of study content of consumer mathematics should be reduced to a minimum.
3. A flexible classroom equipped with the best in teaching devices should be provided.
4. In inaugurating an accelerated program in mathematics, it should be noted that additional funds will need to be allocated for supplementary materials and mathematics libraries.
5. Materials for experiments and pupil projects should be readily available within the classroom.
6. To realize the maximum results in such an accelerated program, class size should be held to the optimum appropriate for a specific school.
7. Consideration should be given to those teachers who are teaching classes in this accelerated program in respect to teacher load.
8. The same teacher should be assigned to teach the class for a full school year.
9. A program of in-service training should be instituted for teachers of the academically talented.
10. Underachievers should be rescheduled into the regular mathematics program.
11. Appropriate tests should be developed to measure pupil progress in the new mathematical concepts.

76. College-Level Courses
for Able High School Students *

Bureau of Secondary Curriculum Development, New York State

College-Level Courses for Able High School Students

Some high schools offer college-level courses taught by high school teachers for sufficiently advanced students. In the past, many able students have found little challenge in their regular courses, or they have had to repeat some of them in college. College-level courses in high schools, with advanced placement examinations, represent an attempt to offer this challenge and through college recognition of such courses to avoid duplication between school and college work. In many colleges, students receive both credit and advanced placement, in others advanced placement only. Some colleges have not as yet formulated their policies in this connection. To date, most students have used their credits and advanced placement for enrichment. In some cases acceleration has taken place and shortened the preparation time necessary for graduate study.

THE STUDY OF ADVANCED STANDING

From 1952 to 1955, several schools and colleges cooperated in the School and College Study of Admission with Advanced Standing, a project led by former President Gordon Keith Chalmers of Kenyon College and financed by The Fund for the Advancement of Education. The two major assumptions were that our schools do not provide sufficiently intensive instruction for our ablest youth and that secondary schools could give such instruction with significant benefit to the students and to the educational system as a whole.

The central committee of the Study experimented with a plan for admission with advanced standing. Subcommittees of school and college teachers were formed to prepare course descriptions for a number of

* From *56 Practices for the Gifted from Secondary Schools of New York State,* pp. 49–55, The University of the State of New York, The State Education Department, Bureau of Secondary Curriculum Development, Albany, 1958. Reprinted with permission, but not copyrighted.

college level courses. These course descriptions were printed in *College Admission with Advanced Standing,* January 1954, and in a supplement circulated by the College Entrance Examination Board, September 1955. These subcommittees constructed and graded two series of examinations upon which colleges might base the granting of advanced credit. The high schools participating in the Study selected competent teachers from their regular faculty, in some instances reduced their teaching load and assigned them to college level courses. Additional books and apparatus had to be provided in most cases.

THE ADVANCED PLACEMENT PROGRAM

The three-year experimental plan of the Study proved so successful that the College Entrance Examination Board has adopted the plan and is developing it on a permanent nationwide basis under the title of the Advanced Placement Program. The number of public and independent schools in New York State giving advanced work has increased each year. The Study and Advanced Placement Program have not only enriched the curriculum of able students at all levels, but have also promoted communication between school and college teachers and articulation between school and college work.

A student may take the advanced placement examinations in one or more fields. The registration fee is $5 for each candidate and $8 for each test taken. Examination papers, questions, and grades, as well as school reports, are sent to the college that the student definitely plans to attend.

Each college makes it own decisions about credit and advanced placement for students who have taken college level courses and the advanced placement examinations.

General information and descriptions of courses and examinations for 12 subjects are given in the new College Entrance Board publication, *Advanced Placement Program Syllabus,* which replaces all previous publications. Copies of it and of the new candidates' bulletin are obtainable from the Program Director, Advanced Placement Program, College Entrance Examination Board, 427 Riverside Drive, New York 27.

Early Admission to College for Selected Students

A number of carefully selected high school students in New York State are admitted to college before they have completed high school. A group of such students is part of the Program for Early Admission to College, an experiment conducted by twelve colleges for four college classes graduating in 1955, 1956, 1957, and 1958.

The basic aims of the experiment were to save the time of the able student and to enrich the quality of his education. It was believed that most high schools are not equipped to offer their ablest students college level work and that, even in high schools that are so equipped, certain of these gifted students who are also socially mature can profit by entering college earlier than usual.

THE EXPERIMENTAL PROGRAM

The Program for Early Admission to College began in the autumn of 1951 when the first group of 420 Early Admission Scholars entered the freshman year at twelve colleges and universities. The students, referred to as Scholars, were selected by the institutions they entered and were granted scholarships financed by the Fund for the Advancement of Education. With few exceptions, the Scholars were 16½ years of age or younger at the time of entering college, and the large majority had not completed high school. Three additional groups of Scholars entered the participating institutions in 1952, 1953, and 1954.

APPRAISAL OF THE EXPERIMENT

The first group of Scholars—those who entered in 1951—were graduated in 1955. The Fund has completed a detailed and comprehensive evaluation of the four-year college experience of the 1951 Scholars both in terms of their academic performance and in terms of their social and emotional adjustment to college life. This evaluation was based on reports from the participating institutions, a substantial body of statistical data gathered and analyzed by the testing experts, and two independent appraisals of the social and emotional adjustment of the Scholars by well-qualified professional people who had no connection with the Fund or with the experiment.

Briefly, these appraisals have shown that the Scholars, despite the gaps in their high school preparation, have academically outperformed not only their classmates but also a control group of "Comparison Students" at the participating institutions who were comparable to the Scholars in aptitude but differed from them in that they had been graduated from high school and entered college at the normal age.

The question that many educators regarded as central to the whole experiment was: How well will the Scholars adjust socially and emotionally to college life in view of their younger age? The two independent studies of this important question showed that the Scholars faced a greater challenge than their classmates in this phase of college life, but that through their own efforts and the wise help of the colleges were able to meet this challenge. Although adjustment varied among the Scholars as it does among students in general, the Scholars as a group did just as well as their classmates.

In extracurricular affairs, athletic as well as nonathletic, the Scholars were as active as other students and at some colleges substantially more so. A large number of the Scholars won academic honors, prizes, and other awards, and, in proportion to their classmates, more were elected to Phi Beta Kappa. Some of the Scholars did not succeed but, at most of the participating colleges, the proportion of withdrawals due to academic and adjustment failures was somewhat lower for the Scholars than for their classmates.

CURRENT STATUS

Although the period of Fund support has ended, each of the participating institutions is continuing to accept carefully selected students for early admission, with varying scholarship arrangements. Admissions and Scholarship policies are determined by the individual colleges. Copies of the Fund's report on the program may be obtained without charge by writing to the Fund for the Advancement of Education, 655 Madison Avenue, New York 21.

Gifted Pupils Attend College Classes

Under a cooperative arrangement between two high schools and a nearby men's college, highly gifted students of both sexes in the junior and senior classes attend freshman courses at the college. The juniors and June graduates go to the college campus for summer courses. The senior boys may attend 8 o'clock classes during the winter. Tuition is charged by the college, which, in turn, gives six credit hours for each course passed. The plan makes it possible for gifted students to avoid duplication of courses and to proceed at an early age to more advanced work than is usually taught in high school.

SUMMER PROGRAM

During the eight-week summer session, the college provides freshman courses in English, mathematics, world history, chemistry, French, and German. Class size is limited to between 10 and 20 pupils. Classes are conducted Monday through Friday from 8 to 9 A.M. and from 11 A.M. to noon. Between the two classes, college professors supervise study periods in the college library. The chemistry course includes also a laboratory session two afternoons a week. Only one course may be taken in one summer.

WINTER PROGRAM

During the regular college year, carefully selected high school senior boys are admitted at 8 A.M. or 2:30 P.M. to freshman courses for which they may receive full credit. The number of pupils admitted to any one course is limited to three so that the atmosphere of the classroom remains essentially that of a college class. The high schools excuse these pupils from first or last period classes and allow them to substitute the college course for the high school course in the subject chosen.

SELECTION OF PUPILS

Selection of pupils for the instruction is based on a composite evaluation of achievement test scores, IQ (minimum 125), data from cumulative records, school grades, rank in class, teacher evaluation, differential aptitude test scores, and College Board score. Guidance counselors interview all eligible pupils individually and evaluate the total information gained from all sources.

High School Students Receive College Credit by Examination

One university extends an opportunity to superior high school students to earn college credit by providing special examinations several times a year. By taking these examinations, which are similar to those given at the end of college courses, students can receive credit at this university for knowledge acquired in high school or through independent study. The procedure is designed to reduce the time required for graduation and for entrance into professional schools by preventing unnecessary duplication of work.

ELIGIBILITY

Both high school seniors and juniors who have the approval of their school principals are eligible to take the examinations. The seniors must have an overall Regents average of 82 per cent and a Regents average of 87 per cent in the field of the examination. If no Regents examinations have been taken, the student must have a superior school average.

For juniors the Regents average must be 85 per cent. In addition 14 units must have been completed.

Students who qualify make arrangements through their guidance counselors and principals to take the examinations. They discuss the preparation for each examination with the high school teacher of the subject and also with the college faculty member in charge of the course.

COLLEGE CREDIT EXAMINATIONS

Students who have, or plan to have, more than 16 units when graduated from high school may take examinations in high school subjects such as modern languages, mathematics, typing, and shorthand.

Students who do not have over 16 units may take examinations in subjects for which they have not received high school credit. For example, they may take examinations in languages, such as Italian, Polish, German, and Russian, which they speak at home (if courses in the languages are offered in the university). Also some students study freshman college English and American history and economics with the aid of outlines provided by the university.

CREDIT ASSIGNED

More than 80 per cent of the students who have taken the college credit examinations have pased and have received credit in the sponsoring university, or in some other college or university. When a student does not pass, the grade is not entered on his record.

ADVANTAGES TO STUDENTS

Advantages of the college credit examinations to superior students as reported by the university are:

1. Some students shorten the time spent earning a college degree by a year or more; many shorten it by a semester.
2. The time and money saved make it possible for students to take more graduate work. Students with limited finances are able to devote more hours to income-producing jobs while they are in college.
3. The examinations help the students to find their true academic level and so keep them alert, interested, and active.
4. Studying for the examinations shows the students early in their academic life how to prepare and master academic data on their own with a minimum of help from others.
5. Students who pass these examinations appreciate the opportunity to take more advanced courses.
6. Students report that earning college credit in advance gives them a feeling of confidence when they enter college.

7. Students who are unable to attend college immediately after high school find the college credit earned through these examinations useful in applying for jobs as well as in the Armed Forces.

College credit examinations are considered to have some broader values. They help to lead into higher education many able young people who otherwise would not consider going to college. They make it possible for superior students to earn additional advanced degrees and to enter early into economic productivity and leadership.

77. Procedures for Class Placement of Gifted Students, Oakland *

M. H. ELLIOTT, *Director of Research*

Identification

Since resources for the education of gifted students are limited, the plans and the program for them in the Oakland Public Schools should include two basic considerations—first, special programs for gifted students should be limited primarily to those who are unquestionably qualified; second, very few exceptions can be made to the admission requirements. The exceptions must be made with care and according to specific criteria and procedures.

A. *Criteria for Admission to Special Courses for the Gifted in Secondary Schools*

1. *Performance*—High quality of performance and achievement in specific courses as indicated by scholarship grades, achievement test scores, and other available data. Prime consideration shall be given to this criterion.
2. *Consent*—Consent of student and parents for placement in the class.

* From a mimeographed document, pp. 1-4, Office of Superintendent of Schools, Oakland Public Schools, Oakland, Calif., 1962-63. Reprinted with permission.

3. *Motivation and interests*—Student shall be motivated toward and interested in the course.

4. *Mental ability*—IQ of 135 or above as measured by an individual test administered by a tester approved by the Research Department. Exceptions may be made where consistence of performance and achievement merit it—i.e., two years over grade level and an A grade in subject. (See page 385 for IQ of 125 and lower as minimum.)

5. *Emotional stability*—History of stability required.

6. *Social maturity*—Student will have social maturity suitable for group.

7. *Physical maturity and health*—Good health and adequate physical maturity.

8. *Chronological age*—Suitable.

9. *Home conditions*—Interest, favorable for study.

10. *Activities outside the school program*—Extensive, balanced, or minimal.

B. *School Approval for Admission to Special Classes for the Gifted*

1. Each student admitted to special classes for the gifted must meet the criteria presented in *A. Criteria for Admission.* However, students meeting these criteria are not automatically included. Each one must receive the approval of the school committee for placement in the program. In making recommendations, the school should consider all the aforementioned factors.

In determining recommendations, the principal and the faculty should keep in mind that the purpose of this program is to provide a special and outstanding opportunity for those students who can and will produce an exceptional performance.

C. *Criteria for Granting Exceptions (IQ 125–34) to Admission Requirements in Secondary Schools*

Approval of the School Committee for Gifted must be obtained before the student for whom an exception is requested is placed in the program.

1. *Performance and achievement*—Appropriate outstanding performance in specific courses as indicated by scholarship grades, achievement test scores, and other available data.

2. *Consent*—School Committee for Gifted should consider the meeting of previously mentioned criteria with a possible minimum of IQ 125 measured by an individual test administered by a tester approved by the Research Department.
3. *Motivation and strong persisting interests.*
4. *Mental ability*—A minimum IQ of 125 or above in secondary schools as measured by an individual test administered by a tester approved by the Research Department.
5. *Underachievers*—Exceptions will be permitted in order to allow school faculties to offer challenging opportunities to low achievers with high IQ's whom they believe will benefit from this placement. However, it must be made clear to parents and student that this is a provisional placement, contingent upon the student's ability to profit from this experience and does not carry with it any implications as to the future placement of the student with similar groups.

   Every effort should be made by the school to provide support for the student and to utilize the appropriate guidance and counseling services from the moment of the original placement.

   Requests for these exceptions should be processed by the school committee in the same way as requests for other exceptions.

In considering cases of students suggested as exceptions to the requirements for admission, it should be remembered that the purpose of this program is to provide a special and outstanding opportunity for those who can and will produce an exceptional performance.

Note: In granting exceptions the school should consider other criteria and other factors of:

> Emotional, social, and physical maturity
> Health
> Chronological age
> Home conditions
> Activities outside the school program
> Work and study habits
> Size of classes, teacher time, and available facilities

D. *Students Meeting Basic Criteria*

1. See *A. Criteria* and *B. School Approval.* Check IQ with Research Department lists or Research Department.
2. In the secondary schools, the principal, counselor, appropriate

subject matter teachers, and the Guidance and Counseling Departments, and the cumulative records should be consulted.

3. Any student with known emotional, health, social adjustment, or home problems should be placed in gifted classes only after consultation with the Guidance Department.

4. The school committee consisting of the principal, the counselor, and two teachers determines the students to be recommended for placement in the program.

5. The placement in the class should be discussed with the student and his parents.

6. If the foregoing conditions are favorable, the student may be placed in the class.

7. In the secondary schools, the student will be assigned to the junior high or senior high school in the attendance area in which he lives. Opportunities are provided in all secondary schools for gifted students. There will be offerings at each junior and senior high school to provide for gifted and highly academically talented students through acceleration in subject matter fields. Each junior and senior high school has teacher allotments for these opportunities.

E. *Students Not Meeting Basic Criteria Who Qualify for Request for Exception (IQ 125–34)*

1. See *C. Criteria for Granting Exceptions.*

2. Each school will organize a committee for the gifted, consisting of the principal, two teachers, and, in the secondary schools, a counselor—these should be people who have had the most contact with the student. The committee should decide not to admit the student, or to admit.

F. *Students Not Meeting Basic Criteria (IQ below 125)*

1. Individual exceptions below 125 may be made, keeping in mind that this is a high potential program, provided exception goes to the Secondary Central Committee.

2. To submit the case to the Secondary Central Committee for Gifted, Request for Exception—Student Not Meeting Basic Criteria, schools will request approval of Director of Counseling on exceptions below 125, etc. The request will include a recommendation from

School Committee for Gifted. More difficult cases will be sent in for the Secondary Central Committee.

3. The Secondary Central Committee for Gifted will report its action in writing on exceptions below 125 to the principal of the school. The school should not place the student in the class nor make any commitment regarding placement before receiving approval of the Committee. In emergencies, a request may be made by telephone to the secondary schools' Director of Counseling.

4. After approval is received, the school will follow the procedure outlined under *D. Students Meeting Basic Criteria.*

5. The Secondary Central Committee for Gifted will consist of:

The Assistant Superintendent of Secondary Schools
Director of Secondary Education
Director of Counseling
Director of Research
A Junior High and/or Senior High School Principal

78. Program Organization and Implementation for the Gifted *

Southern Regional Project for Education of the Gifted

A. Introduction

This section of the report focuses on areas of administrative practice that have particular application to program organization and implementation for the gifted—especially ability grouping, acceleration, and independent study. Descriptions of the many forms of ability grouping and acceleration are available at large in the literature, as are discussions of the pros and cons of these practices. No comprehensive treatment of this easily obtainable normative material will be provided in this *Manual*. The present purpose rather is to discuss the process qualities inherent in these procedures and to indicate a number of general observations regarding these and other administrative matters, which indications comprise guidelines to practice.

It should be recognized that ability grouping, acceleration, and independent study, alone or in combination, do not constitute an adequate program for the gifted. They are merely administrative procedures that allow and facilitate the development of known characteristics of gifted students and that support curriculum development of the kind outlined in the preceding section of this report. . . .

---

* From *The Gifted Student: A Manual for Program Improvement,* pp. 71–78, project developed by the Southern Regional Education Board and supported by the Carnegie Corporation of New York, 1962. Reprinted with permission.

B. Ability Grouping

The desirability of grouping. Observers of special programs come quickly to the conviction that grouping of students according to ability for at least pertinent portions of their school experience is eminently desirable at every grade level. The mere grouping of pupils does not make a program, nor does absence of grouping necessarily mean that a program is absolutely ineffective. Nevertheless, ability grouping greatly increases the school's power to effect a marked improvement in the process of education for gifted students.

Ability grouping *makes possible* many teaching and learning experiences that cannot be accomplished in the typical classroom. This can be seen again and again in specially composed classes in all parts of the country. There is an electric quality, an aura of purposefulness, about such a class—whether it contains the remarkable five and six year olds of the Colfax School in Pittsburgh, lucid, earnest, and intensively engaged in making research reports or the 12th grade social studies students in Portland, Oregon, arguing political theory as though they were the Franklin, Paines, and Jeffersons of their generation. The kinds of intellectual activity that can be engaged in by a group of gifted children under the guidance of a carefully selected and specifically trained teacher simply cannot go on in the typical classroom, regardless of the kind of "enrichment" attempted.

Ability grouping and the teacher. Perhaps the most important and yet the least controllable variable in the grouping situation is the teacher. Ability grouping is of no particular value when teachers do not or cannot capitalize on the fact that they are working with children who have special capabilities and needs. In many classrooms in schools renowned for their programs for the gifted, teachers can be observed using the same plodding, pedestrian techniques that are so often necessary in the typical classroom where students are slow to grasp even elementary facts and concepts—with frustration and boredom as the end products, instead of intellectual excitement and challenge. Whether or not the potential value inherent in ability grouping is realized is to a considerable extent the teacher's responsibility. If the teacher does not recognize these potentialities and fails to modify his or her approach to the teaching-learning situation, the potential value of ability grouping is lost. Too often, one suspects, this is why research data fail to show significant differences between the results of grouping and the results of "enrichment" in the regular classroom.

One common source of failure to translate well-conceived programs into good classroom practice is the administrative procedure of rotating the task of teaching gifted groups through the entire teaching staff of given grades. In many school systems, staff members are required to take turns teaching the bright groups regardless of interest in or ability to work with such children. Teachers should be selected for work with gifted groups on the basis of ability and interest. There can be no doubt that some teachers are better teachers for gifted children than others, just as some teachers are better fitted through training, temperament, experience, and interest to teach retarded children. Teaching each type of student requires the development of skills and knowledge that can best be achieved by special training and by continuous experience of some duration. It is difficult to see what is to be gained by assigning a teacher whose real forte is teaching the gifted to a retarded group one year and an average group the next.

It is a matter of interest to note that in numbers of school systems with a successful pattern of experiences for the gifted, it is established practice to allow teachers of gifted classes additional time for preparation. Effective teaching of gifted children is a demanding task, more so than teaching average children whose range of interests is narrower and for whom drastic departures from standard curriculum and teaching methods already reasonably well-developed need not be made.

Reducing the class loads of teachers of gifted classes need not be destructive of staff morale, provided the whole staff has been led to understand the purposes and the processes integral to this complicated task. *All* teachers should be involved in the planning and development of the gifted program, and the program itself should, of course, be thought of as a part of the total school program. The importance of this approach to program development has already been emphasized.

The feasibility of ability grouping. Some form of ability grouping appears to be feasible (as well as desirable) for any school system regardless of size, wealth, or location. The kinds of grouping practices most suitable for any given system or school will, of course, depend on many factors such as the number of gifted children at various age levels, the number of schools in proximity to each other, and the availability of funds for compensating the factor of reduced teacher-pupil ratios. A sufficient number of "models" are described in the literature so that any school system—those in large, medium, or small cities, and those in suburban or in rural locations —should find help in planning and developing suitable ability grouping procedures. Practically every successful school in this particular has incorporated ability grouping of some kind into its program for the gifted, the forms varying from the massive complex of specialized high schools in

New York City to the weekly seminars for general intellectual stimulation in rural Lewis County, New York. Everywhere the salutary effects of ability grouping upon motivation, achievement, and morale of able students is readily noticeable. There is little evidence in the experience of these school systems to substantiate the fears of those who believe that snobbishness and "elitism" are the inevitable by-products of ability grouping. Nor have they found grading of students in special groups to be an unmanageable problem. The collective experience of teachers and administrators who have worked in the midst of this kind of provision indicates that the common arguments against ability grouping are unfounded in fact.

C. Acceleration

Acceleration a neglected practice.   Despite the fact that research evidence supporting acceleration is unquestionably greater than that supporting ability grouping, systematic acceleration appears to be less often a formal feature of present programs for the gifted. Certain types of acceleration, especially advanced placement, are being increasingly practiced and seem to be gaining in acceptance. Others, such as early admission to first grade, early admission to college, and the "nongraded" primary are less frequently encountered. There seem to be several reasons for this widespread failure of the schools to adopt proven methods of acceleration. State laws prevent early admission to the first grade in some communities. Simple ignorance of existing research findings may account for some of the delay in adopting this and other practices where there are no laws to prevent such action.

Schools that deny, or fail to provide acceleration, frequently operate upon the now discredited belief that "social maladjustment" is the inevitable result of even moderate acceleration. It is not unlikely, however, that much of the reluctance to adopt certain techniques of acceleration may be correctly attributed to administrative inertia—unwillingness to sacrifice the convenience of the chronological age "lockstep" for flexible procedures that more adequately reflect known facts about individual differences in ability and total developmental readiness. Doubtless many gifted five year olds are refused admission to school not because they are not ready in every way but because a flexible admission policy would tend to create administrative "headaches" in the form of parental pressures to admit unqualified children. Such sacrifice of sound procedure to considerations of expediency is indefensible.

Acceleration a desirable practice.   Acceleration, like ability grouping, should be a part of every school program for the gifted. There is nothing startling about this observation, of course. Terman strongly suggested that many able students should be promoted sufficiently to allow them to enter college at age seventeen at the latest, and he claimed that many were ready at sixteen. *Any school system* can make such progress possible for its gifted students, and the experience of those school systems that do practice moderate acceleration indicates that the benefits derived accrue not only to the gifted students but to the school as a whole. Teachers have found that flexible promotion policy can help to reduce the range of variability within the classroom, and at the same time help to lessen the boredom and dissatisfaction of bright students. The anticipated administrative difficulties sometimes do not arise, and in any case they are outweighed by the positive gains derived from elimination of the "lockstep." Finally, and in addition to the benefits of acceleration for students and teachers, it should be pointed out again that society stands to benefit from the earlier entry into productive citizenship of its most able citizens. It seems unlikely that American schools can much longer ignore the compelling logic and impressive empirical evidence that can be marshaled in favor of moderately accelerated progress through the educational system for those who are capable of such progress.

Acceleration alone not a program. It is perhaps unnecessary to point out again that acceleration alone, as with grouping, does not constitute an adequate program for the gifted. This fact is not universally comprehended, however. All too frequently administrators unblushingly talk of "programs" that consist solely of advanced placement classes at the twelfth grade level. While advanced placement is in many ways a useful concept, those who offer it as a "program" hold an impoverished concept of special education for the gifted. Acceleration is an administrative procedure that should be a part of every program for the gifted, but it does not obviate other modifications of the standard school routine, especially in the area of curriculum content and organization.

D. Independent Study

The promise of independent study. It was suggested in the preceding section of this report that the unique characteristics of gifted children make possible a "reversed ratio" of teaching to learning; i.e., gifted students are capable of much learning with relatively little teaching. For this reason independent (individual) study is particularly suited to the needs of gifted students.

The Trump Commission prophesies that in the secondary school of the future even average students will spend perhaps 40 per cent of their in-school time in individual study. How much American schools must change in order to make that prediction come true is apparent to observers who have like the SRPEG participants visited in school after school noting the frequency of given practices. Independent study as a formally recognized procedure, i.e., by inclusion into the administrative plan of the school of independent study courses for which credit is given, is quite rare. While it is true, of course, that teachers everywhere often make individual assignments that involve some degree of independent study, it is doubtful that the true potentialities of this method have been generally recognized. Understanding and acceptance of independent study as a salutary administrative procedure will greatly improve educational opportunity for gifted students. It will mark another step in the direction away from the rigid lockstep procedures still characteristic of American education and toward true individualization of education.

E. Other Administrative Considerations

Articulation. The necessity of assuring continuity in the gifted student's school learning experiences was emphasized in the preceding discussion of curriculum development. Administrative innovations such as ability grouping and acceleration can disrupt established continuity, and therefore the administrator must consider the probable consequences for all ensuing grade levels of any administrative decision affecting a level. Problems can arise, for instance, when junior high schools fail to take account of the high level of motivation, achievement, and expectancy of gifted students entering from valid differentiated elementary school programs. Administrative liaison between levels in the system can help to eliminate or reduce such potential problems. Establishing and maintaining continuity in the gifted student's school experience is extremely important. It can be accomplished only by administrators who can keep in focus the whole school program from kindergarten to college.

Financing special education for the gifted. It is impossible to say how much of a school budget should be allocated to the special education of gifted children. Obviously some provisions are far more expensive than others and may be beyond the reach of many school systems at the present time. On the other hand some provisions such as curriculum revision, most forms of acceleration, and many forms of ability grouping need add little or nothing to the budget.

There can be no question that expenditure of funds for special education of gifted students is fully justified. One of the tenets of the democratic philosophy of education is that each student should have an equal opportunity to develop his potentialities to the fullest. On this basis American schools provide special facilities and equipment for those who are athletically talented, musically promising, and for those who are blind, deaf, crippled, or mentally retarded. When the special intellectual capacities of children demand special educational provisions these should be provided whatever the cost.

F. Conclusions

The unique abilities and needs of gifted students demand unusual administrative provisions. Traditional patterns of pupil and teacher deployment and of pupil progress through the graded sequence are inadequate. It has been suggested in this report that certain administrative procedures embody process qualities that parallel known characteristics of gifted learners. Acceleration implements the gifted learner's ability to accomplish school tasks more rapidly than average students. Ability grouping recognizes his need to engage in activities with his intellectual equals. Independent study capitalizes on his ability and motivation to learn without direct and constant teacher supervision. All of these administrative practices, plus others familiar and commonly reported to be feasible, should be part of every program for the gifted.

The overriding importance of the teacher in the implementation of programs for the gifted is an inescapable observation on the part of persons pointedly studying class upon class. In many cases programs that are outstanding from the standpoint of planning and organization are subverted in the classrooms by teachers who are unable to relate their teaching procedures to the needs and abilities of gifted students.

Ability grouping of some kind is a feature of practically every program for the gifted that has received any attention in the literature. Acceleration procedures, with the exception of advanced placement, are much less often included. The desirability of independent study as a formal administrative procedure has apparently been very largely overlooked by American schools. Thus even in schools noted for their attempts to provide differential education for the gifted there is evidence of inconsistency in philosophy and planning, poor articulation between schools, reluctance to begin special provisions in the early grades, and other evidences of inertia, lack of knowledge of research findings, and lack of imagination. The sum total of the experience of the Project participants suggests that despite the pioneering efforts of a few school systems there is still much room for improvement with respect to administrative aspects of program development for the gifted in American schools.

79. Planning for the Intellectually Gifted, Los Angeles *

EVERETT CHAFFEE, *Associate Superintendent, Division of Instructional Services*

WHEN A program for intellectually gifted pupils is planned, it is recognized that the objectives for gifted pupils do not differ materially from those for all pupils. However, the objectives may be attained at an earlier age and should be developed to a greater depth.

Guidance for Pupils and Parents

One goal of the guidance and counseling program is to provide each intellectually gifted pupil with the assistance that he needs to make the most of his potentialities. The guidance program emphasizes (1) classroom guidance by teachers who have learned to recognize the characteristics of gifted pupils and to provide for their needs, and (2) individual counseling of intellectually gifted pupils as a supplement to group guidance in the classroom.

Parents of intellectually gifted pupils should become aware of the ability of their children as early as possible so that educational planning can be effective. Whenever possible, the principal, teacher, and counselor should hold a conference with the parents when a pupil is identified as gifted.

Individual Study

Counselors are available at all school levels for individual psychological study of gifted pupils who evidence special adjustment problems.

Underachieving gifted pupils present a special adjustment problem. Some underachieving pupils may be gifted but have not been identified because they have achieved relatively low scores on group intelligence and achievement tests. Many other underachieving gifted pupils have been

* From *Education of Intellectually Gifted Pupils in Los Angeles City Schools*, rev., May, 1962, pp. 3–6. Reprinted with permission.

identified but lack the essential motivation to achieve. A complete individual study of all underachieving gifted pupils is important to determine causes for the underachievement and to plan a remedial program.

Cumulative Records

To expedite continuity of planning, cumulative records for intellectually gifted pupils and lists of pupils with special abilities are forwarded to the next educational level from elementary school to college. Information provided in this manner serves as a basis for guidance of pupils identified as intellectually gifted and assists them in making appropriate educational and vocational plans consistent with their interests and abilities.

Evaluation as a Means of Identifying the Gifted

The evaluation program provides an important basis for identifying intellectually gifted pupils by means of the following:

1. Group intelligence tests that are administered at the second-, fifth-, seventh-, ninth-, and eleventh-grade levels
2. Group achievement tests that are administered to all pupils every two years, beginning in the third grade
3. Listings prepared by the Evaluation and Research Section for use in each school that include names of pupils with the 10 highest scores in each subject tested; pupils with an IQ of 130 or above; and pupils in the top 5 or 10 per cent of the total population for both IQ and achievement

Throughout all educational levels, teachers' evaluations supplement the results of standardized tests in the identification process. It is recognized that intelligence tests are only general indicators of scholastic ability and do not measure many facets of pupil ability. Creative and critical thinking are among the important abilities that are not measured by intelligence tests.

Evaluation as a Means of Measuring Growth

Teachers and pupils are aware of the importance of daily performance and of the continual assessment of progress toward educational goals. Intellectually gifted pupils develop self-knowledge, a realistic understanding of their abilities and limitations, and the ability to set goals and evaluate achievement.

Ability Grouping

Ability grouping may be achieved through special classes; through special interest groups or extraclass groupings, such as clubs; and through elective classes. Making provision for the needs of gifted pupils through ability grouping is the most controversial of the various plans that are utilized at the elementary school level. Ability grouping is more common at the secondary level, particularly in the academic subjects.

Acceleration

Results of research indicate that the intellectually gifted pupil tends to be larger physically and more mature socially and emotionally than other pupils of his chronological age. A moderate amount of acceleration is considered as one means of meeting the needs of gifted pupils. When planned on an individual basis, pupils may be accelerated one semester in elementary school, one semester in junior high school, and one semester in senior high school.

Acceleration should be considered early at each educational level and should involve special planning so that essential blocks of learning will not be omitted.

. . . .

Enrichment

Since it is generally recognized that intellectually gifted pupils can learn with remarkable speed and depth and meet normal standards of achievement with relatively little effort, extraordinary measures should be taken by educators to strengthen motivation for learning, to offer experiences appropriate to pupil giftedness, and to provide for individual pacing of learning.

Enrichment requires a learning environment conducive to exploration and originality. An enriched educational program for intellectually gifted pupils is based on the recognition of individual differences and is planned to meet individual needs and challenge abilities. Enrichment emphasizes quality rather than quantity and adds depth and scope to learning experiences. It provides for development of reflective and critical thinking, problem solving, and creative thinking and expression.

The requirements of an enriched learning environment, the kinds of learning experiences that provide depth and scope, and the essential skills in the development of reflective, critical, and creative thinking are listed in *Enrichment for the Intellectually Gifted,*[1] . . .

Homework for Gifted Pupils

Homework is a necessary part of every pupil's educational program. Meaningful homework is reasonable; is related to classwork and the goals of the course of study; emphasizes quality rather than quantity; and is consistent with the ability and maturity of the pupils. Assignments should be purposeful, clear, and based on an analysis of the needs and interests of intellectually gifted pupils.

Homework is purposeful when it permits the pupil to complete assignments begun in class; develops good work habits and a responsibility for completing tasks when they are due; and provides opportunities for pupils to engage in creative projects and research in the areas of their developing interests.

It is the responsibility of the principal to implement the homework policy. It is the responsibility of the teacher to establish clearly defined goals, be specific regarding the work to be completed, and utilize and evaluate the completed assignments.

A guide for secondary schools in developing a homework schedule is provided in *Graduation Requirements and Curricula* (1961 Revision, Publication No. 489) on pages 6–7.

School Marks in Classes for Gifted Pupils

In general, an "A" should be considered as the standard mark for all pupils enrolled in special classes for the intellectually gifted with the exception of grades 7 and 8. Parents and pupils should be counseled that pupils should not continue in the special classes unless they are maintaining work of this caliber. During the first ten weeks of the special class, pupils who do not perform work of "A" quality should receive special counseling and help.

At the junior high school level, policies and procedures should be developed that would assure that the pupil would not receive a lower mark in Honors class than regular class for like quality of work. Specifically this includes for all junior high schools the requirement that except for

---

[1] Copies of *Enrichment for the Intellectually Gifted* may be obtained from any one of the following: Division of Elementary Education, Guidance and Counseling Section; Division of Secondary Education, Office of Special Programs; or Division of Instructional Services, Curriculum Branch, Secondary Section.

unusual circumstances, marks for pupils enrolled in Honors classes should be consistent with marks previously received in the same subject matter field.

If the following steps are utilized in the assignment of pupils for special classes, such difficulties should be minimized:

Selection of pupils based upon predetermined criteria.

Scheduling of parent and pupil conferences prior to the assignment of a pupil to a special class.

Counseling of pupils with marks lower than an "A" at the close of the semester to withdraw from the special class.

Assisting teachers of such classes in recognizing the need for objective evaluation of pupil performance.

At the elementary school level, pupil work of "A" quality is interpreted to mean "A" marks in a majority of the academic subjects.

80. Programs for Intellectually Gifted Pupils, Oakland *

M. H. ELLIOTT, *Director of Research*

I. Outline of K-12 Programs

As part of the concern for appropriate educational opportunity for every pupil, certain special offerings have been made available for those of high academic potential. In line with criteria established by the State Department of Education, gifted pupils are defined as those in the top 2 per cent of the general population in intellectual ability.

The rationale of these programs is based upon the facts that such pupils frequently do not perform at the level of which they are capable, that they need continued challenge and stimulation, and that association and competition with others of similar ability is an obvious source of motivation. Oakland programs for the intellectually gifted are quite varied and inten-

* From a mimeographed document, pp. 1–3, Office of the Superintendent, Oakland Public Schools, Oakland, Calif., 1962. Reprinted with permission.

tionally differ from classroom to classroom, from school to school, and from one school level to another. The emphasis changes with age and grade of pupils. In kindergarten and early elementary grades, the program is one of identification of able pupils and development of opportunities in the regular classroom. Teachers are alert to discover pupils of unusual ability, to arrange appropriate instructional groupings within the class-room, and to provide special enrichment. During these early years any justified extra promotions are encouraged. For example, a plan of more rapid progress through kindergarten and grade one may be initiated for the pupil who is already able to read as he enters kindergarten and who seems to be of appropriate physical and social maturity.

On the basis of teachers' observations, school progress, and results of group tests of ability and achievement, a more intensive identification and study of pupils is carried on in grades four and five. Individual intelligence tests are administered to all pupils whose performance suggests that they may be in the top 2 per cent of the population.

In the sixth grade the program is more structured and centralized. Special classes or centers are organized at certain elementary schools. These classes are typically composed of gifted pupils from several neighboring schools. An attempt is made to keep the enrollments somewhat smaller than usual. The teachers of these classes encourage much individual ex-ploration, promote varied interests, and emphasize the development of communication, study, and independent research skills. This is primarily a program of both enrichment and depth. There is also more rapid progress in such subject matter areas as language and mathematics.

The junior high school programs vary somewhat according to size and resources of faculty and number of gifted pupils. The common element in all junior high schools is the opportunity for qualified pupils to advance more rapidly in specific subject matter areas. Selected pupils may be enrolled in algebra or commence the study of a foreign language earlier than the ninth grade. Thus, some pupils take algebra in the eighth grade, geometry in the ninth grade, etc., and are able to complete four years of high school mathematics by the end of the eleventh grade. Variations in particular junior high schools include special interest groups in science, foreign language, creative writing, etc.

The senior high school programs emphasize rapid progress and ad-vanced study in specific subject matter areas. The most frequent offerings are in the fields of mathematics, science, English, and foreign language. Each senior high school tends to do some experimentation with other types of programs. There are seminars and special groups that vary with the interests and resources of the school and of the pupil population. Regular college courses are available to selected seniors at the University of California, at Merritt Campus of Oakland City College, and in some cases at the high school site. Some pupils may take a single college level course during the senior year and others may take several different courses.

The primary objective in all of these programs is to identify the most able pupils and to provide them with opportunity and with challenge. These programs also furnish a practical and realistic pathway for the most able students to complete the usual high school curriculum ahead of time and to finish part or all of the work of the first college year by the time of graduation from the twelfth grade. The programs are successful to the extent that such pupils graduate from the secondary schools with high levels of achievement, with zest and enthusiasm for further learning, with varied interests, and with the prospect of fulfilling the promise of their potential.

II. Relationships to the General Educational Program

Obviously, any designated special program must be part of the general educational effort and not an isolated endeavor. Pupils do not come in neat and carefully labeled packages. Those in the top 2 per cent in academic ability are different only in degree from their fellows who are in the top quarter of the distribution of ability.

The programs for gifted differ from those for other students of good ability mainly in placing even more emphasis upon high levels of academic achievement, in offering opportunity for more rapid progress in subject matter areas, and in providing time for more intense exploration of special interest fields.

The special programs are not intended to isolate the child identified as intellectually gifted from his fellows, nor are they expected to satisfy all of his educational and developmental needs. Gifted pupils definitely remain as part of the student body of the school and have opportunity for experiences in leadership, in adjusting to and living with others of varied abilities, and in the social and other extracurricular activities. As previously stated, the intention is to avoid isolating these pupils or emphasizing subject matter excellence so much that well-rounded development is prevented.

The fact that subject matter performance is stressed for these pupils does not mean that it is not stressed for all other pupils. The difference between a gifted class and a regular college preparatory class at the high school level is one of degree of emphasis only. The gifted program is not only part of the total educational effort of the school but has also been found to have an impact on the whole. The presence of pupils working at high levels and the experiences of teachers in such classes apparently set a tone and have a favorable influence on other pupils and on teaching.

It is also important to note that while some of the creative and expressive areas such as art, music, dramatics, dance, and writing are not officially labeled as "gifted" programs, they are available as important parts of the educational offerings for these and all pupils with special interests and particular talents.

III. Standards and Grading

When very able students are brought together in a classroom, they are expected to work hard and to reach high levels of achievement. Obviously, such a group—all within the top 2 per cent of the population in general ability—will vary in interest, effort, study habits, and achievement. Even among such pupils there are wide differences in ability and in motivation. One pupil may stand out as far above the others, although these are performing at a high level by usual standards.

It is sometimes difficult to maintain perspective in assigning scholarship marks in such classes. There is a tendency to use something like a normal distribution of grades to distinguish between levels of accomplishment. Thus, pupils in the special program may be penalized by such marking practices and receive lower grades than would have been earned for the same quality work in a regular college preparatory class.

The stated and official policy on assigning marks to pupils in the gifted classes is: *Pupils in a gifted class shall receive the same grade that the quality and quantity of their work would have earned in a regular elementary class or college preparatory class at the secondary level.*

The implications of this policy are obvious. The pupil who has been earning a high grade-point average in regular classes should be expected to maintain at least the same average in the gifted class. The teacher of the gifted class cannot rely upon the implied threat of lowered grades as the principal or sole source of motivation. It is to be hoped that the teacher of the gifted class can communicate some of his own enthusiasm and zest for intellectual accomplishment to these students. Ideally, grades in these courses should almost be taken for granted and have relatively little importance.

81. Program for Able Pupils, Wilkes-Barre City School District *

WALTER C. WOOD

Grade level: 1–12

Number of Pupils in Program: 496

Pupil selection: Kindergarten children are given the California Mental Maturity Test, and those who score above 105 are individually tested on Stanford-Binet or WISC. The kindergarten teacher completes an evaluation form for those children who she thinks might be eligible for the program. However, this is not a criterion for admission. On the basis of the individual test, all the children are listed from the highest score down to 125. The cut-off point is determined by the number of places available in three centers. The parents are invited to a meeting at which they are told that no attempt has been made to evaluate the children's social and emotional maturity and that the program is on a voluntary basis. They are invited to visit classes and to consult the director of pupil personnel and other staff members. They are then asked to make their decision within two weeks. The group continues into junior high school with such change in membership as is found desirable by the principal, the pupil personnel department, the high school guidance director, the seventh grade teachers in the program, and the director of the program.

Tests used include the Wechsler Adult Intelligence Scale, the Leuch Algebra Readiness Test, and Stanford Achievement Test, and the Differential Aptitude Test.

Program: Teachers for the program are selected on the following criteria:

1. They have demonstrated their ability as teachers or have worked with children of high ability in other school systems.

* From *A Report on Local Programs for Able Pupils,* Curriculum Development Series, No. 7, Commonwealth of Pennsylvania, Department of Public Instruction, Harrisburg, Pa., 1962, pp. 45–46. Reprinted with permission.

2. They have demonstrated that they are "adventurous" and are enthusiastic about taking on this kind of assignment.
3. They would not appear to be threatened by dealing with this type of child or his parents.
4. They are willing to enter actively into the local in-service training program, to take appropriate courses when such are available and are anxious to visit other school systems offering programs for able children.
5. They appear able to participate in group work with other teachers.
6. They have at least one strong or consuming interest in education at the elementary level.
7. They have at least one strong or consuming interest in out-of-school activities.

In the secondary grades additional attention is given to the academic preparation and excellence of the teachers.

The elementary program (grades 1–6) operates in three centers that have been established in elementary buildings. In each center the children are combined in first and second, third and fourth, fifth and sixth grade classes. These are termed extra-work classes. Some few children who are in the regular grades and who have demonstrated to their teachers some unusual interest or ability come into the extra work classes for some few activities. All of the children in the extra-work program have their physical education and musical activities in regular classes and some of them also have some art work with regular classes.

Secondary classes (grades 7 and 8) are segregated in all subjects offered in the advanced program (English, mathematics, science, history, French, typewriting, and art). In grades 9–12, the segregated classes include English, mathematics, biology, chemistry, and physics.

82. Program for Able Pupils, Abington Township School District *

M. G. GAFFNEY

Grade level: K–12

Number of Pupils in Program: 1,500

Pupil selection: Those who have unusually high verbal facility as reflected through reading level, writing, and speaking; those who are creative, who can deal efficiently with complex abstractions, and who are able to demonstrate their giftedness in typical school programs.

Criteria used are:

1. Verbal IQ 130 and above.
2. Two grade levels above grade placement on standard achievement tests.
3. Teachers' recommendations.
4. Marks of "H" in major elementary subjects or "A"–"B" in the major secondary subjects.
5. Recommendation of the principal or department chairman.

    In addition to the foregoing, the following are used:

    a. Elementary Seminar—a locally designed talent search test and a sample of creative writing.

    b. For the Science and Mathematics Seminar—the Westinghouse Talent Search Test.

    c. For the Social Studies Seminar—STEP, Cooperative Test Division–Sequential Test of Educational Progress, Forms 2A and 3A, and the Cooperative Test of Social Studies Abilities.

    d. A sample of creative writing and an interview for admission to the senior high school Honors English.

    e. A sample of creative writing for admission to the accelerated junior high school program.

* From *A Report on Local Programs for Able Pupils,* Curriculum Development Series, No. 7, Commonwealth of Pennsylvania, Department of Public Instruction, Harrisburg, Pa., 1962, pp. 48–50. Reprinted with permission.

In the elementary schools—the principal and teachers select the gifted children except those who are to be accelerated in grade in which event the psychologist and guidance counselor meet with the teacher and principal. Students for the Elementary Seminar are selected by a committee consisting of the science coordinator, guidance director, elementary counselor, and school psychologist in addition to the principal and teacher recommendation.

For the Science and Mathematics Seminar and the Social Studies Seminar groups, they are selected by the respective coordinators, guidance counselors, with the help of department heads.

Tests used are: 1. Mental Ability—California Test of Mental Ability, Short Form, 1957, and 2. Achievement—California Achievement Test Battery, 1957. Other tests also used are: Westinghouse Talent Search, Abington Talent Search, Social Studies Abilities, Cooperative Test Division. Sequential Test of Educational Progress, Cooperative Test Division.

Program: The planning is done by:

> A standing committee consisting of the high school principal, one junior high school principal, and one elementary principal. This committee approves all changes and additions to the program.
>
> A committee representing various cross sections of the professional staff that serves as a "sounding board" for the grass roots.
>
> The philosophy of the Abington Program for the Gifted recognizes that gifted students vary in their needs and interests just as all students and therefore require a variety of activities.
>
> Briefly, the following is a summary of these activities:

> > *a.* In the first three grades of the elementary school, the students are grouped within the classroom for reading and in some cases for arithmetic and spelling. Their work is both accelerated and enriched. This practice also applies to those elementary schools where there is only one section per grade.
> >
> > *b.* In those schools that have multiple sections per grade, gifted children are grouped somewhat homogeneously.
> >
> > *c.* Highly selected groups are conducted in each of the three grades in two of our junior high schools. These groups are selected from throughout the district.
> >
> > *d.* Honors groups in each academic area are provided at the senior high school level. An advanced placement course in English (the same as Honors) is conducted in grade 12.

e. Enrichment of course material for gifted students is practiced throughout the program.
f. Seminar programs for those in grades 5 and 6 and 9 through 12, acceleration in grade and accelerated biology, algebra, and foreign language study.
g. Advanced projects in music, art, and vocational education.
h. Cooperative arrangements with colleges for combined high school–college study.

The following curriculum guides are used in teaching the gifted:

1. *A Program for the Gifted Student in the Abington Senior High School*
2. *Teaching the Gifted in the Social Studies*
3. *Teaching the Gifted in the English Language Arts—Junior and Senior High School*

An additional class in theory and composition in music is held at 7:00 A.M. at the senior high school. The a cappella choir is reserved only for those with talented voices. In art and shop, individual projects enable the gifted in these areas to progress according to their abilities.

The Abington Township Association for Gifted Children, which is an independent association of parents, has been in existence for the past seven years. This group serves as a reservoir of ideas and support for all aspects of the program. Community leaders serve as resource people.

Parents—both men and women, in and out of the professions—serve on planning committees of all seminar groups. Parents do not participate in the selection of students.

83. *Instructional Provisions in the Proposed Program for Children and Youth of Superior Ability* *

Division of Curriculum and Instruction and the Department of Psychological Services, Milwaukee Public Schools

1. In the Primary School

It is believed that the Primary School, effectively implemented, offers a highly desirable opportunity to provide for children of superior ability at the primary age level. The opportunities afforded through the Primary School should be continued with special attention given to early identification and desirable acceleration of children of superior ability. . . .

Implementing the philosophy of the Primary School will result in the acceleration by one or two semesters of about 4 per cent of the children above median chronological age and about 1 per cent of the younger children who demonstrate exceptionally high abilities at some point between kindergarten entrance and completion of fourth grade.

2. In the Intermediate Grades

At the fourth grade level, children of superior ability should be kept in regular classes and appropriate enrichment opportunities provided for them. Fourth grade teachers will be informed about children of superior ability in their classes. The regular fourth grade class placement is recommended to provide for the following:

—One year in the intermediate grades in the home school to help the pupils acquire additional growth in independence.

—One year in a regular class in intermediate grades to help children adjust to the expanded curriculum of the intermediate grades before placing them in special classes.

—One year in the intermediate grades to help those accelerated in the Primary School to adjust to the higher grade before placing them in special classes.

* From *Program for Children and Youth of Superior Ability*, pp. 4–14, 21, Milwaukee Public Schools, 1962. Reprinted with permission.

At the fifth and sixth grade levels, children of superior ability are offered placement in special self-contained classes in certain elementary schools, or, in locations where special self-contained classes are not feasible, in a comparable alternative arrangement such as special classes that meet periodically with an itinerant teacher.

The instructional provisions for children and youth of superior ability at the Intermediate Grade level will offer:

(*a*) acceleration to shorten the time spent in grades 4-5-6 when careful study suggests this to be the best means to provide for the pupil.

(*b*) modification of sequential curriculum programs so that children of superior learning abilities may be permitted to progress in a designated subject at an accelerated rate.

(*c*) enrichment to expand and deepen the study beyond the regular pursuits of learning.

At the junior and senior high school level, provisions for youth of superior abilities will include courses in the regular program sequence for students talented in any subject field. In addition, specific opportunities in programs of enrichment, acceleration, and condensed instruction will be available.

The foregoing proposal implies an obligation to define specific differences between regular and advanced or special courses as to content and instructional aims and achievement so that special classes and sectioning will result in more efficient learning by all students. Inasmuch as interests and abilities become differentiated at the junior high school level when applied to the various school subjects and other activities, it is important that the student talented in any subject field receives the same educational opportunity in his area of talent as does the pupil of general superior learning abilities. Careful consideration of these differences among students at the secondary level is essential to planning a balanced program of studies to give breadth and depth to their educational experiences.

The typical superior ability student at the junior and senior high school level would pursue one or more courses one year in advance of the regular sequential program—e.g., ninth grade algebra, general science, and English might be taken in the eighth grade. High school credit toward graduation would be given to eighth grade pupils enrolled in high school courses. The pursuit of courses one year in advance of the regular sequential program will continue on through the senior high school program. Guidance and counseling will play an important role in this phase of the proposed program.

By action of the Board of School Directors, requirements for graduation are as follows:

—A total of 32 high school credits with minimum credit requirements in designated subjects as follows:

English	6
Mathematics	2
Science	2
U.S. History	2

—Enrollment for credit in physical education or health each semester the student is in school.
—A minimum of 6 credits in one subject area other than English *or* 4 credits in each of two subject areas other than English.

For students of superior learning ability, a minimum of 34 credits, including physical education, is recommended. The 13½ or 14 credits, including the credits earned by successfully completing 6 to 8 semesters of physical education or health, specified in the Board requirements plus two additional credits in mathematics, two additional credits in science, two additional credits in social studies, and four credits in a foreign language will constitute 23½ to 24 of the 34 recommended credits. The remaining credits may be distributed among art, business education, health, home economics, industrial arts, and music, in order to provide a more balanced program of studies, or they may be distributed among the subject areas listed in the preceding sentence.

It is not feasible to recommend a minimum number of credits to be completed among art, business education, health, home economics, industrial arts, and music, because, in the pilot programs, programs and courses were not developed specifically for students of superior learning ability and talent in the fine or applied arts. However, continuing study will be given to programs in these subjects. In the meantime, high school counselors should give careful attention to these subjects when planning a well-balanced program of high-school education for each student of superior learning ability.

On an optional basis to students of superior ability at the high school level, provisions will be made for early graduation, advanced placement courses, released time for enrollment at a college or university, and released time for employment.

The guidance function in the individual secondary school will include the coordination of the program for students of superior ability. Upon delegation of responsibility by the principal, the guidance director in each secondary school will be responsible for coordinating the program.

The guidance director will be responsible for the overall program within the school. Responsibility for the individual student of superior ability will be delegated to the appropriate grade level counselor.

Close liaison with the Division of Curriculum and Instruction will need to be maintained in order to ensure the implementation of a consistent guidance and counseling plan on a system-wide basis.

The instructional provisions for children and youth of superior ability at the secondary level will be facilitated by the following:

—Basing special class assignments on uniform criteria. . . .

—Permitting different text materials or dual adoptions for use with advanced groups.

—Planning the pupil load in the best interests of the social as well as the intellectual well-being of the pupil. The number of courses and activities that he carries each year should be determined on the basis of his needs and capacity.

—Making available to students the following options:

  early graduation
  advanced placement courses
  released-time provisions for enrollment at a college or university
  released-time provisions for employment.

—Noting credit earned in special classes on the student's scholarship card.

—Permitting pupils of superior ability to progress one year in advance of the regular sequential program in one or more subject areas.

—Giving high school credit toward graduation to eighth grade pupils enrolled in high school courses.

.   .   .   .

Implementation of the Proposed Program

The gradual expansion of the proposed program as a part of the regular instructional program on a city-wide basis will require additional staff and facilities and certain specific administrative arrangements.

A. ADDITIONAL TEACHERS

Teachers will be needed for the special self-contained fifth and sixth grade classes in the centrally located elementary schools. Presently, eight teachers are assigned to teach special classes. Expansion of the superior ability program on a system-wide basis will approximately double this number.

Itinerant teachers will be needed for the itinerant classes where self-contained classes are not feasible. Presently, two teachers are assigned to teach itinerant classes.

Additional teachers, over and above the number presently allowed by the formula used to staff the secondary schools, will be required if provision is made for small classes in advanced level courses. Small classes should not result in corresponding increases in size of other classes.

Smaller than average classes at the elementary school level, resulting from strict adherence to the selection criteria, will result in a lower than average pupil-teacher ratio in some cases.

B. PSYCHOLOGICAL SERVICES

Sufficient staff will be needed to make it possible for the Department of Psychological Services to incorporate the work incident to the program for children and youth of superior ability as part of its regular work throughout the year rather than as a summer project only. Providing this continuous service will require additional personnel in the Department of Psychological Services.

C. ADMINISTRATION AND SUPERVISION

Administrative coordination and supervisory service for the program will be required. Specific recommendations for staffing the program will be made at a later date.

D. GUIDANCE

Sufficient released time will be needed for the guidance director in each junior and senior high school to assume the function and responsibility of coordination of the program at the individual school level. Counseling of the individual superior student will be done by the various grade level counselors.

E. FACILITIES

The proposed program for children and youth of superior ability requires that special classes be established at the fifth and sixth grade levels in centrally located elementary schools where standard sized classrooms are available.

Presently the Pilot Programs are located in eight such centers that serve approximately 60 elementary schools. The expansion of the proposed program for children and youth of superior ability as a regular part of the instructional program will necessitate approximately twice the number of centers now operating.

F. TRANSPORTATION

An equitable arrangement regarding the use of transportation facilities provided for other children in the Milwaukee Public Schools needs to be authorized for children and youth of superior ability required to travel to special class centers.

G. ADMINISTRATIVE ARRANGEMENTS

The proposed program for children and youth of superior ability needs central staff coordination and supervisory services to ensure consistent procedure and practice.

1. In the Primary School

In the Primary School, the identification and acceleration program will be the joint responsibility of the Department of Psychological Services, Division of Curriculum and Instruction, individual school principal, and the classroom teacher. The principal and classroom teacher will screen the group test results for all pupils according to instructions developed by the Department of Psychological Services. The classroom teacher will complete a rating scale and recommendation sheet for all pupils who meet the criteria. Administrative coordination and supervisory responsibility of the proposed program by the Division of Curriculum and Instruction will be required to ensure a uniform procedure on a city-wide basis.

2. In the Intermediate Grades

At the fourth grade level, pupils of superior ability will be enrolled in regular self-contained classes in their home district school. At the fourth grade level, pupils identified at the Primary School level will be reevaluated by the Department of Psychological Services. The recommendation regarding the placement of these pupils at the fifth grade level will be made by the Department of Psychological Services to the Division of Curriculum and Instruction. . . .

At the fifth and sixth grade levels, identified and selected pupils of superior ability will be enrolled in special self-contained classes in a designated elementary school serving a specified geographic area of the city. Such classes will be established in all areas of the city where it is considered feasible to establish them. In areas where it is not feasible to establish self-contained classes, a comparable alternative provision will be made.

The Department of Psychological Services, the Division of Curriculum and Instruction, the school principal, and the classroom teacher will have joint responsibility for the appraisal and reappraisal of individual pupils enrolled in the special classes. Administrative coordination and supervisory responsibility of the proposed program by the Division of Curriculum and Instruction will be required to ensure a uniform procedure on a city-wide basis.

3. In the Junior High School

The recommendations of the Department of Psychological Services regarding identification and placement will be followed to determine the disposition of each superior ability student regarding special ability grouped class placement. . . .

The Division of Curriculum and Instruction, the individual school principal, the guidance director, and the grade level counseling staff will have the responsibility of proper disposition of each superior ability student regarding course programs. The guidance director of each junior high school will coordinate the program at the individual school level.

Special ability classes in the various subject fields will emphasize enrichment, acceleration, and condensation. Every attempt will be made to provide a schedule of special ability grouped classes for superior or talented students.

Administrative coordination and supervisory responsibility of the proposed program by the Division of Curriculum and Instruction will be required to ensure a uniform procedure on a city-wide basis.

4. In the Senior High School

The recommendation of the Department of Psychological Services regarding identification and placement will be followed to determine the disposition of each superior ability student regarding special ability grouped class placement. . . .

The guidance director and the grade level counseling staff will have the responsibility of proper disposition of each superior ability student regarding course programs. The guidance director of each senior high school will coordinate the program at the individual school level.

Special ability grouped classes in the various subject fields will emphasize enrichment, acceleration, and condensation. Every attempt will be made to provide a schedule of special ability grouped classes for superior or talented students.

The following options may be made available to students:

—Early graduation.

—Advanced placement courses.

—Released-time provisions for enrollment at a college or university.

—Released-time provisions for employment.

Administrative coordination and supervisory responsibility of the proposed program by the Division of Curriculum and Instruction will be required to ensure a uniform program on a city-wide basis.

H. IN-SERVICE EDUCATION OF TEACHERS

Teachers selected to teach the special classes at both the elementary and secondary levels may need to be oriented regarding the nature of gifted students, effective class practices and procedures, and effective enrichment activities. A program of in-service education will be established in order to ensure the most effective results from special classes for superior ability students.

I. WORK WITH PARENTS

Vital to the effectiveness of any special school program is parental understanding and support of it. Continuing and extending the procedures used in communicating with parents during the period of the Pilot Programs, a program will be developed to acquaint parents with the nature of giftedness and to inform them of the special provisions for children and youth of superior ability, to counsel with them as there is need to do so, and to obtain their appraisal of and suggestions for the program. . . .

84. A Policy Guide for the Education of Pupils with Superior Ability *

WARD I. MILLER, *Superintendent of Schools,
Wilmington, Delaware*

The problem—We are now engaged in a three-year special project on the education of superior pupils predicated upon the judgment that educational experiences offered in our schools are not fully adequate to develop to fullest capacity the potentials of pupils with superior abilities. Accordingly, our total program needs to be evaluated in light of this problem.

Who are "superior" pupils?—Superior pupils are those pupils at the upper levels or ranges of ability. Superior ability includes superior mental capacity as well as exceptional ability in areas of "talent" (art, music, dramatics, writing, leadership, and so forth).

Superiority is not to be defined solely on the basis of statistical indices of intelligence. Instead, each school is to direct its concern toward those pupils representing approximately the upper 10 per cent in each category of ability being studied. This definition permits greater flexibility in program development and directs attention to the pupils in each school at the upper levels of ability.

The approach to be used—The approach to be used will be an "enrichment" approach developed within our present framework or philosophy for educational programming. There are two basic aspects of this approach: (1) fullest development of the experiences offered in the regular classroom; and (2) special opportunities for pupils with superior ability. Special opportunities should be designed to meet the unique interests and needs of such pupils and must meet fundamental criteria set forth in *That We May Grow*. These criteria include the following: (*a*) the educational program shall provide for full development of all pupils; (*b*) the educational program shall provide for the physical, emotional, intellectual, social, and spiritual needs of the pupils; (*c*) the educational program should fit a person for living in a democratic society; (*d*) program planning

* From *An Introduction to the Education of the Able Student in Wilmington Public Schools,* Part I, January, 1958, pp. 8–11. Reprinted with permission.

should be consistent with the best existing knowledge about how learning takes place; and (*e*) the program should be evaluated continuously.

Educational programs now offered in the Wilmington schools already provide many exceptional opportunities for superior pupils:

Flexible curricula used in many parts of the system permit pupils to progress at differentiated rates adjusted to their abilities rather than at rates based on rigid grade or subject standards.

A considerable variety of educational resources is available in the system. Special teachers in art, music, physical education, and library services are provided in the elementary schools. A staff of supervisory and specialized instructional personnel is provided in various subject-matter and instructional areas. Guidance, psychological, and health services are available on a broad basis, and classroom teachers are provided with a wealth of instructional materials.

Schools have had considerable experience in the use of community resources. Other instructional procedures—grading and reporting systems, testing programs, and the like—contain much of the flexibility that make them readily adaptable to new programs for pupils with superior capacity.

Wilmington's in-service education program is well developed to a point that permits full consideration of the educational needs of superior pupils.

Placement for superior pupils—Placing superior pupils in special schools and in exclusive classes on a full-time basis within regular schools is rejected. The expected outcomes of such placement are considered to be inconsistent with the educational objectives for our schools. However, this statement does not eliminate special educational provisions for superior pupils that do not require special schools or exclusive school programs on a full-time basis.

Some directions for the program—To implement a more adequate program for superior pupils, the various school divisions in cooperation with the Division of Instruction are authorized to proceed with consideration of the following steps:

Surveys to determine the status of instructional practices for superior pupils.

Development and implementation of practices that more adequately (*a*) identify superior pupils, (*b*) provide educational experiences for superior pupils, and (*c*) reveal problems peculiar to superior pupils.

Determination of need for special staff, equipment, and instructional materials.

Interpretation to the community of our efforts to improve educational opportunities for superior pupils.

Relation to programs for other pupils—Improvement of programs for superior pupils is not viewed as detracting from program development for other students. Instead, planning for superior pupils is an integral part of our total program of curriculum development and should stimulate improvement in educational experiences for all children and youth.

Identification—Schools are authorized to proceed with systematic programs to identify pupils who appear to have superior ability. The following procedures are to be used:

Intelligence, achievement, aptitude, and interest testing as authorized by the city-wide testing committee.

Teacher judgments as expressed in school records, rating scales, interviews, and similar devices.

Parental judgment.

Analysis of products of school work.

Special screening devices developed for "talent" areas.

Individual psychological examination.

Cumulative school records.

Attempts are to be made to identify superior ability as early as possible during the school career of pupils; however identification programs are to be developed on each school level to locate pupils not identified earlier. Information about the superior ability of pupils is to be made part of their cumulative school records.

Enrichment within the regular teaching areas—More adequate provisions for the range of individual differences existing in various teaching situations are to be considered. Instruction in regular classes shall include techniques, materials, and assignments needed to offer stimulating learning experiences for pupils with superior ability. Plans for limited acceleration or for summer educational experiences also may be considered.

Experimental studies and in-service education projects for these purposes may be undertaken.

Special opportunities for superior pupils—To supplement experiences in regular classrooms, schools may develop special opportunities for superior pupils.

In the elementary schools this may take the form of study groups, clubs, or other activities organized around interest and talent areas. When a unit level type of organization is developed for elementary schools, acceleration of pupils in either the primary or intermediate unit is permissible under the policy that now covers procedures for acceleration. Thus a primary pupil, for example, could complete the primary experience in two rather than the three years normally expected.

Secondary schools may develop practices such as seminars operating on a higher qualitative level than the regular classes.

In all instances where pupils are placed in class sections or in activities designed exclusively for superior pupils, appropriately different instructional procedures must be developed. A separation of superior pupils without corresponding instructional changes should not be considered.

Study of special problems connected with the education of superior pupils—Schools also may wish to study certain special problems encountered in the education of superior pupils.

One such problem is that of underachievement. Studies may be made to identify the causes of underachievement and to develop procedures to secure more adequate motivation.

A second problem is related to the vocational plans of superior pupils. Some schools may wish to develop special procedures for assisting superior pupils with future vocational plans.

A third problem frequently encountered is the effect on educational programs of social attitudes toward superiority or giftedness. Social attitudes (of parents, teachers, peers, and the public) exert potent influences on individual pupils and the total school environment. Since social and emotional growth is as integral a part of education as intellectual growth and development of special talents, schools may wish to undertake studies in the area of attitudes and values as these factors relate to the education of superior pupils.

Studies of other problems of this type may be proposed by schools.

Evaluation of practices—Included in all plans for new, additional, or changed practices shall be provisions for evaluating the plans. The most appropriate techniques available are to be used. Examples of such techniques include standardized testing, combined staff judgment, opinion surveys, follow-up studies, case studies conducted in the manner prescribed in the recent workshop on understanding children, and experimental devices specifically developed for the purpose.

Evaluation must be done in terms of aims. . . . Evaluation based solely on objective evidence of growth in achievement is very limited evaluation. Many who consider special programs in terms of possible growth in attitudes, human relationships, research skills, study skills, and thinking abilities feel that too great dependence on test evaluation could well be detrimental.

Thus evaluation will include growth in areas such as critical thinking, interests and motivation, socially desirable attitudes and ability to work with others as well as growth in achievement in specific subject matter understandings.

Administrative procedures for program development—In each school the principal is to take the initiative in program development for superior pupils.

The point at which this action begins will depend on staff readiness for this area of planning. Included in the principal's action will be the following steps:

Preliminary study of the problem as it relates to the school.

Survey of current procedures used to meet the needs of pupils with superior ability.

Selection of a staff planning committee for program development and evaluation.

Determination of special staff, space, equipment, and supplies needed.

In the process of program development the school principal is responsible for making full use of specialized staff resources available in the system. When plans in a particular subject-matter or instructional area are under consideration supervisory personnel concerned are to be involved. Planning involving the need for guidance and psychological services should include personnel from the Department of Child Development and Guidance.

At each step of program development, the respective divisional directors and the director of instruction are to be consulted. The purpose of this requirement is not only to give approval to proposed programs but also to provide a consistent direction for our schools. Changes in program are to be made only with the expressed approval of the directors concerned.

A system-wide steering committee for the project on superior pupils is to be created. This committee will provide central coordination for the project, initiate ideas for program improvement, and serve as a board for evaluating proposals referred by divisional directors.

Superior pupils as envisioned in this document include pupils from all levels of the system—elementary, secondary, and vocational. Programs are not to be confined to college preparatory pupils.

85. A Guide for Teachers' Marks *

W. T. WHITE, *Superintendent of Schools, Dallas, Texas*

1. Elementary Schools

In all groups, heterogeneous and high academic aptitude, the usual marking system is used.

Achievement is the basic consideration in grading.

It it is anticipated that all children in the high academic aptitude groups will earn *1*'s or *2*'s, excepting some who were placed in the group to "fill up" the class, and that in the heterogeneous groups about the usual spread of grades will be found except for fewer top grades.

It is understood also that some schools will show a higher percentage of *1*'s than other schools.

Membership in a high academic aptitude group does not guarantee a *1*.

The so-called curve system is not used in the Dallas schools.

A *1* is not given for effort nor as a stimulus.

Children who are working up to their capacity for their grade level earn a grade based upon the quality of work done, not a *1* based upon effort.

Children who make rapid progress but at a level lower than the grade to which they are assigned do not earn *1*'s.

A pupil of low ability who acquires administrative placement is not given high grades. It might be expected that usually he will receive the lowest passing grade.

* From *A Brochure on Grading,* pp. 3–7, Dallas Independent School District, Dallas, Tex. Reprinted with permission.

Grading and reporting for Grade 1

In grade one a narrative type statement is made on the *Report to Parents.*

The symbols 1, 2, 3, 4 are used on the permanent record card.

First-grade teachers will profit from a study of the *Report of Pupil Progress* for grades 2 and 3, and for grades 4, 5, 6, 7, and 8 with respect to establishing marks for the permanent records. These teachers will also find value in using the same terminology in preparing their narrative statements on *Report to Parents.*

Grading and reporting for grades 2 and 3 and for the intermediate level

The symbols on *Report of Pupil Progress* cards for grades 2 and 3, and for grades 4, 5, 6, 7, and 8 are followed and are explained as:

1—Rapid progress   *3*—Acceptable progress
2—Satisfactory progress   *4*—Little or no progress

EXPLANATION OF SYMBOLS

The pupil who makes "Rapid Progress" usually shows the following practices:

1. Is careful, thorough, and prompt in the preparation of all required work.
2. Is quick and resourceful in utilizing suggestions for supplementary work.
3. Works independently and has the interest and initiative to undertake original projects beyond the assigned work.
4. Performs work without guessing.
5. Expresses thoughts clearly and accurately.
6. Shows leadership in classroom activities.

The pupil who makes "Satisfactory Progress" usually shows the following practices:

1. Prepares all assignments carefully.
2. Is conscientious and dependable.
3. Shows consistent interest.
4. Responds readily in class.
5. Makes a practice of doing all work assigned and makes some use of suggestions for supplementary work.
6. Has good study habits of routine assignments.
7. Is loyal, dependable, and helpful in class activities.

The pupil who makes "Acceptable Progress" usually shows the following practices:

1. Does acceptable work, but may require considerable stimulation from the teacher.
2. Is usually dependable and cooperative.
3. Has good intentions, though interest is not always keen.
4. Does not show a great deal of concern in work beyond minimum requirements.
5. Responds to encouragement and guidance, though sometimes inclined to be careless or slow in accomplishment.
6. Needs to be prompted frequently during discussion or reports.
7. Should develop more independent habits of study.
8. Does work regarded as acceptable according to minimum requirements.

The pupil who makes "Little or No Progress" usually shows the following practices:

1. Does not accomplish the fundamental minimum essentials necessary for success in the subject.
2. Needs to spend more time on the subject.
3. Has study habits that are poor and ineffective.
4. Either will not, or cannot, hold attention to his work.
5. Seldom responds in class and in prepared work.
6. Is too easily diverted from any task.

In all elementary grades, marks are assessed in these broad field areas:

Language Arts
Social Studies
Arithmetic
Health-Science

Within the broad fields, specific skills and understandings that need attention are indicated by an *X*.

2. *Junior and Senior High Schools*

In all groups—heterogeneous, high academic aptitude, honors courses, and advanced placement—the usual marking system is used.

Achievement is the basic consideration in grading.

It is anticipated that all pupils in the high academic aptitude sections, honors courses, and advanced placement courses will earn A's or B's, and that the usual spread of grades, except for fewer top grades, will be found in the heterogeneous groups.

It is understood that some classes in some schools may have fewer top grades than some other classes in other schools.

Membership in a high academic aptitude group, an honors course, or an advanced placement course does not guarantee an A grade.

The so-called curve system is not used in the Dallas schools.

In all secondary schools, final grades are assessed in all courses. Final examinations are given in all courses except Physical Education. Only graduating seniors may be exempt from final examinations.

An *A* is not given for effort alone nor is it to be used as a stimulus.

Students who are working up to their capacity for grade level get a grade based upon the quality of work done, not an *A* based upon effort.

A student of low ability who acquires administrative placement is not given high grades. Usually he will receive the lowest passing grade.

Letter grades are not based upon numerical scores, and there are no numerical equivalents to letter grades. In assessing grades, the teacher will keep in mind these standards:

Excellent Achievement—*A*

Preparation

Careful daily preparation
Promptness and regularity in handling assigned work
Accuracy, good form, neatness, legibility, correct spelling, and thoroughness in all work
Books and materials needed for daily work always in readiness
Good judgment in the use of time

Knowledge of the subject

Ability to make "topic" recitations regularly
Frequent contributions to class discussions
Ability to apply facts and principles pertinent to the subject
High grades on all written work

General

Initiative as shown in attacking new work, with comparative freedom from the aid of the teacher

Quantity and quality of the work above that required for any other grade

Constant use of good English, and ability to read English with comprehension and rapidity

Ability to understand and to follow directions

Good Achievement—*B*

A grade of *B* is earned by pupils who, by reason of better than medium ability and application or of excellent ability and only medium application, rank below the "Excellent Achievement" group. Their work is good, usually correct, and typical of that done by a better-than-average pupil.

Fair Achievement—*C*

A grade of *C* is earned by pupils who, by reason of only fair ability or application, rank somewhat below the "Good Achievement" group. Their work is acceptable, unquestionably passing, and satisfactory in meeting the minimum requirements.

Poor Achievement—*D*

A grade of *D* is earned by pupils who, by reason of poor ability, lack of application, frequent absence, or weak foundation, rank below the "Fair Achievement" group. Their work, although barely passing, can be accepted for credit.

Not Passable Achievement—*F*

A grade of *F* is earned by pupils who, by reason of excessive absence, habitual neglect, or inability to grasp subject matter, have not done satisfactory work and in the judgment of the teacher should not receive a passing grade.

Bad Failure—*G*

A grade of *G* is to be given to pupils whose work is extremely unsatisfactory and to those absent from examination without an excuse acceptable to the dean.

INDEX

Index

Tucson, Arizona, program for gifted in secondary school, 354–56

Underachiever(s), characteristics of, 204–5, 212–14, 218–19
guidance for gifted, 192–97
motivating the gifted, 221–25
as a problem, 214–20
studies of gifted, 198–202, 210–14, 216–20, 394–95
Untereker, A., 112, 115
Utah, 233, 266

Vocational guidance, for gifted, 180–81, 288

Ward, V. S., 6
Weir, E. C., 290

Wetter, A. H., 189
White, W. T., 420
Wichita, Kansas, teaching gifted in grade five, 336–43
Wilkes-Barre, Pennsylvania, program for able pupils, 402–3
Williams, C. W., 89
Wilmington, Delaware, education of superior ability pupils, 415–19
Wilson, F. T., 205, 276
Wilson, R. C., 257
Wisconsin, instructional provisions for children of superior ability in Milwaukee, 407–14
placement procedures in Milwaukee, 57–63
Witty, P., 161
Wood, W. C., 402